D0131474

THE EPISTLE TO THE HEBREWS

THE
EPISTLE TO THE
HEBREWS

by
H. Orton Wiley, S.T.D.

BEACON HILL PRESS
Kansas City, Missouri

First Printing, 1959

Copyright, 1959
Beacon Hill Press

Library of Congress Card Number—59-5493

Printed in the United States of America

Dedicated with heartfelt gratitude to Dr. A. E. Sanner, who made possible my first public exposition of this Epistle, from which there has grown this present study.

FOREWORD

This study of *The Epistle to the Hebrews* had its origin in a fresh spiritual illumination as to the nature of the Melchisedec priesthood of Christ, and the relation of the new covenant to the mediatorship of the divine Son. The key to the understanding of this Epistle, I found to be, not the symbolism of the ancient Tabernacle, as I had formerly supposed, but the new order of priesthood in Christ. My first attempt at a public exposition of this Epistle was at the old Weiser Camp in Idaho under the supervision of Dr. A. E. Sanner.

When I was commissioned to prepare a manuscript which should interpret this Epistle, both for general reading and as a reference book for students, my first thought was to make it a summary of Old Testament symbolism. But the study of the symbolism which largely underlies the text of the Epistle soon became too large for the space allowed me, and the project was abandoned. The work therefore is merely an interpretation of the Epistle from the viewpoint of the Biblical standard of Christian experience, with documentary notes kept at a minimum.

For my chief helps in the preparation I wish to acknowledge my indebtedness to the great critical commentaries of Westcott, Sampson, Vaughan, Lenski, Robertson, Whedon, Clarke, Calvin, Cowles, Ebrard, Chadwick, Lindsay, Lowrie, Stuart, and Lange. In this connection also I owe a debt of gratitude for assistance given me in the use of Greek forms by Dr. Ross E. Price and Dr. Joseph H. Mayfield, both of whom are authorities in this field. References have also been made to the following works: William Jones, *Entire Sanctification;* A. J. Gordon, *The Twofold Life;* Murray, *The Holiest of All;* Meyer, *The Way into the Holiest;* Isaac M. See, *The Rest of Faith;* Wesley, *Arminian Magazine;* J. A. Wood, *Purity and Maturity;* Pope, *Compendium of Christian Theology;* and Miley, *Systematic Theology.*

I am deeply indebted also to Rev. Norman R. Oke, the book editor, for the preparation of the Preface and other assistance in preparing the manuscript, and to Miss Louise Hoffman for the typing and preparation of the Index. To the publishers we extend our thanks for the splendid form in which this work is presented to the public, and we pray that it may prove a spiritual blessing to many.

H. Orton Wiley

Pasadena, California

PREFACE

Every pilgrim—would he be successful—must keep his eyes always on the distant "wicket gate" but not forget the good, strong staff which aids him up the hill. There is the glory of the goal, but there is also the merit of the means by which we attain that goal. Both must be kept in mind and both will be strengthened by a fair reading of this book.

The person of Christ, the priesthood of Christ: these are the central pillars in our citadel of Christian truth.

In His person Jesus is not just one among many, not even a wiser and more pious leader. Of all who ever walked earth's roads—keep this crystal-clear—He alone was God. H. Orton Wiley shouts this out in this book.

And the priesthood of Christ—it is also a cardinal tenet in our structure of faith. He was a better Priest, a timeless Priest, the one sinless Priest. Yea, we find assurance of heaven at last only because of His mediatorial work.

St. Paul felt the full thrust of this truth and fairly exploded as he wrote to the Romans. Listen. "It is Christ that died, yea rather, that is risen again, who is even at the right hand of God, who also maketh intercession for us." This truth seized him and his carefully worded sentences broke forth into a pageant of praise—"Who shall separate us from the love of Christ? shall tribulation, or distress, or persecution, or famine, or nakedness, or peril, or sword? . . . I am persuaded, that neither death, nor life, nor angels, nor principalities, nor powers, nor things present, nor things to come, nor height nor depth, nor any other creature, shall be able to separate us from the love of God, which is in Christ Jesus our Lord."

And this classic outburst from the impassioned heart of Paul came after he saw afresh the high priesthood of Christ.

It is a privilege to commend this book to Christians everywhere. Christ will become even more precious; His priesthood will loom larger and take you to your knees.

When H. Orton Wiley authored the three-volume *Christian Theology* he secured for himself a reputation as one of the foremost theologians in the world of conservative Christianity. Now, in giving us this thoroughgoing treatise on *Hebrews,* his scholarship focuses upon the field of Biblical exposition.

At times your brow will pucker in thought—for the author takes you far below the surface. Your eyes will wet with tears as you climb mountain peaks of divine truth and behold vistas never before dreamed. You may (as I did) blush a bit as you see pictured the worthies of a day long gone by; they suffered so uncomplainingly.

So I plead: Read the book! You will lay it down a better person. You may perchance be ashamed of much that passes under the name Christian in modern life, but you will be deeply proud of Jesus Christ.

NORMAN R. OKE

CONTENTS

CONTENTS

INTRODUCTION

The Epistle to the Hebrews is a divinely inspired commentary on the Old Testament, dealing especially with the Pentateuch and the Psalms. It recounts the journey in the wilderness, the significance of the Tabernacle, and is an interpretation of the various offerings and services in the worship of ancient Israel. The Epistle to the Hebrews begins, however, not with the twelfth, but with the twenty-fourth, chapter of Exodus. The Passover has no place in it. It deals with a redeemed people, and is addressed to "holy brethren, partakers of the heavenly calling" (3:1). It is not concerned with what is represented by bringing Israel out of Egypt, but with what is meant by bringing them into the land of promise. If there is any question concerning this, all doubts should be resolved by St. Paul's declaration "that all our fathers were under the cloud, and all passed through the sea; . . . and did all eat the same spiritual meat; and did drink the same spiritual drink: for they drank of that spiritual Rock that followed them: and that Rock was Christ" (I Cor. 10:1-4). It is clearly evident from this that the people of that day bore some spiritual relation to Christ; and this is still further confirmed by the efficacy of that faith which characterized the worthies named in the eleventh chapter of Hebrews.

No, the symbolism used in this Epistle is not concerned primarily with what we call conversion, for it is not addressed to men in their sins, urging them to accept pardon through faith in Christ, but to those who are already Christians. It is concerned with the second stage of crisis in the work of salvation, the entrance of the sons of God into the fullness of the new covenant. And this covenant, which is twice described in this Epistle, (1) embraces the law of God written in the minds and hearts of His people—hearts so transformed that they are brought into perfect harmony with the will of God. (2) It embraces the remission of sins, which not only includes the pardon of actual transgressions, but the cleansing from "inbred sin" or the "carnal mind"

13

—a cleansing from all sin. And (3) it exalts God as the supreme and sole Object of worship and adoration, the heart being so purified that its affections are set on things above; its will, always obedient to the will of God; and its mind, the "mind of Christ."

The Epistle to the Hebrews is unique in that it begins without the usual salutations, the name of the author, or the churches to which it is addressed. This fact raises many problems, but these belong primarily to the field of New Testament analysis. Since our attention will be directed especially to a series of exegetical and hortatory studies in the Epistle itself, it will be sufficient here to make only a few general observations concerning it, and to follow these with a statement concerning our basic principles of interpretation.

GENERAL OBSERVATIONS

1. *The Importance of the Epistle to the Hebrews.* "The Epistle to the Hebrews," says Dr. Adam Clarke, "is by far the most important and useful of all the apostolic writings: all the doctrines of the Gospel are in it, embodied, illustrated, and enforced in a manner the most lucid; by reference and examples the most striking and illustrious; and by arguments the most cogent and convincing. It is an *epitome* of the dispensations of God to man, from the foundation of the world, to the advent of Christ. It is not only the sum of the *Gospel;* but the sum and completion of the *Law,* of which it is also the most beautiful and luminous comment. *Without* this, the law of Moses had never been fully understood, nor God's design in giving it. *With* this, all is clear and plain; and the ways of God with man rendered consistent and harmonious. The apostle appears to have taken a portion of one of his own epistles for a text: *Christ is the end of the law for righteousness to them that believe;* and has most amply and impressively demonstrated his proposition. All the rites, ceremonies and sacrifices, of the Mosaic institution, are shown to have had *Christ* for their *object* and *end;* and to have had neither *intention* nor meaning but in reference to Him; yea, as a *system,* to

be without *substance*, as a law to be without *reason*, and its *enactments* to be both *impossible* and *absurd*, if taken out of this reference and connection. Never were *premises* more clearly stated; never was an *argument* handled in a more masterly manner, and never was a conclusion more legitimately and satisfactorily brought forth. The *matter* is, throughout, the most engaging; and the *language* is most beautifully adapted to the whole; everywhere appropriate, always nervous and energetic; dignified as is the subject, pure and elegant as that of the most accomplished Grecian authors; and harmonious and diversified as the music of the spheres. So many are the *beauties*, so great the *excellency*, so instructive the *matter*, so pleasing the *manner*, and so exceedingly interesting the *whole*, that the work may be read a hundred times over without perceiving anything of *sameness;* and with new and increased information at each reading. This latter is an excellency which belongs to the whole revelation of God; but to no part of it in such a peculiar and super-eminent manner, as the Epistle to the Hebrews" (ADAM CLARKE, *Preface to the Epistle to the Hebrews*, p. 701). How true and beautiful the above appraisal of this Epistle is, only those can know who have spent years in its study—not only in the English translations, but in the strength, richness, and vivacity of the original Greek.

Dr. Adam Clarke further says that "to explain and illustrate this Epistle, multitudes have toiled hard, and exhibited much industry, much learning and much piety. I also will show my opinion; and ten thousand may succeed me, and still bring out something that is new. That it was written to the Jews, naturally such, the whole structure of the Epistle proves. Had it been written to the Gentiles, not one in ten thousand of them could have comprehended the argument, because unacquainted with the Jewish system; the knowledge of which, the writer of this Epistle everywhere supposes. He who is acquainted with the Mosaic law, sits down to the study of this Epistle with double advantages; and he who knows the *Traditions of the Elders*, and the *Mishnaic Illustrations* of the written and pretended oral law of the Jews, is still more likely to enter into, and comprehend the Apostle's meaning. No man has adopted a more likely way of explaining its phraseology than Schoetgen, who has traced its peculiar diction to Jewish sources; and, according to him, the proposition of the whole Epistle is this: *Jesus of Nazareth is the true God;* and in order to convince the Jews of the truth of this proposition, the Apostle uses but three arguments (1) Christ is superior to angels; (2) He is superior to Moses; (3) He is superior to Aaron."—ADAM CLARKE, *Preface to the Epistle to the Hebrews*, IV, 701.

Continuing the thought of the importance of this Epistle, most modern writers are prolific in their praise, for both its form and its content. Lindsay in his *Lectures on the Epistle to the Hebrews* (p. 1) says: "The Epistle to the Hebrews is one of the most important books of the New Testament. It contains a minute exposition of some of the leading doctrines of Christianity; the plan of it is constructed with great beauty and logical accuracy; and it is written in finer Greek than any other book in the sacred volume." Perhaps one of the best appreciations of this Epistle is that of John Owen. He says: "I found the excellency of the writing to be such, the depth of the mysteries contained in it to be so great, the compass of the truth asserted, unfolded and explained so extensive and so diffused through the whole body of the Christian religion, the usefulness of the things contained in it, so important and so indispensably necessary, that I was quickly satisfied that the wisdom, grace and truth treasured in this sacred storehouse, are far from being exhausted by the endeavors of all that have gone before us. So far did these truths, then, seem from being all perfectly brought to light by them; that I was assured there was left a sufficient ground, not only for renewed investigation after rich ore in this mine, for the present generation, but for all them that shall succeed to the consummation of all things." As previously stated, these estimates of the Epistle will not appear fanciful or overdrawn to the patient and careful student.

2. *The Epistle Was Addressed to Jewish Christians.* While various opinions have been held as to the persons addressed in this Epistle, there can be no question as to its being originally written to the Hebrew Christians. But the question is, To what Jewish Christians? Some have thought that it was written to Jewish Christians in general, but such postscripts as the intelligence that Timothy was set at liberty, and that, if he came shortly, it was the apostle's intention to visit them, all indicate that the Epistle was addressed to a local community. As to the local community, various opinions have also been held—such as Asia Minor, Galatia, Corinth, Thessa-

lonica, Spain, Rome, Antioch, Alexandria, and Palestine.
The use of the allegorical and spiritualizing method applied to the Old Testament has led to the supposition
that the Epistle was addressed to a large Jewish community in Alexandria. The oldest and most generally
received theory is that the Epistle was addressed to the
Palestinian Jews, especially the church at Jerusalem.
The internal evidence seems to favor this opinion, especially the lack of allusion to any danger due to the contact with heathenism. A further evidence is found in
the fact that there were many thousands of Palestinian
Jews which believed and were zealous of the law
(Acts 21:20). These were in constant danger of being
again brought under the ritual worship maintained in
the Temple, and in all probability had not at that time
seen that the acceptance of Christianity meant the abrogation of the Levitical sacrifices. Still further, a letter
addressed to the church at Jerusalem would furnish a
wider circulation of the Epistle, for the scattered Jews
kept in close touch with their capital city of Jerusalem.

The Authorship of the Epistle. The authorship of
this Epistle has been greatly disputed even from the
earliest times. Tertullian referred it to Barnabas;
Clement of Alexandria attributed it, in part at least, to
Luke. He thought Paul to be the author and Luke the
translator. Luther was among those who ascribed it to
Apollos, who was "mighty in the scriptures." Still others
ascribed it to Sylvanus or Aquila, while Dr. Robinson
thinks that it was the work of some other author than
that of the known writers of the New Testament. The

Bishop Chadwick says: "Nevertheless it is the work of some member
of the Pauline School. The resemblances to his style are striking, and
only to be reconciled with the striking differences by the belief that it
was the writing of a disciple who treasured lovingly his master's thought,
and even at times reproduced his phrases, while his individuality remained unimpaired. And this is edifying as well as interesting. We see
the great convictions by which the apostle lived, the Incarnation, the
Atonement, the intercession of our Lord, faith, justification and judgment, influencing another mind, taking new form and color, expressing
themselves otherwise, finding their support in the Old Testament, and yet
continuing the same. It is a fine example of how much difference in
statement, how much originality and independence are consistent with
loving allegiance to the same Gospel."—BISHOP CHADWICK, *The Epistle to
the Hebrews,* pp. 1-2.

Eastern church universally received the Epistle as St.
Paul's, and in the Latin church it was generally received as Pauline until the close of the second century.
In some of the catalogues and ancient manuscripts, such
as the Codex Alexandria, Vatican, Ephraemi, and others,
the Epistle to the Hebrews is found following immediately II Thessalonians in the very midst of the Pauline
Epistles. This gave rise to a theory in the early part of
the century that Galatians was written for the gentiles
and Hebrews for the Jews of the same region. Thus the
covering Epistle would be "To the Galatians," and that
"To the Hebrews" as an enclosure. Eusebius quotes
Clement as saying that the reason St. Paul did not subscribe his name to the Epistle was the fact that he was
the apostle of the gentiles and not of the Jews. Probably
most scholars still feel as did Origen when in the third
century he said, "As to who wrote the Epistle, God alone
knows the truth."

*The Original Language in Which the Epistle Was
Written.* There are two general opinions as to the language in which this Epistle was originally written:
(1) that it was originally written or dictated in Hebrew
and then translated into Greek; and (2) that it was originally written in Greek as we now have it. The ancient
scholars held the former position; the modern incline
to the latter. As in the case of the Epistle to the Romans,
which though addressed to the Romans was written in
Greek, so probably the author thought that it would be
best adapted to common use if written in Greek, even
though addressed to the Hebrews. Those who hold that
it was written originally in Greek do so on the following

In connection with the discussion of the original language, some attention should also be given to the vocabulary, the style, and the imagery
of the Epistle. Westcott states that the Epistle in its language, as to both
its vocabulary and its style, is purer and more vigorous than any other
book in the New Testament. (1) The style is even more characteristic
of a practiced scholar than the vocabulary. (2) The vocabulary is singularly copious and includes a number of words not found elsewhere in
the apostolic writings, and some which are not quoted from other independent sources. (3) The imagery of the Epistle is drawn from many
sources. Some of the figures which are touched more or less in detail
are singularly vivid and expressive. See Westcott, *Epistle to the Hebrews,*
pp. xliv-xlviii.

grounds: (1) it does not have the stiffness of a translation; (2) it quotes uniformly from the Septuagint, which
would not be likely if written in Hebrew; and (3) in
some instances it translates Hebrew words. The Greek
Epistle was very early in circulation, and there is no
evidence that there was a Hebrew original—this being
inferred in order to account for the supposed differences
in style from the other Pauline Epistles.

The Date of Composition. It is evident that the
Epistle to the Hebrews was written before the destruction of Jerusalem, if written or dictated by St. Paul, for
the apostle had died before this date. This appears also
from certain texts (cf. 9: 9; 13: 10) as well as from the
whole scope of the Epistle, which implies that the Temple
was still standing and its worship maintained. Yet it
could not have been written many years before this
time, for there were those who had long been Christians
(5: 12), and it may be also inferred from 13: 7 that their
first teachers were already dead. That impending disaster in the fall of Jerusalem seems to be indicated in
the words, "and so much more, as ye see the day approaching." "For yet a little while, and he that shall
come will come, and will not tarry" (Heb. 10: 25, 37).
The probable date of this Epistle is placed between the
years A.D. 64 and A.D. 67, when the Jewish war began, and
most probably just before the fall of Jerusalem. This
last event marked in a peculiar sense the close of the
old dispensation; and to the Christians it was regarded
as God's final judgment and the sign of His coming.

The Purpose of the Epistle. As generally stated, the
purpose of the Epistle to the Hebrews is to confirm the
Jewish Christians in their faith and to guard them
against an apostasy to Judaism. Sampson in his *Commentary* (p. 35) points out that they were peculiarly
exposed to this danger, and that this "may be known,
(1) from old prejudices and their former education;
Judaism had been the religion of their fathers from
immemorial generations. (2) From the splendor of
the temple service, which appealed to their senses, and
which would be asserted by their enemies to stand in

splendid contrast with the bald simplicity of the Christian worship. (3) From the influence of social relationships; their relatives, neighbors, friends and countrymen were Jews. (4) From the odium attached to the cross, than which there was to a Jew, no greater stumbling block. And (5) from persecutions, which though not unto death were severe."

The purpose of the writer is carried forward by an unfolding of the true nature of Christianity, which he sets forth as the final and perfect religion. This he does, not solely by exhortation and warning, although these are given an important place, but more especially by a splendid and scholarly treatise, in which he dwells upon the glory of Christ, the Son, as contrasted with angels, with Moses, and with Aaron. Here also is set forth in striking contrast the distinction between the old covenant of works and the new covenant of faith. One of the peculiarities of this Epistle is the presentation of Christ as Priest—a truth not found in any other Epistle, although priestly ministrations are mentioned. The real key to the understanding of this great Epistle, therefore, is to view it in the light of Christ, our great High Priest. All other things cluster around this one central thought. So scholarly is the treatment of the material of this great Epistle that it is frequently regarded as a treatise on the high priesthood of Christ.

PRINCIPLES OF INTERPRETATION

In our interpretation of this Epistle we shall emphasize the following points: (1) The primary aim of the Epistle is to bring men into the presence of God. (2) In order to stand in the presence of God, men must be holy. The dominant note of this Epistle, therefore, is holiness; and this personal, spiritual experience is presented under different aspects, and with appropriate terminology related to the person and work of Christ. (3) The people of Israel are viewed as a typical people symbolizing the work of Christ under the new covenant. The emphasis, however, is not upon their deliverance from Egypt, but upon their refusal to enter Canaan, their promised inheritance. Hence the reference to their history is confined chiefly to their journey from Egypt to Canaan, their wanderings in the wilderness, the Tabernacle with its articles of furniture, their priesthood, and the great Day of Atonement—all of these being interpreted in the light of Christ's redemptive work. This redemptive experience is presented under various aspects as it is related to Christ, and with each of these aspects there is an appropriate warning or exhortation. The Epistle when thus analyzed yields the following terminology as applied to experience—an experience known by many scriptural terms, but by Mr. Wesley generally called Christian perfection.

(Aspects of Christ)	(Spiritual Experience)	(Warnings Against)
1. Christ's Deity	The Great Salvation	Neglect
2. Christ's Humanity	Sanctification	Hardening the Heart
3. Christ as Apostle	The Rest of Faith	Unbelief
4. Christ as High Priest	Eternal Salvation	Indifference
5. Christ and the Promises	Christian Perfection	Slothfulness
6. Christ and the Sanctuary	The Holiest of All	Sinning Willfully
7. Christ and the Inheritance	Holiness	Apostasy

It will be noticed that the warnings appear in a gradually descending scale: neglect, hardening the heart, unbelief, indifference, slothfulness, sinning willfully, and apostasy. The term "uttermost salvation" (7:25) gives us another aspect of this gracious experience, but no warning attaches to it. Instead, the writer sets forth the qualifications of Christ as our High Priest, for the restoration of His people to the fullness of their inheritance (7:26-28).

THE HORTATORY NATURE OF THE EPISTLE

The Epistle to the Hebrews is hortatory throughout. Even its most profound arguments and sublime descriptions are all offered in the spirit of exhortation. As previously indicated, these frequently take the form of warnings and admonitions. The supreme concern of the writer is to prevent the Hebrew Christians from returning to Judaism, and to accomplish this he implores them to explore the mysteries of divine grace in Christ Jesus. The writer ever keeps in mind the two great gifts which God has given to man for his salvation: (1) God has given His Son to the world for its redemption; (2) Christ has given the Holy Spirit to the Church for its sanctification and cleansing. As the former is received by faith, so also is the latter.

While the writer emphasizes the crises in Christian experience, he never allows them to exclude growth and development. As conversion is a crisis experience which introduces a life at peace with God, so also sanctification is a crisis which leads to a life of holiness. The latter is especially significant in that it makes a place for the indwelling of Christ in the fullness of the Spirit. To rest in a crisis as an end rather than as a means is the source of much leanness in the hearts of God's people. We do not rest in a holy heart, but in Him who dwells within the holy heart; nor do we labor in our own wisdom and strength, but through Him who works in us both to will and to do of His good pleasure.

As we shall see in the further study of this Epistle, the author is deeply concerned that those who have entered through the veil into the holy of holies shall live lives of full devotion to God. With him, to be filled with the Spirit is to be literally God-possessed; to be anointed with the Spirit is in some true sense to be "Christed," that in our finite measure we shall be true representatives of Christ to the world and to the Church.

May God grant us the help of the Holy Spirit as we study this great Epistle, not only that we may better comprehend the riches of grace in Christ Jesus, but that we shall avail ourselves of these riches through Him who is our Mediator, our great High Priest, who is at once the Surety of the Covenant, and the Minister of the Sanctuary.

CHAPTER I
THE MAJESTY OF THE SON OF GOD

The writer of the Epistle to the Hebrews in a short introduction of four verses states briefly and dogmatically certain basic positions preliminary to his main argument. His intention throughout the Epistle is to prove by reference to the Old Testament Scriptures that Jesus is the Christ, the true Messiah of Jewish expectation. Furthermore, the first two chapters may also be regarded as in some sense introductory to the main dialectic task, which is to show that Jesus Christ perfectly fulfilled the law, and in its place introduced a new and spiritual covenant of grace. Hence we find him giving two chapters to this subject of the God-Man, the one dealing with His deity, the other with His humanity and humiliation.

THE EXORDIUM: GOD HATH SPOKEN

God, who at sundry times and in divers manners spake in time past unto the fathers by the prophets, hath in these last days spoken unto us by his Son (1: 2a).

"We can scarcely conceive of anything more dignified," says Dr. Adam Clarke, "than the opening of this Epistle: the sentiments are exceedingly elevated, and the language harmony itself. The infinite God is at once produced to view, not in any of those attributes which are essential to the divine nature; but in His manifestations of love to the world, by giving a revelation of His will relative to the salvation of mankind; and thus preparing the way, through a long train of years for the introduction of that most glorious being, His own Son. The Son, in the fulness of time, was manifested in the flesh, that He might complete all vision and prophecy, supply all that was wanting to perfect the great scheme of revelation, for the instruction of the world; and to die to put away sin by the sacrifice of Himself. The description which he gives of this glorious personage is elevated beyond all comparison. Even in His humiliation, His sufferings of death excepted, He is infinitely exalted above all the angelic host; He is the object of their unceasing adoration; is permanent on His eternal throne at the right hand of the Father; and from Him they all receive their commands to minister to those whom He has redeemed by His blood. In short, this first chapter, which may be considered the introduction to the whole Epistle, is for importance of subject, dignity of expression, harmony and energy of language, compression and yet distinctness of ideas, equal if not superior, to any other part of the New Testament" (ADAM CLARKE, Heb. 1:1).

This Epistle has no salutation and hence brings before us immediately the wondrous message of God. In this there is a marked similarity to the first words of Genesis. There we read, "In the beginning God"; here it is stated, "God . . . hath . . . spoken." Since this Epistle is addressed to the Hebrews, the writer displays remarkable wisdom in that his first sentence contains an acknowledgment of the divine authority of the Old Testament Scriptures. God hath spoken! Speech is the vehicle of communion and fellowship. By it man reveals the thoughts and dispositions of his mind and heart. So also God, who dwells "in the light which no man can approach unto," speaks to us that He may reveal himself and the infinite purposes of His love. Man's sin interrupted his communion with God, but in the gift of His Son this fellowship has again been restored.

The Euphonious Introduction. The Epistle in the original Greek opens sonorously with two euphonious adverbs joined together by a simple conjunction, *polumeros kai polutropos* (πολυμερῶς καὶ πολυτρόπως). These words at once command the attention of the reader. Translated into English by the expression "in many parts and in many ways," the opening words lose their euphony and much of their stateliness. But this introductory expression is not only designed to command the immediate attention; it gives in a majestic manner the foundational theme of the entire Epistle. The "many

parts" and "many ways" by which God revealed himself in and through the prophets are now summed up
as preparatory to the perfect revelation in the gospel,
which is one and indivisible because it is the revelation of
God in a Person who is the Son.

"At Sundry Times and in Divers Manners" (1:1).
Some of the earlier writers, as Chrysostom, viewed the
words *polumeros* (πολυμερῶς) and *polutropos* (πολυτρόπως) as synonymous terms indicating the single idea
of incompleteness. Later writers view these terms as
expressing different ideas. The first, "at sundry times,"
would then refer to the separate portions in which God
gave the Old Testament to the Hebrews—these being
spread over a thousand years from Moses to Malachi.
The second, "in divers manners," refers to the variety
of ways which God used to make known His will—
visions, dreams, audible voices, Urim and Thummim,
and prophetic utterances. Stuart, while holding to the
view that each term has a separate meaning, points out
that the antithesis is more effective if we translate the
verse as follows: "God, who in ancient times made com-
munications to the fathers by the prophets, in sundry
parts and in various ways has now made a revelation
to us by His Son, i.e., has completed the whole revelation which He intends to make under the new dispensation, by His Son,—by His Son only, and not by a long
continued series of prophets as of old" (STUART, *Epistle
to the Hebrews*, p. 278). This is borne out by the fact
that the Christian revelation was completed in the single
generation which was contemporary with the life of our
Lord on earth.

In Times Past; in These Last Days (1:1-2a). These
expressions denote distinct periods of time. The word
palai (πάλαι), which literally means "of old time" or
"of ancient days," does not simply mean "formerly"
but always describes something completed in the past.
Westcott says that it refers to the ancient teachings, now
long since sealed. The writer therefore by the use of
this term avoids the implication that revelations had

been continued down to the then present time. This would exclude as inspired literature everything from the time of Malachi to the gospel period. "In these last days" appears to have early become a technical designation for the time of the Messiah and His rule. But as generally in the prophecies of the Old Testament, the interval between the two advents is left out of view, and the days of the Messiah regarded as a single manifestation. When however the interval between the first and second advents began to lengthen into years, the expression was modified. Even in this Epistle the expressions "that world" or "those days" is used as a future period, although the Messiah had come. We are told that the Jews divided time into "the present age" and "the age to come," the latter referring to the perfect reign of God. Between these two periods they placed the reign of the Messiah, sometimes connecting it with the former and sometimes with the latter. It was commonly believed, however, that the passage of one age to the other would be marked by the travail pains of a new birth, a period of trial and suffering.

The Divine Revelation: God Spake. Speech is at once the basis of revelation and of fellowship. As a man's words reveal his inner self, so also God, who dwells "in the light which no man can approach unto," reveals himself through His Word in holiness and love—holiness which repels all sin, love which ever draws the sinner to himself. The revelation of God is here stated to have been given in successive stages—the first through the prophets, the second through the Son. Concerning the former, the word *lalesas* (λαλήσας), "having spoken," is an aorist participle, and as such sums up in a single act all the earlier revelations, whether patriarchal, Mosaic, or prophetical. The latter is expressed by the

Lindsay says that "the inspiration of the Scriptures is distinctly affirmed in this opening verse of the Epistle to the Hebrews: it was God who spake to men by the prophets and by His Son; and therefore the penmen of the Old Testament, and those who were employed under Christ to write the New, were infallibly directed by the wisdom of heaven; and what they have written is the truth of God. . . . If it claims inspiration, if it claims infallibility, we must concede the claim."—LINDSAY, *Lectures on the Epistle to the Hebrews*, pp. 28-29.

term *elalesen* (ἐλάλησεν), "spake" or "spoke," which
as an aorist indicative gathers up into one the revelation through the Son, although it does not refer to any
particular event in the life of Christ. The point to be
noted grammatically is that the participial clause "God
having spoken" points forward to the main verb with its
aorist of finality, "God spake," or "God spoke." These
words, therefore, do not mean merely that the God who
spoke in times past is the same God who now speaks;
there is a far deeper significance. It means that, God
having spoken, this earlier revelation now completed
becomes the preparation for the later and final revelation. God spoke, and the message is to us "in these last
times" as truly as when spoken to the apostles and
prophets of the earlier Christian dispensation. What
wonderful condescension that the infinite God should
speak to man! Isaiah cried out, "Hear, O heavens, and
give ear, O earth: for the Lord hath spoken." Let us
then give wholehearted attention to this Epistle, and
with reverence and godly fear be obedient to the words
which God has spoken.

*The Character of the Mediators: "By the prophets . . .
by his [a] Son"* (1:1-2a). The depth and magnitude of
God's revelation of himself depend upon the character
of the medium through which that revelation is given.
Without the medium of a common language there can
be little of communication or understanding. Words as
we know them are but symbols. The truths which they
express lie deeper. Seen in this deeper meaning, words
become spirit and life. Otherwise words are but the
veil which hides both the truth of the message and the
person of the Revealer. Words may tell us something

The word for *last* in the expression "in these last days" is *eschatou*
(ἐσχάτου) in our present version and means "at the end of these days."
In the received text this word for *last* is *eschaton* (ἐσχάτων). Vaughan
suggests that the former means an epoch, the latter an era. Stuart
holds that since both terms are used in the Septuagint they were
regarded as synonyms, and it is a matter of indifference as to the
sense of the text, which reading is used. Westcott says that the expression "in the latter days" is molded from the Septuagint translation
of such texts as Gen. 49:1, "in the last days"; Num. 24:14, "in the latter
days"; and similar texts.

about the truth, but only as they become spirit and life does the glory of the Revealer burst through the veil. Then only are we brought into the presence of Him who is the Way, the Truth, and the Life. If therefore there is to be a perfect revelation of God to man, there must be a perfect medium of communication through which God can reveal himself. The perfection of the Son in whom God spake makes the message perfect. As a word, spoken or written, is an audible or visible representation of an invisible thought, so Christ as Son is the visible Image of the invisible God. This is brought out clearly when the writer tells us that God spake in times past by the prophets, but to us in these last times by a Son. It is evident then that the revelation is continuous insofar as God is the Author of both, but the latter is new and distinct in that it is mediated by Christ as the Son and not by the prophets. The ministry of the prophets could only prepare the way for the Son; it could never satisfy the heart of God or the souls of men. Nor is it the mere words of the Son through which God speaks to us; this would be but to reduce Him to the level of the prophets, who could use only external means of communication. It is through a Son, the Divine Word, the Second Person of the adorable Trinity, that God reveals himself to men. The Son himself, dwelling in the bosom of God (John 1:18), must come to dwell in the hearts of men, bringing to them the depth and rich-

---

The Greek text reads ἐν τοῖς προφήταις and ἐν υἱῷ, that is, "in the prophets" and "in [a] Son." Stuart points out that the frequent use of ἐν with the dative instead of διά with the genitive in the New Testament is a Hebraism; for ἐν corresponds to a Hebrew word which is employed with great latitude of signification, and in cases of the same nature as that in question, for instance, in Hos. 1:2, "The word of the Lord by Hosea." Only an occasional use of ἐν in this way is found in classical Greek writers. Thus the word appears in both the Authorized Version and the Revised Standard Version as by instead of in. Vaughan says that the contrast with ἐν υἱῷ or "in Son" suggests the sense of in the persons of rather than in the writings of. Westcott, using the word in instead of by, says that it was not simply through them as His instruments but in them (4:7) as the quickening power of their life. "In whatever way God made Himself known to them, they were His messengers, inspired by His Spirit, not in their words only but as men; and however the divine will was communicated to them they interpreted it to the people." (Cf. Epistle to the Hebrews: Stuart, p. 23; Vaughan, p. 2; Westcott, p. 6.)

ness of the divine life and inwardly communicating to them His flaming holiness and abounding love. Thus only through the Blood of the atonement and the love of God shed abroad in the heart by the Holy Spirit does God speak to men in a restored fellowship and holy communion.

The Nature of the Covenants. With the difference in the character of the mediators, we are brought at once to a consideration of the essential differences between the two covenants or testaments. Perhaps no one comes to realize the importance of this distinction without the special illumination of the Spirit, certainly not without a deep insight into the nature of the person and work of Christ. We come to see, sometimes by a special flash of divine truth, that the Old Testament was such because it was mediated by human means, God speaking through the prophets. Being mediated by human means, it was necessarily external; being external, it must take form of some kind, and therefore was ceremonial; and being ceremonial, it could only refer to the deeper truths by means of symbols, and therefore of necessity could be nothing more than preparatory. The New Testament, on the other hand, was mediated by the Divine Son, and was therefore internal rather than external; being internal, it was spiritual rather than ceremonial; and being spiritual, it was not merely preparatory but perfect. These distinctions will stand out more clearly if arranged in tabulated form:

The First Covenant	The Better Covenant
1. Human mediators (the prophets)	1. A Divine Mediator (the Son)
2. External (in administration)	2. Internal (in administration)
3. Ceremonial (in character)	3. Spiritual (in character)
4. Preparatory (in purpose)	4. Perfect (in expression)

Thus it is seen that the superiority of the new covenant is due to the superiority of the Mediator. The first covenant, being mediated by human means, the prophets, could be only external and partial; the new covenant, mediated by the Son, is both spiritual and perfect. Only by means of the mediation of the Divine Son could the revelation of the new testament be perfect, and only by the same Mediator could a covenant be introduced which would supersede the old covenant. The Old Testament is still a revelation from God, but preparatory to the "better" revelation of the New Testament. The Old Testament therefore served its purpose as a preparation for that which later was to be given through Christ. The new testament in His blood rests solidly upon the sure foundation of a better and eternal priesthood.

We must then grasp clearly and hold constantly before the mind the difference between the two covenants—the one in which the human element is more prominent, the other the divine; the one more external, the other more internal and spiritual. God speaking through the Son brings us into living contact with himself. It is the glory of this Epistle that it points the way from the initial stage of the Christian life to that of full access within the veil, where dwells the Shekinah of the Divine Presence. Recognizing then the essential difference in the testaments or covenants, three things follow: (1) The covenants represent two historical periods in the revelation of God to men—law and grace. (2) They represent two levels of Christian experience— life and love; and (3) They represent two stages in the spiritual progress of the Christian—the Word and the Spirit. These three aspects of the two covenants have far-reaching implications but can be given only brief treatment here.

Two Historical Periods of Revelation. God spoke as truly in the Old Testament as He does in the New. The prophets were God's messengers as well as the Son. But in the former the word was spoken *to us;* in the latter it is spoken *within us* by the Indwelling Word. The prophets' being finite precluded the full revelation. An infinite God can be fully revealed only by an infinite Mediator. Yet every truth of the New Testament has its roots in the Old and cannot be understood without it. The Spirit worked in both dispensations and His purposes in any age can be known only as they appear in every age. The Old Testament was a dispensation of law as over against a dispensation of grace. It was at once a preparatory and a disciplinary period in preparation for the fullness of times, a schoolmaster to bring us to Christ. This is still its office, for discipline must ever precede liberty; repentance, forgiveness; and a death to sin, the new life of holiness.

Two Levels of Christian Experience. Not only do the two testaments represent two stages in historical revelation; they also represent two levels of Christian experience—*life* and *love.* Life is given in regeneration or the new birth, and this life is a holy life, embracing as it does all of the graces of the Spirit, and manifesting itself in love to God and man. But this life is implanted in a soul which by inheritance from the race is infected with a depraved nature commonly known as inbred sin or the carnal mind. One who is regenerated or "born again" comes to see that which St. John so clearly taught, that fear may exist in the heart along with love. He sees also that there is an experience where perfect love casts out the fear that has torment (I John 4: 17-18). This experience must be his if he is to have boldness in the day of judgment. It is here that the meaning of the two testaments becomes intensely personal. If one sincerely seeks the experience of perfect love, he will realize afresh that the Old Testament was meant to show him his own impotence and bring him to that lowly plane of helplessness where alone grace operates. Through the Spirit he will then realize the truth of the expression of the saintly Fletcher, "Thy helplessness is no hindrance to my loving kindness," and by faith enter into the life within the veil, where perfect love casts out fear. Thus the purification of the heart from sin follows a testing time after conversion, to see whether or not the newborn soul will gladly and willingly surrender all in order to obtain the fullness of the blessing. This experience of perfect love is wrought by grace alone, through the atoning blood of Jesus and the sanctifying power of the Holy Spirit (Acts 15: 8-9). Love thus be-

comes the ruling motive of the sanctified life, and this
love is capable of infinite increase.

Two Stages of Spiritual Progress. The two testaments are likewise vitally related to progress in grace.
The life imparted in the new birth has a capacity for
continuous growth and development. When the hindrances are removed by the purification of the heart
from inbred sin, growth is more rapid and Christian experience more stable and secure. Progress is essential
to the well-being of every Christian. He must not only
be saved from his sins, but he must come to know Christ
in the deeper experiences of the spiritual life. St. Paul's
great desire was to "know him, and the power of his
resurrection, and the fellowship of his sufferings, being
made conformable unto his death" (Phil. 3:10).

In the onward progress of grace, the two testaments
represent the letter and the spirit, or in a deeper sense
the Word and the Spirit. Two dangers are apparent.
There are those who rest in the letter and soon become
devoid of spiritual life; "for the letter killeth, but the
spirit giveth life." On the other hand, there are those of
a more mystical tendency who would advance in the
Spirit but who overlook the fundamental necessity of
simple trust in the Word of God. One can never reach
the true inwardness of the Spirit without first passing
through the outwardness of the letter. This is as true of
each individual person as it is of historical revelation
generally. There is no other way. Simple faith in the
written Word of God brings the help of the Spirit, and
with the Spirit comes the true inwardness of prayer and
supplication. Perhaps just here is to be found the greatest obstacle to Christian progress. We tend to pray
merely in hope instead of faith. But faith alone is God's
method of answering prayer, whether for salvation or
for progress in the Christian life. To struggle in self-
effort in order to make one's self believe is not God's
plan. His plan is simple trust in the written Word, which
He then makes spirit and life to our souls.

Following the exordium, the writer begins his argument for the superiority of the Son, which is set forth in

three stages. (1) *The Son in His Pristine Glory* (1: 2b),
which has reference primarily to the Son in His cosmic
relations as the Heir of all things and the Creator of the
worlds. (2) *The Beautiful Gate to the Temple* (1: 3),
which refers more to the personal relation of the Son
to the Father. These are set forth in five chief characteristics, and furnish as strong a demonstration of the
deity of Christ as can well be conceived. Here as in the
prologue to St. John's Gospel (John 1: 1-18), the Son is
viewed as the Word which forms at once the ground of
God's revelation to man and man's access to God. He
is the Gateway into the temple of the Divine Presence.
(3) *The Majesty of the Son in His Mediatorial Kingdom*
(1: 4-14). This is an argument for the superiority of the
Son, first over the angels because of the better name, and
them over man as being the redemptive Head of the race.
These subjects must now be given further consideration.

The Son of God in His Pristine Glory

*Hath in these last days spoken unto us by his Son,
whom he hath appointed heir of all things, by whom also
he made the worlds* (Heb. 1: 2).

We have seen that the distinction between the Old
and New Testaments is based upon the character of the
mediators. The new covenant, mediated as it is by the
divine Son, not only fulfilled and brought to a close
the older dispensation, but is in itself the final stage of
revelation. It will be noted by the thoughtful reader
that the writer has so arranged his brief comparison of
the dispensations that the statement ends with the mention of the Son, whom he now proceeds to extol in a
continuous flow of thought. It is a unique and interesting characteristic of the author of this Epistle that when
he mentions the name of the Son he lingers long, either
to elaborate the theme or to meditate upon it in humble
devotion. Here he dwells upon the glory of the Son of
God, through whom the new dispensation is mediated.
The glories thus set forth will, to those who, like the
author, meditate long and quietly upon them, burst

forth into inner spiritual glory and fill with light the broad horizons of the believing soul. Let us then not be merely content with what He has done for us, but seek to enter into a deeper and more perfect fellowship with Him. "To be justified is great," said Mr. Bramwell, "to be sanctified is great, but oh to be filled with all the fulness of God!" God grant that we may continue to gaze into the divine glory until we all, "with open face beholding as in a glass the glory of the Lord, are changed into the same image from glory to glory, even as by the Spirit of the Lord" (II Cor. 3:18).

The Significance of the Word Son. The author of the Epistle to the Hebrews uniformly uses the word Son for Christ, while St. John in his prologue to the Fourth Gospel (1:1-18) uses the Greek term *Logos* or Word. It may be said that in general the term *Logos* is used for Christ in His preincarnate state, while the word *Son* is used for the *Logos* or Word incarnate. Both of these terms have basic trinitarian implications. As St. John uses the *Logos* or Word, it is both eternal and personal. "In the beginning was the Word, and the Word was with God, and the Word was God" (John 1:1). It is therefore the full objectification of the Father as God. As thus used, the Word bears only a necessary, not a free, relation to the Father except it be considered in relation to a Third, the Spirit, which as the "bond of unity or perfection" glorifies this necessary relationship into one of perfect freedom and love. Since a word is a necessary means of communication, the Incarnation, or the Word made flesh, becomes the sole gateway to communion and fellowship with God. It is also the gateway to the full meaning of human life. Hence our Lord could say, "He that hath seen me hath seen the Father" (John 14:9).

In this Epistle the word "Son" is used, but with the same trinitarian implications. Ideas are generated in the mind as truly as plants produce plants and animals generate animals. The difference lies in this, that in the mind the generation is spiritual. An idea or a thought is, before its expression, an internal work; and while distinct from the soul, is not separate from it. The mind can generate thought without losing anything of itself. Thus the Word or the Son is coetaneous and coeternal with the Father. The Father is not first and then thinks; for as a Person, God is never without thought. And this thought or Word of God as the Son is likewise distinct from the Father without being separated from Him, in the same manner that my thought is distinct from my soul without being separated from it. As an object held before a mirror reveals itself without destroying the original, so in an infinitely sublime manner the Son is eternally generated from the Eternal Father; and while distinct though not separate, the Son never diminishes the perfections of the Father. Thus the Father can say, "Thou art my Son; this day have I begotten thee"— today, in the eternal present, God engenders His Son in an act which will never end as it has never begun.

1. *Christ as the Heir of All Things* (1: 2a). The word "heir" refers to the original purpose of creation. God did not first make the worlds and then place them under the dominion of the Son; hence heirship is mentioned previous to creatorship. And since the Son was

The doctrine of the Scripture (John 1:14) is not that the eternal Son was united to a son of Mary, to a human nature in the concrete sense; but that the eternal, hypostatical Logos became man, assumed human nature in the abstract sense, concentrated itself by a free act of self-limitation prompted by love, into an embryo human life, a slumbering child-soul, as such formed for itself unconsciously and yet with creative energy a body in the womb of the Virgin, and hence He who in Scripture is called υἱός which incarnate is one and the same subject with that which with respect to the relation of oneness with the Father is called ὁ λόγος (or Word) or ὁ μονογενής (the Only-Begotten). Nay, even which incarnate He can only be called the Son of God because in Him the eternal μονογενής became man. And hence in the second place, we must guard against explaining the idea involved in υἱός from the relation of the incarnate man to the Father, as if He were called "Son" in the same sense in which other pious men are called "children of God."—EBRARD, *Epistle to the Hebrews*, pp. 15-16.

John Wesley in his *Notes* says: "Thou art my Son, God of God, Light of Light. This day have I begotten Thee,—I have begotten Thee from eternity, which by its unalterable permanency of duration, is one continued, unsuccessive day." Of this Dr. Adam Clarke says: "Leaving the point of dispute out of the question, this is most beautifully expressed; and I know not that this great man ever altered his views on the subject." Mr. Wesley retained Dr. Adam Clarke's own statement in the article "An Arian Antidote" in the fourth volume of the *Arminian Magazine*, published in 1781.

"appointed heir of all things" previous to their creation, the Son himself must likewise so have existed. The word "heir" as used here does not carry with it the thought of coming into possession after the death of a former possessor; instead it appears to have been derived from a Hebrew word which simply means "to acquire" or "to possess." In its simplest form it means Lord, Possessor, or Sovereign. It seems evident that there is a further connection between heirship as here stated and the words "when he had by himself purged our sins, sat down on the right hand of the Majesty on high" (1:3b). There is a twofold heirship. The Son is Heir by creation; that is, He embodied in himself the purpose of the Father; and He is Heir by the redemption of the purchased possession also. "How proper and natural it is," says Ebrard, "that He through whom the universe was made, after having humbled Himself and accomplished the gracious will of the Father, should as His reward be also invested with the dominion over the universe as a permanent inheritance" (EBRARD, *Epistle to the Hebrews*, p. 19). The word "heir," therefore, carries with

Although the infinite essence of the Word is united in one person with the nature of man, yet we have no idea of its incarceration or confinement. For the Son of God miraculously descended from heaven, yet in such a manner that He never left heaven; He chose to be miraculously conceived in the womb of the Virgin, to live on the earth, and to be suspended on the cross; and yet He never ceased to fill the universe, in the same manner as from the beginning.—CALVIN, *Institutes*, II, xiii, 4 (Vol. I, pp. 525-26).

As in Christ the personal union of the divine and human natures is in the most perfect manner accomplished, while yet the two natures are in no way confounded, the two thus remain always distinguishable, yet are never to be conceived as actually separated. We must regard therefore, as erroneous the language of so many earlier writers who limit the exaltation exclusively to the human nature of Christ. It applies rather to the person of the God-man.—LANGE, *Commentary on Hebrews*, p. 31.

The word *heir* marks the original purpose of creation. The dominion originally promised to Adam (Gen. 1:28; Psalms 8:6; 2:7) was gained by Christ . . . The term is used in relation to the possession, as marking the fulness of right, resting upon personal connection and not as implying a passing away and a succession, in relation to a present possessor. The heir as such vindicates his title to what He holds. . . . The heirship of the Son was realized by the Son incarnate through His humanity; but the writer speaks of the Son simply as Son being heir. In such language we can see the indication of the truth which is expressed by the statement that the incarnation is in essence independent of the Fall, though conditioned by it as to its circumstances.—WESTCOTT, *Epistle to the Hebrews*, p. 8.

it something more than the universal power bestowed upon Christ by which He enables His people to triumph over sin and to preach effectively to the nations during the gospel age. It means also that this power shall come to perfect fulfillment, according to the Messianic promise of Rom. 4: 13, when, at the Second Advent, He shall banish sin and its consequences from the race, remove the curse from the earth, and reign in universal power and glory.

2. *The Son as Creator.* "By whom also he made the worlds" (1: 2b). The purpose of the creation having been stated, the writer proceeds to show that the Son is also Creator. Not only were the worlds made on account of Him as to their purpose, but by Him as the instrumental cause of their existence. St. John states this emphatically: "All things through him came into being (or existence); and without him came into being not one (single thing) which has come into being" (John 1: 3). It is evident, therefore, that God's relation to all things without himself is through the Son, who is the Beginning and End of all existence. In the fact that He made the worlds lies the possibility of harmony between natural and historical revelation. This harmony does not now exist because of man's sinfulness, nor can it be effected merely by natural development. It can be accomplished only through the special divine acts of the Incarnation and the Second Advent, by which sin and its consequences are removed from the world. Christ is not only Head of the Church, but the Head of all things to the Church. Were this not true, there would be no sound basis for Christian experience and no providential security for the Church.

The term for "worlds" is *aionas* (αἰῶνας) or "the ages," while in the Septuagint the word is *gen* (γῆν) or "earth." The universe may be regarded either as to its actual constitution or as an order which exists through time. The world as material is *cosmos* (κόσμος); the world as temporal is *aion* (αἰῶν) or "the ages." Both of these Greek terms are used in the Epistle to the

Ephesians (2:2), where St. Paul speaks of the "time-state," *aiona* (αἰῶνα), of this "matter-world," *kosmou* (κόσμου). When the singular of this world is used it generally means "age." When the plural is used, as in the case of "the worlds," it suggests the idea, not of a continuous, but of an aggregate, duration, or the world as marked by successive periods of distance. St. Paul speaks of the "the ages to come." The Son as the Word incarnate is He who has made all things, and if His glory was hidden while in the tabernacle of the flesh, we must ever bear in mind that He is still the Creator, and therefore learn to recognize Him in this lowly guise.

These two statements concerning Christ as Heir and as Creator when taken together form an important transition in the author's thought. They are not to be considered co-ordinate. The phrase "heir of all things" is a universal, under which is to be subsumed the particular statement, "by whom also he made the worlds" or ages. This places the Son in the position of an Agent or sovereign Authority, preparing the way for one of the chief aims of the Epistle—the bringing in of a new age to supersede the old. It looks forward to the glorious position of the Son, who, having ascended to the Father, received of Him the promised Spirit, which He poured out upon His waiting disciples at Pentecost—the great inauguration day of the Holy Spirit.

The Beautiful Gate to the Temple

Who being the brightness of his glory, and the express image of his person, and upholding all things by the word of his power, when he had by himself purged our sins, sat down on the right hand of the Majesty on high (Heb. 1:3).

The glories of the Son of God in His cosmic relations having been established, the writer now proceeds to set forth the glories of the Son in His personal relations with the Father. Here He is shown to be at once the revealing and the enabling Word of God. God having spoken to us through His Word as the incarnate Son, this Word becomes the Gateway into the temple of communion and fellowship with God. The Son is consequently portrayed under the figure of the beautiful gate to the Temple. Josephus tells us "that the temple had nine gates, which were on every side covered with gold and silver; but there was one gate, which was without the holy house, and was of Corinthian brass, and greatly excelled those which were only covered with gold and silver. The magnitude of the other gates were equal one to another; but that of the Corinthian gate, which opened on the East, over against the gate of the holy house itself, was much larger, for its height was fifty cubits, or about seventy-five feet, and it was adorned after the most costly manner, as having richer and thicker plates of silver and gold upon them than the other. This last is probably the gate that is called beautiful, because it was on the outside of the temple, to which there was an easy access, and because it was evidently the most costly."

We may say that "the brightness of his glory" is symbolized by the polished Corinthian brass, more precious than gold; the "express image of his person" may well be signified by the firm foundation upon which the gate rested, for the word *hypostasis* meant originally the foundation, the substratum, which came to be interpreted as steadfastness, purpose, resolution, or determination. "Upholding all things by the word of his power" is clearly a reference to the gateposts which upheld the crown of the structure. The glorious light

That the historical Mediator of the final revelation of God is the ante-mundane Mediator of the creation of the world, imparts to Him a special majesty and dignity beyond that of all mediated creators. The comparison of Him with the angels shows that He is not, in this relation conceived as unconscious, intermediate cause, but has exercised mediating agency in a personal existence. And the declaration that He is the beaming image of God's glory and the impress of His substance, shows that the Mediator who is distinguished above all beings, and even above the angels, by the name of "Son," does not bear His filial name in a conventional and theocratic sense.—LANGE, *Commentary on Hebrews*, p. 31.

Westcott states that the position of the participle ὤν, which means "being" or "bearing," gives emphasis to the expression, and further points out "that this participle describes the *absolute* and not simply the present essence and action of the Son. In particular it guards against the idea of 'adoption' in Sonship, and affirms the permanence of the Son during His historic work."—WESTCOTT, *Epistle to the Hebrews*, p. 9.

which shone through the gateway reveals at once the darkness of the world in sin and the supreme redemptive act by which He purged our sins and returned in His mediatorial exaltation to "the right hand of the Majesty on high." The glory of the Son as set forth in the sublime and lofty expressions of this scriptural passage is worthy of the most careful and profound study. The scriptural order will be followed in this preliminary discussion of the person and work of the Son.

The Son Is the Brightness or Effulgence of the Father's Glory. The word *apaugasma* ($\dot{\alpha}\pi\alpha\dot{\upsilon}\gamma\alpha\sigma\mu\alpha$), which occurs only here in the Scriptures, signifies the radiation of light flowing from a luminous body, and comes from a root word meaning to shine or emit splendor. The word effulgence perhaps most closely expresses the thought. Some have held that this brightness or effulgence is to be interpreted as a reflection of light, that is, the reflected image thrown upon a smooth reflecting surface. Others view it as active light, or the rays which continually emanate from a luminous body. Ebrard points out that the former view presupposes the distinct hypostatical existence of the Son, the emphasis here being on the qualitative sameness with the Father. The second view, which appears to be the most worthy, regards the Son as the perpetual and continuous life-act of the Father. His own view is that the word "denotes not the brightness received from another body, and thrown back as a reflection or mirrored image, nor the light continually proceeding from a shining body as a light streaming out and losing itself in space, but it denotes a light, or a bright ray which is radiated from another light in so far as it is viewed as now become an independent light." Vaughan also holds that the word expresses the results rather than the act of shining, and is therefore more suitable as a word for the Person

---

The expression ray-image best answers to the original; as a ray-image, it is a living image composed of rays not merely ones received and reflected, but it is conceived of as independent and permanent. It is more than a mere ray, more than a mere image; a sun produced from the original light.—EBRARD, *Epistle to the Hebrews*, p. 21.

in whom all the rays of the divine glory are concentrated. "Effulgency may be the nearest English word, but it lacks the characteristic idea of the embodiment of the emitted splendor."

The Son Is the Express Image of the Father in His Person or Essence (1:3b). This is the second statement concerning the Son, and is directly related to the preceding, as substance or essence is related to brightness or out-shining. These words are sometimes translated "the impress of his substance," from *charakter* (χαρακτήρ, "impress") and *hypostasis* (ὑπόστασις, "substance, essence, person"). Thus as *apaugasma* (ἀπαύγασμα, "brightness, out-shining") has reference to the appearance of God externally, so *hypostasis* (ὑπόστασις, "substance, essence, person") has reference to the Son as the exact expression of the substance or essence of the Father internally. In the language of the theologians, the former may be said to be *ad extra*, the latter *ad intra*. The *glory* and the *substance* are therefore related to each other as are the *effulgence* or brightness and the *express image of His person*.

But these words are of sufficient importance to demand fuller treatment. The word *charakter* (χαρακτήρ) comes from the idea of a seal or an engraving. Westcott says that there is no word in English which exactly renders it. "If there were a sense of 'express' (i.e., expressed image) answering to 'impress,' this would be the best equivalent." The word may refer to the agent or the instrument for engraving, but more commonly refers to the stamp or the engraved letter or figure which is used to make an impression on wax. It therefore means an "exact likeness" or "characteristic repre-

---

Generally speaking χαρακτήρ may be said to be that by which anything is directly recognized through corresponding signs under a particular aspect, though it may include only a few features of the object. It is so far a primary and not a secondary source of knowledge. Χαρακτήρ conveys the representative traits only, and therefore is distinguished from εἰκών which gives a complete representation under the condition of earth of that which it figures; and from μορφή which marks essential form. (Cf. I Cor. 11:7; II Cor. 4:4; Col. 1:15; 3:10).—WESTCOTT, *The Epistle to the Hebrews*, p. 12.

sentation." For this reason the translation "express image of his person" seems to convey the truth more accurately than the words "impress of his substance." The latter rather implies the *wax* than the *seal* by which the impression is made.

This sublime expression, therefore, suggests the exact resemblance of Christ to the Father in His substance or essence and not merely in outward appearance. This *express image* is an infinite and eternal fact, and not merely something stamped upon Christ at His incarnation. No, Christ is invested with the same attributes as the Father, and is of the same nature and essence. He is the full "objectivation" of the Father; and since the Father is infinite and eternal, the Son, in order to be His exact image or full expression, must likewise be infinite and eternal. For this reason the Son is the Mediator of the spiritual world. Externally for the world and for man, He is the Being in whom all the rays of the divine glory are concentrated for communion, and who therefore mirrors forth the Deity in all His perfections of wisdom and power, of holiness and love. Internally, the ground of this revelation lies in the fact He is of the Divine Essence—"the only begotten Son, which is in the bosom of the Father" (John 1: 18).

The word *hypostasis* (ὑπόστασις), which is here translated *person*, literally means "to stand under," and was used by the fathers in the sense of *substance* or *essence*. The word *person* as used in the Authorized Version is better expressed by the Greek word *prosopon* (πρόσωπον). Since the word *hypostasis* came to be ap-

Westcott says that the word *hypostasis* properly means "that which stands beneath" as a sediment or foundation or ground of support. From this general sense come the special senses of firmness, confidence, that in virtue of which a thing is what it is, the essence of any being. "When this meaning of essence was applied to the Divine Being two distinct usages arose in the course of debate. If men looked at the Holy Trinity under the aspect of the one Godhead, there was only one *hypostasis*, one divine essence. If on the other hand they looked at each Person in the Holy Trinity, then that by which each Person is what He is, His *hypostasis*, was necessarily regarded as distinct, and there were three *hypostases*. In the first case *hypostasis* as applied to the one Godhead was treated as equivalent to *ousia;* in the other case it was treated as the equivalent of *prosopon*."—WESTCOTT, *Epistle to the Hebrews*, p. 13.

plied to each of the three Persons in the Trinity only
after a long period of theological development, these distinctions cannot be read into the text. The meaning of
the word *person* as here used is simply essence or *ousia*
(ovσία), and thus brings the divine nature of the Son
immediately before us. Christ is the "express image"
or "exact expression" of God. In Him and by Him is
God fully and perfectly revealed, and this by such a
likeness as originates in perfect identity. All the perfections of God belong to and dwell in the Son, who is the
self-manifestation of God. It would seem that no stronger
language could be used to express the deity of the Son.

*The Son Upholds All Things by the Word or Utter-
ance of His Power.* The Greek term translated here as
"word" is not *logos* (λόγος), the term applied to the preincarnate Christ by St. John (1:1); but *remati* (ρήματι),
"utterance" or "saying." The thought conveyed is not
that He bears up all things by effort as a dead weight,
but as done without effort, by the simple utterance of
His own power. The expression "word of his power"
seems to have been a form of speech common among the
Hebrews, and is brought over into the New Testament
with the simple meaning "powerful word." It has its
parallel in the "God said" of Genesis in which the worlds
were spoken into existence by a simple utterance. The
word *pheron* (φέρων) signifies the bearing, upholding, or preserving of "all things" which are previously
ascribed to Him as Creator. Thus the writer brings before us in this expression the infinite energy and all-

---

Adam Clarke points out that the Jewish writers frequently express
the perfection of the divine nature by the phrases, "He bears all things
both above and below; He carries all His creatures; He bears His world;
He bears all worlds by His power." This is borne out by Isa. 63:9, where
it is said that God bare His people and carried them all the days of old;
and again by St. Paul in Col. 1:16, where he declares that "by him all
things consist" or are made to stand together.

Lindsay states the matter well when He says that "the preservation
of the universe indeed, requires the continual exercise of the very
same power which first brought it into being; and if the sustaining arm
of Christ were for one moment withdrawn, the innumerable suns and
systems which people space would crumble into dust, and return to
the nothing from which they sprang."—LINDSAY, *Lectures on the Epistle
to the Hebrews,* pp. 37-38.

pervading power of Almighty God in a manner awe-inspiring and worthy of our highest praise.

"When He Had by Himself Purged Our Sins" (1: 3d). Having declared the glory of the Son, first in His absolute nature (ὤν), and then in His relation to finite being (φέρων), the writer immediately states the purpose for which He was sent into the world—that He might purge or make expiation for sin. The word *katharismos* (καθαρισμός) usually means *purification*, as in Heb. 9: 14, "purge your conscience from dead works"; and I John 1: 7, "the blood of Jesus Christ his Son cleanseth us from all sin." In the Septuagint the word sometimes bears the sense of *atonement*, as in Exod. 29: 36, "Thou shalt cleanse the altar, when thou hast made atonement for it." However in Hellenistic Greek the word is often used in the sense of *expiation*, and the text would then read, "having by himself made expiation for our sins." Lowrie says that it means the expiation of sins by blotting them out. This is probably the sense in which it is used here, as seems to be indicated by a later assertion that "this man, after he had offered one sacrifice for sins for ever, sat down on the right hand of God" (Heb. 10: 12). The words "by himself" indicate that the expiation was made without the help of angels or others, He being Priest and Sacrifice, Altar and Incense, and everything needed to make full atonement. This is further shown by the use of the middle voice of the verb, which indicates that what He did was of himself and as His own work. The language in which this fact of expiation is presented is evidently a reference to the purification by sacrifice under the Levitical economy, and is a fulfillment of that which was accomplished in symbol on the great Day of Atonement. This purification, therefore, is a provision and potency for the taking away of sin, whether in act or nature. That which has the virtue of purging or cleansing away sin was done once for all by Christ's vicarious sacrifice on earth and before His ascent to heaven. This prepares the reader for the main teaching of the Epistle—the high priestly work of Christ.

"Sat Down on the Right Hand of the Majesty on High" (1:3*e*). The Heir of all the ages, the Creator of the worlds, having become incarnate and through His sufferings and death made expiation for sin, is now in His human nature as man—and continuing to be man— exalted to the throne of God, and is seated at the right hand of the Majesty on high. To sit at the right hand of God not only signifies honor, approbation, and reward, but in a deeper sense participation in dignity and authority. This participation, as well as the thought of a finished work, is expressed in the words "sat down." No priest under the old covenant ministered except in a standing position, for his work was never finished. But Christ, "after he had offered one sacrifice for sins for ever, sat down on the right hand of God; from henceforth expecting till his enemies be made his footstool. For by one offering he hath perfected for ever them that are sanctified. Whereof the Holy Ghost also is a witness to us" (Heb. 10:12-15*a*). It must be clearly understood that this conferred exaltation and authority are granted Him as a reward of His humiliation. In His divine nature the Son could not be exalted, for He was already infinite in majesty, glory, and power; while on the other hand, had our Mediator not been the Divine Son, He could not thus have shared in the divine glory and government. The elevation of Christ, therefore, to the seat of sovereign power at the right hand of the Father can only refer to what has been called the mediatorial Kingdom, for it is described as the result of His expiatory sacrifice. Having made expiation, He "sat down."

Concerning the expression "sat down at the right hand of the Majesty on high," Ebrard says: "Never and nowhere does the Holy Scripture apply this expression to denote that form of world-government, which the Logos (or eternal Son) exercised as eternally pre-existent; the sitting at the right hand of God rather denotes everywhere, only that participation in the divine majesty, dominion and glory, to which the Messiah was exalted after His work was finished, therefore *in time*, and which is consequently exercised by Him as the glorified Son of Man *under the category of time.* Already in Psalm 110:1 where the expression first occurs, it applies to the future, the *second David*, at a future time exalted."—EBRARD, *Biblical Commentary on the Epistle to the Hebrews,* p. 27.

THE MAJESTY OF THE SON OF GOD AS MEDIATOR

From a discussion of the glories of the Divine Son in His pristine state, and His personal relations with the Father, the writer now turns to a consideration of His supremacy over the angels in His mediatorial estate as the God-Man. The abruptness with which a new subject is introduced, and which we meet here for the first time, is a phenomenon peculiar to the Epistle to the Hebrews. But despite the apparent abruptness of the approach there appears to be in the mind of the writer a sufficient reason for the transition. The Son seated at the right hand of the Majesty on high implies the thought of myriads of angels bending prostrate in worship before Him, and hence the writer is led at once to make a formal comparison between them. But aside from this, the argument is directed at the high concept of angels as held by the Jews. They believed, as was stated by Stephen, that their law "was given by the ministration of angels" (see Acts 7:53), and St. Paul asserts that the law "was ordained by angels in the hand of a mediator" (Gal. 3:19). The Jews therefore

The Jews had the highest opinion of the transcendent excellence of angels; they even associated them with God in the creation of the world, and suppose them to be of the private council of the Most High; and thus they understood Genesis 1:26. "Let us make man in our own image in our own likeness"; and the Lord said to the ministering angels that stood before Him, and who were created on the second day, "Let us make man in our own image." (*Targum of Jonathan ben Uzziel*) And they even allow them to be worshipped for the sake of their Creator, and as His representatives; though they will not allow them to be worshipped for their own sake. As therefore, the Jews considered them next to God, and none entitled to their adoration but God; on their own ground the apostle proves Jesus Christ to be God, because God commanded all the angels of heaven to worship Him. He therefore, who is greater than the angels, and the object of their adoration is God. But Jesus Christ is greater than the angels, and the object of their adoration; therefore Jesus Christ must be God.—ADAM CLARKE, *Commentary*, IV, 687.

Lowrie says: "The suddenness with which this subject of comparison, viz., the angels, is introduced occasions some perplexity. But in the sequel we notice that Moses (2:2) and Melchizedek (5:10; 6:20), and Levi (7:5) are in turn brought into comparison with as little preface." "We shall also have occasion to notice in the author a similar manner of introducing turns of thought and obvious applications, and conclusions from statements made. We may therefore treat this as a matter of style with him."—LOWRIE, *An Explanation of Hebrews*, p. 11.

prided themselves on the fact that thousands of angels
had been employed in the establishment of their law,
and consequently cherished a strong attachment for it.
But they drew from this a false conclusion. They argued
that since the law was given by beings so glorious, it
would never be abrogated. The writer does not deny
their premises, but he holds their conclusion to be false.

Having traced Christ's work of expiation to His
exaltation to the right hand of the Father, it becomes evident at once that He who has ascended the seat of sovereign power is manifestly "higher than the angels" and
superior to them in influence and authority. The writer
therefore assures the Jews that the new dispensation
now introduced is superior to that of the angels; and
that whatever glory the old dispensation may have acquired through them, the new is vastly superior in that
it is administered by the mediatorial King. But the
writer also supplies somewhat of a measure which would
enable the Jews to form some idea as to the extent of
Christ's superiority. He does this in the words "as he
hath by inheritance obtained a more excellent name than
they." This name not only carries with it eminence,
honor, and distinction, but *more* eminence, *more* honor,
and *more* distinction. Furthermore, the name here used
not only indicates a difference in degree but also a difference in kind. He is high above the angels in that His
name is ascribed to Him by the Father as an inheritance,
on the ground of His being the only begotten Son. He is
therefore "so much better than the angels."

"But why was it of so much importance to him to carry
out that comparison of the Son with the angels?" This
is the question asked by Ebrard, who before giving the
answer to it reviews the opinions of Bleek, Tholuck, and
others. While Bleek is of the opinion "that the belief of

The Jews believed that God at one time held court on earth in order
to give grandeur to the scene, and had committed to the angels the execution of the law. "The Lord came from Sinai," they said; ". . . from his
right hand went a fiery law." "The chariots of God are twenty thousand,
even thousands of angels." To the Jews, therefore, it would be a fearful
thing to violate the sanctity of such a dread covenant.

the Israelites in the cooperation of angels in the giving of the Sinaitic law, led the author to speak of angels," Ebrard thinks that the true motive lies deeper. He says, "The entire Old Testament is related to the New as the angels are to the Son." Since in the Old Testament, God had condescended to approach His people as "the angel of the Lord," and since Moses was exalted to speak "face to face" with God, it was necessary that the author should show that these two mediators of the Old Testament should find their higher unity in Christ. Hence he proposes to show that the Son was greater than the angels as the problem of the first part, and that He "was counted worthy of more glory than Moses" as the problem of the second part.

"The mediation in the Old Testament is a double one, a chain consisting of two members, Moses and the Angel of the Lord." There stands a man who is raised above other men with whom he stands on the same level as a sinner, and brought nearer to God, yet without partaking in the divine nature. Here stands the form of an angel, in which God reveals himself to His people, become like to men yet without becoming man. God and man thus approach nearer to each other, but there is as yet no real union of God with man. But in the Son, God and man have become personally one—not merely outwardly near to each other, but revealing His fullness in the Man Christ Jesus. And in the person of this incarnate One, not merely a member of humanity has come near to God, but as He was born of a virgin, He is himself eternal God. In Him as the First Fruits of the new humanity has mankind been exalted to the inheritance of all things. (Cf. Ebrard, *Commentary on Hebrews*, p. 30.) Since the Word is the medium of communication between God and man, the Incarnation is the sole gateway into the communion and fellowship with God. And since Deity and humanity have been combined in the one Person of the Son, He becomes not only the Gateway into the presence of God, but the Gateway also into the full meaning of human life.

THE SEVENFOLD ARGUMENT FROM THE OLD TESTAMENT

The writer of this Epistle in comparing the Son with angels divides his argument into two parts, with what is known as the "First Warning" separating between them. The first section (1: 4-14) deals with the Son as superior to angels by virtue of His eternal existence as the Son of God. As there are seven statements concerning the eternal Son as the Second Person of the Godhead, so here are seven statements in proof of the superiority of the Son over the angels. This refers especially to the Son in His incarnate or mediatorial state. Then follows the warning against neglect of the "great salvation" (2: 1-4); and after this the argument is resumed (2: 5-8, 16), where Christ is now seen to be superior to men. Since the Jews had denied the sonship of Jesus, it was necessary that the writer should show that this was not a new

The presentation of the deity of Christ from the standpoint of the Old Testament would have peculiar weight with the Jews, and would lend completeness and finality to the Christian position. The following are the scriptures cited.

1. The Divine Son and His Inheritance. "I will declare the decree: the Lord hath said unto me, Thou art my Son; this day have I begotten thee. Ask of me, and I shall give thee the heathen for thine inheritance, and the uttermost parts of the earth for thy possession" (Ps. 2:7-8).

2. The Divine Son and the Davidic Covenant. "I will be his father, and he shall be my son" (II Sam. 7:13). A similar expression is found in Ps. 89:26-27. "He shall cry unto me, Thou art my father, my God, and the rock of my salvation. Also I will make him my firstborn, higher than the kings of the earth."

3. The Divine Son and His Glorious Second Advent. "Confounded be all they that serve graven images, that boast themselves of idols: worship him, all ye gods" (Ps. 97:7).

4. The Divine Son and the Majesty of His Kingdom. "Who maketh his angels spirits; his ministers a flaming fire" (Ps. 104:4).

5. The Divine Son and the Perpetuity of His Kingdom. "Thy throne, O God, is for ever and ever: the sceptre of thy kingdom is a right sceptre. Thou lovest righteousness, and hatest wickedness: therefore God, thy God, hath anointed thee with the oil of gladness above thy fellows" (Ps. 45:6-7).

6. The Divine Son and the Immutability of His Kingdom. "Of old hast thou laid the foundation of the earth: and the heavens are the work of thy hands. They shall perish, but thou shalt endure: yea, all of them shall wax old like a garment; as a vesture shalt thou change them, and they shall be changed: but thou art the same, and thy years shall have no end" (Ps. 102:25-27).

7. The Divine Son and the Triumphant Consummation. "The Lord said unto my Lord, Sit thou at my right hand, until I make thine enemies thy footstool" (Ps. 110:1).

revelation, but had its basis in their own Old Testament Scriptures. His total argument is enforced by seven scripture quotations found chiefly in the Psalms. It is worthy of note that the author of this Epistle at no time refers to the human agents of revelation, but only to its divine source. In the seven quotations used in this chapter are the words "He saith"; and later in the Epistle is found the expression, the "Holy Ghost saith."

Two truths are closely related to this emphasis upon the divine authorship of the Scriptures. *First*, these wonderful expositions must have been inbreathed by the Spirit, who alone could have given the author the depth of meaning and insight to unfold the unique truths found in these Old Testament texts. *Second*, and co-ordinate with the first, is the fact that the presence of the Spirit who inspired these truths in the Old Testament is likewise necessary to unfold and interpret them in the New Testament. Hence we have the climactic promise of the New Testament, that Jesus on His departure would send "another Comforter" who as the Spirit of truth would guide us into all truth.

The Divine Son and the Superiority of His Inheritance. "Being made so much better than the angels, as he hath by inheritance obtained a more excellent name than they. For unto which of the angels said he at any time, Thou art my Son, this day have I begotten thee?" (1:4-5a) These verses are taken from the second psalm, in which the course of thought is of extraordinary brilliance and force. The imagery is doubtless taken from

---

The reference to the second psalm is as follows: "I will declare the decree: the Lord hath said unto me, Thou art my Son; this day have I begotten thee" (2:7). The inheritance is mentioned in the following verse. "Ask of me, and I shall give thee the heathen for thine inheritance, and the uttermost parts of the earth for thy possession" (2:8). St. Paul applies the first text to the Resurrection in the words, "God . . . raised up Jesus again; as it is also written in the second psalm, Thou art my Son, this day have I begotten thee" (Acts 13:33); and also that He was "declared to be the Son of God with power, according to the spirit of holiness, by the resurrection from the dead" (Rom. 1:4). St. John so uses it also in Rev. 1:5, "Jesus Christ . . . the first begotten of the dead, and the prince of the kings of the earth." The argument from the inheritance is based on both the better name and the universality of its extent.

the anointing of David as king over Israel, but the psalm itself is Messianic. This is evident because (1) it is in harmony with numerous other Messianic prophecies, and (2) it was explicitly referred to by the apostles as applying to the Messiah (Acts 4: 25-28). To rightly understand the argument which the writer draws from these passages, it must be constantly kept in mind that the word "Son" as here used does not primarily refer to the Son as the Second Person of the adorable Trinity, although this underlies each of the scriptures quoted, but to the Divine Son as having become man. This embraces not only the Incarnation, in which the Divine Son assumed a human nature, but also to the full scope and dignity of the God-Man as further manifested in His resurrection, His ascension, and His session at the right hand of the Father. This brings us to the first point to be proved, i.e., Christ's superiority over the angels in His mediatorial work. The argument as drawn from this text includes three important steps: the name, the inheritance, and the first-begotten.

1. The word *onoma* (ὄνομα), here t r a n s l a t e d "name," is by some rendered "title," and by others "dignity." The name sets before the mind that which a person is in himself, the name of God or of Christ being that which embraces the whole of the revealed nature, attributes, and work. Hence the "name" designates that which the Messiah should be according to the Scriptures. Westcott says: "By the name we are to understand, probably not the name of the Son simply, though this is applied to Christ as part of it, but the Name which gathered up all that Christ was found to be by believers, Son, Sovereign and Creator, the Lord of the Old Testament." The word *kreitton* (κρείττων), translated "better," frequently means "different" (Rom. 12: 6), or "excellent" (Heb. 8: 6), but as here used means "being different by superiority." The word *genomenos* (γενόμενος), "having become" or "having been made," is further evidence that the reference here is to Christ as the incarnate Son. As previously indicated, however,

the divine nature is not excluded, for it lies at the foundation of His mediatorial work, in this and all the following passages.

2. The inheritance explains how the name "Son" came to belong to Jesus in a unique sense, different from that of any creature. This inheritance by which He transcends the angels in dignity and glory is directly connected with His incarnation. The name "Son" was His from all eternity as the Second Person of the Trinity; but when in the Incarnation He assumed a human nature and became the God-Man—truly divine and truly human —His human nature acquired or inherited the name "Son" also. This was by virtue of the union of the human nature with the Divine Person, and also by virtue of the work done in and through this human nature. Thus St. Luke says, "He . . . shall be called the Son of the Highest" (Luke 1: 32). The use of the perfect tense, "has inherited," implies that the title "Son" which He bore in the eternal order continues to be His in the temporal order of His incarnate life. The human nature which He assumed is so inseparably joined to His person as the God-Man that it is exalted to the right hand of God, and there becomes an intercessory presence for us. The essence of the argument therefore is this, that Jesus Christ as the incarnate Son of God infinitely excels in glory. For to which of them has He ever said, "Thou art my Son, this day have I begotten thee"? The Son is far greater in excellence than the angels; to that same degree His heavenly administration is superior to theirs. Angels may minister to us; only the Son can minister the Spirit within us.

3. The words, "This day have I begotten thee," (1: 5a) are applied by St. Paul to the Resurrection in Acts 13: 33, and by St. John in Rev. 1: 5. The Son was indeed the "only begotten of the Father before all worlds, and the deity of the Son necessarily underlies the Incarnation and the Resurrection; otherwise it would exclude His work as Mediator. But the Son was also

begotten again in the Resurrection, which marked the
full out-birth of the humanity of Jesus from its state of
humiliation to that of its glorification and exaltation. It
was in the Resurrection that Christ overcame death as
the penalty of sin. Here the Son of God as the Son of
Man enters into His glory. This is clearly indicated in
the high priestly prayer of Jesus: "And now, O Father,
glorify thou me with thine own self with the glory which
I had with thee before the world was" (John 17: 5). St.
Paul makes a similar statement when he speaks of Christ
as "made of the seed of David according to the flesh;
and declared to be the Son of God with power, according
to the spirit of holiness, by the resurrection from the
dead" (Rom. 1: 3-4). The words "this day" refer most
properly, then, to the day of Resurrection, in which
God gave the fullest proof that Jesus was both innocent
and righteous. The miraculous power by which He was
raised from the dead declares Him to be the Son of God;
and His body, which never saw corruption, was raised
a spiritual body—the first-born from the dead, and the
first fruits of them that sleep.

The problem which faces the Jewish Christians
concerning the deity of the Son in His Messianic aspect
is perhaps most ably set forth by Ebrard in his *Commentary* (p. 46) as follows: "Two things must not be
forgotten if we would rightly apprehend the meaning
and the argument of the verse before us; *first,* that the
author simply testifies to the Godhead of Christ (1: 2-3)
as a thing already known by his readers through the
apostolic preaching, and acknowledged by them, without deeming it necessary to adduce proofs for this doctrine; *secondly,* that for this very reason, the aim of
verse 6 is not to prove that the Messiah is the Son of
God, but that the Messiah, who is known to be identical

The perfect *kekleronomeken* (κεκληρονόμεκεν) "inheritance" lays stress
upon the present possession of the name which was inherited by the
ascended Christ. That which had been proposed in the eternal counsel,
was realized when the work of redemption was completed. The possession
of the name—His eternally—was in our human mode of speech, consequent on the Incarnation, and the permanent issue of it.—WESTCOTT,
Epistle to the Hebrews, p. 17.

54   THE EPISTLE TO THE HEBREWS

with the Son of God, is, even in the Old Testament
dispensation, placed higher than the angels. For it was
on this point that the readers needed to be instructed.
They had no doubts about the Messiahship of Jesus
and the divinity of the Messiah, but this whole Messianic
revelation was still in their eyes but an *appendix* to the
Mosaic revelation, given only on account of Moses and
Israel, only a blossoming branch of the religion of Israel.
They had yet to be brought to know, that the divinity
of Him who was the organ of the New Testament revelation necessarily involves His infinite elevation above the
organs of the Old Testament; that the old dispensation
was ended on account of the new, and that this new
dispensation was on account of all mankind, not on
account of the old. This they had yet to be taught, and
this is precisely what is designed to be proved in these
verses, the proof being drawn from the divinity of Christ,
already acknowledged by the readers."

The Divine Son and the Davidic Covenant. The
writer follows with another quotation intended to show
the superiority of the Son over the angels. This text,
however, approaches the subject in reverse order. "I
will be to him a Father, and he shall be to me a Son"
(1: 5b). The words are quoted immediately from
II Sam. 7: 8-17, but the same thought, and in the same
order, is found in Ps. 89: 26-27. Historically these
words are associated with the Davidic covenant, and
God's promise to David of a son—Solomon—who should
reign in his stead and whose kingdom should excel in
glory. But the words have always been held to have a
wider meaning, and look forward to the pre-existent
Son, as the idealized "seed of David" upon which the
glorious kingdom of Christ should be founded. This
Kingdom our Lord established in its initial stage while
on earth, and it consists of a spiritual reign in the hearts
of men. Thus St. Paul speaks of the Kingdom as within
—a reign of righteousness and peace and joy in the
Holy Ghost. But this Kingdom must come to its full
completion in a reign, not only within the hearts of

men, but over all things. Only as all things are brought
in subjection to Him can the Kingdom be said to have
fully come. It is to this then that the writer hastens
as the next stage in the progress of his thought.

The Divine Son and His Glorious Second Advent.
"And again, when he bringeth the first begotten into
the world, he saith, And let all the angels of God worship him" (1: 6). The peculiar construction in Greek
has led to much controversy concerning this verse. Dr.
Adam Clarke translates it, "But when he bringeth again,
or the second time, the first-born into the habitable
world." Perhaps Stuart's paraphrase brings out the
thought most clearly. He says, "Moreover when on another occasion, he introduces his first-begotten into the
world, he saith, And let all the angels of God worship
him." The proofs of the Son as superior to the angels
drawn from verse 3, concerning the inheritance of a
better name, are in effect closed, and arguments
drawn from other considerations are now to be offered.
The first of these concerns the majesty of the Son, and
refers to the Messianic kingdom, in which the place
assigned to the angels is merely that of worshiping
spectators.

This new phase of the argument is based on a verse
in what is known as *The Second Advent Psalm* (97: 7).
In our Authorized Version, which follows the Hebrew
text, the words quoted are "worship him, all ye gods";
but since the writer quotes from the Septuagint, he
uses the word "angels," as it is found there. Evidently
he intends to use the words in the same sense as presented by the Psalmist, and therefore refers not to Christ
as the "only begotten" Son in His essential deity, nor
yet to the incarnate Son in His humiliation, but to the
Son in His glorious return at the Second Advent. Two
words of great importance furnish the basis for this

The word *gegenneka* (γεγέννηκα), "begotten," marks the communication
of a new and abiding life, represented in the case of the earthly king
by the royal dignity, and in the case of Christ by the divine sovereignty
established by the resurrection of the incarnate Son in which His ascension was also included. (Cf. Acts 13:33; Rom. 1:4; 6:4; Col. 1:18;
Rev. 1:5.) Cf. Westcott, *Epistle to the Hebrews*, p. 21.

interpretation. The *first*, which is translated "world" in our version, is *oikoumene* (οἰκουμένη) and means "habitable" or "inhabited world"; and is thus distinguished from *kosmos* (κόσμος), which refers to the earth apart from its inhabitants. The word used of our Lord's coming into the world at the time of His incarnation is *kosmos*, but in this instance *oikoumene* is used to express His second appearance. The *second* word is translated "first begotten" or "firstborn" and comes from *prototokos* (πρωτότοκος), which must be carefully distinguished from *monogenes* (μονογενής), or "only begotten." The first describes the relation of Christ to man in His glorified humanity; the latter describes the unique relation of the Son to the Father in the Holy Trinity. Had the word Son (υἱος) been used in this text, it might have appeared to refer to the Resurrection, which in some true sense was a second appearing of Christ among men. However, the word "first begotten" is used, and since this term refers to the Resurrection, the expression "again . . . he bringeth the first begotten into the world" can apply only to His glorious appearing at the Second Advent.

The writer's argument may be summed up as follows: (1) Both St. Paul and St. John regard the term "first begotten" as referring to the Resurrection. (2) The quotation indicates "that on another occasion" He introduces His Son as the "first begotten" into the "habitable world." This could take place, therefore, only after the Resurrection and Ascension. (3) The words "again he bringeth the first begotten into the world" can refer

Westcott says that "it follows that all interpretations which refer this second introduction of the Son into the world, to the incarnation are untenable. . . . The patristic commentators rightly dwell on the difference between 'only-begotten' which describes the absolutely unique relation of the Son to the Father, and 'first-begotten' which describes the relation of the risen Christ in His glorified humanity to man."—WESTCOTT, *Epistle to the Hebrews*, pp. 22-23.

Dr. Adam Clarke states that the Resurrection was indeed a second bringing of the Son into the world, but the first bringing of the "first begotten" as the very name "firstborn" implies. But the second bringing into the world is not the Son as such, but the First-born, which as we understand can be applied only to the Second Advent, for this alone is the second time that the First-begotten comes into the world.

only to the glorified Christ returning to the world which
He has redeemed, and out of which He has called many
sons to glory. (4) The term world as used here means
the habitable world of men. A careful study of this
psalm shows that the Lord Jehovah as King will reign
over the inhabited earth, the hills will melt like wax,
the heavens will declare the righteousness of God, and
all people shall see His glory. Everything in heaven and
earth will bow before Him. Is it any wonder then that
the highest beings we know—the angels are sometimes
called Elohim or gods—should likewise be commanded
to worship Him who is the brightness of the Father's
glory and the express Image of His person? (5) But
the highest evidence that this psalm refers to the Messianic reign, and is so used by the writer, is to be found
in the words of Christ himself, who says, "When the
Son of man shall come in his glory, and all the holy
angels with him, then shall he sit upon the throne of
his glory." "For the Son of man shall come in the glory
of his Father with his angels; and then he shall reward
every man according to his works" (Matt. 25: 31; 16:
27; cf. I Thess. 4: 13-18; II Thess. 1: 7-10; Jude 14; Rev.
1: 7).

The Divine Son and the Majesty of His Kingdom.
"Who maketh his angels spirits, and his ministers a
flame of fire." Having spoken of the glorious advent
of the Son, the writer now advances to the thought of
the majesty of His kingdom. Here he quotes from the
104th psalm, sometimes known as the *Oratorio of Creation.* In this psalm the name Jehovah occurs ten times,
and in each instance is descriptive of the greatness of
God in creation. God is very great, is clothed with honor

Dr. Adam Clarke gives us this from the Jewish writings. "The angel
answered Manoah, I know not in whose image I am made, for God
changeth us every hour; sometimes He makes us *fire,* sometimes *spirit,*
and at other times, *angels.*" Commenting upon this he says, "It is very
probable that those who are termed *angels* are not confined to any
specific form or shape, but assume various forms and appearances according to the nature of the work on which they are employed and the
will of their sovereign employer. This seems to have been the ancient
Jewish doctrine on this subject."—ADAM CLARKE, *Commentary on Hebrews,*
1: 7.

and majesty, covers himself with light as with a garment, and stretches out the heavens like a curtain. He lays the beams of His chambers in the waters, makes the clouds His chariot, and walks upon the wings of the wind. Then comes the great climax—He "maketh his angels spirits; and his ministers a flaming fire." This could not fail to suggest to the Hebrew reader the awful accompaniments of the giving of the law at Sinai, and is later developed in the contrast between Mount Sinai and Mount Sion (12: 18 ff.).

There are various interpretations of this text as it concerns the nature of angels. (1) It is interpreted to mean that angels serve God as truly in a spiritual sense as do the winds and the lightnings in the physical realm. (2) It is interpreted as referring to the character of the work of angels. He makes His angels winds, i.e., swift as the winds; and His servants lightning, i.e., rapid, terrible, and resistless as the lightning. (3) It is sometimes interpreted to mean messengers in the general sense—the term embracing all ministrants, from the lowest impersonal forces to the highest intelligences near the throne. This appears to be Bishop Martensen's position, who further holds that angels differ from men in that they represent a single great power, while in man, though in a finite measure, play all the forces of the divine nature. (4) These words have been further interpreted to mean that angels are evanescent beings which God can change into winds and lightnings, and therefore are not immutable, as is the Son. Westcott notes that the variableness of the angelic nature was dwelt upon by the Jewish theologians, who supposed that angels lived only as they ministered. He quotes this remarkable passage, "The angels are renewed every morning and after they have praised God they return to the stream of fire out of which they came" (Lam. 3: 23). But the purpose of the writer of this Epistle is not primarily to discuss the nature of angels, but to exalt the lordship of the Son and the ministry of angels in subjection to Him. The greatness of the angels, swift as the winds in obedience, and destructive as the light-

nings in power, serves to exalt the majesty of the King
and the powerful forces at His command.

The Divine Son and the Perpetuity of His Kingdom.
"But unto the Son he saith, Thy throne, O God, is for
ever and ever: a sceptre of righteousness is the sceptre
of thy kingdom. Thou hast loved righteousness, and
hated iniquity; therefore God, even thy God, hath
anointed thee with the oil of gladness above thy fellows"
(1: 8-9). This text marks another step in the gradation
of thought concerning the dignity of the Son. First,
there is a reference to the glorious return of Christ,
then a description of His majesty and power as King,
and now a reference to the splendor of His millennial
reign. This quotation is from the forty-fifth psalm,
which has always been regarded as thoroughly Messianic. The Chaldee Targum interprets the second verse
of the above as, "Thy beauty, O king Messiah, is greater
than the sons of men" (Ps. 45: 2); while Theodoret,
speaking for the Early Church, says, "This is a Psalm
of the beloved, i.e., for the beloved Son of God." The
author of this Epistle gives his emphatic endorsement
of the psalm by quoting verses 6-7 entire. Three things
challenge him: the perpetuity of the Kingdom, the righteous rule of the King, and the anointing with the oil
of gladness.

1. The perpetuity of the Kingdom is expressed in
the words, "Thy throne, O God, is for ever and ever."
Here the Son is addressed as God—a statement of great
significance. "It is worthy of notice," says Lowrie,
"that in verse 8, the apostle does not hesitate to write
unequivocally, *O God*, as addressed to the Son, in the
vocative. And as he weaves the quoted language together, this so involves verse 9 that the same construction must be retained there, and we must read: *O God,
thy God*. The application in the verses 10-12 of language
originally addressed to God is in the same spirit. All
of verses 8-12 therefore, are most unequivocal apostolic
testimony to the divinity of Jesus Christ" (Lowrie, *An
Explanation of Hebrews*, pp. 23-24). Here also we find

another contrast between the Son and the angels. The Son has a divine throne; the angels have none. He is their Lord; they are His subjects.

2. The righteousness of the King's reign is based upon His true character as shown in His humiliation—"Thou hast loved righteousness, and hated iniquity." In the verses preceding the comparable Old Testament statement the Psalmist describes the majesty of the King in glowing terms. "Gird thy sword upon thy thigh, O most mighty, with thy glory and thy majesty. And in thy majesty ride prosperously." This martial display is not merely through the possession of power, but as the Psalmist is careful to add, "because of truth and meekness and righteousness" (Ps. 45: 3-4). The glory of His rule lies in the fact that it is a moral influence on His subjects; He is the Founder of a Kingdom of righteousness. Throughout His kingdom, wherever the scepter is borne, it is a righteous scepter, and all thrones and dominions, human and angelic, hold righteous sway under His majestic reign of righteousness.

3. The anointing with the oil of gladness above His fellows typifies for the author of this Epistle the Christ to whom the Spirit was given without measure. He has spoken of Christ as an eternal King, and as a King of righteousness, and now he presents Him as an anointed King. There are two words for anointing: one from the verb *aleipho* (ἀλείφω), which means to anoint with oil, festally, medicinally, or as homage to another; the other from *chrio* (χρίω), which has reference to a conferring of power, as in the case of priests or kings. In the New Testament this latter word always refers to the anointing of the Holy Spirit, which in the life of our Lord on earth took place at His baptism. Then it was that officially He entered in upon His ministry. The meaning of the two words appears to be blended in the expressions "the oil of gladness" or "the oil of joy."

But Christ was not only anointed with the oil of gladness above His fellows; He was also anointed to give the oil of joy for mourning (Isa. 61: 3). The word *ech-*

risen (ἔχρισεν), "anointed," as used in the text, appears
to have been drawn from the crowning of a sovereign
with joy, as at a royal banquet. So our author makes it
plain that Christ was anointed because of the fact that
He loved righteousness and hated iniquity. This righteousness was not only His because of His deity, but also
because of His faithfulness on earth; likewise the throne
was His by virtue of His being the Heir of all things;
but, as the Son of Man, He was required to win it afresh.
So when at the Ascension He sat down at the right hand
of the Father, we must view the anointing as the consummation of the royal glory, at which time He received the
promise of the Father. It is of this that St. Peter speaks
in his sermon at Pentecost when he says, "Therefore
being by the right hand of God exalted, and having received of the Father the promise of the Holy Ghost, he
hath shed forth this, which ye now see and hear"
(Acts 2: 33).

The gift of the Holy Spirit, then, is Christ's gift to
the Church and not to the world. This truth, which is
so clearly set forth in St. John's Gospel, appears here in
the expression, "Therefore God, even thy God, hath
anointed thee with the oil of gladness above thy fellows."
The word "fellows" is from *metochos* (μέτοχος), which
means a partaker, a participant, or an associate; and
while sometimes applied to angels, may apply also to
those whom Christ has redeemed from their sins. As He
was anointed with the oil of joy, so He anoints His people
with the oil of joy; for the Kingdom is one of righteousness, and peace, and joy in the Holy Spirit.

The Divine Son and the Immutability of His Person.
"And, Thou, Lord, in the beginning hast laid the foundation of the earth; and the heavens are the works of thine
hands: they shall perish; but thou remainest; and they
all shall wax old as doth a garment; and as a vesture
shalt thou fold them up, and they shall be changed: but
thou art the same, and thy years shall not fail"
(1: 10-12). This reference is a quotation from the
102nd psalm, which has as its title, "A Prayer of the
afflicted, when he is overwhelmed, and poureth out

his complaint before the Lord." It is the appeal of an
exile, who out of his deep distress looks confidently to
Jehovah for His personal intervention in behalf of Zion.
In the Septuagint, from which the author quotes, the
word "Lord" is found in the first part of the sentence,
giving rise to the tradition that God was thus addressing
the Messiah as God. This is clearly the position of the
writer. The psalm finds its perfect fulfillment in the
sufferings of Christ. The cry of the afflicted one finds
its greatest moment of intensity in the words, "O my
God, take me not away in the midst of my days." How
strangely like the agonizing cry of our Saviour in Gethsemane, as He faces the ignominy of the Cross! In the
midst of this strong crying and tears come the comforting
words "Thou, Lord," and again God addresses God.
Then, reverting to His preincarnate existence as Creator
of the heavens and the earth, comes the assurance that
these are the work of His hands, and though they perish,
He remains. He shall fold them up as a vesture and
they shall be changed, but He is forever the same, and
His years shall not fail.

There is here, as in the previous quotations, a remarkable advance in thought. It lies in this, that as

The word *diamenein* (διαμένειν) indicates the abiding in one condition
through all the vicissitudes of time (Ps. 119:90; II Pet. 3:4).

The Scriptures indeed teach a *telos* (τέλος) or end of the world
(Matt. 24:14); a change of its present form (σχῆμα) (I Cor. 7:31); a
passing away of heaven and earth (Matt. 5:18; Luke 21:33; I John 2:17;
Rev. 20:11); a dissolving of the elements (II Pet. 3:12) yet by no means
teaches an annihilation of its existence, but rather a regeneration, a new
birth of the world, with the transformation naturally attending it. The
doctrine of the eternity of the world is equally to be repudiated with
that of future annihilation. Its transformance into a new and nobler
form of existence is effected by means of the same Lord, and that according to divine purpose and will, so that its destruction also is to be
referred to no exhaustion of originally supplied powers, wrought by age
and the natural decay of years, nor to any regularly recurring cycles of
revolution, by which at definite intervals and according to unchangeable
laws, creation is resolved into its elements, and again remoulded into
new forms and combinations for other destinies.—LANGE, *Commentary
on Hebrews*, p. 41.

As the world was not created by naturalistic evolution, so also it will
not be changed by a process of exhaustion. As the natural body of man
is to be changed into a glorified body by the resurrection, so also the
earth (out of which man's body was created) will pass through a similar
change, involving both the physical earth, which will be glorified, and
the moral order, which will be one wherein dwelleth righteousness.

Jesus faced death and triumphed over it, being begotten
into a new and eternal order, so also, as Creator, He
has power to change the heavens and the earth to conform to this new order of being. Christ is declared to
be "the firstfruits of them that slept"; and in the resurrection, the saints shall be given bodies like His own
glorious body, immortal and incorruptible. This new
order demands a new environment. Like a garment the
present heavens and earth will have waxed old, and no
longer will serve their purpose. But Christ, who had
power to lay His life down and to take it again, has power
also to fold up the present order as a vesture and change
it, and out of the old to usher in according to His promise "new heavens and a new earth, wherein dwelleth
righteousness" (II Pet. 3: 13). But whether in the crisis
of death or that of the universe, our Lord remains the
immutable and unchanged.

The Divine Son and the Triumphant Consummation.
"But to which of the angels said he at any time, Sit on
my right hand, until I make thine enemies thy footstool?
Are they not all ministering spirits, sent forth to minister
for them who shall be heirs of salvation?" (1: 13-14)
This final quotation is from the 110th psalm, of which
Luther once said that "it is worthy to be overlaid with
precious jewels." This is the psalm which mentioned the
priesthood after the order of Melchizedec, to which
the writer gives much attention in the later chapters of
the Epistle. It is the psalm also which Jesus pondered
and which He quoted to the Pharisees to prove that the
Messiah was David's Lord. It was quoted by Peter on
the Day of Pentecost in proof of the ascension of Jesus
and the promised gift of the Holy Ghost (Acts 2: 33-35);
and it is referred to twice in this Epistle (1: 13 and 10:
12-13). It is clearly evident that the reference here is
not merely to the eternal *Logos,* or the pre-existent Son,
but to the Son incarnate, who through His humiliation,
death, and resurrection now returns to the throne of His
Father; and on the seat of honor at the right hand of
God, He is expecting until His enemies are made His
footstool in the day of His second and glorious appearing.

Concerning the clause, "Until I make thine enemies thy footstool," the question arises as to whether it is intended to mark the close of the mediatorial reign or whether it merely refers to the completeness of the previous triumph. St. Paul in his Corinthian correspondence evidently refers to this when he says, "Then cometh the end, when he shall have delivered up the kingdom to God, even the Father; when he shall have put down all rule and all authority and power. For he must reign, till he hath put all enemies under his feet" (I Cor. 15: 24-25). The Kingdom which the Son is here said to deliver up to the Father must of necessity be the mediatorial Kingdom. In its initial stage it is the reign of grace in the hearts of believers; in its consummation it is the reign of glory ushered in at the Second Advent. The present reign of grace is the preparation for the coming reign of glory. Nor will the Messianic prophecies have found their fulfillment until the curse shall have been removed from the created universe and the perfect dominion of God re-established. To use Lange's apt expression, "The Christocracy is the fully unfolded, world-embracing form of the Theocracy."

But St. Paul continues with a further statement. He says, "And when all things shall be subdued unto him, then shall the Son also himself be subject unto him that put all things under him, that God may be all in all" (I Cor. 15: 28). Here we must understand that there is no reference to the Son as the eternal Logos, but to the Son as the incarnate Christ, whose redemptive economy will at His second coming be brought to a close. He comes then, not with a sin offering, but to judgment; and there will be a return of the government to the form in which it existed previous to the present reign of mercy. God will then be "all in all"; and the blessed Trinity will reign in a fully redeemed and restored universe—a better country and "a city which hath foundations, whose builder and maker is God."

Finally, there is the reference to angels as ministering spirits, sent forth to minister to those who shall be heirs of salvation (1: 14). There is a distinction

here which is not brought out in the Authorized
Version. The first word for ministering is *leitourgika*
(λειτουργικὰ), which implies a sacred or liturgic service (8: 6; 9: 21); while the second word is *diakonian*
(διακονίαν), which implies personal helpfulness. The
sentence may be properly rendered, "ministrant spirits
sent forth for service." The present participle *apostel-
lomenoi* (ἀποστελλόμενοι) means "habitually sent forth,"
that is, commissioned to serve in that habitual form
of action which springs from their nature and corresponds to their destination. The sum of the argument
therefore is that Christ is greater than angels in that He
is the Son of God incarnate; they are but ministrant
spirits in God's providential care of the redeemed. Jacob
in vision saw the angels of God ascending and descending; and Elisha's servant, with eyes touched by the
prophet, saw the mountains filled with the chariots of
God and the horsemen thereof. Doubtless were our eyes
so touched we too should see what the apostle teaches so
clearly, that the pathways of the air are filled with angels
as messengers of mercy to the people of God.

The Scriptures are filled with references to angels, which should give
us a new vision of God's protective care. "The angel of the Lord en-
campeth round about them that fear him, and delivereth them" (Ps. 34: 7).
"For he shall give his angels charge over thee, to keep thee in all thy
ways" (Ps. 91: 11). Angels came and ministered to Jesus after His temptation in the wilderness, and during His struggle in the Garden of
Gethsemane.

CHAPTER II

THE HUMANITY AND HUMILIATION OF CHRIST

We have seen that the first chapter of this Epistle deals with the majesty of the Son of God, and this whether in His pristine state or in His personal relations with the Father. Further still, He is seen to be greater than the angels in dignity and power even in His incarnate or mediatorial state. The writer now turns to consider another aspect of Christ—not now His deity, but His humanity as the Son of Man in relation to the world of men. The theme of the second chapter, therefore, may well be entitled *The Humanity and Humiliation of Christ.*

The second chapter opens with an admonition and a warning. "Therefore we ought to give the more earnest heed to the things which we have heard, lest at any time we should let them slip" (2:1). The word "therefore" links the teaching of the first chapter concerning the glory of the Son and His supreme dignity as Mediator with the admonition to give "more earnest" or "more abundant attention" to the things which have been heard; not only because of the superiority of the revelation itself, but also because of the supreme greatness of the Divine Revealer. The adverb *perissoteros* (περισσοτερος), "more abundantly," is in the comparative form and indicates, as Westcott points out, the absolute rather than a merely relative excess. The writer then pauses to enforce the practical consequences of this great truth.

Lowrie gives us this translation. "For this reason we must more abundantly give heed to the things that were heard, lest haply we drift away" (from them). By "more abundantly is denoted a comparison. But it is not more earnest heed than had been given to a previous revelation; nor more than might have been needed had the present revelation come by an agent not superior to previous agents. There is progress in thought to an *additional motive* for hearing, derived from what has been represented of the service of angels. The meaning is: more abundant heed than might have been needful if the angel had not been charged with such a service."—Lowrie, *An Explanation of Hebrews,* p. 31.

66

The First Warning: Against Neglect

This warning against neglect is the first of a series of warnings of deepening import scattered throughout the Epistle. The increasing vehemence of these warnings marks the stages of natural decline in spiritual things, and can but prove of value to those who would "hold fast the confidence and the rejoicing of the hope firm unto the end." The warning is found in the midst of the discussion concerning the angels and separates the argument into the former portion, where Christ is presented as superior to angels (1: 4-14), and the latter part, in which angels are regarded as superior to men. (2: 5-7)

The Meaning of the Term Neglect. The word *amelesantes* (ἀμελήσαντες), translated "neglect," literally means a "drifting away," a "drifting by," or a "missing the mark" as a "ship that in stress of weather fails to make its haven" (Luther). "The idea is not that of simple forgetfulness but of being swept along past the sure anchorage which is within reach. The image is singularly expressive. We are all continually exposed to the action of currents of opinion, habit, action, which tend to carry us away from the position we ought to maintain" (Westcott). Vaughan points out that this word is used of the invited guests in Matt. 22: 5, and conveys the thought of slighting rather than refusing the invitation. In the case of the Hebrew Christians, the drift of old associations was carrying them back to Judaism, the religious system which they had renounced and from which they had withdrawn. It is easier to drift than to struggle against the currents of evil, but the result is disastrous. We are warned that one of the greatest dangers to the Christian is precisely that of being at ease in Zion, thus allowing the soul to be removed by imperceptible degrees from prayerfulness,

---

Stuart says that the word "neglect" (ἀμελήσαντες) is plainly emphatic, and means "to treat with utter disregard" or "contempt," such namely as would be implied in apostasy. . . . The word "salvation" (σωτηρία) refers to the Christian religion with all its promised blessings and tremendous threats.—Stuart, *Commentary*, p. 285.

meditation, spiritual communion, and the clear consciousness of the presence of God. Like a fading picture, our experience imperceptibly becomes vague and unsatisfying. It appears that more souls are ruined by drifting carelessly and unconsciously from their moorings than are overcome by sudden satanic conflicts.

The Word Spoken by Angels (2:2). The comparison of Christ with the angels is here continued but from a different point of view. Not now is it a comparison between two classes of agents—the Son and the angels —but is designed to stress the wide and essential difference in their manifestations. The chief characteristic of the agency of angels, the writer intimates, is that of prohibitions and commands, for this is implied in the words "transgression and disobedience." The Israelites received a "just recompence of reward," by which the writer evidently means the punitive judgments inflicted upon them during the wilderness period (3:7 ff.). The work of Christ the Son, however, is that of salvation, and hence is later expressed as "so great salvation." The contrast between the words "spoken by angels" and those spoken by Christ carries with it the same thought as the terms law and grace as used in the more abstract sense by St. Paul in the Epistle to the Galatians. Here however the terms "angels" and "Christ" are more concrete and personal. As the law was our schoolmaster to bring us to Christ, so the dispensation of angels which ushered in the law with all its glorious sanctions was preparatory to the work of the Son; and as the law was given by the dispensation of angels, so also they were charged with the execution of it.

This is brought out clearly in two of our Lord's parables: (1) *The Parable of the Tares*, where it is said that "the Son of man shall send forth his angels, and they

---

The word "transgression," *parabasis* (παράβασις), is from the root word *para-baino* (παρα-βαίνω) and means to cross over the line, to transgress, also to depart or desert (Acts 1:25). The word for "disobedience," *par-akoe* (παρ-ακοή), is from *par-akouo* (παρ-ακούω), which means to hear negligently or to disregard (Matt. 18:17). The punishment of *recompense of reward* was for those who crossed over the line, or who heard negligently—and this of the word spoken by angels.

shall gather out of his kingdom all things that offend, and them which do iniquity; and shall cast them into a furnace of fire: there shall be wailing and gnashing of teeth" (Matt. 13: 41-42). (2) *The Parable of the Net,* where our Lord says, "So shall it be at the end of the world: the angels shall come forth, and sever the wicked from among the just, and shall cast them into the furnace of fire: there shall be wailing and gnashing of teeth" (Matt. 13: 49-50). Here it is clear that the angels gather out the wicked for punishment, so that in some true sense it may be said that the "great salvation" of Christ is an escape from the word spoken by angels. It is the redemption through grace of those that are under the law.

How Shall We Escape? "How shall we escape, if we neglect so great salvation?" (2: 3a) F. B. Meyer calls this "The Unanswerable Question." There is no possibility of escape. The eye of God detects every sin, and every sinner is under the wrath of God. Where the blood was not on the doorposts, the first-born of every family in Egypt died; when Israel refused to enter the promised land, their carcasses fell in the wilderness. Some have assumed that there is an undue softness about the religion of the New Testament, that a God of love will not punish wickedness, and faith is merely a sunny consciousness that all will somehow be well. Instead, the Christian life is earnest and intense, the very opposite of drifting with the currents of this world. If they of the former dispensation to whom God spoke through the prophets were punished with sore destruction for their sins, how shall we escape who live in the dispensation of Him who is the Light of the World and the Author of so great salvation? Nor is the warning necessarily concerned with actual transgressions and sins; it is against merely drifting. Not taking earnest heed, failing to trust in the Blood of the atonement, neglecting to give God His full measure of devotion—it is these things that not only make escape impossible but intensify the severity of the punishment in those who neglect "so great salvation."

The Great Salvation

"How shall we escape, if we neglect so great salvation; which at the first began to be spoken by the Lord, and was confirmed unto us by them that heard him; God also bearing them witness both with signs and wonders, and with divers miracles, and gifts of the Holy Ghost, according to his own will?" (2: 3-4) Faber, in his deep devotional spirit, says: "Salvation! what music there is in that word; music that always rouses, yet always rests us! It is vigor to us in the mornings and in the evening it is peace. It is a song that is always singing itself deep down into the delighted soul. Angelic ears are ravished by it up in heaven, and our eternal Father Himself listens to it with adorable complacency. It is sweet even to Him of whose mind is the music of a thousand worlds. What is it to be saved in the fullest and utmost meaning? Eye hath not seen nor ear heard. It is a rescue, and from such a shipwreck! It is rest, and in such an unimaginable home! It is to lie down forever in the bosom of God in an endless rapture of insatiable contentment."

This great salvation is the answer to every human problem. It is born out of the majesty of the Son at the right hand of the Father; it is provided through the all-atoning blood of Jesus, and is administered in the Church by the Holy Spirit as the gift of the glorified Christ. It is the love of God shed abroad in the heart that casts out fear; it is the peace of God that passes all understanding and that keeps the heart and mind through Christ Jesus; it is the anointing that abideth. This great salvation is the answer to careless drifting in the Church, to lukewarmness in personal experience, and to lack of unction in the ministry of the Word. It has transformed weak Christians into towers of strength; it has given radiance to the countenances, and put joy into the hearts of its recipients; it has made its ministers flames of holy fire, and inspired such devotion to Jesus Christ as made martyrs the seed of the Church. To fail to lay hold of this great salvation by faith in Christ is but to reveal the enormity of the sin of neglect or careless drifting in the Christian life. How then shall we escape if we neglect so great salvation? It is the unanswerable question. There is no escape.

Three things stand out clearly in the author's summary of the elements entering into this great salvation: its announcement by the Lord, its confirmation by His hearers, and its divine attestation by miracles and gifts of the Holy Spirit.

The Announcement of the Great Salvation. "Which at the first began to be spoken by the Lord," (2:3b) or more literally, "having first been spoken by the Lord." The prophets have been called the chords through which the heavenly music sounded, but the Son was the perfect instrument which gave to men the melody of heaven. Every prophet added his own touch to the glorious picture of the days of the Son of Man, until after the elaboration of the main figure the painters all withdrew, and the curtain fell for a while. But the Person who shall raise the curtain again has already been revealed and He will trace with His own hand for His contemporaries the complete fulfillment of all prophecy. But the expression "first began to be spoken by the Lord" carries with it something more than the utterance of His words during His earthly ministry. It implies that His teaching was the true origin of the gospel, and it would be easy to show that all the doctrines set forth and amplified in the Epistles had their beginning in some truth found in the Gospels. We may well believe that any truth

Adam Clarke in his comment on this verse sets forth the greatness of this salvation by a comparison with that granted to the Jews. (1) The Jewish dispensation was provided for the Jews alone; the Christian dispensation, for all mankind. (2) The Jewish dispensation was full of significant types and ceremonies; the Christian dispensation is the substance of all those types. (3) The Jewish dispensation referred chiefly to the body and outward state of man, washings and external cleansings of the flesh; the Christian, to the inward state, purifying the heart and soul and purging the conscience from dead works. (4) The Jewish dispensation promised temporal happiness; the Christian, spiritual. (5) The Jewish dispensation belonged chiefly to time; the Christian, to eternity. (6) The Jewish dispensation had its glory; but that was nothing when compared with the exceeding glory of the gospel. (7) Moses administered the former; Jesus Christ, the Creator, Governor, and Saviour of the world, the latter. (8) This is a great salvation, infinitely beyond the Jewish—but how great, no tongue or pen can describe.

which the apostles have given us came first from the lips of the Son of Man. The teachings of the prophets which preceded Him were by His own words interpreted and sealed, while the future opened by His brief statements and the apostles' amplification is certified to us by manifestations of the divine presence. Thus it is that the prophets on the one hand and the apostles on the other are forever justified and maintained in their teachings by the words of Him who stood between them.

The Confirmation of the Gospel. "And was confirmed unto us by them that heard him" (2: 3c). The announcement of the great salvation "took commencement of being spoken through the Lord," but the apostle would not have us understand that these words were limited to those spoken during His earthly ministry. Jesus himself said, "I have many things to say unto you, but ye cannot bear them now." The earthly ministry was but the beginning of the great salvation. This is confirmed by St. Mark, who opens his book with the words, "The beginning of the gospel of Jesus Christ, the Son of God." St. Luke also in his first volume (the Gospel) speaks of the things that were delivered to them "which from the beginning were eyewitnesses, and ministers of the word"; and in his second volume (the Acts) writes of the things "that Jesus began both to do and teach, until the day in which he was taken up." This is followed by the words, "after that he through the Holy Ghost had given commandments unto the apostles whom he had chosen" (Acts 1: 1-2). This can mean only that the apostles and others were through the inspiration of the Holy Spirit to continue the revelation in which God had spoken in a Son. The inspired word of these who had heard Him and were eyewitnesses becomes also in the New Testament teaching the "word of the Lord."

The word *ebabaiothe* ($\dot{\epsilon}\beta\alpha\beta\alpha\iota\dot{\omega}\theta\eta$), translated "confirmed," expresses the emphatic phase of thought in this passage, and is the verb form of the same word translated "stedfast" in verse 2. Thus the author says that this salvation which God spoke through the Son became as steadfast as the word spoken by angels which made

certain the punishment of every "transgression and disobedience." Special consideration should be given to the
fact that it is the salvation that is confirmed, and not
merely the declaration of it, for the gospel is "the power
of God unto salvation." The confirmation by them that
heard Him is in the steadfastness of the salvation, and
is thus vindicated by its own claims in the lives of its
recipients.

The Divine Attestation of the Truth. "God also bearing them witness, both with signs and wonders, and
with divers miracles, and gifts of the Holy Ghost, according to his own will" (2:4). The writer has considered the origin of the great salvation in the Son, its
confirmation in the experience of His hearers, and now
turns his attention to the method by which this salvation
is imparted to others. When those who personally had
heard the Lord began to preach this great salvation, God
bore them witness in the sense of supporting them with
additional testimony. The words "bearing witness with
them" are in Greek a double compound word, *sune-
pimarturountos* (συνεπιμαρτυροῦντος), which occurs only
here in the New Testament. In this word *sun* (συν),
"with," is associative, but frequently used with the idea
of additional support; *epi* (ἐπι), "upon," carries the
thought of God's own testimony added to the preached
word; while *marturountos* (μαρτυρουντος), "witness" or
"testimony," is given in a fourfold manner—by signs,
wonders, divers miracles, and gifts of the Holy Spirit.

The word *semeiois* (σημείοις) refers to the purpose
of a miracle as signifying some one or some thing, and
is the broader term because of its ethical nature. The
term *terasin* (τέρασιν) is a narrower term and does not
occur alone in the New Testament. It refers primarily
to the marvelousness of the miracle, or the astonishment

Ebrard has an excellent interpretation of the word συνεπιμαρτοῦντος.
He says μαρτυρεῖν means to bear witness of a thing which is still under
question or doubtful; ἐπιμαρτυρεῖν, to testify of a thing already established; and συνεπιμαρτυρεῖν, to give additional testimony to a thing in
itself certain and confirmed by proofs from other sources.—EBRARD, *Commentary on the Epistle to the Hebrews*, p. 68.

which it creates in the beholder. The word *dunamesin*
(δυνάμεσιν), "miracles," means "powers" or the "exercise of power," and marks especially the super-
human agency involved—here combined with *poikilais*
(ποικίλαις), which means "variegated" or "many-
colored," and is rightly interpreted "manifold powers"
or "various acts of power," and in the Authorized Version is translated "divers miracles."

The final means of attestation mentioned in this verse
is found in the expression "gifts of the Holy Ghost."
The word translated "gifts" is *merismois* (μερισμοῖς) or
"distributions" of the Holy Spirit. Westcott points out
here that there is progress inward from that which is
most strikingly outward, as signs and wonders to that
which is most decisively inward, the Holy Spirit. Greater
than signs and wonders and divers miracles is the gift of
the Holy Spirit given to the Church at Pentecost. The
Son has His seat at the right hand of God and is our
Advocate above; the Holy Spirit has His seat in the
Church and is our Advocate within. The Greek word
Paraclete, translated "Comforter," is from *para,* to go
along with, and *cletos,* the called, and signifies one who

Vaughan says that the article is missing in Heb. 1:4 (πνεύματος ἁγίου),
as it usually is when the communication of the Holy Spirit is the point
in view. The Holy Spirit *personally* is τὸ ἅγιον or τὸ πνεῦμα ἅγιον. Lenski
says that it takes more than the plural "apportionings" or "distributions"
and the absence of the Greek article with the Holy Spirit to make this
an objective genitive, which divides the Holy Spirit into "portions" that
God distributes. Words ending in μος expressing action make it obvious
that this is not an objective but a subjective genitive; the Holy Spirit
makes the apportionings exactly as in I Cor. 12:11, "dividing to every
man severally as he will" the different gifts proceeding from the Spirit.
Westcott takes the former position but regards God as giving the Holy
Spirit in different degrees.
  The final phrase, "according to his own will," is generally supposed
to refer to all that goes before it. Lenski says that it modifies the participle of the genitive absolute, and that this makes it apply to all the
datives. Westcott says that it applies to all that precedes it. Lowrie,
however, says that this phrase applies only to "distributions of the Holy
Spirit, and not to all the other particulars that precede, and is intended
to denote not only that these free distributions proceeded from the
free grace of God, but that they were in great variety as to their nature
and degree, and in great abundance. What is referred to is primarily
the miraculous manifestations that attended the preaching of the Apostles
and were the proof of the presence of the Holy Spirit: and then
charismata generally" (*Hebrews,* p. 41). (Cf. Acts 2:1-4; 4:31; 10:44; I Cor.
12:4-11.)

goes along with the called to do anything that needs to be done. The Holy Spirit is God dwelling in the Church, the Third Person of the Trinity, the Lord and Giver of Life, the Agent of cleansing, inspiration, guidance, and comfort. The Holy Spirit is both a Gift and a Giver. He is the Gift of the glorified Christ, and in turn He distributes His own gifts, or *charismata*, severally as He will.

While some authorities have differed in their interpretation, the evident meaning approved by all is that the "distributions of the Holy Ghost" denotes those powers or graces which the Scriptures tell us were bestowed upon those early Christians in their transmission of the gospel. These gifts as enumerated in the Corinthian correspondence were diverse and yet all were the work of that "selfsame Spirit, dividing to every man severally as he will" (I Cor. 12:11). The expression "according to his own will" is generally understood to refer to all that precedes it. How impressive then must be these great teachings in respect to the warning which he presents with such urgency! If the neglect of the law, which was given by the disposition of angels, was punished with such severity, is it not impossible to suppose that a system introduced by the Son, attested by the Father, and made effective by the Holy Spirit, should be left so undefended that men might reject it with impunity? How then shall we escape if we neglect? There is no escape.

Westcott says that *thelesis* (θέλησις) is the active exercise of the will as distinguished from *thelema* (θέλημα), which is a definite expression of the will. *Thelesis* (θέλησις) is will in action; *thelema* (θέλημα) is the object willed—a command or a desire. So also Lenski points out that the word *thelesis* (θέλησις) is used in order to express action, "according to his willing," and not *thelema* (θέλημα), as an object willed. The apostles never wrought miracles at will, but only as God willed, and this as to the time, place, and manner.

Having represented the urgency of the situation that requires his readers to escape from the word spoken by angels, in other words, from the inevitable consequences of transgression and disobedience of that word, and having pointed to the Gospel of Christ as the only salvation, in terms that display the greatness of it, *the Apostle proceeds to represent how there comes to be such a salvation,* i.e., a dispensation that is escape from the foregoing dispensation revealed by the agency of angels. —LOWRIE, *An Explanation of Hebrews,* p. 42.

THE EMERGENCE OF A NEW HUMANITY IN CHRIST

Having warned his readers of the danger of neglect or mere drifting, and having presented the great salvation as its remedy, the writer again takes up the subject of angels—not at this time to set forth the majesty of the Son, but as a transition to his teaching concerning man. "For unto the angels hath he not put in subjection the world to come, whereof we speak" (2:5), but He has given this dominion or lordship to man (2:6-8). Then in verse 9 the writer draws a parallel between man in his original or unfallen condition, and the emergence of a new humanity in Christ. These positions must be considered somewhat at length.

The Use of the Term Emergence. In our consideration of the new humanity in Jesus, we use the term "emergence" in a thoughtful and guarded manner. Christ was not created separate and distinct from the Adamic race, but was a new creation resulting from the incarnation of the Word. God and man therefore did not merely approach each other through the "angel of the Lord" on the one hand and Moses, the divinely inspired mediator, on the other. God and man were now conjoined in one Person, a theanthropic Being, one who was both God and man in the full sweep of the consciousness of both. Man did not evolve out of nature. God used the lower as a foundation upon which should rest His higher creative purposes. His body was formed from the dust of the earth, but His spiritual nature was divinely inbreathed. So also Christ did not evolve from this present human race. He was a Root out of dry ground, and came to the plane of human history through the race but not from it. And as man conjoined in himself the physical and the spiritual, so Christ conjoined in one Person the divine and the human. St. Paul makes this distinction when he speaks of Adam as a "living soul," but of Christ as a "quickening spirit." On the one side He is one with the Father in majesty and power; on the other He has lifted man to a new redemptive level, and having quickened him

into life, makes man holy and again brings him into
communion with the Father.

Transitional: The Supreme Headship of Christ. The
apostle has abundantly proved the vast superiority of
Christ over the angels and to the dispensation given
through their ministration. He now assumes the point
which he intends to prove, the headship of Christ over
the new dispensation. These are the principles which
underlie the claims of the gospel which the writer has
so eloquently set forth in the preceding verses of this
chapter. The transition is made in the fifth verse, "For
unto the angels hath he not put in subjection the world
to come, whereof we speak" (2:5); and it is made with
the author's usual beauty of style. Here he bridges over
the space between the majesty of the Son and the frailty
and weakness of man, and he does so by suggesting a
further idea in which Christ transcends angels. This
new idea is that the dominion of the future Kingdom
or the "world to come" is not to be given to angels but
to man. Man is to be at the head of the new economy,
but man in Christ, as will be seen in the following verses.
The expression "world to come" has been the subject
of much debate, many of the earlier commentators holding that it refers to the gospel age. The word for "world"
as used here is not *kosmos* (John 3:16), nor *aeon,*
meaning "age" (as in Matt. 13:49 and Heb. 9:26), but
oikoumenen (οἰκουμένην) or "economy." This, as we
have pointed out in a previous chapter, means the
"habitable earth." It would seem therefore to refer to
the millennial age, the world to come being the present
earth, renovated and redeemed from the curse and
made subject to the Son of Man. This return to the
earth we are told will be sudden and glorious. "For as
the lightning cometh out of the east, and shineth even
unto the west; so shall also the coming of the Son of
man be" (Matt. 24:27).

It is to be understood, then, that not only Christ
as the only begotten Son is greater than the angels, but
that man in Christ is also higher, because it is possible

for man to be brought into immediate union with God, a potentiality that does not belong to angels. The words "whereof we speak" refer to 1:14, where it is distinctly stated that the angels are to minister to them who shall be heirs of salvation. Man shall sit with Christ on His throne; the angels shall be his ministers.

A further step in the transition is to be found in the wonder of the Psalmist that God should visit frail man. "But one in a certain place testified, saying, What is man, that thou art mindful of him? or the son of man, that thou visitest him?" (Ps. 8:4) This verse is taken from the Septuagint, and is word for word except the omission of one clause. The omission is probably due to the fact that it is merely a repetition of the last clause, and is not found in the original Hebrew text. The indefinite approach in the words "but one in a certain place" in no wise implies that the writer was ignorant of the proper citation; rather it is a tribute to the familiarity of the Hebrews with their own Scriptures. This indefinite approach is found in Heb. 4:4 and was also used in the writings of Philo. Chrysostom says that "it is neither meant to hide or reveal the one that testifies, but indicates that the source was well known, and the readers, as well versed in Scripture." Above all, it is immaterial to the writer as to who said these words; they are found in the Scriptures and are therefore the inspired word of God. This is the all-important fact. The word used for "man" is the term which indicates a frail being, perhaps man in his fallen estate. This would only increase the Psalmist's wonder that God should visit him. The terms "man" and "son of man" are perhaps used to form the poetic parallelism so common in Hebrew literature.

The question arises, "Why did the writer use the eighth psalm instead of the original statement found in Gen. 1:26-28? It is because the word "angels" is found in it, and this assists him in making the transition we have been considering. Here the distinction between angels and man makes it clear that man has

THE HUMANITY AND HUMILIATION OF CHRIST

a glory all his own. This breaks down the assumption
that might be drawn from his previous statement, that
everything which is concerned with human affairs is
subject to angels. No, man has a distinct rank and
sphere of his own, and this as well as his universal
dominion furnishes a reason for his being crowned with
glory and honor.

Man in His Original State as God Made Him. "Thou
madest him a little lower than the angels; thou crownedst
him with glory and honour, and didst set him over the
works of thy hands: thou hast put all things in subjection under his feet. For in that he put all in subjection under him, he left nothing that is not put under
him" (Heb. 2: 7-8*ab*).

1. "Thou madest him a little lower than the angels." In the Hebrew text (Ps. 8: 5) the word for angels
is *Elohim,* sometimes rendered "the sons of Elohim," or
frequently merely as "the Elohim" or "the gods." The
usual Hebrew word for angels is *malak* or "messenger,"
and the use of the word *Elohim* in this place is evidently
intended to convey the idea of angels as supernatural
beings. Translated literally, the Hebrew text would
read, "Thou hast made him less than God"; but the
writer quotes from the Septuagint, where it reads, "a
little lower than the angels." Our Lord in His controversy with the Jews appears to substantiate the former
position when He quotes a verse from the eighty-second
psalm, "I said, Ye are gods? If he called them gods,
unto whom the word of God came, and the scripture
cannot be broken; say ye of him, whom the Father hath
sanctified, and sent into the world, Thou blasphemest;
because I said, I am the Son of God?" (John 10: 34-36;
cf. Ps. 82: 6.) Probably the real meaning of the words
"a little lower than the angels" is "something above
nature but less than God"—hence the use of the word
angels in the Septuagint. However this translation does
not bring out as forcibly as the Hebrew the idea of the
divine nature which is couched in the expression, "Man

was created in the image and likeness of God"—words
spoken of no other creature, either in heaven or on
earth.

The words *brachu ti* ($\beta\rho\alpha\chi\acute{v}$ $\tau\iota$), literally "little
some," may mean either "a little while" as to time or
"a little less in degree." Westcott and others maintain
that it has reference to degree, and this appears to be
one's first impression in reading either the text or the
psalm from which it is taken. Many commentators,
however, favor the temporal aspect, maintaining that
"a little while" refers to man's present condition but
not to his ultimate goal, which in Christ will transcend
even the glory of angels. The verb "madest," *elattosas*
($\dot{\eta}\lambda\acute{\alpha}\tau\tau\omega\sigma\alpha\varsigma$), "didst make," is interesting in that it carries with it the idea of a decrease of that which was
originally created. It is the same verb that John the
Baptist uses when he says," "He must increase, but I
must decrease." But while angels are endowed with
greater gifts than man, and being incorporeal are not
bound by a body of clay, nevertheless man has something in common with angels, that is, immortality. Our
Lord made this clear when in speaking of the children
of the resurrection He said, "Neither can they die any
more: for they are equal unto the angels" (Luke 20:
36). The "little while," therefore, applies most probably to man in his fallen estate as subject to death.

There are two other things of interest in this connection: (1) The fact that man is classified with angels
indicates that he is more closely related to the spiritual
order above him than to the order of brutes beneath
him. This is proof that he is of divine sonship, rather
than the end of a merely naturalistic process. (2) Man
has a rank and glory all his own, which is distinct from
that of angels and in its ultimate purpose transcends
them. Man is capable of receiving the Saviour in the
person of the Son of God as an integral Member of the
race, and through Him entering into a transcendent
fellowship which the angels have never known nor can
know.

2. "Thou crownedst him with glory and honour, and didst set him over the works of thy hands" (2:7b). To be crowned means to be elevated to the highest possible position. There are two words for "crown" in the Scriptures: *diadema* (διά-δημα), which always symbolizes royalty; and *stephanos* (στέφανος), which means the festal garland of victory or achievement. It is in the latter sense that the word is used here—crowned as a conqueror. To be crowned with glory carries with it the thought of true dignity and outward splendor; to be crowned with honor suggests the high esteem due to true excellence. Because of this crowning with glory and honor, God set man over the works of His hands, thus climaxing the picture of man's high place in the created world.

3. "Thou hast put all things in subjection under his feet. For in that he put all in subjection under him, he left nothing that is not put under him" (2:8ab). The eighth psalm, from which these words are taken, is a beautiful pastoral. David, gazing into the vastness of the heavens, beholding the moon and stars as the work of God's fingers, felt how small is man, and how help-

---

Dr. F. B. Meyer in a wonderfully descriptive passage says: "There you have royal supremacy. Man was intended to be God's vicegerent and representative. He was king in a palace stored with all to please him, monarch and sovereign of all the lower orders of creation. The sun to labor for him as a very Hercules; the moon to lighten his nights, or lead the waters around the earth in tides, cleansing his coasts; elements of nature to be his slaves and messengers; flowers to scent his path; fruits to please his taste; birds to sing for him; fish to feed him; beasts to toil for him and carry him. Not a cringing slave, but a king crowned with glory of rule, and with the honor of universal supremacy. Only a little lower than the angels; because they are not like him encumbered with flesh and blood." Of man as sin has made him Meyer says: "His crown is rolled in the dust, his honor tarnished and stained. His sovereignty is strongly disputed by the lower orders of creation. If trees nourish him, it is after strenuous care, and they often disappoint. If the earth supplies him with food, it is in tardy response to exhausting toil. If the beasts serve him, it is because they have been laboriously tamed and trained; whilst vast numbers roam the forest glades, setting him at defiance. If he catch the fish of the sea, or the bird of the air, he must wait long in cunning concealment. Some traces of the old lordship are still apparent in the terror which the sound of the human voice and the glance of the eye still inspire in the lower creatures, as in the feats of the lion-tamer or the snake-charmer. But for the most part anarchy and rebellion have laid waste man's fair realm."—MEYER, *The Way into the Holiest*, pp. 42-43.

less in contrast with the forces of nature. And yet God is mindful of him and visits him. Then seeing beyond, "all sheep and oxen, yea, and the beasts of the field; the fowl of the air, and the fish of the sea, and whatsoever passeth through the paths of the seas," the author with the pen of divine inspiration wrote, "Thou madest him to have dominion over the works of thy hands; thou hast put all things under his feet" (Ps. 8:6). Dr. Adam Clarke observes that, if this be spoken of man as he came from the hands of his Maker, it places him at the head of all God's works—Thou hast made him less than God. God had said, "Have dominion"; man was therefore destined to rule this present world as well as the world to come.

Man as Sin Has Made Him. "But now we see not yet all things put under him" (2:8c). In these brief words is to be found the story of man's fall through unbelief and sin. Here the application throughout is to man in his present state; the references to Christ do not begin until the following verses. The dominion given to man at his creation and the wisdom with which he was endued to rule as the vicegerent of God were lost through his fall into sin. His will became perverse, his intellect was darkened, and his affections alienated; and through fear of death, all his lifetime became subject to bondage. But there is even here a ray of hope. The word *outo* (οὔτω), translated "not yet," and used by St. Paul only in one other place (I Cor. 3:2), suggests that even yet the promise may be fulfilled. Man has failed but the promise has not failed. The writer is about to tell us that in a new Man, even Jesus, the words of the Psalmist shall eventually and abundantly have their perfect fulfillment. There are prophetic glimpses of this even in the earthly life of Jesus. The nature parables indicate His transcendent power. He spoke to the winds and waves, "Peace, be still," and they obeyed Him. To His disciples who had toiled through the night, He said, "Cast the net on the right side of the ship," and shoals of fish filled it to the break-

ing point. The fig tree withered at His command, and
water was turned into wine. Disease and devils felt His
power, and death could not hold Him. At the close of
His earthly life as He gave the Great Commission to
His disciples, He said, "All power is given unto me in
heaven and in earth." But the writer hastens on to this
further triumph in Christ.

*Jesus, the Representative Man, or Man in His Re-
deemed State.* "But we see Jesus, who was made a little
lower than the angels for the suffering of death, crowned
with glory and honour; that he by the grace of God
should taste death for every man" (2:9). Here the
writer in a single masterly statement meets every point
of objection to the superiority of Christ in His incarnate state. What a glorious contrast! Man, though
fallen in Adam, is redeemed through Christ. The Son
of God took upon Him our human nature, and through
suffering and death has entered into the possession of
that glory promised to man; and what He has achieved
for us may be ours in union with Him through the impartation of the Holy Spirit. As the nexus of the race
fallen in Adam is known as the "old man," so also the
nexus of the redeemed race in Christ is known as the
"new man," "which after God is created in righteousness and true holiness" (Eph. 4:22-24; Col. 3:9-10).
Those who "have heard him, and have been taught by
him" are commanded, therefore, to put off the one and,
through the renewing of the spirit of the mind, put on
the other. All that man lost in the Fall shall be fully
realized in Christ, and more; for "where sin abounded,
grace did much more abound" (Rom. 5:20*b*).

There is an interesting use of the two Greek words
for *see* found in this and the preceding verse, and the
change of words is not without significance. In verse
8 the word for "see" is *horomen* (ὁρῶμεν), from the
verb *horan* (ὁρᾶν), and signifies a continuous exercise
of sight; while in verse 9 the word is *blepomen*
(βλέπομεν) and means a particular exercise of sight,
such as turning the attention to some particular person

or thing. What the writer says, therefore, is that what we observe or see constantly before us is not the whole of it; we are to *take a glance* or *fix our gaze* upon Jesus, and see in Him the promise and pledge of man's ultimate triumph. But these words do not only apply in their ultimate sense to the coming age; they are also the ground of personal faith in the development of Christian experience. In the midst of weakness, perplexity, sorrow, and disappointment, with darkness and discouragement all about us, we have but to glance at Jesus, who is even now crowned with glory and honor, and we too shall participate in that glory which comes from the infilling of the divine Spirit. This is the glorious hope which comes from turning our eyes to Jesus in the midst of a confused and dying world.

The Parallel Between Man and Christ. As the first Adam was head of the natural race, so Christ, "the last Adam," is Head of the redeemed race. The writer then sets the two over against each other in a parallel passage—man in his original and unfallen state, and Christ in His redemptive mission. Of man he says:

He was made "a little lower than the angels."

He was crowned "with glory and honour."

He was set over the works of creation.

Nothing was left that was not put under him.

Then comes the great defection, "But now we see not yet all things put under him"—only a few words from the pen of the writer, but all history spells out the awful disaster. But in even briefer words the writer says, "We see Jesus." Here the human name is used, and the parallel lays a foundation for the life of faith. Of Christ he says:

He was "made a little lower than the angels."

He was "crowned with glory and honour."

"For the suffering of death."

"He by the grace of God should taste death for every man."

In this parallel, the expressions "a little lower than the angels" and "crowned with glory and honour" are

both considered in the psalm as predicates of man; so
also they must both be considered predicates of Jesus
as man. Furthermore, since both were the result of the
one divine act, they must refer to the one divine act in
the case of Jesus also. In the latter case these expressions, while including His humiliation and exaltation,
are written primarily to prove that Jesus was as truly
man as was Adam. That there are distinctions in the
parallels is true, and these will now be given consideration.

Jesus Was Made a Little Lower than the Angels
(2:9). The writer now turns to the remaining portion
of the parallelism which he introduces with the words
"But we see Jesus," using significantly the human name
instead of those used previously, such as the "Son," the
"first begotten," and "Lord." Jesus Christ, as at once
Son of God and Son of Man, was infinitely superior
to the angels, and to be made a little lower than them
meant for Him a humiliation. This cannot be said,
however, of man in his original creation, but only of
man in his ultimate glory through Christ. It was only
by means of His union with us in the Incarnation, and
voluntarily taking upon Him our nature, that He was
able to claim and achieve the glory that God had promised to man. On the other hand, it is only as we receive
this new nature from Him through the Spirit, by virtue
of His work both on earth and in heaven, that what He
has achieved for us can become ours in reality. "Let
us here at the very outset of our Epistle," says Andrew
Murray, "get well hold of the truth that what Christ
does for us as our Leader and Priest, our Redeemer, is
not anything external . . . All that Adam wrought in
us is from within, by a power that rules our inmost life.
And all that Christ does for us, whether as Son of God
or Son of man, is equally and entirely a work done
within us. It is when we know that He is one with us
and we with Him, even as was the case with Adam,
that we shall know how truly our destiny will be realized
in Him. His oneness with us is the pledge, our oneness

with Him the power of our redemption" (ANDREW MUR-
RAY, *The Holiest of All*, pp. 73-74).

Jesus Crowned with Glory and Honor. Do the words
"for the suffering of death" attach to the expression
"made a little lower than the angels" or to "crowned
with glory and honour"? If to the first, the meaning is
that Christ was crowned with glory and honor because
of, or on account of, the suffering of death; if to the
latter, He was crowned with glory and honor that He
might suffer death. The first would express the purpose
of His being made a little lower than the angels; the
second, the reason for His being crowned with glory
and honor. Both positions are equally true, and both
find confirmation in this Epistle. Christ has received a
twofold glory: one by right, that of becoming man;
and one by the grace of God, that of personal achievement. It must be borne in mind that the use which
the writer makes of this psalm depends entirely upon
this conception. This twofold glory is brought out
clearly in the response to Christ's prayer, "Father, glorify thy name. Then came there a voice from heaven,
saying, I have both glorified it," (with the glory bestowed upon man in his original creation) "and will
glorify it again" (in the gracious acceptance of His
humiliation and triumph). What is this glory and honor?
Evidently the honor is that bestowed upon Him by the
Father, while the *glory* is that of His personal manifestation, and consists in the acceptance of His death as
an adequate propitiation for the sins of all mankind.
This leads to what may be called "the foregleams of
the atonement," a subject which later is given extended
treatment in two chapters of great importance.

Foregleams of the Atonement. We turn now to the
purposive clauses of the text and ask, How did Jesus
thus come to be crowned with glory and honor? The
answer is, Through "the suffering of death." What was
the purpose of this suffering? "That he by the grace
of God should taste death for every men" (2:9). It
is not the purpose of the writer at this point to discuss

the atonement, but to reveal the greatness of Jesus. Insofar as the sufferings of Jesus and their purpose are concerned, this verse is but a foregleam of that which is to follow. The writer here gives a masterly reply to the two main objections urged by the Jews: (1) They objected that Jesus was but a man and not the Son of God; and (2) that He suffered an ignominious death on the Cross. He could not therefore be greater than the angels. The writer declares that these, so far from proving Him to be inferior to angels, by which the law was given, prove that they were immediately connected with His own exaltation to glory, and with the salvation of men. It is sometimes objected that the two last clauses in this parallel between man and Christ —"for the suffering of death" and "taste death for every man"—are but repetitions. This objection however is only apparent. For the first is personal and furnishes the ground by which He was advanced to glory and honor; the second is purposive—He tasted "death for every man" that provision might be made for the salvation of all men. We must now examine these purposive clauses more at length.

"For the Suffering of Death." The suffering of death means more than mere dying. It means that Christ's death was not an easy one, but a death of suffering accompanied by inward agony and outward torture. As expressed in the words of St. Paul, He was "obedient unto death, even the death of the cross" (Phil. 2:8). Vaughan points out that the words *tou thanatou* (τοῦ θανάτου), "of the death," are peculiar in that they define the word *pathema* (πάθημα) or "suffering," and may therefore be translated "the suffering consisting of death." It should be noted also that both the words *suffering* and *death* are preceded by the definite article, thus reading *the suffering* and *the death*. This indicates that Christ's suffering and death are unique and therefore to be distinguished from that which pertains in general to mortal men. Jesus underwent a sacrificial, vicarious, propitiatory death. It was such a death as

fully satisfied the demands of infinite holiness and righteousness, and it is because of this that He is crowned with glory and honor. This links the crowning with the subjection of all things to himself, and thus fulfills the original promise by restoring man to his regnancy through Christ. But there is another statement of great importance here. This unique suffering and death is said to be by the grace of God, *chariti Theou* (χάριτι Θεοῦ), or by God's appointment. This statement by the emphatic position which it occupies implies a strong denial of the opposite, that is, that it was a death under the wrath of God. Fallen and sinful men die under the wrath of God, but not Christ; otherwise His death could not be for the benefit of those subject to death. This is a further reason as to why Christ was crowned with glory and honor.

"That He by the Grace of God Should Taste Death for Every Man" (2:9b). In the council of divine grace concerning man's redemption, the chief purpose of the Incarnation was to provide Christ with a propitiatory offering. Both events were miraculous, the Virgin Birth being for the sake of the vicarious Offerer and His offering. To taste of death is, as we have previously pointed out, a stronger statement than the simple verb "to die." It carries with it the thought of consciously undergoing all the dread bitterness of death, and in the case of our Lord the humiliation and reproach of a death on the Cross. As the preceding clause, "the suffering of death" tells us *what* was done for us in removing the bar to the glory of full dominion, so here the writer tells us *how* this is accomplished—He tasted "death for every man." He tasted death, not merely by sipping the cup, but by draining it to its dregs. The words *hyper pantos* (ὑπὲρ παντὸς), "for all," make it clear that this vicarious death was for the benefit of every member of Adam's fallen race. Ebrard points out

It should be noted that there is an alternate reading here, and Ebrard says that the reading wavers between χαριτι Θεοῦ, which is translated here "the grace of God," and χωρις Θεοῦ, which would mean "apart from" or "except God."

that the word *hyper* as here used should not be rendered "in place of" or "instead of," but "for" or "in behalf of." This universality is expressed in the enumerative singular "for every one," and while the Authorized Version adds the word "man" as presupposed, the Revised Version omits it, as does the Greek text. Since in verse 8 the writer laid emphasis upon *ta panta* (τὰ πάντα) or "all things," so here we find all things reconciled; that is, He tasted death for everyone or for everything, including the angels. Although they need no atonement, yet the angels enjoy in adoring contemplation the fruits of the death of Jesus and rejoice over every sinner that repents.

THE CAPTAIN OF OUR SALVATION

Jesus is called the Captain of our salvation because He marches in the van. He goes before us, not only as a Leader, but as a Conqueror. The subject is introduced by the words, "For it became him, for whom are all things, and by whom are all things, in bringing many sons unto glory, to make the captain of their salvation perfect through sufferings" (2:10). The word "for" links this verse to the previous clause, the "death of Christ," which opened up the way to God for us and made it possible for Him to become our Captain or Leader. The word *eprepen* (ἔπρεπεν), "it became" or "it was becoming," describes what God does as something befitting to Him. Here it describes the suffering and death of Jesus as something necessary to save men, and as taking place through the grace of God, not through His wrath. And although God is sovereign, it is here stated that the only way to secure the glory of man was through the suffering and death of the Son.

A further explanation of what is becoming to God is found in the words, "For whom are all things, and by whom are all things" (2:10*a*). It lies in this: (1) the thing done, "bringing many sons unto glory"; and (2) the manner in which this is done, through the sufferings and death of Christ. But instead of saying that

He was crowned with glory, it is said that He leads "many sons unto glory"; and instead of speaking of the death of Christ, the writer speaks of Him as being perfected through suffering. Christ is therefore at once the End or Purpose of our lives, and the efficient Agency by which all things are accomplished. Andrew Murray points out that this reduces to a comprehensive, yet simple, principle of holy living: "All for God" and "All through God."

THE NATURE OF SANCTIFICATION

In this section (2: 11-13) the writer continues his discussion under a different terminology. The Captain of our salvation becomes the One who sanctifies; and the "many sons" brought to glory are the sanctified. The present participles *hagiazon* (ἁγιάζων) and *hagiazomenos* (ἁγιαζόμενος) as used with the articles become substantives, and hence the Sanctifier and the sanctified, these parties being designated by their relative positions. It is very evident therefore that He who leads many sons to glory does so by sanctifying them, and that the only way to glory for the sons of God is through sanctification. "Let none deceive themselves," says John Owen, an ancient writer. "Sanctification is a qualification indispensably necessary unto them who will be under the conduct of the Lord Jesus Christ unto salvation. He will lead none to heaven but whom He sanctifies on earth. The holy God will not receive unholy persons; this living Head will not admit of dead members, nor bring them into the possession of a glory which they neither love nor like" (OWEN, *Hebrews*, p. 28). We must understand the term sanctification as used here in its fundamental sense, as the setting apart of a person or thing from common use and devoting it to the holy, such as is befitting the nature of God and His service. The word *koinon* (κοινόν), or "common," means "belonging to anyone"; the word *hagios* (ἅγιος), or "holy," means "belonging to God only." The holy person is a "God-possessed person," cleansed from all sin and unrighteousness, and fully devoted to God.

The Sanctifier and the Sanctified Are All of One. The expression *ex henos* (ἐξ ἑνὸς) is an ablative of source and means literally "out of one" or "originating in one" which is God the Father. Thus the Sanctifier and the sanctified, originating in one source, are in some sense "all of one piece." Some have attempted to confine the expression solely to the humanity of Christ, while others refer it to His deity as well as His humanity. Calvin holds that the word *henos* (ἑνὸς) is in the neuter gender, and therefore refers to a common nature, as though it were said, "They are made out of the same mass." Generally however the word is regarded as masculine and therefore as referring to God the Father of all. Our Lord, as at once the Son of God and the Son of Man, is "from the Father"; and therefore it may be equally said that the Son of God and the sons of men have one common origin as being both from the Father, but in a widely different manner. Christ is the "only begotten" and "eternal" Son, of the same essence as the Father and equal in power and majesty. Men are sons of God by creation through the divine inbreathing of life. Christ's sonship is original and infinite; man's is derived and finite; but the being of both is of God. Man however fell into sin and lost the moral image of God, fellowship was broken, and depravity like a dread disease permeated the entire race, finding its issue in suffering and death. It "became him," therefore, to partake of men's natural condition that He might deliver them from their sinful condition. It is a glorious thought that Christ, being our Elder Brother, could not rest in glory while we were in sin without making provision for our redemption. As His unity with us made possible the Incarnation, so also our unity with Him makes possible our spiritual restoration. So great is His sanctifying power through the Holy Spirit, and so great the spiritual restoration of the sanctified, that He is no longer ashamed to call us brethren.

The Meaning of the Word Sanctification. Since we have the statement that the Sanctifier and the sanctified are brethren, we must now examine more closely the meaning of these terms. The word *hagiazein* (ἁγιάζειν), "to sanctify," is used in both an objective and a subjective sense. In its objective sense it has reference to the work which Christ has done *for* us in expiating sin or in making atonement. This objective and provisional aspect is sometimes referred to as "the finished work of Christ." But this is not the full sense of the word sanctification, for it also has its subjective aspect, by which is meant that which Christ works *in* us by His Holy Spirit. It is not enough to say that Christ has provided an atonement *for* us; we need Christ *in* us as much as we need His atoning work *for* us. It is not alone what Christ did on the Cross that saves us; it is what He does *in* us by virtue of what He did *for* us on the Cross. Christ not only expiates our sins; He dwells within us through the Holy Spirit; and it is His personal presence within that sanctifies us in the deeper meaning of the word *hagiazein* (ἁγιάζειν). Here the word *hagios* (ἅγιος) or "holy" signifies not only the act of purifying or cleansing, but the indwelling presence of Christ in His cleansed temple; and it is this Presence within that sanctifies and makes us His possession.

We must understand, therefore, that the word *sanctify* as used here refers primarily to the objective work of Christ in the expiation of sin, the atonement which finds its ultimate issue in the divine declaration that "the blood of Jesus Christ his Son cleanseth us from all sin" (I John 1:7). It denotes the total act by which Christ separates His people from a life in sin and places them in the sphere of a new life which rests upon His atoning death and His resurrection unto life. Dr. Adam Clarke points out that the Sanctifier, *ho hagiazon* (ὁ ἁγιάζων), has reference to One who expiates sin, or makes atonement, and therefore agrees with the word *caphar*, which in Hebrew means "to expiate sin." The "sanctified" are those who have received the atonement, which in its fullness includes the forgiveness of sins, the impartation of the new life in regeneration; the purification of the heart and the indwelling presence of the Holy

Spirit in entire sanctification; and in the resurrection of the just, the glorification of His people with himself.

Christ Not Ashamed to Call His People Brethren. "For which cause he is not ashamed to call them brethren" (2:11b). When we consider the immense difference between the eternal Son as the "only begotten" of the Father and the sons of God by creation, and when added to this is the sinfulness of these sons, we clearly see the marvelous, condescending love of our Saviour in calling us brethren. Despite the fact that He is infinitely above us, He considered this "no disparagement to Himself." As He is the Sanctifier, He sanctifies His people and makes them like himself. Holiness then is the bond of union, the ground of approving grace.

The word holy is of deepest meaning, and is used in three main forms in the Scriptures. (1) It is used of God, who alone is absolutely holy, the Fountain of all good, and who manifests himself in love and righteousness. The Holy Spirit is so called because His office work is to make men holy. He is the Bearer of divine love, which He sheds abroad in the cleansed heart of man, and the bond of communion, not only in the Trinity itself, but likewise between God and man. (2) In the derived sense, as it respects persons and things, holiness is the separation from the common and the devotion to the holy. This may refer to things which are withdrawn from a natural or profane use and, after cleansing, devoted to the service of God. In the case of persons, it refers to a withdrawal from the natural and sinful life and being set in a redemptive relation to God. It does not always mean entire sanctification, and this accounts for its use in reference to those in the Church, which as an organization is separated to God. (3) The word is also used in the sense of a gracious personal experience. Here it is the purification of the heart from all sin, and the infilling of divine love by the Spirit. This love becomes the motive of devotion to God, and comprehends what is commonly known as entire sanctification. Holiness, therefore, means to be "God-possessed," and finds its issue in the name "brethren" which Jesus gives to His redeemed people.

The Idea of Brotherhood in the Old Testament. It was prophesied in the Old Testament that the Messiah would enter into a relation of brotherhood with the subjects of His kingdom, and that He would exalt them to a participation in sonship with himself. The writer now turns to the Old Testament to substantiate his claim. He finds his material in the twenty-second psalm, where a suffering king becomes typical of the Messiah, who as the Anointed of God comes to His own through suffering; and to Isaiah, where a prophet as a member of Israel suffers with those to whom he prophesies. The writer presents the truth drawn from these passages in a dramatic manner which is at once unique and inspiring.

1. "I will declare thy name unto my brethren" (Heb. 2:12a; Ps. 22:22a). Here is the first act of the drama, in which the Son is pictured as starting on a revealing mission, that of declaring or manifesting the name and nature of the Father. That this mission was abundantly fulfilled is set forth in our Lord's high priestly prayer, "I have manifested thy name . . . and will declare it: that the love wherewith thou hast loved me may be in them, and I in them" (John 17:6, 26). It is supposed that this psalm was written about the time of David's persecution by Saul; and though David had been anointed king, his kingdom, established through suffering and sorrow, was later turned to joy in a kind of gospel. This scripture, therefore, takes on great significance in that the typical king and the true King attain their sovereignty under like conditions, and both alike in their triumph acknowledge kinship with the people whom they raise to brotherhood.

2. "In the midst of the church will I sing praise unto thee" (Heb. 2:12b; Ps. 22:22b). Here a new particular is added. The glorified Christ is not only the Son revealing the Father; He is also its Precentor, leading its worship. He is found in the midst of the Church, a unity of Christ with His brethren expressed in a new form, that

of a common worship of the Father. The "congregation" in which the typical king and his brethren exercise their common privilege as citizens of the commonwealth is here lifted to the true King and His brethren in the divine commonwealth and glory of the New Testament Church.

3. "And again, I will put my trust in him" (Heb. 2:13a; Isa. 8:17; II Sam. 22:3). Here a further advance is taken. The Son is not only a Brother and a Fellow Worshiper, but also a Fellow Believer. He is represented as in the same condition with those to whom He was sent, and as saying along with them in this dramatic presentation, "I will put my trust in him." The fitness of the allusion lies in the fact that the prophet Isaiah, through whom the word of the Lord came, was himself as resigned to the hope that God would fulfill His promises as were the people to whom he spoke. As this was true of the Old Testament prophet, so also in the New Testament we hear Jesus saying, "I can of mine own self do nothing . . . I seek not mine own will, but the will of the Father which hath sent me" (John 5:30, 38). Our Lord during His incarnation as Son of Man lived a life of faith. Hence while in this chapter He is called the Captain of our salvation, in Heb. 12:2 He is called the Author and Perfecter of our faith. The Greek word for Captain and Author is however the same, but the emphasis is not now upon the necessity of leadership, but upon the quality of faith which makes that leadership effective. The Old Testament worthies represented different aspects of faith; Christ exhibited faith in its full-rounded perfection. For this reason He can perfect our faith in every exigency of life.

4. "Behold I and the children which God hath given me" (Heb. 2:13b; Isa. 8:18a). This is the final act in the drama, in which the Son returns to the Father with the many sons He leads to glory. Here again the reference is to Isaiah the prophet and his children, who had become signs to an unbelieving people (Isa. 8:4). The typical prophet and his children thus become the basis

for the statement, "Behold I and the children which God hath given me." And in this final act He returns to the Father and presents them at the threshold of glory, where once He was without them. He went out singly and alone; He returns with the multitude of His saints. We turn to the high priestly prayer of Jesus again for the fulfillment of this typical prophecy. "And now, O Father, glorify thou me with thine own self with the glory which I had with thee before the world was. I have manifested thy name unto the men which thou gavest me out of the world: thine they were, and thou gavest them me; and they have kept thy word" (John 17: 5-6). But this is not all. "Father, I will that they also, whom thou hast given me, be with me where I am; that they may behold my glory, which thou hast given me: for thou lovedst me before the foundation of the world" (John 17: 24). To be with Christ for ever and ever, and there behold the infinite glory which He had with the Father before the world was—this is the high estate to which Christ has lifted us as His brethren; this is the heritage of the sons of God.

A MERCIFUL AND FAITHFUL HIGH PRIEST

The writer has spoken of Jesus as the "captain of our salvation" (2: 10) and thereby introduced the subject of the apostolic work of Christ, which he will later treat under the symbol of Moses, the apostle of the Old Testament; here (2: 14-18) he introduces the subject of Christ's priestly work, which will later be treated under the symbols of Aaron and Melchisedec. Man in order to be a true follower of Christ has three specific needs: (1) he is a sinner and needs to be saved from sin; (2) he is in an enemy's country and needs power to overcome his enemies; and (3) he is liable to break down in the way because of his own weakness and infirmity. In this brief section, Christ as a merciful and faithful High Priest will be shown as meeting every need of man. (1) He redeems us from sin and lifts us to the plane of salvation and fellowship with God; (2) He gives us victory over our enemies and lifts us to the plane of

spiritual freedom; and (3) He strengthens us by His
Spirit in the inner man and thereby lifts us to the plane
of gracious security. Thus He fulfills to us "the oath
which he sware to our father Abraham, that he would
grant unto us, that we being delivered out of the hand
of our enemies might serve him without fear, in holiness and righteousness before him, all the days of our
life" (Luke 1: 73-75). The section now under consideration is an amplification of the above great truths, with
special attention to the necessity and purpose of the
Incarnation.

*The Incarnation and Deliverance from the Fear of
Death.* "Forasmuch then as the children are partakers
of flesh and blood, he also himself likewise took part of
the same; that through death he might destroy him that
had the power of death, that is, the devil" (2: 14*ab*).
Two things stand out clearly in this text and demand
special consideration: (1) The Necessity of the Incarnation and (2) The Purpose of the Incarnation.

1. *The Necessity of the Incarnation.* "Forasmuch
then as the children are partakers of flesh and blood,
he also himself took part of the same" (2: 14*a*). It has
been previously pointed out that from the divine side
it was necessary for Christ to become incarnate in order
to call men His brethren; here however we have the
necessity of the Incarnation from the human aspect.
This necessity arises from the fact that Christ must be
made like His brethren in all the circumstances of life,
its trials, its temptations, its suffering and death. It
should be noted (1) that the reality of the Incarnation
is here reaffirmed. Christ's humanity was as real as
ours. His was no mere Christophany or appearance, as
early Docetism taught. He took part in our flesh and
blood. (2) The Incarnation becomes the ground of personal fellowship between Christ and His people. He
knew hunger and bodily fatigue; He was a "man of sorrows, and acquainted with grief." In all things He was
made like His brethren, sin only excepted. (3) This
text preserves for us the uniqueness of the Incarnation.

The writer carefully guards the distinction between the
nature of Christ and that of man in his fallen estate.
He does not say that Christ was "a partaker of flesh and
blood" as is mankind, but that He "took part of the
same." Two different Greek words are used in these
two clauses. The first is *kekoinoneken* (κεκοινώνηκεν)
and has reference to the human nature shared in common by all individuals as a permanent inheritance. The
second word is that used of Christ, *meteochen* (μετέοχεν),
and expresses the uniqueness of the Incarnation as a
voluntary acceptance of humanity in its present state
of humiliation, but with the added thought of transitoriness. Thus Holy Writ preserves for us the distinct nature
of Christ as the Holy One. Though as truly man as He
was very God, yet He was different from mankind in
general in that His human nature was not permeated
with the virus of sin, as is man in his fallen state. From
His birth He was called "that holy thing," and later
in this Epistle is said to be "holy, harmless, undefiled, separate from sinners, and made higher than the
heavens" (7: 26).

2. *The Purpose of the Incarnation.* "That through
death he might destroy him that had the power of death,
that is, the devil" (2: 14b). This is a purpose clause
which states another reason for our Lord's assumption of flesh and blood. It is to bring to nought or to
break the authority of him who had the *kratos* (κράτος),
"power," "might," or "dominion," of death. As a guilty
man is confined as a prisoner by the pronouncement of
a judge, so Satan held men in bondage by virtue of the
law of sin and death. Legally, there is no release. The
only possibility of deliverance from Satan and death is
found in putting off the fallen nature over which they
had authority and power. This man could not do, and
hence God sent His own Son "in the likeness of sinful
flesh, and for sin," and thereby "condemned sin in the
flesh" (Rom. 8: 3). Christ, as enduring death for sin,
acknowledged the righteous judgment of God and secured for us the promise of deliverance: (1) from death
as a penalty for our own transgressions, (2) from our

own sinful nature as a life in the flesh, and (3) from the fear by which Satan held us in bondage. This He did by destroying or bringing to nought the power of Satan over death.

The word "destroyed" as used here is often interpreted to mean "annihilation," and for this reason the Revised Version has "bring to nought." The Greek word is *katargesei* (κaταργήσῃ), used many times by St. Paul and variously translated "bring to nought" (I Cor. 1: 28), "without effect" (Rom. 3: 3), "make void" (Rom. 3: 31); and also "to abolish," "put away"; and in its highest form, "to destroy." In our Authorized Version it is rendered by at least seventeen different phrases. It is declared that it was through death that Christ rendered of none effect him that had the power of death. It will be noted that the word "his" is not used in this connection, the Greek words being *tou thanatou* (τοῦ θανάτου), or "the death." The writer does not use the pronoun, for he would emphasize the fact that the devil was overcome by that which was his own sphere of power. Thus Christ turned Satan's own weapon against himself, and delivered us from his bondage without a weapon except the endurance of all that the enemy's weapon could inflict. It was this that led Chrysostom to say, "Herein is the wonder, that Satan is worsted by that which he overcame."

The Incarnation and Deliverance from Our Enemies. "And deliver them who through fear of death were all their lifetime subject to bondage" (2: 15). Christ came not only to expiate our sins but to deliver us from our enemies and thereby lift us to the plane of gracious freedom. Here His triumph over the devil is traced to its full consequences; and having overcome the last enemy, which is death, the great Captain of our salvation is able to deliver us from every enemy that would hinder our progress in the way of holiness. Our last great enemy is death. It is not said that Christ destroyed death, but by overcoming it in the Resurrection He has so changed our position toward it that it no longer holds us in the bondage of fear. And yet death is still our enemy—the last enemy, a conquered enemy, but still an enemy. There are few homes where the chill of death has not been felt, where loving bonds have not been torn asunder, and where the pain of parting has not been felt. Jesus wept at the grave of Lazarus. But through Christ's death and resurrection we can triumphantly exclaim, "O death, where is thy sting? O grave, where is thy victory?" Death is still here but we can now say that both life and death are ours; and we look forward with confidence to that "better country" where there shall be no death, neither sorrow nor crying.

The Incarnation and Preservation Through Weakness and Infirmity. In addition to deliverance from sin, and from the fear of enemies, man has a third great need, that of preservation in times of weakness and infirmity. Sin must be removed in this life or not at all; but the consequences of sin, such as weakness and infirmity, are removed only at the time of the resurrection. St. Paul recognizes these two types of perfection when he says, "Not as though I had already attained, either were already perfect"—the resurrection perfection; and, "Let us therefore, as many as be perfect, be thus minded"—Christian perfection (Phil. 3: 11-15).

The aspect of bondage, whether to the law of sin or to Satan, is not often given the prominence in theology that it is accorded in the Scriptures. Dr. Pope states it in this manner: "Mankind, as the object of redemption, is ransomed from captivity to sin primarily; subordinately and indirectly, from captivity to Satan and to death the penalty of sin. Sin holds man in bondage both as a condemnation and as a power. (1) The condemnation is the *curse of the law. As the strength of sin is the law,* so the strength of the law is sin. It binds every moral creature to perfect obedience; and, that being found wanting, it shuts the transgressor up to the sentence of doom from which, so far as legal ordinance goes, there is no release. (2) Sin is an internal power in human nature; enslaving the will, and affections, and mind. (3) The atoning intervention of Christ has *put away sin* as an absolute power in human life. He hath *obtained eternal redemption for us;* an objective, everlasting, all sufficient redemption from the curse of the law and from the necessary surrender of the will to the power of evil." Continuing this thought, he says that Satan and death are subordinate but real representatives of the power of evil, Satan representing at once the condemnation of the law and the inner bondage to iniquity. Here it is seen how closely related are sin and our enemies. Christ's redemption has made provision to set man free, both from sin and from Satan, our enemy who administers it through death. The Epistle to the Hebrews connects both of these truths with the atonement in a remarkable manner. Cf. Pope, *Compendium of Christian Theology,* II, 289.

In Christian perfection Christ purifies the heart and dwells within it through the Spirit, thus enabling us to follow Christ in pressing toward the perfection given in the resurrection. We not only need Christ as our Aaronic High Priest to atone for our sins; we need Him also as our Melchisedec High Priest through whom we may live our earthly lives; or stated in a deeper sense, that Christ may live His life through us. It is in this connection that we not only see the need for such a priesthood, but it is here also that we have the first mention of Christ as our High Priest. This priestly work is accomplished through the indwelling of the Holy Spirit as Paraclete or Comforter, the Promise of the Father and the Gift of the glorified Christ.

What a gracious gift to the Church is this Gift of the Holy Spirit! When Satan tempts us to think that we have never been forgiven of our sins, or cleansed from all unrighteousness, we are able to reach out by faith and span the promise that "the blood of Jesus Christ his Son cleanseth us from all sin" (I John 1:7). When we are beset about with enemies, having fightings without and fears within, we can reach out even wider by faith and claim "the oath which he sware to our father Abraham, That he would grant unto us, that we being delivered out of the hand of our enemies might serve him without fear, in holiness and righteousness before him, all the days of our life" (Luke 1:73-75). And when we are all but overcome by weakness and ready to fall from weariness and our many infirmities, we find that the Comforter still abides within, ever present to strengthen us in our weakness, guide us in our perplexities, hold us steady in every temptation and trial, and comfort us in our times of sorrow and bereavement. "Thanks be unto God for his unspeakable gift."

The Incarnation and the New Order of Priesthood. "For verily he took not on him the nature of angels; but he took on him the seed of Abraham. Wherefore in all things it behoved him to be made like unto his brethren, that he might be a merciful and faithful high priest in things pertaining to God, to make reconciliation for the sins of the people. For in that he himself hath suffered being tempted, he is able to succour them that are tempted" (2:16-18). We have seen that the Incarnation, in which Christ became man, furnishes the ground for various aspects of the one great salvation. (1) He became man that He himself might be perfected through suffering in order to become the Captain of our salvation, thus preparing a way of life by which He might lead many sons to glory. (2) He became man that through His death and resurrection He might bring to nought the power of Satan and deliver His people from the fear of death. (3) The writer now offers another aspect of the manhood of Christ—"that he might be a merciful and faithful high priest in things pertaining to God." It is to this aspect that we now turn our attention.

1. *The Seed of Abraham.* "For verily he took not on him the nature of angels; but he took on him the seed of Abraham" (2:16). This text has been understood to mean that, by way of contrast, Christ did not assume the nature of angels but only a human nature as expressed in the words "the seed of Abraham." This idea evidently influenced the translators of the Authorized Version; for the words "the nature of," as indicated by the italics, are not found in the Greek text. While it is true that Christ did assume a human nature, this is not here the point of emphasis. Lindsay in his *Lectures on Hebrews* (p. 106) states that the word *epilambanesthai* (ἐπιλαμβάνεσθαι) coupled with the genitive of person denotes to lay hold of the person for the sake of helping him, and hence means simply to help, to assist, or to support; and it cannot possibly mean to assume the nature of a person. The same word is used in Matt. 14:31, where Christ reached out His hand to help sinking Peter; and again in Mark 8:23, where He took the blind man by the hand. Since the law mediated

The word *epilambanesthai* (ἐπιλαμβάνεσθαι) sometimes occurs as *epilambanetai* (ἐπιλαμβάνεται) and means always to lay hold of in the sense of rendering help or assistance. There is no thought that the gentiles are not included, but also Israel likewise needs the same help. Neither is there any thought of unconditional election of Israel or of a refusal to save angels.

by angels was imposed upon the race, it was necessary for Christ to lay hold of the seed of Abraham in order to make propitiation for them, and through them for the whole world. St. Paul tells us that the true Seed of Abraham is Christ, that they which are of faith are the children of Abraham, and that in Him shall all nations be blessed (Gal. 3: 7-9, 14). Christ therefore "lays hold" of all believers to expiate their sins, and as the Captain of their salvation, to lead many sons to glory. The word *epilambano* (ἐπιλαμβάνω) in its various forms appears nineteen times in the New Testament, and twelve of these are in the Gospel of Luke. No further mention of angels is made in this connection.

2. *Christ as High Priest.* "Wherefore in all things it behoved him to be made like unto his brethren, that he might be a merciful and faithful high priest in things pertaining to God, to make reconciliation for the sins of the people" (2: 17). The word *archierus* (ἀρχιερεύς), "high priest," is here used for the first time—a word not found elsewhere in the New Testament except in this Epistle, where it furnishes the central theme of the discussion. The term is significant in that it refers primarily to the ministry of the high priest on the great Day of Atonement. There the high priest was separate from his offering; in Christ the two are conjoined. Christ was both Offerer and Offering. As High Priest, He offered himself without spot to God. This Offering was himself, at once vicarious and substitutionary. His sacrifice was His own blood, and beneath that sprinkled Blood, mercy is extended to all mankind. For this reason He is said to be a "merciful and faithful high priest." The word "merciful" is frequently interpreted as His attitude toward men, in whose likeness He had been made; and "faithful," as referring to His ministry in things pertaining to God. Perhaps a more accurate interpretation would emphasize the fact that Christ was primarily merciful, this word being mentioned first and with emphasis in the Greek; and that as a consequence He is faithful in the sense of being reliable or worthy to be trusted.

3. *Christ as Our Propitiation.* The word "reconciliation" as found in the Authorized Version is not the best translation of the Greek term *hilasmos* (ἱλασμός), which when used as a noun is translated "propitiatory" or "expiatory." Both of these terms refer to the "mercy seat," which was the covering of the ark of the covenant in the holy of holies. The word "reconciliation" comes from the Greek *katallasso* (καταλλάσσω), and refers to a state of peace existing between man and God. The Greek words used in connection with the atonement may be arranged in this order: (1) propitiation or expiation, *hilasmos* (ἱλασμός), which is the sacrificial offering made to God as the ground of atonement. Propitiation refers primarily to the sacrifice, and expiation to the result. The wrath or displeasure of God is propitiated; the sin is expiated. (2) Redemption, *lutro* (λύτρω), is the redemptive price paid for the salvation of men. (3) Reconciliation, *katallasso* (καταλλάσσω), is the state of peace consequent upon the expiation of sin. (4) There is another word also which is used in Heb. 9: 28, *anaphero* (ἀναφέρω), which means "to take upon one's self and bear our sins," in order to make expiation. Here the priestly act and the priestly offering are combined in one Person, who is our "propitiation." "Christ was once offered to bear the sins of many; and unto them that look for him shall he appear the second time without sin unto salvation" (9: 28).

In the text under consideration, however, the word "propitiation" must be regarded chiefly from the objective point of view. The primary emphasis is upon

Redemption once for all effected on the cross, and redemption now in process, are described by the same terms. Those terms may be arranged in four classes: first, those in which the λύτρον or ransom price, is included; secondly, those which mean purchase generally, such as ἀγοράζειν; thirdly, those which imply only release, as from λύειν: and lastly, those which indicate the notion of forcible rescue, ῥυέσθαι. It will be obvious that, as we are now discussing the Atonement in relation to the finished work of Christ alone, the first of these classes belongs more strictly than the rest to our present subject. Sometimes the distinction is expressed as redemption by price and redemption by power. This is a beautiful and true distinction; though it is well to be on our guard against too sharply distinguishing these two, whether in the Lord's external work or in the believer's internal experience of it.—POPE, *Compendium of Christian Theology*, II, 288.

expiation, as on the great Day of Atonement, sin was expiated by the sacrificial offerings of the high priest. But this is not the full meaning of the term. Christ not only redeemed us by the sacrifice of himself upon the Cross, but arose again to become the Executor of His own will. As such the risen Christ becomes our merciful and faithful High Priest, ministering *to us* from His throne in the heavens the salvation He wrought out *for us* at Calvary. What the writer seeks to emphasize here is that Christ not only died for all men, but personally ministers this salvation to everyone who trusts in Him. A clear grasp of both the Cross and the Throne is essential to a full understanding of Christ as our Propitiation.

This is brought out further in the Christian doctrine of redemption, which holds that Christ did not make a propitiatory offering merely to release us from bondage and let us go; instead He recovers for himself that which He has purchased. He ransoms us back into His own regal rights over us as God; and herein lies the significance of the new priestly order of Melchisedec, who was at once a priest and a king. Furthermore, Christ has not only released us from bondage negatively, but positively has restored our inheritance to us. This inheritance is the restoration to man of the Holy Spirit, by whom that communion with God which he forfeited in the Fall is again restored. What greater inheritance could man possibly possess than the indwelling of God the Holy Spirit, the Third Person of the adorable Trinity, sanctifying, illuminating, energizing, and empowering the soul, bringing it into holy fellowship with both the Father and the Son!

4. *Christ and Temptation.* "For in that he himself hath suffered being tempted, he is able to succour them that are tempted" (2:18). Here we have a still further

St. Paul brings out this twofold aspect of propitiation very clearly in his Epistle to the Galatians: "Christ hath redeemed us from the curse of the law, being made a curse for us: for it is written, Cursed is every one that hangeth on a tree: that the blessing of Abraham might come on the Gentiles through Jesus Christ; that we might receive the promise of the Spirit through faith" (Gal. 3:13-14).

advance in the life of the suffering Saviour, that is, His temptation. Two more or less distinct positions concerning the temptation are found in this verse: (1) that the sympathy of Christ is to be found in the fact that He felt temptation whenever exposed to suffering; or (2) it may be based on the fact that His whole life was one of suffering, to which the temptation now mentioned is an added factor. The latter position is the more plausible. In Greek the word *autos* (αὐτός), "himself," precedes the word *peiratheis* (πειρασθείς), "tempted," instead of the word *peiponthen* (πέπονθεν), "suffered," which places the emphasis upon the temptation of Christ rather than upon His suffering. While in a sense the word "himself" may properly apply to each of the terms, for Christ both suffered and was tempted, it has previously been stated that Jesus suffered, and the emphasis is here shifted to the temptation as an added occasion of suffering

Lenski points out that there is an interesting study of tenses found in this verse. (1) The word "tempted" is in the aorist tense, which simply denotes as a past fact that Jesus was tempted. (2) The word "suffered" is in the perfect tense, and therefore has reference to the whole period of His suffering down to the time of His death. (3) The words "he is able" are in the present tense and therefore express His continuous ability to give help to those who are tempted. (4) The expression "those who are tempted" is a participle and iterative, which means "being tempted from time to time." (5) "He is able to succour them that are tempted" is a final and effective aorist, which means literally, "He is actually and effectively able to help."

While the subject of temptation is of the utmost importance, it is not in this place acute, and will be given further treatment in connection with Heb. 4:15. The present purpose of the writer is to point out the qualifications of our High Priest for the personal care of His people. While the chief work of Christ is atonement and intercession, the one accomplished on earth, the other in heaven, both of these find their culmination in Him as a merciful and faithful High Priest. As it is by the atoning Blood that we are redeemed and sanctified, so also it is by His priestly intercession that we are enabled to live the life of holiness and righteousness. What a glorious thought it is that we may live our lives through our great High Priest! It is not by our own power or holiness, not by strength of will or wisdom of mind, that we live a life of spiritual triumph, but by Him who through the Spirit dwells within the holy heart, and thereby lives His life through us. Christ assumed our human nature and suffered being tempted, that He might fully enter into our experiences, and thus His earthly life becomes exceedingly precious to us. His humanity gives us the assurance of His understanding and sympathy, and His deity assures us of His abiding and unfailing presence. He is a merciful High Priest in that we may approach Him just as we are with all our problems and temptations; He is a faithful High Priest in that He is abundantly and effectually able "to succour them that are tempted." The life which we now live, therefore, we live by "the faith of the Son of God" (Gal. 2:20), always bearing in mind that "those who trust Him wholly will find Him wholly true."

CHAPTER III

THE APOSTLESHIP AND
HIGH PRIESTHOOD OF CHRIST

We are now about to leave the beautiful gate of the Temple and enter into the spiritual temple itself. The writer has lingered long at this gate, noting both the divine and the human aspects of Christ, and drawing from both phases valuable lessons in Christian experience. He has also uttered serious warnings against the neglect of the great salvation from the standpoint of the deity of Christ, and now is about to utter a similar warning against hardening the heart, in reference to the humiliation of Christ. But as we leave the gate to enter the temple, we shall find that it is but the expanding life of Christ himself, again viewed from the twofold aspect of His divine and human natures. Here however Christ is considered more in the light of what He has done for us than what He is in himself, although the latter is always the foundation of the former.

THE SPIRITUAL TEMPLE

Wherefore, holy brethren, partakers of the heavenly calling, consider the Apostle and High Priest of our profession, Christ Jesus (3:1).

The divine-human nature of Christ is the gateway into the temple of fellowship with God, and the temple itself is the ever-expanding grace of God in Christ. In entering this temple of grace and truth, the writer will have us consider the nature and work of Christ in relation to Moses, the apostle of the Old Testament, and to Aaron, its high priest. The subject, therefore, is to be presented under the symbolism of the ancient Tabernacle and its service; and the writer's discussion may be viewed as an inspired commentary on the Old Testament, its history and ritual, its laws and legal precedents. Under the aspect of an Apostle, there is the thought of

108

transcendency which has its issue in "revealing grace" and marks a change in relation; under the aspect of the High Priest, there is the thought of immanency which has its issue in "enabling grace" and marks a change in condition. These are combined in the Incarnation from which they flow, and are united again in the final purposes of God. In the temple of spiritual fellowship which we are about to enter, there will be, therefore, an ever-expanding increase of light and truth on the one hand; and comparable to it, an ever-expanding increase of love and power on the other, both of which are revealed through the grace of our Lord Jesus Christ.

The word "wherefore" forms the transition from the two preceding chapters to the two which immediately follow. In it is implied all that has been said in the former chapters concerning the superiority of Christ to the angels, even in His incarnate state; and further, it lays the foundation for the superiority of Christ to Moses, the mediator of the former dispensation and the founder of an earthly theocracy.

"Holy Brethren." This form of address is evidently taken from a statement in the preceding chapter, where it is said, "For both he that sanctifieth and they who are sanctified are all of one: for which cause he is not ashamed to call them brethren" (2: 11). The two words, therefore, are combined in the expression "holy brethren," which forms a fitting characterization of those who are about to pass through the gate into the spiritual temple. It is Jesus who sanctifies us and thereby makes us holy; we are His brethren, by both creation and redemption. What then could be more natural than that these two great thoughts should be joined together? Holiness is common to both Christ and His people, and marks the bond of their union and the ground of their fellowship. The primary idea of holiness is that which God separates to himself, and is sometimes used in an external or corporate sense, as is the Church. But we may not infer from this that every member of this external organization is possessed of inward holiness. There are babes even in the Church of Christ who have not entered into the experience of heart purity or perfect love. Inward holiness demands the concomitant truth of inward purity. What God has separated to himself in order to be "sanctified in truth" (John 17:17) must also be inwardly purified from sin, and made to conform to the image of His Son, who is "holy, harmless, undefiled, separate from sinners" (Heb. 7:26).

"Partakers of the Heavenly Calling" (3:1). The Christian's calling is heavenly—not only because it proceeds from heaven as to its origin, nor yet because it is a call to heaven as a supreme goal, but because it is a spiritual quality of life which finds its ultimate fulfillment in heaven. Andrew Murray speaks of this heavenly calling as that in which the power of a heavenly life works in us to make our lives heavenly. In its full conception, therefore, it is the power of the Holy Spirit first bestowed at Pentecost, by which men were delivered from all sin and transformed into the spiritual likeness of Christ. The Word *metochoi* (μέτοχοι), or "partakers," means literally "sharers" or those who hold things in common. Christians are the "anointed" ones and therefore in some true sense the "Christed" ones who share with Him the "power of an endless life." The voice from heaven to Moses was an earthly calling, a call to the fulfillment of an earthly life in the establishment of a theocracy. Christians are called to be sharers in the establishment of a spiritual Kingdom, the initial stage of which is an inner condition of righteousness, peace, and joy in the Holy Ghost.

"Consider the Apostle and High Priest of Our Profession" (3:1). This expression may be stated more emphatically as follows: "Therefore, because Jesus is the Apostle and High Priest of our confession, consider Him well" (Lowrie). The word "consider" is an astronomical term derived from the Latin root *sidus*, meaning a star or a constellation, and thus we have *sidereal* as pertaining to the heavens. "Consider" carries the thought that, as astronomers gaze long and intently at the heavens in order to inform themselves concerning the solar system, so also as Christians we are to continu-

ously gaze with wonder and adoration at Jesus Christ. The Greek word for "consider" comes from the verb *katanoeo* (κατανοέω), which does not mean primarily to lay anything to heart, but to bring it before the mind, in the sense of fastening the attention upon it or weighing it thoroughly. Westcott says that it expresses attention and continuous observation and regard. This regard is directed toward Jesus as our Apostle and High Priest, and more remotely to His faithfulness as compared with that of Moses. These are now to be the objects of attentive consideration.

The word *katanoesate* (κατανοήσατε) is in the imperative mood, but is generally regarded, not so much as an exhortation, but as a proposition designed to exhibit the subjects which the writer later intends to discuss. In fact, the entire Epistle from this point on forms a logical and compact discourse on the very subjects to which attention is called in the first verse of the chapter. It is to this discussion that he now invites attention as worthy of close and prolonged consideration.

Christ Our Apostle (3:1). The apostolic work of Christ has reference primarily to its objective phase as Revealer and Leader, the latter previously mentioned as the Captain of our salvation (2:10). As Moses brought Israel out of Egypt and across the desert to the borders of their material goal, the Canaan rest, so Christ our Apostle not only brings us to the borders of our divine rest, but as our great Joshua, actually brings us into that rest that awaits the people of God. Canaan therefore symbolizes the "rest of faith" which God has prepared for His people, but which ancient Israel failed to enter through unbelief and hardness of heart. Four phases of the apostolic work are presented in this and the following chapter under the symbolism of (1) the house, (2) the voice in the house, (3) the land, and (4) the throne in the land. Here too the Sabbath is mentioned as explanatory of the type of spiritual rest which God from the beginning has provided for His people. It will be noted that these symbols represent a deepening and broadening conception of the apostolic work of Christ. "We shall not rightly consider Him as Apostle," says Bishop Chadwick, "until we remember the fidelity, the pathos, the homeliness of His teaching, the blessings He scattered with both hands, and His long endurance of sinners against Himself; until we reflect upon the gentle majesty with which He revealed the Father, and remind ourselves that all His ministry was for us in the twentieth century, as truly as for Galilee and Judaea in the first." He is the only One who can reveal to us the condition of our hearts and bring us to the place of self-surrender. He it is who alone can bring us to the all-atoning Blood of His priestly sacrifice, and through His Spirit take up His abode in our hearts. His prophetic work must always precede His priestly atonement; and in receiving Christ and His salvation, we must accept Him in all His offices, as Prophet, Priest, and King.

Christ Our High Priest (3:1). The two terms applied to Jesus, Apostle and High Priest, have but one article, thus indicating that He is the Subject of both offices, and the One great Object of our confession. As an Apostle, Christ has access to the Father and reveals Him to us; as High Priest, He pleads our cause with the Father and brings us into the presence of God. In both offices He is merciful and faithful (2:17)—merciful to men in that, having become incarnate, He understands our weaknesses and temptations; faithful to us and to God in that He spoke only the words that He heard the Father speak, during the time He tabernacled among us. It is this faithfulness that makes Him trustworthy, and resting in Him we find the inward confidence and joyful assurance that He will fulfill all of God's promises to us. In Chapters III and IV, the apostolic work of Christ will be presented under four main heads as previously indicated; in Chapters VII through X, His priestly work will likewise be presented in four divisions: (1) the priesthood, (2) the promises, (3) the sanctuary, and (4) the inheritance. These Old Testament types are given spiritual interpretations in the light of the new covenant; and joined with them are four corresponding warnings against indifference, slothfulness, sinning willfully, and apostasy.

THE HOUSE OF GOD

The writer has previously characterized Jesus as "a merciful and faithful high priest" (2:17); and having mentioned briefly His mercy, he now proceeds to consider Jesus as faithful. Later more attention will be given to the aspect of mercy. Christ "was faithful to him that appointed him, as also Moses was *faithful* in all his house" (3:2). The word *oikos* (οἶκος), translated "house," does not merely apply to a building and its furniture, but also to the resident family or household, including the establishment of servants. The text which forms the basis of the argument is found in the Book of Numbers (12:7), where it is said, "My servant Moses . . . who is faithful in all mine house." The "house" as used in the Old Testament refers to the people of Israel; as used in the New Testament, it is the Church, which is expanded to include all believers, the middle wall of partition having been broken down. In relation to God, the house is essentially one; but considered in reference to its administration, it is twofold—the Old Testament economy under Moses and that of the New Testament under Christ.

Christ as Superior to Moses. It is the writer's purpose to show the superiority of Christ by a threefold argument: (1) The builder is greater than the house; (2) The master is greater than the servant; and (3) The fulfillment is greater than the type.

1. The first argument is based upon the superiority of the builder to the house, and is thus stated: "For this man was counted worthy of more glory than Moses, inasmuch as he who hath builded the house hath more honour than the house" (3:3). The glory of which Christ was counted worthy is a reference to His eternal sonship; while the word *doxes* (δόξης), translated "glory" in the first part of the verse, becomes *timen* (τιμήν) in the latter part, as being more applicable to

a house. Moses was indeed faithful, but he was a part of the household, not the founder of it; hence we have a significant change in the prepositions from "in" (ἐν) to "over" (ἐπί). Moses was faithful *in* the house; Christ was faithful *over* the house. The words "hath more" honor than the house are *kath hoson* (καθ᾽ ὅσον), which mean "how much more." This however is a general statement and is not intended as a comparison of the honors bestowed. The writer reinforces the argument in the next verse by saying, "For every house is built by some man; but he that built all things is God" (3:4). There is here a deep spiritual insight that sees in the incarnate Christ the *Logos* or Eternal Word by which all things have been made. Thus Christ as the Divine Son is not only Sovereign but Founder of the house and hence greater than Moses, who was part of the economy over which he presided.

2. The second argument is drawn from the contrast between Moses as a servant and Christ as the Son. "And Moses . . . was faithful in all his house, as a servant" (3:5a). The task of exalting Christ above Moses was a delicate one, for Moses was held in high veneration by the Jews. Their religious life, their law with its varied observances, their knowledge of Jehovah, and their hope of the future were all connected with Moses, the servant of God. Furthermore, Jehovah himself had testified that Moses was "faithful in all his house," and that "with him will I speak mouth to mouth" (Num. 12:8). But the skill of this writer, inspired by the Holy Spirit, never fails him. He lays hold of the words "house," "servant," and "Son," and develops them in a masterful manner. Moses is a *therephon* (θεραπων), or free servant, one who serves voluntarily and carries out his master's wishes in the conduct of the household; not a *doulos* (δοῦλος), or a slave who has no will of his own. Moses therefore is characterized by all the dignity which attached to his high office. Again, Moses was a servant who was faithful in *all* his house. Other servants were used in various parts of the household—prophets,

priests, and kings dealt with different and limited aspects of truth and life—but to Moses was entrusted the entire economy, the regulation and care of the whole family of Israel. The point then of the argument is this: Moses was a servant over a household of servants, he himself being a part of the household; but Christ is a Son over a household of sons, He himself being the Author and Founder of the economy over which He is Sovereign.

3. The third argument is this: Moses' ministry was "a testimony of those things which were to be spoken after" (3:5b). Moses therefore not only witnessed to the truth of his own legislation, but he ordered the typical worship of his house in a manner that would afterward be a witness to that which was to be more fully exhibited in Christ. Hence our Lord says, "For had ye believed Moses, ye would have believed me: for he wrote of me" (John 5:46); and to the disciples on the road to Emmaus, "beginning at Moses and all the prophets, he expounded unto them in all the scriptures the things concerning himself" (Luke 24:27). The Mosaic dispensation, therefore, was typical of, and witnessed to, both the person and work of Jesus in the gospel age.

"Whose House Are We." "But Christ as a son over his own house; whose house are we" (3:6a). Both in a corporate sense and as individuals, we are His house, "builded together for an habitation of God through the Spirit" (Eph. 2:22). Since in spiritual things each part is likewise a whole, then each individual as a living stone in the spiritual house is indwelt by the Spirit and manifests the holiness of God. In a corporate sense these living stones are builded together into a habitation of God, and through their personal relationships with each other show forth His glory. If therefore we would know the faithfulness of Christ and the joy of His fellowship, we must surrender to Him the keys of our lives. He must be the abiding Presence within our hearts; and this, not as a Guest, but as Host. We are His house and He must have access to every room, and the management

and control of all must be in His hands. The test of genuine consecration is the keeping of the keys in His hands, not only during the periods of success and joy, but also in the times of sorrow and adversity. We are His house over which He watches with peculiar care. What a great honor is this! What peace of mind, what freedom from worry and care are ours while the keys are in His hands! He is not only the Head of the Church, but the Head of all things to the Church, and orders the universe for its progress and care. Let us then rely upon Him wholly and expect from Him all that He has undertaken for us.

The Necessity for Steadfastness. When the writer says, ". . . whose house are we," he adds the significant condition, "if we hold fast the confidence and the rejoicing of the hope firm unto the end" (3:6b). This portion of the verse is sometimes rendered, "if we hold the boldness and the glorying of the hope firm unto the end" (Moulton). "There is no question," says Bishop Chadwick, "that exercises the earnest minister of the Gospel in our days, as in earlier times, more deeply than what may be the reason that so many converts grow cold and fall away, and what may be done that we may have Christians who can stand and conquer." Perhaps a critical study of the words *parresian* (παρρησίαν), translated "confidence," and *kauchema*

True consecration, by a thorough yielding to God of all we have, and are, and expect to be; of our time, past, present and future (we say past time, for there are many who secretly wish for a return to past surroundings), settles all questions in favor of the full control of God in all the concerns of our life; and in favor of His regulation, as to time, place and manner of the circumstances connected with them. . . . The reader will see at once the difference between everything being at God's disposal, and our holding it so. He is the Sovereign, and doeth what He will with His own, but men do not always acknowledge Him as such. . . . He must have all, because He cannot do anything with you while you desire to keep back a part of yourself or your goods. For anything you set your heart upon is an idol, and it cultivates covetousness which is idolatry, thus keeping you most effectually in such a state that He can do no mighty work within you. This demand for a full consecration to the measure of your light is not an arbitrary rule of tyranny, but the necessary outgoing of pure love. God desires to bless you, and you can only enjoy a delightful sense of His presence when you know He is your supreme good.—Isaac M. See, *The Rest of Faith,* pp. 17-18.

(καύχημα), "rejoicing," will give us an insight into both the nature and the necessity of steadfastness in the Christian life. The former word denotes "open and intrepid speaking without any fear of consequences," and hence has come to mean confidence or boldness. The idea of freedom of speech is never absent from the word, but as used here it is a sincere and reverent freedom which springs from a purified heart, enlarged and set at liberty (Ps. 119:32). To set off the meaning of this word more clearly another Greek word, *hedone* (ἡδονή), denotes a joyous experience awakened by favorable circumstances, while *parresian* (παρρησίαν) is exactly the reverse, signifying that boldness which comes from within and triumphs over all unfavorable circumstances. It is that freedom and boldness which comes from the anointing of the Holy Spirit, and which so qualified the waiting disciples at Pentecost that they "spake the word of God with boldness."

The word *kauchema* (καύχημα), translated "rejoicing," and all the words of the same family, carry with them the idea of "boasting" or "glorying." That the word is translated "rejoicing" in the Authorized Version is due perhaps to the fact that in the Septuagint the Hebrew words denoting joy or gladness are generally rendered by these terms. The word *kauchema* (καύχημα), as used here, refers more especially to the subject, while the word *kauchesis* (καύχησις) refers to the act. Our hope then is not in our inward feelings but in the great Object which inspires them, and the purpose of the writer is to show what abundant ground we have for boldness and glorying in the person and work of Jesus Christ. This hope is steadfast in itself and treasured up in God, but the glorying in it and the making a boast of it are our privilege and duty. Westcott points out that "hope is related to faith as the energetic activity of life is related to life." Hope can come to its perfect fulfillment only when it inspires boldness in those who possess it. It is this abounding hope that is the point of the active agency, the secret of steadfastness, and the source of courageous exultation. This hope we must hold firm to the end if we would live Spirit-filled lives. The word *kataschomen* (κατάσχομεν), or "hold," is an aorist subjunctive which Westcott translates, "if we shall have held fast"; and Vaughan puts it, "if when the great day comes, we shall be found to have held fast." The way to steadfastness, then, is the way of simple faith. It draws from Him who is our Life the joy of His presence, and finds its boldness in Him who is the unfailing Ground of every hope. He gives us honey out of the rock, health in the midst of disease, the oil of joy for mourning, and the garment of praise for the spirit of heaviness. The power of the Infinite is in the way of simple faith.

There is an important lesson here for all who would succeed in the Christian way of life. Steadfastness and perseverance strike deep into essential Christian character and find their only root in the boldness of hope. St. Peter gives us the foundation for this hope when he says that we are "begotten . . . again unto a lively hope by the resurrection of Jesus Christ from the dead" (I Pet. 1: 3). Both St. Paul and St. John link this hope with divine love. St. Paul states clearly that all who are justified by faith have in Christ also a deeper and more abounding grace "wherein we stand, and rejoice in the hope of the glory of God. And not only so, but we glory in tribulations also" (Rom. 5: 2-3). St. John also links boldness with the experience of perfect love. "Herein is our love made perfect," he says, "that we may have boldness in the day of judgment." "He that feareth is not made perfect in love." Here it is clear that fear may be mingled with love in the experience of Christians; but there is a deeper experience in which fear arising from doubt and distrust is cast out, and love is made perfect. Shall we not then, as God's house, allow Him to cleanse our hearts, cast out fear, and perfect our love? Are we not commanded to love the Lord our God with all the heart, soul, mind, and strength? And does He command something that He is not able to accomplish? Let us then hold fast the boldness and the glorying of our hope firm unto the end.

THE SECOND WARNING: AGAINST HARDENING THE HEART

The second warning is against hardening the heart, and is drawn from the experience of Israel in the wilderness. The faithlessness of the people of Israel under Moses becomes the ground of warning to the Hebrew Christians, whom the writer evidently regards as being in imminent danger of falling after the same example of unbelief. The history of the past was eminently fitted to prepare them against the unbelief which destroyed the ancient fathers. The second warning is at the opposite pole from the first, and is directed against a condition more subtle and dangerous. The first warning was against neglecting the great salvation, seen in the light of the majesty of the Son of God; the second is against hardening the heart as a consequence of undervaluing the person and work of the Son as seen in His humiliation. The Son of God is the same, whether seen as a King in His majesty or as a Servant in His humiliation; whether seen in the strength of a lion or the meekness of a lamb; as the Ancient of Days or the Babe of Bethlehem; as the Scepter Bearer of heaven or the Burden Bearer of the world. For this reason the writer reaches immediately into Israel's history for the ground of his warning. This warning extends from chapters 3: 7 to 4: 13 with various applications of the one truth to the Hebrew Christians. Since this section involves, as it does, other important truths, it must be analyzed and considered in its several divisions.

"The Holy Ghost Saith." The writer according to his custom refers directly to the Author of the Scriptures instead of the human instrument, and thus expresses his unqualified belief in the inspiration of the Old Testament. He appears to approach this warning with some hesitancy, and viewing the Scriptures as the voice of God breathing in every part, he introduces the subject with this deeply significant expression, "As the Holy Ghost saith" (3: 7a). The Holy Spirit, who inspired the Scriptures, is their authoritative Interpreter. What is spoken by the Holy Spirit can be under-

stood only by the presence of the Spirit in a fully yielded and obedient heart. We pointed out in our discussion of the first verses of this Epistle that in olden time God spoke through the prophets, and the consequent revelation was therefore external, ceremonial, and preparatory. In these last times God has spoken to us through the Son, and this revelation is internal, spiritual, and perfect. Christ now dwells in the hearts of His people through the Spirit, and thus speaks not only *to* us but *within* us. The Holy Spirit reveals Christ in us, and He alone makes the truth vital and real in our experience. Only through the Holy Spirit is it possible to have fellowship with the Father and the Son; and the writer would strongly impress upon us that the Spirit speaks only to those who with yielded and obedient hearts hearken to His voice.

"To Day if Ye Will Hear His Voice" (3:7b). There are two important words which the Spirit uses freely— "to day" and "harden not your hearts." Satan's word is "tomorrow," and delay always hardens the heart. Here the word "to day" speaks of the eternity of God. To Him there is no past or future, but all His blessedness is gathered up into one eternal "now." So also every believer who would avail himself of the riches of God's grace must respond to this "now" with a present trust. Mr. Wesley once said, "Hereby know we whether we are seeking by works or by faith; if by works, there is always something to be done first; but if by faith, why not now?" This wondrous truth which the Holy Spirit speaks through Christ, the living Word, is here directed, not to sinners, but to believers. It is a call to the "rest of faith" which the writer is about to introduce, and which he will treat more fully in the following chapter. To those who have received the Holy Spirit as the abiding Comforter, He becomes the Guide into all truth. With every promise for temporal or spiritual blessings, the Holy Spirit says, "To day," and breathes into us the spirit of faith by which we lay hold of the promises of God and make them real in our lives. As used here, however, the Spirit comes with words of warning to

"harden not your hearts." He speaks only to trustful and obedient hearts, and to harden the heart is to close every avenue of communion with God.

"Harden Not Your Hearts." "Wherefore (as the Holy Ghost saith, To day if ye will hear his voice, harden not your hearts, as in the provocation, in the day of temptation in the wilderness" (3: 7-8). The writer does not voice this warning in his own words, but turning to the ninety-fifth psalm, he presents it in the words of the inspired Scriptures. The quotation is taken from the Septuagint, which is generally regarded as the writer's own comments, as he applies this scripture to the Hebrew Christians. The words *me sklerunte* (μὴ σκληρύντε) are in the aorist subjunctive and express in the most forcible manner a single act of hardness. The use of the aorist subjunctive with the negative μὴ means to forbid in advance whatever may be contemplated. In effect this expression means, "Do not even start it," or, "Do not do it even once." In a sense, this combination is even stronger than the simple imperative.

The figure is drawn from the drying up or stiffening by disease or cold that which should be supple and pliable. It is applied in scripture (1) to a man's own action in refusing grace and (2) to the judicial sentence which at last endorses it (Vaughan). The same root word, *sklerunthei* (σκληρυνθῇ), as used in 5: 13 expresses a state of hardened unbelief or of obstinate opposition to God's word. The word "heart," *kardias* (καρδίας), is not limited to the affections in the Old Testament, but is used of the whole person—intellect, feeling, and will. (Cf. also Eph. 4: 18.) Since the use of the aorist with the subjunctive denotes merely negative demands, these words may be interpreted, not as the peremptory demands of the imperative, but in the sense of a longing or wish. "Oh, that today ye would not harden your hearts!" Ellicott points out that the Greek will not allow the sense in which the words are naturally taken by the English reader, "if ye are willing to hear." The meaning of the Hebrew is either, "Today, oh, that ye would hearken to [that is, obey] His voice!" or, "Today if ye hearken to His voice." The words thus become more tender as a hortatory command or an exhortation.

THE WILDERNESS STATE

Attention has previously been called to the fact that no mention is made of the Passover in this Epistle, for Israel had already been delivered from death in Egypt by the blood on doorposts; and with "a mighty hand and by a stretched out arm" had been led out of bondage. They were a redeemed people, journeying across the wilderness to their promised inheritance in the land of Canaan. Never did Israel occupy greater vantage ground than that morning when through the power of God they stood victorious over their enemies on the farther shore of the Red Sea. Egypt with its bondage was behind them forever. Before them was the pillar of cloud and fire that guided them by day and lighted them by night. The glory of the Divine Presence hovered over them, and the land of promise was just in sight, a land of vineyards and olive groves, a land that flowed with milk and honey. But they failed, and of those six hundred thousand men, flushed with their first victory, only two were permitted to enter the land. Of the rest, the simple account is that their carcasses fell in the wilderness.

There are two distinct epochs in this earlier history of Israel. The first was deliverance from the bondage in Egypt; the second was the establishment of the people in Canaan. So also there are two types of life initiated by these crises: the temporary life in the wilderness, and the permanent life in Canaan, both necessary to the growth and glory of David's kingdom. The Scriptures tell us that "all these things happened unto them for ensamples: and they are written for our admonition, upon whom the ends of the world are come" (I Cor. 10: 1-4, 11). These historical events symbolize two crises in Christian experience and two types of the

Christian life. The first crisis is called by St. Paul "justification" or the deliverance from the guilt and power of our own actual sins; the second is here called the "rest of faith" and is a deliverance from the inner conflict between the new life imparted in regeneration and the "flesh" in the sense of the "carnal mind" or inbred sin. That sin, the sense of inherited depravity, remains in the heart of the regenerate is admitted by all the great creeds of the Church and is clearly set forth in the Scriptures. For this reason it is said, "The Lord brought us out . . . that he might bring us in"; or to use Mr. Wesley's statement, "We are justified that we may be sanctified." Christ redeems us from all iniquity, and this He does in order that He might "purify unto himself a peculiar people, zealous of good works" (Titus 2:14). If a sinner can be conscious of the peace which follows justification (Rom. 5:1), so also a believer may be conscious of an inward state of purity when sanctified wholly (Acts 15:8-9). Furthermore, it must be noted that the processes in the attainment of these two stages in salvation are distinct and different—passing from a state of rebellion to one of sonship, and from that of uncleanness to one of purity. These two are never confused in the Scriptures, and are clearly indicated by a distinct terminology.

The Provocation in the Wilderness. "Harden not your hearts, as in the provocation, in the day of temptation in the wilderness: when your fathers tempted me, proved me, and saw my works forty years" (3:8-9). The Hebrew text has the words "Meribah" and "Massah" (cf. Deut. 33:8), but in the Septuagint these words are translated according to their meanings, and appear as *parapikrasmoi* (παραπικρασμῷ), "provocation," and *peirasmou* (πειρασμοῦ), "temptation." There were three outstanding events in the journey from Egypt to Kadesh-barnea with which God was displeased. First, the outbreak in the Wilderness of Sin: there was no bread; second, the outbreak at Rephidim: there was no water; and third, the most serious was at Kadesh-barnea, from which point the Israelites were to

enter the promised rest. Here they listened to the voice
of unbelief and discouragement, and throughout the
entire night wept and murmured against Moses and
Aaron. Nevertheless in each of these crises they saw
the wonderful works of God. They were without bread
but God fed them with manna, the bread from heaven.
They were without water, but from the smitten rock
God gave them streams in the desert. And further,
God gave them every evidence that He would overcome all hindrances and bring them safely into the
land of promise.

The character of their unbelief is shown in the words
epeirasan (ἐπείρασαν), "tempted me," and *edokimasan*
(ἐδοκίμασάν), "proved me." The former word is from
the verb meaning "to judge" either with no anticipation
of the result or with the anticipation of finding it bad;
while the latter is "to prove" in expectation of finding
good. As used here, therefore, it is the trial of God
by men, experimenting on His power and forbearance,
and thus revealing the pride and self-sufficiency of
their own hearts. This attitude of mind is far from that
of reverence, humility, and trust. The writer further
characterizes them by saying, *"Planontai"* (πλανῶνται),
"They do alway err in their heart;" (or are "led
astray") "and they have not known my ways."

God Was Grieved with That Generation. "Wherefore I was grieved with that generation, and said, They
do alway err in their heart; and they have not known
my ways" (3:10). The word "grieved" as used here
is sometimes translated "provoked" or "indignant"; and
since the Greek word is strong, some think it should
be translated as "disgusted" or "abhor." The Greek
word is *prosochthisa* (προσώχθισα), compounded of *pros*
(πρὸς) and *ochte* (ὄχθη), a "bank," and was applied in
post-Homeric Greek to ships running aground. As applied to the mind it denotes the aversion or dislike
which one person has for another, although this meaning is generally found only in the Septuagint. Hence
God was displeased or indignant with that generation,
by which is meant all who came out of Egypt above

twenty years of age. The Holy Spirit indicates that the seat of their error and wanderings lay in "an evil heart of unbelief," which cannot see or understand or know God. Hence it is said that they "alway err in their heart"—an expression signifying that in every trial and on every occasion they persistently wandered from God, seduced by corrupt wills and corrupt affections. In all God's dealings with them they had never risen to a conception of faith in the providence of God. Such is the power of "an evil heart of unbelief."

"They Shall Not Enter into My Rest." "So I sware in my wrath, They shall not enter into my rest" (3:11). As verse 10 described the feeling which God bore to the unbelieving generation of the Exodus, so in conformity with that fact verse 11 announces the decision which God pronounced against them. The finality of this is indicated by the word "sware," which in Greek is the word *omosa* (ὤμοσα) means "to take an oath." The conditional particle *ei* (εἰ), "if," in the expression "if they shall enter" was a part of the Hebrew formula for any oath, and may be interpreted, "If they shall enter, then I am not Jehovah." God takes pleasure in His children, but is grieved with those who take evil courses. Hence He rewards those who serve Him and punishes the incorrigible, all of which is done in accord with the principles of justice and holiness. The word "rest" is from the compound word *katapausin* (κατάπαυσιν), the verb *pauo* (παύω) meaning to restrain, to cease, or to give rest, which compounded with the preposition *kata* (κατά), or "down," conveys the idea of permanency or a "settling down" in the promised inheritance. It is the opposite of *anapausis* (ἀνάπαυσις), which means rest by a cessation of labor and may be only temporary. The "rest" mentioned here is the land of Canaan, a rest at once from the bondage of Egypt and from the weary journeyings in the desert. It is called "my rest" because God had promised it to His people, and had delivered them from bondage in Egypt that He might bring them into this goodly land as a place of permanent abode.

Forbidden to enter the land of Canaan because of unbelief, Israel was condemned to wander in the wilderness for a period of forty years. These wilderness journeyings were characterized by aimlessness, unrest, and dissatisfaction: aimlessness, in that the Israelites had no fixed goal in life; unrest, in that they moved from place to place with no certain possession of their own; and dissatisfaction, arising from the deep longings for better things. All of these are likewise characteristic of those who, having begun in the Christian way, and even having made some progress in it, are through fear and unbelief turned back from the "rest of faith" promised them, to the hopelessness of a wilderness experience.

An Exhortation and a Warning. "Take heed, brethren, lest there be in any of you an evil heart of unbelief, in departing from the living God" (3: 12). Here the warning is continued in hortatory form, the emphasis being upon unbelief as the cause of the hardening of the heart. The warning against unbelief comes to its full statement in the following chapter. The word "brethren" indicates the close of the previous quotation from the ninety-fifth psalm, and makes it clear that the writer is speaking out of his own heart the concern which he has lest the Hebrew Christians fall after the same example of unbelief. The word *blepete* (βλέπετε), translated, "Take heed," is in the present imperative and expresses duration—"Be always watchful." The abruptness of the introduction is not in line with the author's concern for smoothness of diction, but it may have been his intention to awaken his readers to the seriousness of the warning. The expression *en tivi humon* (ἔν τινι ὑμῶν), translated, "in any of you," may equally well be translated, "in some one of you," and shows the deep concern for each individual to whom he writes. This individualizing of the text is a plea from a fraternal and loving heart which would not have even one lost. But there is a further meaning also. The writer fears lest a start should be made by "some one" that might easily spread to the others. It is the same thought which he later expresses as a fear "lest any root of bitterness springing up trouble you, and thereby many be defiled" (12:15).

The "Evil Heart of Unbelief" (3:12). The writer attributes the failure of the ancient Israelites to an evil heart of unbelief, and therefore warns the Christians against the real seat of the trouble, an impure or uncleansed heart. The word for evil here is not *kakos* (κακός), a term applied to evil according to its nature; but *ponera* (πονηρὰ), or evil according to its effects. The synonyms are "depraved," "malignant," or "wicked." The original word for evil denotes one who is industrially wicked; and hence Satan is called *ho poneros* (ὁ πονηρός) or that "Wicked" (one). The word for unbelief is *apistias* (ἀπιστίας) and is in direct opposition to *pistis* (πίστις) or "faith," the contrast showing more clearly in the Greek than in the English. It carries with it the thought of "disbelief" or a "refusal to believe" rather than the mere idea of unbelief. The evil heart, *kardia ponera* (καρδία πονηρὰ), is manifest in unbelief or distrust of God, in persistent error or perversity of will, and in a darkened intellect, or a failure to understand the ways of God. Thus the wickedness does not lie solely in the will or in the affections or in the understanding, but in the corruption of the whole heart or being, as the term is used by the Hebrews. It is "an evil heart of unbelief."

The "evil heart of unbelief" is therefore but another name for that odius thing which St. Paul calls "the old man," "the body of sin," "the law which is in

Some recent writers following a superficial psychology have asserted that it is impossible to know that the heart has been purified from sin; for, they say, sin may lie in the subconscious realm and therefore be out of the range of consciousness. This is a false position but not a new one. Dr. J. A. Wood in his *Purity and Maturity*, published previous to 1876, says that Dr. Curry in a lecture to the New York Preachers' Convention expressed a doubt regarding the cleansed state being one of consciousness. He said, "Consciousness takes notice of the soul's processes, but the range of its observance does not extend to the quiescent states." To this Dr. Wood replied: "What are *rest, freedom from condemnation, peace* and *repose*, but 'quiescent states of the soul,' of which we may be as clearly and positively conscious as of any of the soul's processes . . . The sanctified may be as positively and fully conscious of *purity,* as the unsanctified of *impurity*" (p. 109).

my members," and "the carnal mind," which is enmity
to God. It is, as Mr. Wesley calls it, "a bent to sinning,"
for it tends to issue in actual sins, which bring guilt
and condemnation. Our Lord made this distinction clear
when He said, "Even so every good tree bringeth forth
good fruit; but a corrupt tree bringeth forth evil fruit"
(Matt. 7:17). The character of the tree determines the
quality of fruit it bears. Christianity teaches that there
is a nature back of the act, and both need atoning Blood
—the act to be forgiven, the evil nature cleansed.

This "evil heart" or sinful nature manifests itself,
the writer tells us, "in departing from the living God."
The word for "departing" is *apostenai* (ἀποστῆναι) and
is sometimes translated "falling away"; hence our word
"apostasy," which suggests the dreadful end to which
unbelief or distrust in God naturally leads. The verb
form is a compound word, *apistemi* (ἀπίστημι), which
in the aorist infinitive expresses definiteness and actual-
ity, thus making it necessary to understand the word
"unbelief" in the sense of "having believed in" and then
turned away or "departed" from the living God. The
expression "living God" is *anarthous,* there being no
article in the Greek. It is a Hebraism and is common
in the Old Testament as contrasting Jehovah with the
lifeless idols of the heathen, and literally means "God
full of life." He is a gracious Being who loves and is
to be loved, full of goodness and truth, loving-kindness
and tender mercy, a very present Help in time of need.
The expression occurs four times in this Epistle.

"Exhort One Another Daily." "But exhort one another daily, while it is called To day" (3:13a). The
Hebrew Christians were apparently in danger of apos-
tatizing from Christ; hence the writer suggests a means
to be employed by which help might be given to preserve every individual in the faith. The basis of this
is brotherly affection which leads to mutual admonition,
and thus maintains the integrity of the entire body.
These Christians were to encourage themselves. The
word for "encourage" is *parakaleite* (παρακαλεῖτε), derived from the noun *Paracletos* or "Comforter" as the

term is applied by our Lord to the Holy Spirit. The word for "yourselves" is *heautous* (ἑαυτούς) and is used instead of *allelous* (ἀλλήλους), as found in Eph. 4: 32. There is practically no difference between the terms, says Vaughan, for the former is a reference to the closely knit body of believers, and when each encourages himself, he is encouraging the entire body of which he is a member. The word "daily" is *hekasten hemeran* (ἑκάστην ἡμέραν)—literally "every day"—and suggests that these mutual admonitions must be frequent and continuous. In the expression "while it is called To day," the definite article is used, "the To day," and evidently is intended to refer to the previous quotation from the psalm (3: 7). The whole expression means "so long as it is called the Today." Lindsay indicates that the time referred to is the present life, which on account of its brevity and uncertainty may well be styled a day. He says: "The present moment is ours: we know not what shall be on the morrow; and if we waste our day of merciful visitation, we can have no future opportunity of turning to the Lord and rising to glory."

"Lest Any . . . Be Hardened Through the Deceitfulness of Sin" (3: 13b). The emphasis here is not so much on the moral quality of deceit as upon deceitfulness as a means by which the heart is deceived. The word *apate* (ἀπάτη), translated "deceitfulness," is in the instrumental case and means a "fraud," or a "lying deceit" by which one is led into error and sin. This "deceit," however, is not purely passive in the sense that it leaves the person guiltless, for it is associated with *tes hamartias* (τῆς ἁμαρτίας) or "the sin," which implies self-deception. It makes the person at once the deceiver and the deceived, and therefore incurs guilt. It is sometimes said that the sin mentioned here is to be identified with either the unbelief or the apostasy mentioned in the context. This cannot be, since the words *apostenai* (ἀποστῆναι) and *sklerunthei* (σκληρυνθῇ) both describe a state of hardened unbelief, and therefore *hamartia* (ἁμαρτία) cannot mean the same thing unless it is supposed that the apostle confounds

the cause and the effect. But the writer is specific; he
calls it *tes hamartias* (τῆς ἁμαρτίας) or "the sin" and
thus identifies it with the cause. It is the "evil heart"
which manifests itself in the unbelief to which he refers,
the inbred sin or inherited depravity which remains
even in the regenerate, until the heart is cleansed by
the blood of Jesus Christ (I John 1: 7, 9). It is "the
sin" of which St. Paul writes when he says, "Shall we
continue in 'the sin,' that grace may abound?" to which
he gives the laconic reply, "God forbid." "How shall
we, that are dead" or "have died to the sin," "live any
longer therein?" Here again we have the article used
with the word sin, *tei hamartiai* (τῇ ἁμαρτίᾳ). "The sin"
here mentioned, the writer later tells us, is removed by
"the sanctification."

"Partakers of Christ." "For we are made partakers
of Christ, if we hold the beginning of our confidence
stedfast unto the end" (3: 14). The word *metochoi*
(μέτοχοι), translated "partakers," is also translated
"partners," "sharers," or "companions." The expression "companions of Christ" would seem to refer to the
fact that as ancient Israel in the journey to the promised
land were the companions of Moses, so in the spiritual
journey of life we are to become companions of Christ.
However there appears to be more solid ground for the
translation "partakers" in that, as Christ in partaking of
our flesh and blood (2: 14) became one of us, so we
spiritually are likewise partakers of Him. This is a
precious thought, that our salvation consists in the possession of Christ himself. He is our Way, our Truth, and
our Life. We are not merely companions in an outward
sense, but sharers of a common life. Christ dwells within
us through the Spirit in a deeper, richer fellowship; and
this inward, spiritual fellowship is a continuous experience, fragrant with new manifestations of His presence
day by day. There is an error more or less prevalent,
that salvation is a mere thing, wrought by Christ indeed, but something to be maintained apart from Him
and the merits of His atoning blood. This is a dangerous
error and necessarily leads to darkness and confusion.

Genuine Christian experience is a conscious fellowship with Christ, and it is solely in recognition of this fellowship that the Blood of Calvary's cross cleanses the heart from all sin and keeps it blameless before the throne of God (I John 1: 7).

It will be noticed that there is a similarity between the expressions "if we hold fast the confidence" (3: 6) and "if we hold the beginning of our confidence stedfast unto the end" (3: 14). In each case the reference is to individuals who have entered into salvation through Christ, although the language is somewhat varied. The word *kataschomen* (κατάσχωμεν) or "hold" is the same in both verses, as is also the word *bebaian* (βεβαίαν), which in the former verse is translated "firm" as referring to the house of God, and in the latter as "stedfast," which is a nautical term for maintaining a steady course (Acts 27: 40). The word "made" as referring to "partakers of Christ" is *gegonamen* (γεγόναμεν) and is not the equivalent of *esmen* (ἐσμέν). It is from the verb *ginomai* (γίνομαι), and being in the perfect tense denotes a past action, the effects of which continue to the present moment. Translated literally, it is "have become and continue to be" partakers of Christ. The word "confidence" as used in the former sense is *parresian* (παρρησίαν) and signifies "boldness of speech"; here the word is *hypostaseos* (ὑποστάσεως) or "assurance."

The beginning of our confidence was by faith in Christ, the Spirit of adoption enabling us to cry from our inmost beings, "Abba, Father." To this was added another witness, that of the Spirit bearing witness with our spirits that we are the children of God. But the pardon of sins and the impartation of a new life are but the beginning of fellowship with Christ. There is another and equally significant term connected with this progress in fellowship. It is the word "cleanseth," which is never used interchangeably with either of the foregoing terms. It refers specifically to the completed act of purification, the removal of "the sin" or the cleansing of the "evil heart of unbelief," and thus becomes the ground of a deeper and more abiding fellowship. "If we walk

in the light, as he is in the light,"—and only Christians
have the light, and only the spiritually alive are able to
walk—"we have fellowship one with another, and the
blood of Jesus Christ his Son cleanseth us from all sin"
(I John 1: 7). But the "if" involves the whole thought
of spiritual progress. "If we hold the beginning of our
confidence stedfast," "if we walk in the light," then this
divine fellowship is sustained and the precious Blood
avails for all past sins, ignorant or deliberate; all past
impurities, contracted or inherited; and all weaknesses
and infirmities to which fallen man is heir. What is the
end which we would attain? It is twofold. The immediate end is the "rest of faith," to which the writer will
now direct our attention; the ultimate end is the heavenly
rest in a "better country."

The technical study of these two verses serves to
correct two common and hurtful errors: (1) that it is
by our own perseverance that we are made partakers
of Christ—a salvation sought by works and not by faith;
and (2) perhaps a more seductive and subtle error,
that those who fail to persevere to the end have never
made a true beginning. This denies the witness of the
Spirit given to all who are born into the family of God;
and further still, renders groundless any need for these
warnings.

The Concluding Parallel and Exhortation. "While it
is said, To day if ye will hear his voice, harden not your
hearts, as in the provocation. For some, when they had
heard, did provoke; howbeit not all that came out of
Egypt by Moses. But with whom was he grieved forty
years? was it not with them that had sinned, whose
carcases fell in the wilderness? And to whom sware he
that they should not enter into his rest, but to them
that believed not? So we see that they could not enter
in because of unbelief" (3: 15-19). As in the preceding
verses, the writer again directs his exhortation and
warning to the Hebrew Christians by referring once
more to the ninety-fifth psalm. Here however the warning is presented in interrogative form. Before the time
of Bengel it had scarcely occurred to anyone that the

word *tines* (τινες) at the beginning of the verse was the interrogative *tines* (τίνες) and not *tines* (τινὲς), the indefinite pronoun "some"—the sole difference being in the accent. The series of dramatic and rhetorical questions are as follows:

1. Who having heard provoked? Was it not the very people who had been redeemed out of Egypt? (An exception is made in the case of Caleb and Joshua.)

2. With whom was He sore vexed for forty years? "Was it not with them that had sinned, whose carcases fell in the wilderness?"

3. "And to whom sware he that they should not enter into his rest"; was it not with "them that believed not?"

"We must admire his skill," says Lowrie. "He points the application with laconic and nervous vigor, that must have fallen on the hearts of his readers with bewildering impetuosity, that nothing could ward off, and that must have been most effective with every one who was not already hardened" (LOWRIE, *Interpretation of Hebrews*, p. 109).

CHAPTER IV

THE REST OF FAITH

The rest of faith! What a wonderful experience awaits the people of God! It may be compared to a beautiful spring morning in the country: the grass fresh with dew, the trees fragrant with blossoms, the birds warbling their songs of praise, the flowers lending their beauty to the scene, and over all, the mellow light of the dawn and the holy hush of a new and beautiful Sabbath day. So also when the Spirit enters the inmost sanctuary of the soul, He illuminates it to its farthest horizons with a sense of purity, and fills it with the presence of God. Is it any wonder that the saintly Bramwell testified, "My soul was all wonder, love, and praise"? or that Bishop Foster exclaimed, "What a wonderful deliverance God has wrought! Ought not I to praise Him? Ought not I to publish this great salvation? What a rest He hath found for my soul!"

It is in this fourth chapter of the Epistle that the writer treats of the "rest of faith" as an important and scriptural aspect of a holy life. It is a rest not only from the guilt and power of sin, but also from the inbeing of "the sin" itself. Attention is sometimes called to the historical contrast between the third chapter with its wilderness experience and the fourth with its promised rest in Canaan, but the spiritual contrast thus symbolized is far greater. Gone are the doubts and fears, and instead, "the love of God is shed abroad in our hearts by the Holy Ghost which is given unto us" (Rom. 5: 5). Of this experience Lady Maxwell in glowing words said, "I rest in Him; I dwell in Him. Sinking into Him I lose myself, and prove a life of fellowship with Deity so divinely sweet I would not relinquish it for a thousand worlds. . . . When I look back, I rejoice to see what I am saved from; when I look forward, it is all pure expanse of unbounded love. Surely the heaven of heavens is love." We turn now to an exegetical study of this important chapter.

The Goal of Christ's Apostolic Work. In considering Jesus as the Apostle of our profession (3:1) we have seen that the comparison shifts from that of Christ and the angels to that of Christ and Moses. Under the symbolism of Moses as the apostle of the old covenant, the writer now sets forth the work of Christ as the Apostle of the new covenant. The goal of Moses as he led the people out of Egypt was the land of Canaan, their promised inheritance. But Moses failed to bring the people into the land, a task that was left for Joshua. Christ, the Apostle of the new covenant, is not only our Moses to lead us out of bondage, but our great Joshua, the Captain of our salvation, who will bring us into our spiritual inheritance. He brought us out that He might bring us into this "rest of faith," or "rest in God," this being the supreme goal of our earthly spiritual experience. These two stages or crises in experience must be fully realized in order to properly understand God's wondrous plan of salvation. Calvary and Pentecost are the two mountain peaks of redemption. But Pentecost follows Calvary, is dated from it, and draws all its virtue from the shed Blood on that rugged Cross. Calvary marked the completion of Christ's earthly ministry, the finished atonement. Pentecost marked the coming of the Holy Spirit and the beginning of Christ's heavenly ministry. The rending of the veil of Christ's flesh not only opened up the way for us into the holy of holies of God's presence, but through the Spirit so purifies our hearts that through that veil also God comes to dwell within us. The "rest of faith," therefore, is our rest in God and God's rest in us.

THE THIRD WARNING: AGAINST UNBELIEF

The third warning is against unbelief as the source of hardness of heart, and taken together these warnings are the most solemn of which language is possible. The ancient people of the Exodus would not be persuaded, and turned back on the very eve of victory. They had faith to leave Egypt but not faith to enter Canaan. They had not seen that their murmuring at Meribah and Massah would deepen into open rebellion at Kadesh-barnea; and that these would form a bridge to the general disposition of unbelief, which was the source of their disobedience. Ancient Israel refused the highest that God had for them and perished miserably in the wilderness. The Hebrew Christians at this time were tempted to return to the law imposed upon them from without, and were not pressing on into the new covenant in Christ, in which through the Spirit the law would be written in their hearts and in their minds. With this Old Testament example before him, the writer warns them, and us, lest we too should fail through unbelief.

When God gave the promise to Abraham and renewed it to those whom He called out of Egypt, it was in some sense a call to the spiritual rest of faith. God could have realized this promise in connection with Canaan, for this inference presents no greater difficulty than our Lord's lament over Jerusalem: "If thou hadst known, even thou, at least in this thy day, the things which belong unto thy peace! but now they are hid from thine eyes" (Luke 19: 42). Who can say what would have taken place if the Jews had accepted their Messiah? But that generation failed, and the result—the fall of Jerusalem with all its horror, devastation, and death. It is not a matter of option whether or not a converted person presses on into this rest that awaits the people of God. Nothing holy or unclean, whether in act or condition, can stand in the presence of God's flaming holiness. And so it is enjoined upon every believer to possess the best that God has for us; and this because without holiness "no man shall see the Lord" (Heb. 12: 14).

Let us therefore fear, lest, a promise being left us of entering into his rest (4: 1a). The writer addresses his readers in the first person, "Let us . . . fear"; but immediately following, changes to the second person and says, "lest . . . any of you should . . . come short of it." His purpose is to bring upon the people that fear which he himself possesses. This is shown by the fact that the imperative *phobethomen* (φοβηθῶμεν) is an aorist, which if ingressive could well be translated, "Let us get this fear." He would have them realize the seriousness of their position as he feels it. This concern is further emphasized by the use of the word *mepote* (μήποτε), which generally indicates anxiety. While this verse enjoins diligence and watchfulness on the part of the Hebrew Christians, it does so only on the assumption that there is still a promise of rest awaiting them. Since the promise in the foregoing chapter referred directly to their inheritance in the land of Canaan, from which ancient Israel was debarred by unbelief, it is evident that the writer conceives of the promise as being broader than the material inheritance and as containing something higher and nobler—a spiritual "rest of faith" or a "rest in God." This includes a state of purity and holiness in this life, and in the life to come a perfect rest from all the consequences of sin: ignorance, infirmities, sickness, suffering, and death.

Lest . . . any of you should seem to come short of it (4:1b). The word *dokei* (δοκῇ) or "seem" is a difficult one and has been interpreted in many ways. Thayer calls this a polite expression used in place of an outright statement, "have actually come short of it." Westcott considers it a comprehensive warning, such that the mere appearance or suspicion of failure is to be earnestly dreaded. Vaughan views it from the forensic standpoint, the word being used in the sense of a verdict. It would then read, "Lest any of you should be judged to have missed it." The use of the word *mepote* (μήποτε) would seem to indicate "lest he continue to think or imagine" himself to have come too late for it. Another interpretation, which however appears to be inadequate, makes the word "seem" to be merely a mitigating or weakening of the term in order to avoid a forthright statement. Another difficult word is *husterekenai* (ὑστερηκέναι), which means "to arrive on the following day," "to come too late," "to be behind," and tropically "to miss," "to lack," or "to come short." When this text is interpreted in the traditional manner, "lest any of you should seem to come short of it," it is evident that the purpose of the writer is to prevent his readers from falling short of the promised rest. But the text may also be rendered, "lest any of you should suppose himself to have come too late for it"; then the writer's aim is to show that they are not too late, for this rest remains or is "left over" and still awaits the people of God. There is a general tone of caution and concern here also, which implies that neither is it too late to be excluded from the Christian rest of faith, as were their fathers in ancient times.

For unto us was the gospel preached, as well as unto them (4:2a). This translation is very confusing to the English reader in that it supposes that what we technically call the gospel as presented in the New Testament was previously preached in the same sense to ancient Israel. This is not true. The word *euaggelion* (εὐαγγέλιον) is used in a twofold sense. The primary meaning of the word is "good news" or intelligence of any description; the secondary meaning is that particular "good news" which we call the gospel. The verb form is used in the same broad sense, and there can be no doubt that in this passage it is used in its primary sense. Furthermore, the verb is used in the perfect tense, which indicates the continuance of the message and not merely a single announcement in the past. The meaning therefore is that we have been favored with "good news" as well as they, for we like them have also received the "good news" of a promised rest. The Jews of course could say that they were living in the land of promise, but their entrance into Canaan in nowise perfectly fulfilled the original promise. Along with their rest in Canaan, and included in the promise as first given, is a spiritual rest such as could not come to fulfillment under the old covenant; but the way having been opened to us by Christ, we may now enter through the veil into the holiest of all, into the presence of God through the Spirit. This point is taken up again in a didactic section, giving consideration to the four rests mentioned in the Scriptures (4:3-11).

But the word preached did not profit them, not being mixed with faith in them that heard it (4: 2b). The *word* has often been compared to food for the body, and *faith* to the processes of digestion by which it is combined with other essential elements to render it nutritious. The "word of hearing" had entered their minds, but it had not been so combined with faith as to become wholesome to the soul. There are two readings of the Greek word translated "having been mixed with." The first is *sunkekerasmenos* (συνκεκερασμένος), agreeing with *logos* or the "word," and is here used in the negative form. It is frequently combined either with the dative of person (instrument) or of a thing (reference). In the former sense it means that the word was not combined with faith in the hearers; that is, they heard the message outwardly but, due to their lack of faith, were not inwardly inspired by it. In the latter the meaning is that the word and faith were not so mixed with one another in their hearts as to become effective in their lives. In the first instance the faith is connected more closely with the word; that is, the word itself was not quickened in their hearts by faith. This is the most generally accepted position. The second reading *sunkekerasmenous* (συνκεκερασμένους), the same root word but ending in "ous," thereby showing its agreement, not with *logos* or the "word," but with *ekeinous* (ἐκείνους) or "them." According to Ebrard, the text would then read, "The word did not profit those persons, because they did not unite in the faith with them that obeyed," viz., with Caleb and Joshua. Lindsay renders it more elaborately as, "They were not profited by the word, not being associated with those that heard it in faith; they stood apart from the faithful hearers, and therefore died under the curse." In each of the above constructions, however, it will be seen that faith is a necessary element in the acceptance and fulfillment of the promises of God.

For we which have believed do enter into rest (4: 3). Faith alone gives entrance into this rest of God, the works of which "were finished from the foundation of the world." It cannot now refer to the Canaan rest, for the oath is repeated that ancient Israel should not enter. This "rest of faith" is a personal, spiritual rest of the soul in God; and it is promised as an inheritance to all who are the sons of God by the "new birth"—a second definite crisis in the lives of true believers. This position is frequently supposed to be the peculiar tenet of the Wesleyan tradition, but commentators of the various denominations have in their exegetical studies advocated the same great truths. Thus John Owen, an early writer and a strong Calvinist, says: "The rest here spoken of (4:1) cannot be the rest of heaven and glory, as some have affirmed, wholly misunderstanding the argument of the apostle, which is the superiority of Christ over Moses. The rest here intended, is that rest which believers have entrance into by Jesus Christ in this world." Bishop Westcott, one of the most learned of commentators, and an unbiased exegete, points out that the words *eiserchometha gar* (εἰσερχόμεθα γὰρ), "for we enter," assume that actual experience establishes the reality of the experience. "The writer seems to say, 'I speak without hesitation of a promise left us, for we enter, are entering now, into the rest of God,—we who have believed.' The above verb is not to be taken as a future, but as the expression of a present fact. Furthermore, the efficiency of the faith is here regarded in its critical action, and not as might be expected, in its continuous exercise. At the same time, he does not simply say 'we enter in having believed;' but he regards believers as a definite class who embraced the divine revelation when it was offered. This effective faith works its full result while it continues" (WESTCOTT, *Epistle to the Hebrews*, p. 96).

THE FOUR RESTS

There are four rests mentioned in this chapter, which must be given some preliminary consideration. These rests are as follows:

1. The Creation Rest   (4:4)
2. The Sabbath Rest   (4:4, 9, A.R.V.)
3. The Canaan Rest   (4:8, A.R.V.)
4. The Divine Rest   (4:1-3, 10-11)

Dr. Edwards suggests that the Greek mind was ever on the alert for something new. Its character was movement. But the ideal of the Old Testament was rest; and this ideal finds its truest and highest realization in Christ, who began His ministry with a call to rest.

1. The Creation Rest. "And God did rest the seventh day from all his works" (4:4). The word "rest" does not mean a refreshing from weariness (Isa. 40:28) but a cessation from operation. Here also the emphasis is not so much on the activity of creation as upon its completion and perfection. "And God saw every thing that he had made, and, behold, it was very good" (Gen. 1:31a). This follows from the participle *genethenton* (γενηθέντων), which is used in the sense of *teleisthai* (τελεῖσθαι), meaning to finish, to bring to completion, to perfect. God's work was finished not only outwardly, but inwardly and qualitatively. There was no sin, no corruption. Everything was new and fresh from the hands of its Creator. This text further indicates that God bears a twofold relation to His work. There is first His creative activity, which ceased when He had finished all that He had "created and made"; and second, His rest, which is but a new and higher form of activity, that of taking delight in His perfected work. It is this rest by faith in the perfected work of God—a rest like His— that He calls His people to enter.

2. The Sabbath Rest. The Genesis account further states that "God blessed the seventh day, and sanctified it: because that in it he had rested from all his work which God created and made" (Gen. 2:3). It is evident from this scripture that there is a close and vital relation between the creation rest and the Sabbath rest. Two things characterize this Sabbath rest: (1) It is a rest after six days of labor; and (2) It is a rest in which God dwells, and this indwelling Presence sanctifies and makes holy both the rest and the day. That only in which God rests is holy, and that soul in which He rests through the Spirit is likewise holy. But what is the seventh day in which God rests? It is that which follows

the six days of creative activity marked by a beginning
and an ending, but in the Genesis account neither evening nor morning is predicated of the seventh day. It
is a limitless, an eternal day; and the rest is an eternal
rest. For this reason it is spoken of as God's rest, "my
rest," "this rest," and in one instance, "that rest." While
the creation rest is God's eternal "To day," He also appointed the seventh day, as man reckons time, as a
"holy Sabbath," or "rest day," at once the symbol and
type of God's eternal rest.

3. *The Canaan Rest.* "For if Joshua had given them
rest, he would not have spoken afterward of another
day" (4: 8, A.R.V.). It should be explained that the
words "Jesus" and "Joshua" are identical in Greek, and
that the word "Jesus" in the Authorized Version should
have been translated Joshua. This is evident from the
context, and is so translated in the Revised Versions.
A new step in the argument begins with the sixth verse,
and is intended to meet an objection of the Jews that
the Canaan rest fulfilled the promise. The Canaan rest
was the material inheritance promised to Abraham, a
land which should be the dwelling place of Israel after
the bondage in Egypt and the wearisome desert journey.
It is described as "a land of hills and valleys, and drinketh water of the rain of heaven: a land which the Lord
thy God careth for: the eyes of the Lord thy God are
always upon it, from the beginning of the year even
unto the end of the year" (Deut. 11: 11-12). It was a
second Garden of Eden, and one of the most beautiful
and fertile spots of ancient times. But as pointed out in
the preceding chapter, the generations of Israel contemporary with Moses refused to enter because of their
unbelief and hardness of heart. It is true that the second
generation of those who were rescued from Egypt entered into the material inheritance that was refused to
their fathers, but the land of Canaan was not the "rest"
with which the writer is concerned. Joshua gave the
people many things, but he could not give them the spiritual rest that they craved; otherwise the Holy Spirit
would not have spoken through David of another day

to denote this rest. The Psalmist, dwelling in the troubled land of Canaan, could well understand that this was not the rest God ultimately designed for His people, and therefore pointed to a rest as yet unattained and unfulfilled, still awaiting the people of God. Like the Sabbath, Canaan could be only a type of that rest which God has prepared for His people.

The land of Canaan is frequently considered as a type of heart purity, but the opponents of such symbolism point out that this cannot be true, for enemies still remained within the land. We need, therefore, to clearly understand in what sense Canaan becomes a symbol of the "rest of faith." It will be noted that both a finished work and a continuous work are associated with each member of the Trinity. With the Father, the finished work is creation; and the continuous, preservation and providence. With the Son, the finished work is atonement; and the continuous, intercession. With the Holy Spirit, the finished work is purification and sanctification of the soul; the continuous work is His constant indwelling as the Comforter, the Revealer of Christ, the Guide into all truth, and the Anointing with power for service. So also there are two symbols to represent these two phases, the Sabbath and the land. The Sabbath is the symbol of the finished work, the "rest of faith" in which the believer ceases from his own works or carnal self-life; the land is the type of the continuous work or that state of constant victory over his enemies. It is a life of holy conquest through the Spirit. The law of the Sabbath is that we believe and enter in; that we cease from our own works, that God may work in and through us. The law of the land is, "Every foot of ground which your feet shall press shall be yours." Hence we are to possess our possessions. But these victories cannot be self-won; they must be God-won through

Under the promise of Canaan lay, for the believing Israelites, that other promise without which the former would have been transitory and illusory. This thought runs through the chapter, and finds its parallel in the unhesitating assertions of the eleventh chapter as to the far-reaching faith of the saints of the earlier dispensations.—VAUGHAN, Epistle to the Hebrews, p. 73.

faith and obedience. Canaan, then, is typical of a life of spiritual conquest and victory for those who have entered into the "rest of faith," the sabbath of the soul.

4. *The Divine Rest* (4:1-3, 6-11). The divine rest is the central theme of this chapter, and all other references are merely incidental to it. The creation rest is mentioned as its foundation, and also to account for the Sabbath, which more fully defines this rest. The Canaan rest from the weariness of the desert wanderings is mentioned as a type also, but even this did not exhaust the promise; for Abraham "looked for a city which hath foundations, whose builder and maker is God" (11:10). We must now turn to the following didactic section, and study more fully the nature of this Divine Rest.

THE NATURE OF THE DIVINE REST

The didactic section (4:4-11) marks a new stage in the argument, its purpose being to show that the divine rest is not limited to the possession of the land of Canaan. There is also a return to a consideration of the superiority of Jesus over Moses. In the first comparison (3:2-6) the contrast is between the two persons: Moses as a servant, Christ as the Son. The present contrast is between the work of these two persons. The writer points out the weakness of Moses in that: (1) his work imparted no power for its fulfillment, and hence he could not bring the people into the promised rest; (2) the rest itself into which they were later brought was an earthly rest, and merely typical of the true divine rest. Christ is superior to Moses in both these points: (1) He is able through the Spirit to actually bring us into this spiritual rest; and (2) this rest is real and substantial, and corresponds in nature to the Sabbath rest of God. Having analyzed carefully this statement concerning the divine rest (4:1-3), it will now be helpful to analyze in the same manner the writer's argument concerning the nature of this rest.

The Rest That Remaineth. "Seeing therefore it remaineth that some must enter therein, and they to whom it was first preached entered not in because of unbelief"

(4:6). We have seen that neither the Sabbath nor the Canaan rest exhausted the fullness of God's promise. This is borne out by the terms used for the verb "remaineth." The infinitive clause *tinas eiselthein* (τινὰς εἰσελθεῖν) is the subject of the verb "remaineth," and means literally "some to enter." It is more in harmony with the context, however, to translate this "for some to enter," and it is so translated in the Revised Versions. While God in His infinite wisdom never provides for His people without implying that some will accept His mercy and rest upon His promises, the word "must" is not to be interpreted as implying necessity. The text properly interpreted offers a fresh, unrealized opportunity to all who will believe and enter into rest. The word *apoleipetai* (ἀπολείπεται) is in the present passive indicative, and means "to be left over" or "to remain." The same thought is conveyed by the word *kataleipomenes* (καταλειπομένης) in verse one, which, being in the present tense, expresses a successive or continuous leaving over for others until the promise is finally fulfilled. The offer made to the Exodus generation was again made to David's generation, some five hundred years later. Westcott points out that, while the rest is the same, there are now two conditions instead of one— another day being appointed. This brings afresh to our minds that the writer is still comparing Christ with Moses; and since no mention is made of a new promise to Joshua, or any acceptance of it by David's generation, we may well conclude that the writer has in mind two generations only, that of Moses and that of Christ. Moses failed because there was no faith mixed with the word; Christ succeeds because He ministers the Spirit. It is the presence of the Holy Spirit that brings us into that supreme spiritual rest which is the heritage of every child of God.

The Appointment of Another Day. "Again, he limiteth a certain day, saying in David, To day, after so long a time; as it is said, To day if ye will hear his voice, harden not your hearts. For if Joshua had given them rest, then would he not afterward have spoken of another

day" (4: 7-8). The writer again refers to his psalm text
(95: 7-11), not so much for a continuation of the main
argument as for its confirmation by the Scriptures before
stating his final conclusion (4: 10). Here also he notices
some of the errors that may have attached to the interpretation of this psalm. (1) If it is interpreted to
mean the promised land of Canaan, then it could be
supposed that those who entered with Joshua did enter
into rest; but since another day is mentioned later, the
Canaan rest cannot be the "my rest" spoken of in the
psalm. (2) On the other hand, if the rest meant more
than Canaan, it might be inferred that the oath, "They
shall not enter into my rest," was the withdrawing of
the promise altogether. The writer here corrects these
false positions by asserting that another day had been
appointed with its promise of entering into His rest.
The words "limited a certain day" mean to determine,
to define, to mark out or fix; and may be determined
either as (1) a prophetic prediction or (2) an authoritative institution. When God speaks of another day, this
is not to be interpreted as another rest, but as the "my
rest" of the psalm which was not exhausted by all that
had gone before, and still awaited the people of God.
The seventh day was defined and fixed for the Exodus
generation at the time of the giving of the manna (Exod.
16: 22-30). This new day, therefore, cannot refer to
the entrance into Canaan under Joshua, for Israel had
already dwelt there "for so long a time." Furthermore,
they were still living under the seventh day Sabbath,
which in itself is evidence that they had not entered
into the rest symbolized by the new day. This new day,
which the writer later explains (4: 10), points to the
new and spiritual rest—a rest still open to be accepted
or rejected, and hence the exhortation, "Harden not
your hearts."

A Rest for the People of God. "There remaineth
therefore a rest to the people of God" (4: 9). This
verse marks the conclusion of the main argument, and
the writer will turn next to the provisions made for
entrance into this rest. The word used in this text for

rest is *sabbatismos* (σαββατισμὸς), one which in its noun form is not found elsewhere in the Scriptures. It is formed from a Hebrew word with a Greek ending and thus becomes a comprehensive term. The original Hebrew word meant "to rest" and is used in Gen. 2: 2-3, where it is said that God rested or "sabbatized" on the seventh day. The change in terms, therefore, is evidently intended to identify the "rest" of God with the rest promised to His people; otherwise the word *katapausis* (κατάπαυσις) would have been used as in 3: 11, 18; 4: 1, 3, 5, 10-11. The writer doubtless sees in *sabbatismos*, not an isolated Sabbath day, but a sabbath life. It is God's own rest in himself—His delight in His perfections, and His eternal satisfaction in all His works. Hence to express this *sabbatismos* or "Sabbath-life" the observance of another day has been defined or determined as a pledge and token of it.

But what is this rest? It is a present, personal, spiritual, and practical experience of rest in God, and is marked by the following characteristics. (1) It is a *Rest for the People of God*. It is not for sinners, but the rich heritage of every true child of God. As in the previous chapter it was stated that we become "partakers of Christ," so here it is said that God's people enter with Him into rest. (2) It is a *Rest of Faith*. By this we mean a full reliance upon God through the redemptive work of Christ. It is a perfect rest in a finished atonement. There are some who seem to regard faith as a self-effort, or a struggle to believe; this is not faith but a subtle form of works. Faith is rest and repose, not effort and struggle. It is a rest in God because it is His bestowment. The work wrought is all His. There is no merit in faith. Faith does not of itself save us; Christ saves us through faith. The power and the glory belong to Him. (3) It is a *Rest from Sin*. That inbred sin or depravity remains in the heart of the regenerate is a generally admitted fact, and from this inward pollution the heart is purified by the baptism with the Holy Spirit (Acts 15: 8-9). This therefore is a removal of the conflict between the flesh or carnal mind and the Spirit;

for those who are Christ's in the full new covenant sense
"have crucified the flesh with the affections and lusts"
(Gal. 5: 24). (4) It is a *Continuous Rest in God* through
the atoning work of Christ. Only the pure in heart see
God, and only those who walk in the light have constant
fellowship with Him. Here the "blood of Jesus Christ
his Son cleanseth us from all sin," that is, cleanses and
continues to cleanse or keep clean. This rest is not apart
from the atonement; instead, it is a constant and continuous resting in the merits of the shed blood of Christ.
With such high privileges afforded us, is it any wonder
that the writer urges us to give all diligence to enter into
this rest?

THE REDEMPTIVE WORK OF CHRIST

The creation rest was disturbed and marred by sin,
and man lost that inner spiritual rest in God, the true
sabbath of the soul. No longer could he find rest through
works or a cessation from them, for both the works and
himself were inwardly stained with sin. Hence God
does not now rest in His creative work for man, of which
the seventh day is a symbol, but in His redemptive work
through Christ. Thus the Psalmist says, "For the Lord

The two Greek words rendered faith and believe occur in the New
Testament over five hundred times. *Pistuo* is the verbal root, and
expresses action; it occurs two hundred and fifty-six times in the
New Testament, where it is translated believe; it signifies an act of the
creature but is never predicated of God. The other form of the Greek
text is *pistis,* translated faith. It occurs two hundred and forty-seven
times in the New Testament, where its only legitimate meaning is "an
act of trust performed by the creature." The perfect idea embraced in
these two words formulates itself in the mind as an act of the creature
by which the will subordinates the affections, actions and life to his
Creator. It implies the surrender of the whole man in the fullest sense
to his Redeemer, for His use and glory. . . . The most fatal error in
regard to faith is the assumption that it is a Divine gift; that it is some
indefinable influence, mysteriously infused into the soul; the penitent
struggles and waits and wonders, but does not advance. The professor
looks at his spiritual moods, tries to analyse his emotions and becomes
anxious and discouraged because God does not give him faith. He
mourns over his leanness and dies of starvation in the midst of plenty,
because he insists upon reversing the divine order of salvation. We
refuse to accept the fact that having faith in God and believing on His
promise is the same act expressed in two different ways.—WILLIAM
JONES, *Entire Sanctification, Scripturally and Psychologically Examined,*
pp. 63-64.

hath chosen Zion; he hath desired it for his habitation. This is my rest for ever: here will I dwell; for I have desired it" (Ps. 132: 13-14). God now rests in His new creation, which is inward and spiritual.

The Redemptive Rest in Christ. "For he that is entered into his rest, he also hath ceased from his own works, as God did from his" (4: 10). There is a noticeable change in the pronouns from the plural to the singular in this text, which makes it, not general, but specific. "He that is entered into his rest" does not refer to man in general, but specifically to Jesus; and every unprejudiced reader, says Ebrard, "must also, on account of the aorist *katepausen* (*κατέπαυσεν*), understand the 'rest' in the same way." The author does not expressly mention the name of Jesus here because in verse eight the same word was used to designate Joshua. It is evident that Joshua did not give the rest which the writer mentions in this verse, else another day would not have been appointed.

We have previously indicated that when God rested on the seventh day His work had been finished inwardly as well as outwardly. Jesus mentions this when He says, "Did not he that made that which is without make that which is within also?" (Luke 11: 40) This rest is therefore to be taken qualitatively as including the work of redemption which was accomplished by Christ; for it is said that "the works were finished from the foundation of the world." St. John states this same truth as "the Lamb slain from the foundation of the world" (Rev. 13: 8). This indicates that the work of redemption was planned for man in case he should fall, even previous to the entrance of sin into the world.

It is very evident that Isaiah regarded the true Sabbath as a cessation from sin. He says, "If thou turn away thy foot from the sabbath, from doing thy pleasure on my holy day; and call the sabbath a delight, the holy of the Lord, honourable; and shalt honour him, not doing thine own ways, nor finding thine own pleasure, nor speaking thine own words: then shalt thou delight thyself in the Lord" (Isa. 58:13-14). It is because of the disturbing element of sin that men regard God's day as a weariness. Only when God's will is done in us, and His rest has been introduced into our disordered natures, are we able to speak of the Sabbath as a "delight," as "the holy of the Lord."

Ebrard further states that when the words of verse three are translated in their grammatical exactness we have this: "For he who has entered into his rest, himself rested in like manner from his works, as God did from his," thus setting forth a striking parallel between God's work in creation and Christ's work in redemption. Christ's work outwardly and inwardly were both completed when on the Cross He cried, "It is finished." After the finished atonement and the passing of His humiliation, He left the state in which His soul was separated from His body in death, arose again in the Resurrection, and assumed His body now glorified. For forty days He remained in a transitional state, visiting His disciples from time to time; then in their presence He ascended until a cloud received Him out of their sight, and is now seated at the right hand of the Father on high.

The parallel, however, must be carried even further in that His appearances are chiefly related to the keeping of the Sabbath. With the resurrection of Christ began the Sabbath of the Son; and because a sabbatism requires that after every six days of activity one day of rest must be devoted to our heavenly calling, the Church has reckoned the seventh day, not from the Sabbath of God in creation, but from the Sabbath of the Son, who arose on the first day of the week. The Christian Sabbath, frequently called the Lord's day, takes on great significance. In itself it is not only an institution set up as a memorial of God's rest after the finished work of creation, but celebrated on a new day it becomes also a memorial of the finished work of Christ in redemption.

Dr. Wardlaw in his treatise on the Sabbath says, "As God's resting from the works of creation gave rise to the ancient Sabbath, so Christ's completion of the work gave rise to the Sabbath which is now observed in the church." He further states, "I am of the opinion, with some eminent critics, that we have in these verses (4:9-10), a direct intimation and express authority for the change of the Sabbath" (from the seventh to the first day of the week. "I am perfectly satisfied as to the meaning of the passage, as an intended and explicit declaration of the change of the Sabbath" (quoted in Lindsay, *Lectures on the Epistle to the Hebrews*, pp. 177-78). This matter is also referred to by Dr. Adam Clarke in his *Commentary on Hebrews*.

A Cessation from Works. "He also hath ceased from his own works, as God did from his" (4:10*b*). Having finished His earthly work and ascended to His throne in the heavens, Christ now continues His work from that throne in a ministry through the Spirit. As previously the writer speaks of man as not having all things put under him, and then says, "But we see Jesus" (2:8-9), so here we see man in the person of the Saviour entering into the divine rest, and thus opening the way into the holiest for all His people. As the Captain of our salvation, Christ, leads many sons to glory through sanctification (2:10-11), so here it is said that He brings them through the "rest of faith," or that eternal repose of soul which is found only in fellowship with the Father and with the Son. This is the prophetic aspect of Christ under the symbol of Moses; later the writer will present the same truth under the symbol of Aaron, the high priest.

How does the child of God enter into this divine rest? He enters (1) by ceasing from his own works and then (2) by resting in simple faith on the finished work of Christ. These two are coincident in time, for it is impossible to rest at once in our own dead works and in the shed blood of Christ offered as an atonement for us. The earthly life of Jesus affords us an example of continuous and absolute dependence upon the Father. "The Son can do nothing of himself," He says, "but what he seeth the Father do: for what things soever he doeth, these also doeth the Son likewise" (John 5:19). Christ is the Light of the world; and so transparent was His

Mr. Wesley maintained that, as we are justified by faith, so also we are sanctified by faith. In making a distinction between seeking this blessing by works or by faith he said, "If by faith, why not now?" There is no other way into this "rest of faith" than a simple, heartfelt trust in the Blood of the atonement. One of the best illustrations of the power of simple faith is found in the *Memoirs of Carvosso,* an early Methodist class leader. He says: "Just at that moment a heavenly influence filled the room; and no sooner had I uttered or spoken the words from my heart, 'I shall have the blessing now,' than refining fire went 'through my heart, illuminating my soul, scattered its life through every part, and sanctified the whole.' I then received the full witness of the Spirit that the blood of Jesus had *cleansed me from all sin.* I cried out, 'This is what I wanted. I have now got a new heart.' I was emptied of self and sin, and filled with God."

nature during the time of His humiliation that everything coming from God to man passed through Him
without any obstruction, and everything that was presented to God through Him likewise reached the throne
undiminished. Christ is Light, and down to the infinite
depths of His being there is no darkness at all.

But what does it mean to cease from our own works?
It does not mean a cessation of all activity as in a life
of pure contemplation; rather it means a life of intense
activity. It is the ceasing from those works which flow
from our own self-life, that, like Jesus, we may live
wholly in the will of God—a yielding up of our own
wills that the works of God may be wrought in us. As
Jesus died to bring us out from under the penalty of sin,
so we must die to the old self-life if its works are to cease.
There must therefore be a death of the sinful self, a
crucifixion with Christ, a cleansing from all sin, or whatever other scriptural term may be used to designate this
experience. In the last analysis, it means such a purification of the heart that God can work in us "both to will
and to do of his good pleasure." "No greater mistake
can be made in regard to holy living," says Isaac M. See,
"than that we do the living." It is not we who live; it is
Christ living in us, and the life which we now live in the
flesh we live by the faith of the Son of God (Gal. 2:20).
Faith is rest in Another. How many there are who
struggle in their own strength to live a life worthy of
Christ, only to find bitter disappointment and failure!
No, it is Christ that lives in us and manifests His life
through us, and this life is by faith in Him who dwells
within.

St. Paul had learned the secret of holy living and
laboring. He says, "Whereunto I also labour, striving
according to his working, which worketh in me mightily"
(Col. 1:29). The Greek words are strong. They read:
agonizomenos (ἀγωνιζόμενος), "agonizing," according to
His *energeian* (ἐνέργειαν), "energy," which energizes in
me in *dunamei* (δυνάμει), "might" or "power." It is not
by "our own power or holiness" that we are to live and
labor, but by Him who dwells within the holy heart.

One of the greatest dangers which we face is to rest in that which Christ has done for us rather than in Him who continuously works within us. Only as we are cleansed from all sin, and cease from our own works, will the stream of divine energy flow through us according to our measure, as it did in its fullness through Christ; and only thus is it possible to live a holy life and labor effectively for Christ.

An Exhortation to Diligence. "Let us labour therefore to enter into that rest, lest any man fall after the same example of unbelief" (4:11). The words "Let us labour" are a translation of *spoudasomen oun* (σπου-δάσωμεν οὖν), which means "to be diligent," "to hasten," or "to be eager and alert." The reference is primarily to an intensity of purpose or the utmost eagerness to enter into that which God has so richly provided for His people. Here it is not a blessing given *for* the keeping of His commandments, but a blessing *in* keeping them—one which flows solely from divine grace. The two expressions, "Let us . . . fear," (4:1) and, "Let us be diligent," (4:11) are aorists and therefore decisive and effective. The former is negative, appealing to the motive of fear; the latter is positive, appealing to the greatness of hope. Again, the word "lest" touches the negative side, but the word "in" (ἐν) does not so much mean "after," as our Authorized Version has it, i.e., falling after the pattern of those who have gone before; rather it means that if anyone fall he is adding to the pattern or example of disobedience, as did the Israelites who refused to enter Canaan because of unbelief. Ebrard translates it, "Let us beware therefore, lest we neglect the second more excellent and more powerful call of grace, and lest we also in our turn, become an example of warning to others."

The "rest of faith," as we have shown, is a personal and spiritual experience of resting in God through the Spirit; but that it is not the Christian's final rest is indicated by the fact that it is still associated with the keeping of a typical Sabbath day. It is sometimes held that the words "that rest" are used instead of "God's rest" in order to comprehend in a single statement both the Sabbath rest of the soul and the observance of the day to commemorate it. There is a similarity here between St. Paul's teaching concerning the earnest of our inheritance and the entrance into the "rest of faith." The earnest is not merely a type but a true portion of that which later is to be bestowed in a richer, fuller measure. It is a portion of the inheritance but not the whole of it. So also this "rest of faith" is only the beginning of that which later will be merged into the "rest in glory," the ultimate goal to which the Captain of our salvation leads those whom He sanctifies here (2: 10-11). It is the foretaste of that which is to come, when "hope shall change to glad fruition, faith to sight, and prayer to praise."

The Sabbath celebrated on the seventh day commemorated God's rest in creation and His proprietorship in all His works; the Sabbath celebrated on the first day commemorates the redemptive work of Christ and is the assurance of our resurrection and final glory. There will be another Sabbath in the world to come—the Sabbath of the Holy Spirit. As the original Sabbath in which God rested had neither evening nor morning, so the Sabbath in the world to come will be an eternal day, for there will be no night there. It will be an eternal rest, for in the new heaven and the new earth which are to come, there dwelleth only righteousness. The "rest of faith" and the "final rest in glory" meet and merge at the portals of death and in the glories of the first resurrection. Thus St. John writes, "Blessed are the dead which die in the Lord from henceforth: Yea, saith the Spirit, that they may rest from their labours; and their works do follow them" (Rev. 14: 13). The word here translated "labour" is kopon (κόπων), which signifies labor, toil, or trouble. In that bright land all the consequences of sin will be removed, for "God shall wipe away all tears from their eyes; and there shall be no more death, neither sorrow, nor crying, neither shall there be any more pain; for the former things are passed away" (Rev. 21:4). We shall rest forever in the place which Jesus has gone to prepare for us, but best of all, we shall rest with Him in resplendent glory. For "we know that, when he shall appear, we shall be like him; for we shall see him as he is" (I John 3:2b). We ask again, Is it any wonder that the writer exhorts us to give all diligence to enter this "rest of faith" which shall find its ultimate issue in the glories of the world to come? or that he warns us against becoming a pattern of unbelief as did those to whom first the "good news" was preached?

The Living and Powerful Word of God

This section (4:12-13) must be regarded as a reinforcement of the preceding warning and exhortation. The reference here is primarily to the written Word of God. But God never separates himself from His Word; hence there is always a close relation between the personal Word (John 1:1, 14) and the spoken or written Word (Luke 5:1; Mark 7:13). We may note the following characteristics of the Word of God.

1. "For the word of God is quick, and powerful" (4:12a). The word "quick" is an obsolete term for "living." The Greek word *zon* (ζῶν) or "living" is placed first in the sentence for emphasis. The Scriptures are so called because they are the Word of the living God. They are the outflow of divine life and therefore themselves instinct with life. Jesus emphasized this great truth when He said, "The words that I speak unto you, they are spirit, and they are life" (John 6:63b). The word *energes* (ἐνεργής), translated "powerful," means power in action as over against merely potential power. It is therefore expressed by such words as "active," "energetic," or "efficient." The writer is speaking of the written Word which the Jews possessed, and this he views as the active power of God as shown by the personal pronouns in the following verse. What presumption, therefore, to tamper with the Word of God, or subject it to the narrow, if not fallacious, opinions of men! It is folly to criticize that by which we must ourselves be judged before an assembled universe.

2. "And sharper than any t w o e d g e d sword" (4: 12b). The word *distomon* (δίστομον) means literally "two-mouthed," and is a reference to the short sword or *machaira* (μάχαιρα) used by the Roman legionnaires (Eph. 6: 17) The word *pasan* (πᾶσαν) may equally well be translated "every" instead of "any," and is a stronger term. The sword is used as an illustration of the penetrating power of the Word of God. As a sword can cut through the flesh parting it asunder, and cut through the bones exposing the marrow, so the Word of God can cut through the soul and spirit to the innermost thoughts and intents of the heart.

3. "Piercing even to the dividing asunder of soul and spirit, and of the joints and marrow" (4: 12c). The chain of ideas here is well paraphrased by Ebrard as follows: "The word of God is sharper than every two-edged sword, inasmuch as it penetrates to the dividing asunder as well of spirit as of soul, thus resembling a sword which pierces even to the separation of the parts, as well of the marrow as of the joints." The word translated "pierce" is *diiknoumenos* (διικνούμενος) and means "to cut right through" or "to go the whole length." The use of the word *merismou* (μερισμοῦ), "dividing" or "separating," in connection with the words *te kai* (τε καὶ), "both, and," cannot mean a separation *between* soul and spirit, but a dividing of both soul and spirit, and also of both the joints and the marrows (plural). Westcott says that the simplest explanation of this text is to regard the two compound clauses as coupled by the *te*, so that the first two terms represent the immaterial part of man's being, and the latter two the material part. Thus it may be said that the divine Word or revelation penetrates through the whole of man's being.

4. "Soul and spirit" (4: 12c). The use of the terms soul and spirit demands further consideration. It is well known that the Greek word *psuche* (ψυχή) is not the exact equivalent of the English word soul. The former is often used by Greek writers to signify merely the life which animates the body, and hence the source of carnal

appetites and desires. But the English term soul con-
notes a far higher idea and is regarded as the immaterial
or spiritual part of man. Man is therefore composed of
a material part, the body, and an immaterial part known
either as the soul or the spirit. The immaterial part, however, is itself regarded by St. Paul in a twofold manner
—the soul in that it animates the body, and the spirit as
the source of our relation to God. It is this that gives
rise to his teaching concerning a *functional* trichotomy,
while still holding to an *essential* dichotomy. It is well
to bear in mind that the soul is spirit in relation to body,
the spirit being the *principle* of life, and the soul the *seat*
of life. When however these two terms are distinguished
from each other, the soul or *psuche* (ψυχή) is the life of
the body which the spirit gives it; and the spirit or
pneuma (πνεῦμα), the same immaterial portion regarded
as divinely inbreathed and therefore the sphere of God's
regenerating and sanctifying power. Sin has wrought
moral disorder in man and produced a state of unrighteousness, in which the higher principle of the spirit has
been brought under the dominion of the *psuche* or
natural life. To this condition the apostle applies the
term *psychical* or *soulish*, the *psuche* being the seat of
the thoughts, feelings, and volitions merely as they pertain to bodily existence. But the Word of God pierces
far beyond this into the very thoughts and intents of
the heart, and thus is able to renew and sanctify the
very spirit of man's mind (Rom. 12:2). To this latter
condition the apostle applies the term *spiritual* as opposed to the merely *psychical*.

5. "A discerner of the thoughts and intents of the
heart" (4:12*d*). This statement adds materially to the
thought of the penetrating power of the Word. Here
the term heart is used and not soul and spirit as previously, the heart being the active center of the personal
being. From the heart or inmost being there arise
enthumeseis (ἐνθυμήσεις) or the natural desires, passions, reflections, and meditations which find undis-
turbed play in the natural mind; and the *ennoiai* (ἔννοιαι)
or the conscious thought life, the opinions, principles,

and ideas formed on the basis of the former reflections and which find issue in intentional activity. Thus we have the "word" as permeating both the *thoughts* and *intents* of the heart. The word for discerner as found here is not *krites* (κριτής), which would mean a judge, but *kritikos* (κριτικὸς), which means one skilled in judging. God's Word therefore exercises a separating and critical effect upon the whole moral character of man, and its discernment, its judgments, warnings, and consolations are always infallibly and unimpeachably true.

The Word of God enables us to distinguish between that which is merely natural and that which is wrought in us by the Spirit. As the joints connecting the limbs are dead without the inner marrow of life, so the soul is dead in trespasses and sins until vitalized by the lifegiving Spirit. The impartation of spiritual life in regeneration does not, however, remove the principle or seed of sin which St. Paul calls the "flesh" or the "carnal mind." But the Word of God pierces into the inmost recesses of the heart and makes manifest that which is spiritual and that which is carnal. It does not call the flesh Spirit, but condemns the carnal mind as "enmity against God" (Rom. 8:7). This piercing of the heart, this cutting away of the "flesh," is painful surgery, but it leads to the health of the soul—to "wholeness" or holiness of heart and life. It is of the greatest importance to recognize these two stages in Christian experience and in the personal knowledge of God. The first conveys the gift of life, which gives us power to walk in the Spirit, and thus not fulfill the desires of the flesh, although the conflict remains in the soul (Gal. 5:16-17). The second is the higher plane in which the "flesh" or "carnal mind" is itself crucified, thus removing its outreachings of evil desires and inordinate affections. Thus purity spreads throughout the whole being, and the soul enters in to the fullness of the blessing of Christ.

6. "Neither is there any creature that is not manifest in his sight: but all things are naked and opened unto the eyes of him with whom we have to do" (4:13).

Here God and His Word appear to be identified by the use of the two personal pronouns *autou* (αὐτοῦ), which may be a gathering up of the thought of the preceding verse where the expression "word of God" is used. The transition from the manifestation of God through His Word to that of His person is perfectly natural, and is further sustained by the last clause. The preposition here is *pros* (πρὸς) or "face to face," which makes it clear that we are ever under the all-seeing eye of the Almighty. There can be no doubt that this statement connects effectively both God and His Word, and gives content to what is said in this connection. The words "manifest in his sight" are in Greek stated in the negative form, *aphanes* (ἀφανὴς), "unapparent," being a strong statement that there is nothing that is not apparent to Him. Thus the eye of God in His providence extends to all His creatures, so that not even a sparrow falleth without the knowledge of the Father. Every creature is constantly in His sight, and there is nothing that can hide or obscure His vision. The intensity of this vision is further strengthened by the word *gumna* (γυμνὰ), "naked"; and by the additional word *tetrachelismena* (τετραχηλισμένα), which means "opened" or "laid bare," hence stripped of all disguise. This last sentence is especially strong in that it contains a double negative, "not a creature" (singular) is unexposed; and

---

Ebrard has this pertinent paragraph concerning the discerning power of the Word. "This power it has, because as the word of that *grace* in the highest manifestation of which the *holiness* of God remained altogether unscathed, it both forgives and judges the same sin in the heart of man, at one and the same time, and by one and the same act. On the cross of Christ the guilt has been atoned for, and the sin which brought Christ to the cross at the same time condemned, and held up as an object of abhorrence to all who love the propitiator. Thus has this word of wonder, the wonder of all words, the power to comfort without seducing into levity, to shake without plunging into despair. It draws while it rebukes, it sifts while it draws; the man cannot set himself free from it who has once heard it; its gentleness will not allow him to cast it from him, and as he holds it fast he escapes not also from its sifting severity. It has in one word—a barb. The law of Moses rebukes the deed done; the word of the Gospel works upon the source whence actions proceed, the mind, the heart; it judges *before* the deed is done, not *after;* it is living; its judging consists in making better, in sanctifying the inner man of the heart, and thus extending its efficacy to the outward life."—EBRARD, *Biblical Commentary on the Epistle to the Hebrews,* p. 163.

"all things" (plural) are laid bare, or not disguised. It appears that no stronger emphasis could be given to this great truth of the all-seeing eye of Him to whom we must give account.

7. The writer has now reached his second conclusion. He has shown that Christ is superior to angels, and has now proved that He is superior to Moses. Further still, he is about to show us that Christ has conjoined in himself, not only the apostolic office of Moses, but also the high priesthood of Aaron, lifting them both out of the realm of types and shadows into a new and heavenly order. But his theme is still the "rest of faith." Alas that not only ancient Israel, but many in the churches today, have failed to press forward into holiness of heart and life! They too, through unbelief, have turned back at the very borders of this spiritual rest.

THE TRANSITIONAL PASSAGE

The closing section of this chapter (4: 14-16) is a transitional passage which sums up the past and prepares the reader for the great truths to be unfolded concerning the high priesthood of Christ, and the sacrificial offering of himself for our sins. The superiority of Christ to angels has been likened to one pillar of a great archway; the second, to the superiority of Christ over Moses; the arch spanning the two being a new and eternal order of priesthood. The Keystone of the arch is Christ, who embraces in himself both the Aaronic priesthood of death and the Melchisedec priesthood of life, and thus becomes a true High Priest for man in things pertaining to God. That this is a transitional passage is further indicated by the fact that the verses are introduced by the Greek word *oun* (οὖν), or "therefore," and are an inference from what precedes; and the word *gar* (γὰρ), "for," which indicates that they are a preparation for the more extended discussion of the priesthood in the following chapter. Luther however held that 4: 14 should have marked the beginning of the next chapter. The incidental manner of introducing new subjects has been shown to be peculiar to this Epistle. (Cf. 1:4; 3:2.) The whole section is hortatory, and its truths among the richest of the entire Epistle.

We Have a Great High Priest. "Seeing then that we have a great high priest, that is passed into the heavens, Jesus the Son of God, let us hold fast our profession" (4:14). Four things are mentioned as constituting the greatness of Jesus as our High Priest. (1) He is great because He is a High Priest, and not a subordinate. Furthermore, He is of the high order of Melchisedec and therefore a King-Priest. As a King, He condescends to minister as a Priest; as a Priest, He ministers with the authority of a King. (2) He "is passed into [literally 'through'] the heavens." The reference is to the high priest passing through the inner veil into the holy of holies (or holiness of holinesses), where dwelt the Shekinah of God's presence. So also Jesus ascended in the presence of His disciples, and passing into the physical heavens, was screened from their vision by a cloud like a veil. Behind that cloud all the physical heavens that we know were but the vestibule through which He passed into the ineffable glory and inaccessible light, into the immediate presence of God.

What the Aaronic priests could not do except in type and symbol, Jesus has done in fact, passing through, not a material veil, but the upper heavens, penetrating to the very throne of God. For this reason the writer speaks later of His having been made "higher than the heavens" (7:26). Jesus is great as a High Priest because He has access to God, and is seated as our Mediator at the right hand of the Majesty on high, ministering for us in a greater and more perfect tabernacle, that is, in heaven itself. (3) He is a sympathetic High Priest. The writer first mentions His earthly name, "Jesus," before calling Him by the august title of the "Son of God." The first gives us the assurance of His sympathetic presence; the second, the ground of our confidence. (4) He is the "Son of God," the Second Person of the adorable Trinity, and yet was made flesh that He might be the "propitiation for our sins: and not

for ours only, but also for the sins of the whole world"
(I John 2:2; 4:10).

The writer, having presented our great High Priest
as the ideal of priesthood fully realized, now turns to
consider in a hortatory manner the benefits accruing to
us. The Holy Spirit tells us that this great High Priest
is ours, our very own. God himself has appointed Him
for this very purpose. We are to put our full trust in
Him, and follow implicitly His guidance and direction.
We are not our own; we have been bought with a price.
He has ordained that we live our lives through His
priesthood; and so identical must our wills be with His
that it can be said that Christ lives in us and manifests
His life through us (Gal. 2:20). Let us then hold fast
our profession, the writer exhorts us, and not allow ourselves to be deprived of our inheritance through the
deceits of Satan. The Holy Spirit strongly reassures us
of His help by using the double designation of our great
High Priest—He is Jesus, the Son of Man, and fully
understands and sympathizes with us; and He is the
Son of God with sovereign power, enabling us to triumph in all things.

The Sympathy of Jesus. "For we have not an high
priest which cannot be touched with the feeling of our
infirmities" (4:15a). This verse is introduced by a
double negative in order to emphasize and strengthen
the contrary position. Cowles points out that this is
somewhat peculiar, but is adopted for a reason not far
to seek. Suspicion might arise as to whether One "so
superlative in dignity and glory" could possibly have

This double negative the reader will notice is somewhat peculiar,
but it is not adopted without a reason which we need not go far to seek.
Sometimes perhaps, even in Aaron's line, there might be high priests
who would feel their personal dignity in a way which would crush out
all natural sympathy with the lowly. Hebrews who had had experience
with such high priests, would perhaps recoil from one who came recom-
mended for His superlative greatness, dignity and glory. . . . Anticipat-
ing and forestalling this fear, the author would say: True there might be
a high priest who could not be touched with the feeling of our infirmities, but *we have not such an one.* You need never fear that Jesus will
be unfeeling, unsympathizing . . . For He "was tempted in all points
like as we are, yet without sin."—Cowles, *Epistle to the Hebrews,*
pp. 55-56.

sympathy with lowly and frail sufferers. To such the writer replies, "We have not such an one." It never can be true that the heart of Jesus will be untouched with the feeling of our infirmities.

There are two verbs translated "to sympathize," each of which occurs but twice in the New Testament, never in the Septuagint. The first is *sunpaschein* (συνπάσχειν) and means literally "to suffer with" or along with another. It rises no higher than a mere community of suffering in which fellow creatures participate. The second verb, *sunpathein* (συνπαθεῖν), the one used in this text and in 10:34, comes through *pathos* (πάθος) and *sumpathes* (συμπαθής). It thus takes on a higher meaning, that of fellow feeling rather than fellow suffering. With men it is possible that the springs of sympathy may be effectually quenched through lack of understanding; but Jesus as the God-Man, with His deeper theanthropic consciousness, fully understands us and is unfailing in His sympathy.

Miley in his chapter on the sympathy of Christ says: "We thus reach the very sure ground of the sympathy of Christ as it is revealed in the Scriptures and apprehended in the deepest Christian thought and feeling. This ground does not lie in the experiences of a mere human consciousness, with all the limitations and disabilities of the human. Nor is it subject to the law of time and changing conditions, as grounds of all human sympathy must be. The trials of Christ which constitute the ground of His sympathy have their place in His theanthropic consciousness. Therein they ever abide, and for all the requirements of His sympathy are living facts still, just as they were in the hours of His trial. . . . It is here that we find in the sympathy of Christ the true doctrine of His personality. He must be a theanthropic Person, else He could not have the consciousness of trial and suffering which is necessary to His sympathy. He is a theanthropic Person as in personal oneness He unites a human nature with His divine nature, and through the human enters into the consciousness of trial and suffering like our own. The theanthropic consciousness of Christ is the central truth of His personality. . . . The divine consciousness of the human is an intrinsic fact of the theanthropic character of Christ. . . . He is theanthropic in His personality, not in His natures. In His natures He is divine *and* human, but in the unity of personality He is divine-human, God-man. In the unity of personality there must be the unity of consciousness, but in the theanthropic consciousness there must be both divine and human facts. In the theanthropic consciousness of Christ, the divine facts come with the divinity of the Son; the human facts, through the human nature in which He was personally incarnated."—MILEY, *Systematic Theology,* II, 40-41.

For the use of the words συνπάσχειν and συνπαθεῖν see Vaughan, *Epistle to the Hebrews,* p. 84.

The Temptation of Jesus. "But was in all points tempted like as we are, yet without sin" (4:15b). The words *choris hamartias* (χωρὶς ἁμαρτίας), here translated "without sin," are found also in 9:18, but with an entirely different connotation. There they have reference to Christ's second coming, which will be apart from all sin-bearing or propitiatory offering. For this reason the words "without" or "apart" from sin are interpreted to mean that He will come at that time without a sin offering. Here however, in the text before us, the words "without sin" mean a personal "apartness" from sin, by either contact or contagion, in either act or condition. They may mean (1) that Jesus endured temptation without in any wise being stained with sin; or (2) that Jesus was tempted in all points as we would be were we, like Him, without sin. Westcott says that the former of these thoughts is not excluded from the expression "without sin," but the latter appears to be the dominant idea. Other Biblical scholars take the same position. Von Hoffmann says, "Not only did the temptation produce no sin in Him, but it attached to no sin." Vaughan tells us that "He was tempted in all points like us, but in absolute severance from any, the least admission of sin." Lowrie takes the position that the added expression "without sin" limits the notion of likeness to us. It is not merely that He did not sin "but that the temptation was wholly unattended by sin in Him." Dr. Adam Clarke comes to the same con-

Dr. Adam Clarke has this further note on the expression "according to the likeness." He says of Christ: "For though He had a perfect human body and a perfect human soul, yet that body was perfectly tempered, and free from all morbid action, and consequently free from all irregular movements; and His mind or human soul, being free from all sin, being every way perfect, could feel no irregular temper, nothing that was inconsistent with infinite purity. In all these respects He was different from us; and cannot as man, sympathize with us in any feelings of this kind; but as God, has provided support for the body under all its trials and infirmities; and for the soul He has provided an atonement and a purifying sacrifice; so that He cleanses the heart from all unrighteousness, and fulls the soul with His Holy Spirit, and makes it His own temple and continuous habitation. He took our flesh and blood, a human body and a human soul; and lived a human life. Here was the likeness of sinful flesh (Rom. 8:5); and by thus assuming human nature, He was completely qualified to make an atonement for the sins of the people.—ADAM CLARKE, *Commentary*, IV, 733 ff.

clusion by translating the words *kath' homoioteta* (καθ' ὁμοιότητα), "according to the likeness," that is, "as far as His human nature could bear affinity to ours." The words "according to the likeness" and "without sin" mark the distinction between the true humanity of Jesus and ours in its fallen estate. Not only did He not yield to sin under the pressure of temptation, but there was no sin in Him to respond to it. Neither were there any habits of sin to overcome, as is common with mankind. But He did have all the God-given, normal, and innocent desires and affections pertaining to pure human nature. These in contrast with the divine nature are called *astheneia* (ἀσθένεια) or "weaknesses," for the scripture tells us that He was crucified through weakness (II Cor. 13:4). It was through these that He was tempted, suffering poverty, hunger, and thirst, weariness, reproach, shame, and the "contradiction of sinners against himself." Satan sought to turn these innocent desires into those which were inordinate and which

Like us, He was wearied with toil, faint from hunger, chilled by the winter's cold, oppressed with the summer's heat, having not where to lay His head; and passing from these to other ills, harder by far to be borne,—He met the contradiction of sinners against Himself; slanders upon a spotless life; cavils against the kindest appeals and the strongest arguments; persistent repulsion alike to His most faithful rebukes and to His most tearful entreaties. He came unto His own and His own received Him not. Moreover, all there can be of darkness and horror in the fiercest temptations of Satan He passed through once and again— we cannot know how often; all that human weakness which makes angelic ministration so precious, He certainly felt and had occasion to welcome its sweet comfort and consolation.—Cowles, *Epistle to the Hebrews*, pp. 55-56.

"Now it is quite clear that a man may, in this way find himself in the situation of *being tempted*, without its being necessary to suppose that there is therefore in him an *evil inclination*. . . . So it was in reference to Christ's temptation; He was tempted "in every respect," in joy and sorrow, in fear and hope, in the most various situations, but *without sin*; the being tempted was to Him purely *passive*, purely *objective* throughout the whole period of His life; He renounced the pleasures of life *for which He had a natural SUSCEPTIBILITY*, because He could not retain these only in compliance with the carnal hopes of the Messiah entertained by the multitude, and He maintained His course of conduct in spite of the prospect which became ever more and more sure, that His faithfulness and persecution would lead Him to suffering and death, *of which He felt a natural fear*. That susceptibility of pleasure and this fear, were what tempted Him,—not sinful inclinations but pure, innocent, natural affections, belonging essentially to His human nature." (For an extended and excellent treatment of this subject, see Ebrard, *Biblical Commentary on the Epistle to the Hebrews*, pp. 169-70.)

mark the beginning of sin. But Jesus proved in every point the malice of the tempter and defied his power, for He knew no sin. Although so great a High Priest, and ministering from the heavens, He still understands our temptations, and the greatness of His sympathy and help exceeds the utmost of His people's need.

The Throne of Grace

The writer, having described Christ as the ideal High Priest, His temptation, and His sympathy for His people, now considers Him as administering grace from His throne in the heavens. "Let us therefore come boldly unto the throne of grace, that we may obtain mercy, and find grace to help in time of need" (4:16). Rich as this verse is to the hearts of God's people, it takes on deeper significance when the Greek words are seen in their varying shades of meaning.

The Throne of Grace. The word "throne" comes from an old Greek word brought over into the English language to signify the seat of kings. This throne of grace is the same as that of the Majesty on high, previously mentioned (1:3), but it is presented in a different aspect because the Son, our Mediator, is seated at the right hand of the Father to administer grace and truth. We are to draw near to God, not as our Judge, but through Christ, as our gracious Heavenly Father. The allusion is to the entrance of the high priest into the holy of holies on the great Day of Atonement; but the greatness of Jesus as our High Priest does not consist in entering through any material veil, but into heaven itself, there to minister in the greater and more perfect tabernacle. Having made His propitiatory offering, He "passed through the heavens" into the presence of God, there to appear for us. To this throne of grace all men may now draw near with confidence and assurance.

Let us come boldly. The w o r d *proserchometha* (προσερχώμεθα), here translated "come," is in Acts 7:31 and again in Heb. 10:22 rendered "draw near." The first reference is to Moses, who was admonished to "draw near" to the burning bush in the wilderness. It is a word used in the Old Testament for the service of the priests in the sanctuary, especially that of the high priest. The word is in the present tense, active and volitive, and means, "Let us keep on coming," or, "Keep drawing near to God through our great High Priest." Christ has made infinite provision for us, and we honor Him when we come boldly to receive the purchased and promised grace. The word "boldly" does not imply presumption, but rather the opposite. It comes from the root word *parresias* (παρρησίας) and means "saying all." The invitation therefore is to draw near as you are, say what you wish, and ask with confidence for what you need. What a gracious invitation is this! Those who approach the throne of grace in a halting and fearful manner show but little confidence in the wondrous provisions Christ has made for us through grace.

The repetition of the word *proserchometha* or "draw near" (10: 21) is significant in that it is a further exposition of the "rest of faith" under the symbolism of the heavenly sanctuary. Then too, it emphasizes more especially the mode of its accomplishment rather than the finished work. The writer will there treat of the rent veil of Christ's flesh, His entrance as Forerunner into the greater and more perfect tabernacle, and His opening for us a way into the most holy place of God's presence. As the apostolic work of Christ leads to the rest of the soul in God, so His priestly work provides for us within the veil a fullness of life and blessing. The writer has not yet come to his teachings concerning the sacrificial offering of our great High Priest, the better promises, and the heavenly sanctuary; and we must therefore regard this first "draw near" in the light of simple prayer, which the weakest believer cannot possibly misunderstand. But those who "keep on coming" to the throne of grace will soon be brought to the second "draw near," where life within the veil is spent "in the fulness of the blessing of the gospel of Christ" (Rom. 15: 29).

*That we may obtain mercy, and find grace to help
in time of need* (4:16b). The word *labomen* (λάβωμεν),
here translated "obtain," in its simplest form means
merely "to take." Christ has tasted death for every
man, and now every man is free to go to the propitiatory
of the Cross, and take freely the mercy that has been
purchased for him, and which awaits him there. The
term "mercy" refers more especially to the pardon of
sins, while "grace" is that which we seek to purify the
heart and uphold us in all the trials and disappointments of life. Hence the verb *heuroman* (εὕρωμεν)
means "to find" in the sense of "to discover" or find
out by test, in times of need. Because Jesus has made
a finished atonement, we are sure of mercy; and because He is our High Priest on the throne, He is able
to make all grace abound toward us in all things. The
expression "in time of need" is from the Greek word
eukairon (εὔκαιρον)—*eu* meaning well, and *kairon*
meaning opportunity—so that the term means "season-
able" or "well-timed" help; that is, help that is needed,
when needed. It is what Rev. Will Huff, one of the
great preachers of the past generation, called "nick o'
time" grace. The word *boetheian* (βοήθειαν) or "help"
may equally well be translated "assistance" or "support"; but there is a deeper and even more precious
meaning. It signifies "to run at the cry for help." We
may understand therefore that, even from the throne
of grace, support will not be given without the cry for
help. But how good to know that, when in trouble and
sorrow we cry for help, our great High Priest, full of
sympathy and compassion, hastens to our side and never
fails to give grace in time of need. But let us also
remember that the cry must be for immediate help,
and not for help in the distant and unknown future.
The only warrant that we have for approaching this
throne of grace is that we have a need. It may be a
need now, and a need the next hour, or still further
when the morrow comes; it matters not how great that
need nor how small, "God is able to make all grace
abound toward you; that ye, always having all suffi-

ciency in all things, may abound to every good work" (II Cor. 9: 8).

The Final Exhortation. In this closing exhortation a final word needs to be said concerning the boldness with which we are to draw near to the throne of grace. We have seen that the Greek word does not admit of presumption, but neither can it be interpreted as a mere state or condition produced in ourselves by self-effort or determination. The word here translated boldness occurs in two other places in this Epistle where it is rendered "confidence." In 3: 6 we are exhorted to "hold fast the confidence," and in 10: 35 we are warned to "cast not away" our "confidence." Confidence implies faith in another. This confidence therefore is not merely our own, but was purchased for us by the blood of Jesus, and inspired within us by the Holy Spirit. St. John tells us that it flows from perfect love in a heart purged from all unholy fear, and that it is this which gives boldness in the day of judgment. This is further illustrated by Peter and John, who in healing the lame man denied that this miracle was due to their "own power or holiness"; and yet their boldness astonished the priests and Sadducees, who took note of them that they had been with Jesus (Acts 3: 12; 4: 13). Here then is the secret of boldness in the work of God—it is the constant fellowship with Jesus, who breathes into the soul the strength and courage of perfect love. Let us therefore, with the boldness born of confidence, draw near to the throne of grace, "that we may obtain mercy, and find grace to help in time of need."

CHAPTER V

THE OFFICE AND WORK OF A PRIEST

Leaving chapter four we enter upon the third and largest division of this Epistle. We have previously discussed the prophetic work of Christ under the symbol of Moses and the promised inheritance interpreted spiritually as the "rest of faith." Now we enter the division concerned with the priestly work of Christ under the symbol of Aaron, which embraces three main subdivisions: (1) the priesthood, (2) the sanctuary, and (3) the sacrifice. While these subjects are treated in chapters five to ten inclusive, it is difficult to offer a fixed outline, for the subjects shade off and merge into one another. There is first a consideration of the Priest, then the sanctuary as the sphere of His operations, and lastly, the service rendered in the sanctuary —that of gifts and sacrifices. In general we may say that the priesthood is considered primarily in chapters five, six, and seven; the sanctuary in chapters eight and nine (including the covenant); and the sacrifice in chapter ten. As Leviticus sixteen is the great atonement chapter of the Old Testament, so Hebrews nine and ten are the great atonement chapters of the New Testament—chapter nine viewing Christ as the priestly Offerer, and chapter ten as the sacrificial Offering.

The fifth chapter continues the subject begun in the transitional passage of the previous chapter (4: 14-16), but the manner in which the two passages are related depends upon the interpretation of the word "for"—whether chapter five is merely explanatory of the former passage or whether it is an independent section in the continuation of the argument. If the former, then the previous statements concerning Christ's priesthood are confirmed by showing that they fully meet all the requirements of the Aaronic priesthood; if the latter, then chapter five is an independent state-

ment of the basic requirements for the priesthood—
one of course under which the Aaronic priesthood would
qualify. We shall consider the chapter in the latter
sense.

THE QUALIFICATIONS AND WORK OF A PRIEST

There are six qualifications essential to the high
priesthood as stated in the first section of this chapter
(5:1-5). These may be enumerated as follows: (1)
He must be "taken from among men," and therefore
must be of the same nature as those whom he serves.
(2) He is ordained or appointed for men; that is, he
is a representative man, and while his office pertains
to God, it is concerned always with men. (3) He must
not come before God empty-handed, but must "offer
both gifts and sacrifices for sins." (4) He must manifest an attitude of compassion or moderation toward
those that are ignorant and out of the way. (5) Because he is taken from among men and partakes with
them of infirmities and sins, he must make an offering
for himself as well as for the people. (6) He does not
take to himself the honor of being a high priest, but is
called and appointed of God, as was Aaron. It is evident
that these six qualifications can be easily reduced to
two main essentials: he must be chosen from among
men, and he must be appointed by God. In this case
the other four are merely explanatory. However, in
our more thorough discussion of the Aaronic priesthood, we shall for greater simplicity follow the scriptural order found in the first section (5:1-3) as above
indicated.

1. A high priest must be *taken from among men*
(5:1a). This is the primary qualification for the high
priesthood. Ebrard states that this sentence may be
arranged logically as follows: "Every high priest can
appear before God for men, only in virtue of his being
taken from among men." To be taken from those he
is to represent is necessary for true fellowship, understanding, and sympathy. For this reason the writer has
previously stated that Christ "took not on him the

nature of angels; but he took on him the seed of Abraham" (2:16). But this very expression "taken from among men" suggests the thought that there is another Priest of which a different description might be given—Christ, who, though as a man He is connected with the human race, is nevertheless at the same time of heavenly origin (7:28).

2. He *is ordained for men in things pertaining to God* (5:1b). The word *kathistatai* (καθίσταται) is the usual term for appointment to an office. Here however the reference is primarily to the nature of the office, and hence the words "constituted" or "ordained" are proper terms to express the office thus established. The clause "appointed for men" is the emphatic part of this statement. The high priest, though taken from among men in order to act in things pertaining to God, is still vitally related to men. When appearing before God in the fulfillment of the functions of his office, he is there solely for that which concerns men. To turn aside from this purpose or even to be negligent in it would violate the very nature of his office.

3. *That he may offer both gifts and sacrifices for sins* (5:1c). Perhaps the best authorities interpret *thusia* (θυσία) or "sacrifices" as restricted to bloody sacrifices of slain beasts; and *dora* (δῶρα) or "gifts" as applied to freewill offerings, such as the meat offerings, drink offerings, and thank offerings. However, while the word for sacrifices is restricted to bloody sacrifices or offerings, the word for gifts is not so restricted in the Scriptures and is sometimes applied to the sacrifices of slain beasts, as in 8:4, where the word *dora* is made to cover both gifts and sacrifices, as indicated in the preceding verse. The theory generally held is that *dora* is a general term applied to all offerings, and that *thusia* is a specific term for sin offerings; but when used together, then *dora* is used to distinguish freewill offerings from sin offerings. The word *prospherei* (προσφέρῃ) means "to bring forward" and is the term frequently used of the priest's act in bringing the victim forward

to the altar of sacrifice. Technically, the work of the priest was not in the slaying of the victim, which was frequently done by others, but in the "presentation" of the sacrifice before God at the altar of burnt offering.

4. *Who can have compassion on the ignorant, and on them that are out of the way* (5:2a). This qualification has reference to the frame of mind in which the high priest is to make his offering. It is comprehended in the statement that he is appointed "from among men," in order that he may be able to bear with them. The word *metriopathein* (μετριοπαθεῖν) does not occur elsewhere in the New Testament, nor is it found in the Septuagint. It is of later Greek origin and appears to have been first used in opposition to the Stoics, who held that the wise man should be free from passion of *apathes* (ἀπαθής). The formation of the word indicates that it is a mean between passionless and the violent indulgence of passion. It is therefore translated "to exercise forbearance" or to show "moderate feeling" —the opposite alike of violent anger and utter indifference. The high priest, then, is "to feel gently toward" or "to bear gently with" those who are ignorant and out of the way. The difference between the word *sumpathesai* (συμπαθῆσαι), used of Christ (4:15), and the present *metriopathein* (μετριοπαθεῖν) is that the former indicates sympathy as a positive feeling of kindness while the latter more specifically indicates the restraint of unkindly feelings. Lindsay indicates that "perhaps the selection of the terms may have been designed to express the idea, that a more positive and purer sympathy reigned in the breast of Christ—a sympathy produced by no feeling of His own frailty, but resulting from the divine compassion of His nature. In the case

---

Lindsay further says that "the selection of this word will appear the more happy still, when it is recollected that men often have a tendency to censoriousness strong in the inverse ratio of their own goodness. The worst of the two thieves was the most bitter against Christ. The earthly priest with all his sinfulness and imperfections, is more prone to harshness than the heavenly, and therefore he needs to restrain himself; and for this purpose he ought habitually to recollect that he is a sinner, like those for whom he ministers."—LINDSAY, *Lectures on the Epistle to the Hebrews*, I, 201

of the earthly priest, the moderation of his feelings of displeasure against the the sinner is produced by the consciousness of his own sinfulness" (*Lectures on Hebrews*, I, 201).

By the expression "ignorant and erring," the writer does not imply that the work of the priest is concerned only with "mild sinners" and that others are excluded. The term covers all sins which the people commit and for which the high priest offers atonement. The first term, "ignorance," *agnoousin* (ἀγνοοῦσιν), is used in the Septuagint in its various forms to translate those Hebrew words which signify a more or less aggravated and sinful content, as in Ps. 25:7, where David prays for the forgiveness of the sins of his youth and his transgressions. It is probably related to the expression "deceitfulness of sin" (3:13), where the thought is not that of absolute ignorance, but the confused idea of sin brought about through deceit. The word for "erring," *planomenois* (πλανωμένοις), carries with it the idea of straying or roving from the right way or from the true owner. For this reason it is found in the Authorized Version as "them that are out of the way." It is used in this sense also in the expression, "They do alway err in their heart; and they have not known my ways" (3:10). Stuart suggests that the two words *agnoousin* and *planomenois* are employed in order to designate offenders of various kinds. However, the priest must "feel gently" for the wanderers or the deceived, and seek by every possible effort to restore them to the way of truth.

5. *He ought . . . also for himself, to offer for sins* (5:3). "And by reason hereof . . . as for the people, so also for himself, to offer for sins." The reference is to the great Day of Atonement, at which time the high priest first offered for himself and then for the people. The regular preposition used for the sin offering is *peri* (περὶ) and it occurs three times in this verse, "for the people," "for himself," and "for sins." The word for "ought" is *opheilei* (ὀφείλει) and carries with it the sense of obligation, in that the relation the high priest

had assumed required it of him in order to be consistent. The words "for that he himself also is compassed with infirmity," spoken of the high priest in the previous verse, are here made the ground of necessity for an offering for himself. The word for "compassed" is *perikeitai* (περίκειται), which means "lying around one," or "surrounded by"; while the word for "infirmity" is *astheneian* (ἀσθένειαν) and means primarily "weakness," but is here used in the sense of moral weakness or sin.

Two great truths stand out clearly here: (1) The high priest had no one to expiate his sins or atone for them, and hence, being encompassed with infirmity as were the people from whom he was taken, he must make atonement for himself. This of course calls attention to the imperfections of the Levitical priesthood, and prepares the way for the presentation of the inherent perfections of Christ as the Son of God. (2) Closely related to this is the necessity of personal fitness as a qualification of the priesthood. The high priest must stand free from guilt before God himself and be acceptable to Him before he can present the needs of the people. In the case of the Levitical priesthood, this was a ceremonial purification, and pointed forward to the need of One who himself was without sin, personally and inherently, as is the Son of God. The Levitical priesthood therefore is typical and temporary; that of Christ, real and eternal.

6. *No man taketh this honour unto himself, but he that is called of God* (5:4). Not only is the office of high priest constituted, and the qualifications and functions of a high priest enumerated, but here it is shown that the final and crowning characteristic of the high priest is that he as a particular person is specifically called of God to serve in this capacity. In confirmation of this position the writer appeals to Aaron, and in doing so refers to the office as originally constituted, and therefore in its purity and simplicity. That which perfects the qualifications of a high priest, then, is the call of God. This alone could give the ancient Levitical

high priest confidence in approaching God, and this alone could create that confidence in the people as would enable them to entrust him with their eternal interests. No one can legitimately take this honor to himself, and those who have presumed to do so have suffered the vengeance of God. God is the offended One, and only He can name the high priest through whom the people may approach Him. These three verses (5:1-3) with the transitional verse (5:4) have shown that Christ fully meets every qualification of a high priest as set forth in 4:14-16; and that with greater dignity and glory than that which attached to the ancient Levitical priesthood. Christ has been shown to be free from all moral defect and to be of far greater sympathy than Aaron ever felt. This verse which has furnished the crowning qualification of a high priest now becomes the introduction of a new section, "Christ and the New Order of Priesthood" (5:5-10).

CHRIST AND THE NEW ORDER OF PRIESTHOOD

While this section of the chapter (5:5-10) is a continuation of that which precedes—the presentation of Christ under the symbolism of Aaron—it will be recalled that the six qualifications and functions of a high priest mentioned in 5:1-4 were said to be reducible to two, that is, "taken from among men," and "called of God." They are so treated in this section, but in reverse order, the call of God being first mentioned, and later by easy transition, the possession of a human nature. Like many other transitions, these are introduced in a natural and almost casual manner. But there is introduced in this section a new element, that of a new order of priesthood after the order of Melchisedec and not after the Levitical order.

So also Christ glorified not himself to be made an high priest (5:5a). This is a continuation of the previous verse and completes the parallel between Aaron and Christ. Since "no man taketh this honour unto himself, but he that is called of God, as was Aaron," so also Christ glorified not himself to be made an High Priest. There is here an ellipsis which needs to be supplied in order to complete the antithesis—such as "God glorified Him," or as others have suggested, "But God has glorified Him in that He has spoken to Him." In 4:14 the word Jesus is used in connection with "the great high priest," but here the word Christ is associated with the priesthood. This is due perhaps to the fact that the high priest was anointed with oil, and since "Christ" means "the Anointed One," this term better expresses His official capacity. Again, in connection with the Levitical high priest, the term "honour" is used; here the richer term "glorified" is used of Christ. That God should count it an honor for His Son to become the High Priest through whom a lost and guilty world should not perish, but through faith in Him have everlasting life (John 3: 16), manifests a love that passes all understanding, for it flows from the infinite heart of God. That Christ should leave the glory which He had with the Father before the world was, and count it a higher glory to redeem us by His death on the Cross, cleanse us from all sin through His precious blood, and give us His Spirit to dwell in us as an abiding Comforter—this, mortal man can never fathom, but only wonder and adore. Nor will our wonder and adoration cease, but rather increase throughout the eternal ages.

The ceremonial of consecration, as used by Moses, began with the washing at the door of the tabernacle; followed by investiture with the high priestly array; and upon the sacred person thus washed and clothed the oil of anointing was poured forth. In connection with this a sin-offering was sacrificed for the removal of guilt, a burnt-offering to express entire consecration, and a peace-offering to show God's acceptance. But the oil was the sanctification: and he *poured the anointing oil upon Aaron's head, and anointed him, to sanctify him.* (Lev. 8:12) The high priest was the priest who was higher than his brethren, *upon whose head the anointing oil was poured,* poured in abundance. (Lev. 21:10) Our Lord was consecrated to His office by the Holy Ghost whom He received without measure; *Him hath God the Father sealed.* All other particulars of the consecration fell away, unless the baptism of Christ responded to the washing of the high priest. But the essential difference was in this, that Christ, while He received as incarnate the Spirit of anointing, did also consecrate Himself: *for their sakes I sanctify myself.* (John 17:19) By the divine glory of His Sonship He dedicated His person and His being to the propitiation of the sins of men.—POPE, *Compendium of Christian Theology,* II, 219-20.

But he that said unto him, Thou art my Son, to day have I begotten thee (5:5b). There is no specific mention here of an appointment to the priesthood. Some hold that the Messianic office comprehends in itself the prophetic, the priestly, and the royal functions. Bruce regards the office of the priesthood as coeval with sonship, and the terms so interwoven that to say, "Thou art my Son," is equivalent to saying, "Thou art a priest." Ebrard maintains that the reference to the second psalm contains an address to that Son of David who soon came to be identified with the Messiah; and since the Messiah must be a Priest, it follows that Jesus, being the Messiah, was also a Priest.

It would seem, however, that the truth lies far deeper than this. The writer in the earlier portion of this Epistle (1:1-3) presents the Son as the Heir of all things; that by Him the worlds were made, that He is the brightness of the Father's glory and the express Image of His person; that He upholds all things by the word of His power; and that, having by himself purged our sins, He sat down at the right hand of the Majesty on high. The Son therefore is the sole Entranceway into the temple of fellowship with God, into the very life of God himself. He alone has the necessary qualifications for a spiritual priesthood. This He exercises by making us partakers of himself, and through Him of the glory which He has in and with the Father. For this reason no one could be our great High Priest but the Son of God. These words not only reveal Christ's priestly work as based upon His divine sonship, but also the nature of His priestly work which is through sonship, to restore men to fellowship with God.

The words "To day have I begotten thee" are of utmost importance also in this connection. Both St. Paul and St. John regard the expression "first begotten" as referring to Christ's resurrection (Col. 1:18; Rev. 1:5). The offering of himself on the altar of the Cross having been made, "the Resurrection," says Vaughan, "was the virtual investiture of Christ with the Priesthood. The exercise of it waited for the Ascension, which was to the Resurrection, as the coronation is to the accession of a sovereign" (*Epistle to the Hebrews*, p. 92).

As he saith also in another place, Thou art a priest for ever after the order of Melchisedec (5:6). The foundation having been laid in the words "Thou art my Son," which form at once the basis for, and the nature of, the priesthood of Christ, the writer now confirms His direct appointment. He does this by another quotation from the Psalms (110:4)—a psalm that has ever been highly regarded as Messianic, and to which both our Lord and His apostles referred as a prophecy concerning the claims of Christ. The words are these, "Thou art a priest for ever after the order of Melchizedek," words which are constituting, authoritative, and emphatic. But this psalm not only confirms the fact that Christ was as truly appointed to the priesthood as was Aaron, but it introduces an entirely new element—that Christ was a Priest of a different order. The emphasis however in this place is solely upon the thought of the appointment. It will be noted that the word "priest" *hiereus* (ἱερεύς) is used instead of high priest, *archiereus* (ἀρχιερεύς), for there were no subordinate priests in the order of Melchisedec. Again, there are two words used in the Hebrew for "order," the one used in this psalm differing from that concerning Moses and the order of priests. The Greek word *taxin* (τάξιν) is used to translate both of these words. It is therefore used as "order" in Luke 1:8 and many other places. But the word also means "quality," "kind," "rank," or "position"; and these terms better express the truth intended than the word "order" since Melchisedec had neither predecessor nor successor. The whole verse is quoted, partly to a better understanding of it, but primarily because it is a pedagogical principle of this writer to mention briefly beforehand a subject which he later intends to treat more fully. Thus this expression is used three times (5:6, 10; 6:20) before being discussed in the seventh chapter, where it is used twice more (7:17, 21).

The following particulars concerning Melchisedec illustrate the character of Christ as the true Melchisedec

Priest. (1) He was a priest in his own right and not by
virtue of his relationships with others. (2) He was a
priest forever, without substitute or succession. (3) He
was not anointed with oil but with the Holy Spirit, a
priest of the most high God. (4) He did not offer animal
sacrifices but bread and wine, symbols of the Supper
which Christ later instituted. And (5), perhaps the
principal thought in the mind of the writer at this time,
he conjoined in himself both the priestly and kingly
functions, a thing strictly prohibited in Israel, but to be
manifested in Christ—a Priest upon His throne (Zech.
6: 13).

Who in the days of his flesh (5: 7a). The writer,
having abundantly shown that Jesus was a High Priest
by divine appointment, now turns to the second essential of the priesthood, that of human sympathy through
the possession of a human nature. Here it will be shown
that Christ as perfectly fulfills this qualification as the
former, having learned through the actual experience
of suffering to sympathize to the utmost with human
weakness. As is common with the writer, this subject
is informally introduced by the word "who," *hos* (ὅς),
which refers to Christ in verse 5. The phrase "in the
days of his flesh" refers to the whole period of Christ's
earthly life, including also His death. The word *sarx*
(σάρξ) marks the distinction between the creature and
the invisible God. It refers not so much to the essential
elements of humanity as to the conditions of the present

It was on the eve of the Sacrifice of the Cross that our Lord solemnly
assumed His sacerdotal function: first, by the institution of the Supper,
the memorial sacrifice of Christianity; and secondly, by what is sometimes called the High-priestly prayer; the symbolical Feetwashing
having been interposed with an affecting relation to both. The sacramental
institute is pervaded by sacrificial ideas: it exhibits the true Paschal
Lamb whose blood is at the same time shed for the remission of sins in
virtue of a new covenant ratified by the blood of propitiation, and the
benefit of whose death is celebrated in a continual peace-offering feast.
The High-priestly prayer was the self-consecration of Jesus to the final
endurance of the sorrows of expiation. All the Messianic offices are
hallowed in that supreme Prayer. The prophetic: *I have given them thy
word;* the regal: *as thou hast given him power over all flesh;* the priestly:
I sanctify myself, that they also might be sanctified. But it is preemi-
nently the consecration prayer of the High Priest; the formal assumption,
in the presence of the Cross, His altar, of His atoning work.—POPE,
Compendium of Christian Theology, II, 217-18.

life. It is a term which refers to human nature in its frail and suffering state. St. Paul uses the term *sarx* (σάρξ) for sinful human nature, or human nature as it exists after the Fall; but since the writer in 4: 15 states that He was "without sin," we must exclude every trace of sin in His nature, attributing to it only the sinless infirmities of human nature, such as the sorrows and afflictions of life. Into the whole picture of human life with its frailties and sufferings, Christ fits perfectly with this one exception: He was "without sin."

When he had offered up prayers and supplications with strong crying and tears (5: 7b). There seems to be a parallel with the writer's previous assertion that a priest must offer up both gifts and sacrifices, reinforced by the words "with strong crying and tears." It has been said that by a gift, *doron* (δῶρον), we honor God, and by a sacrifice, *thusia* (θυσία), we are delivered from danger which only God can avert. In the case of a sinner this danger arises from his sin, which must be forgiven; in the case of Christ it arose from the crushing burden of the sins of the world, in which God alone could sustain and preserve Him until the completion of His mission. There appears to be in the mind of the writer also a parallel between the Levitical priesthood and that of the Melchisedec order. The Levitical priest was a sinful representative of a sinful people which needed to be purified; hence he must sacrifice for himself before offering the sacrifice for the people. Christ was "without sin," but in the agony of His supplication He sweat as it were great drops of blood—the beginning of the shedding of that Blood which later flowed from His thorn-crowned brow, from the hands and feet nailed to the Cross, and from the spear-thrust in His side. It is this Blood shed on the cross of Calvary which is "the propitiation for our sins: and not for ours only, but also for the sins of the whole world" (I John 2: 2). Who can fathom the infinite depth of the words, "He hath made him to be sin for us, who knew no sin; that we might be made the righteousness of God in him" (II Cor. 5: 21)!

The ordinary word for prayer to God is *proseche* (προσεχή), and the word for a simple petition or request is *aitema* (αἴτημα). But the word used here is *deeseis* (δεήσεις), which means humble or pitiful pleadings or beggings, and for this reason is sometimes translated supplications (Phil. 4: 6). The word usually translated "supplications" is *hiketerias* (ἱκετηρίας) and is generally understood to be more formal. It is the term used when ambassadors are sent with outward tokens of entreaty. As a noun it is derived from the custom of a suppliant binding an olive branch with wool and holding it forth as a token of his character or mission. It is therefore humble or lowly pleading, and is sometimes translated "entreating." The word of "crying" is *krauges* (κραυγῆς), and the word translated "strong" is *ischuras* (ἰσχυρᾶς), which means strong, powerful, vehement, or mighty. The word for tears is *dakruon* (δακρύων).

These expressions must without doubt refer to some particular occasion, and the mind naturally turns to the Garden of Gethsemane, where the Evangelists tell us of the agony which our Lord there endured. Matthew tells us that He said, "My soul is exceeding sorrowful, even unto death" (Matt. 26: 38); Mark in addition to this tells us that He "began to be sore amazed, and to be very heavy" (Mark 14: 33-34); while Luke says that "being in an agony he prayed more earnestly: and his sweat was as it were great drops of blood falling down to the ground" (Luke 22: 44). Some have thought that the words *krauge ischura* (κραυγὴ ἰσχυρά), "loud or vehement cries," refer to the Cross, when Jesus cried out, "My God, my God, why hast thou forsaken me?" and again just before He died when He cried with a loud voice, "Father, into thy hands I commend my spirit." While the Garden scene best fits the descriptions here given, there is no reason why the writer might not have drawn from all the varied scenes during the days of His flesh, and probably intended the clause to refer to both the scenes of sorrow.

In the use of these strong terms, the supreme purpose of the writer is to describe the agony of Jesus in its full intensity. It is a picture of Jesus in the deepest depths of His humiliation. The tears start unbidden as we read of His pitiful pleadings or beggings, His humble and repeated entreaties, His loud outcries, the flood of tears that accompanied His agony of soul, and the sweat starting from His every pore, falling to the ground, as it were great drops of blood. Here in the Garden the veil is lifted a little, and we begin to see His holy being shrink with sheer dread of the curse. He saw death as penal. In a few hours He would face the Cross, and had He not read in the Scriptures, "Cursed is every one that hangeth on a tree"? Yet He was to be nailed to the tree, and thus be made a "curse for us" that He might redeem us from the curse of the law and that we might receive "the Spirit through faith" (Gal. 3:13-14). He was exquisitely alive to suffering, and His very purity in a world like this laid Him open to sources of sorrow to which we are strangers. All accordingly that we read in the Scriptures leads us to suppose that the closing scene of His life was accompanied with sufferings such as had never been before experienced in this world. Who does not feel that if no such scenes as Gethsemane were recorded for us we should be apt to suppose that in some way His divinity would have prevented Him from feeling the full agony of His burden; and would not His example of patient endurance have then been lost to us? Besides there was this peculiarity in the sufferings of Christ, that He knew beforehand every step of the rugged road He was to travel. Sufferings that develop gradually can never exert the same influence upon the mind as those which are foreseen from the first. "Need we wonder then," says Lindsay, "that the foreseen sorrows of Christ filled His soul with so great an agony?" It cannot be doubted that the nearer He approached the scene of Calvary, the more acute became His suffering, until the angelic ministration brought Him the calmness of soul with which He approached the Cross.

The writer set out to prove the second essential of the priesthood as being fulfilled in Christ—that He was taken from among men, and was in deepest sympathy with those whom He was to represent. Here has been shown that He bore the weight of the sins of the world, and in doing so, suffered such as no other in this world. He has fully sustained His position.

Unto him that was able to save him from death, and was heard in that he feared (5: 7c). Having spoken of the intense agony of Jesus, His prayers with a loud cry and tears from a heart torn with anguish, the writer now turns to the nature of His prayer and the answer it received. For what did Christ pray? What was the answer received? These are questions which have found various answers on the part of interpreters. The differences lie in the interpretation of the two main expressions, "to save him from death" and "was heard in that he feared." Concerning the former, *ek thanatou* (ἐκ θανάτου), the preposition *ek* means "out of," "egress," "unfolding," or "out from within," and is here used instead of *apo* (ἀπὸ), which means "from." Two different meanings are thus set forth: (1) to be saved from death, so as to escape it or be exempted from it; and (2) to bring out of death into a new life, or a prayer for resurrection. The second main clause is *apo tes eulabeias* (ἀπὸ τῆς εὐλαβείας), and here also the word *eulabeias* (εὐλαβείας) has two meanings. (1) It may denote godly fear or reverence; or (2) it may mean fear, dread, or terror in the face of some impending calamity. Both of these meanings are used in classical Greek and also in different versions of the Bible. The former, "godly fear," is used in the Latin Vulgate, by the Greek writers generally, and in most of the English versions, including the marginal notes of the Authorized Version. On the whole it is preferable to the latter idea of fear or dread, which through Calvin's and Beza's influence found its way into the Genevan text, the Bishops' Bible, and then into the Authorized Version of 1611. It is translated "godly fear" in both the American Revised Version (1881) and the Revised Standard Version.

It is evident that any interpretation of this text must take into account the various meanings of the two participial clauses "to save him from death" and "in that he feared." The following are some of the attempted solutions of the problems involved in this text.

1. The first solution depends upon the use of *ek* as "out of" and *eulabeias* (εὐλαβείας) as "godly fear." The prayer of Jesus, therefore, was not to be delivered from physical death, but to be delivered out of it by the Resurrection. Thus the prayer was answered, for on the third day He arose and came forth crying, "Behold, I am alive for evermore" (Rev. 1:18). This is the solution presented in Ellicott's *Commentary*, in which it is said: "The prayer, we are persuaded, was not that death might be averted, but that there might be granted deliverance out of death. This prayer was answered: His death was the beginning of His glory" (2:9).

2. The second solution, which widely differs from the preceding, is that of Lowrie (*An Explanation of Hebrews*, pp. 155-57). Here the expression "able to save him from death" is viewed as bringing in additional notions important to the text. It is not said that Christ prayed for deliverance from physical death, but that He prayed to Him that "was able to save him from death," but with the consciousness that He would not, for He was created for the suffering of death (2:9). Here *eulabeias* (εὐλαβείας) is used in the sense of fear or dread. The writer has previously spoken of Christ as being "in all points tempted like as we are, yet without sin" (4:15); now he portrays Him as undergoing that temptation which had become the lifelong fear of those He had come to save (2:14-15). The meaning is that Christ was allowed to be overwhelmed by the fear of death as were other men, sympathizing with their infirmity in that He too shared with them a human nature. Why He shrank back can be explained only by supposing that He saw in death the penalty of the curse and a conflict with all the powers of sin, even hell itself. The second part of the participial clause tells us, not only that He was heard, but also how His prayer was answered—"He was heard from his dread."

The answer then was a deliverance from that dread which had overwhelmed Him. An angel came and strengthened Him, and from that time forward He faced the closing events of His earthly life in perfect serenity, even to the Cross. Now that Christ has triumphed over death, it has ceased to be the dread of the people of God.

3. The third solution holds that Jesus prayed only with an "if," so that the real burden of His prayer was for the will of God. This view regards *eulabeias* (εὐλα-βείας) as reverent or godly fear—not the fear of death, but the fear of God, a fear which shrinks from contravening the will of God. The real prayer of Jesus therefore was, "Thy will be done," and this prayer was fully answered in His life.

4. Westcott points out that Christ's prayer was for victory over death as the fruit of sin, and that the hearing of prayer, which teaches obedience, is not so much the granting of specific petitions as the assurance that what is granted does most effectively lead toward the end. Thus Christ learned that every detail of His life and passion contributed to the work which He came to fulfill, and so He was most perfectly heard. In this sense He was heard for His godly prayer (*Hebrews*, pp. 128-29).

Though he were a Son (5: 8a). There is necessarily a close connection between this and the preceding verse; and the Son is mentioned here, not only to guard His dignity and glory, but also to enhance it. While the word "Son" is generally used of the Incarnation, it is here used of the eternal Son, or the Son as related to the Father in the Holy Trinity. This however is always implied in the use of the word Son in connection with the Incarnation. The writer, having previously stated that the Son is "the brightness of his [the Father's] glory, and the express image of his person," now portrays Him as a humble Suppliant approaching the Father with strong crying and tears. This time of humiliation does not detract from the glory of the Son, for it is seen that these sufferings are vicarious and propitiatory, and find their perfection in the death on the Cross. This

redemptive work of Christ is a new and added glory,
for in that He became obedient even unto the death on
the Cross, "God also hath highly exalted him, and given
him a name which is above every name: that at the
name of Jesus every knee should bow, of things in
heaven, and things in earth, . . . and that every tongue
should confess that Jesus Christ is Lord, to the glory of
God the Father" (Phil. 2: 8-11).

*Yet learned he obedience by the things which he suf-
fered* (5: 8b). These words in Greek are an alliteration,
emathen aph hon epathen (ἔμαθεν ἀφ᾽ ὧν ἔπαθεν), that
is, "He learned by what He suffered." The emphasis
however is to be placed on the latter term *epathen*, "He
suffered." It is not said here that He learned to obey,
for He was always obedient. Neither is it said that the
lesson of obedience was forced upon Him through suffering, for it is written of Him, "I delight to do thy will,
O my God" (Ps. 40: 8; Heb. 10: 7). It will be noted
also that the definite article is used with the word obedience, *ten hupakoen* (τὴν ὑπακοήν), which gives it the
significance of a special or completed obedience as distinguished from obedience in general. The definite article is omitted before the word Son because it is the
predicate, and in our Authorized Version the indefinite
article is substituted for it. The text may well be translated, "Though He were (the) Son, He learned obedience." Lindsay expresses the true meaning when he
says "that He acquired the actual experience of what
it means to obey in circumstances of overwhelming distress. A great work has been entrusted to Him; one
difficulty after another rose to oppose Him; unspeakable
sufferings were accumulated upon His head near the
close. His heart was overwhelmed with agony at the
prospect, but He never once wavered in His obedience
to God. With perfect resignation He met the hour and
power of darkness, and thus was His obedience tried to
the utmost; and by sore experience He learned what it
is to obey; how bitter, how trying when suffering and
death lie in the pathway of duty" (*Lectures on Hebrews*,
p. 219). We may say then that to learn the obedience

is to experience the full length and breadth of that suffering to which He as the Saviour was required to yield in
order to secure the full redemption of mankind.

And being made perfect (5:9a). This is the second
time the writer uses the expression "perfect through
sufferings." In 2:10 the word is *teleiosai* (τελειῶσαι)
and is in the aorist active with respect to the Father, who
is said to "make the captain of their salvation perfect
through sufferings." Here however the word is *teleio-
theis* (τελειωθείς) and is used passively with respect to
Christ, indicating the effect of these sufferings upon
Him. Again, in the first instance the statement is made
with reference to the symbolism of Moses, or the apostolic work of Christ. In this He identifies himself with
His people, and goes before them as a great Leader to
bring many sons to glory. Here the reference is to the
symbolism of Aaron, in which Christ as High Priest
offers himself as a Propitiation for the sins of the people.
The words "having been made perfect" (A.R.V.) cannot refer to the perfection of Christ's moral character,
for this would be inconsistent with all that has been
previously represented of Him. Neither can it refer to
His relationship with the Father, for this was inherently
and eternally perfect. Had He remained as He was in
the original glory of the Father, He never could have
become the Author of salvation nor could He have led
many sons to glory. It was His love to the Father that
constrained Him to become man, for that was the will
of the Father (John 14:31); and Christ having through
love to us also assumed our nature and entered into
our conditions of life, the way to glory for Him as well
as for us lay through sufferings, death, and resurrection.
The perfection of the God-Man must be viewed from
both the natural and the supernatural aspects.

1. From the natural or human aspect, the very
necessity of the case required that Christ be perfected,
not in reference to moral excellence, as previously indicated, but in the sense of official qualification. It was
necessary for Him as the Son of Man to offer up to God

the sacrifice of a *perfect humanity*. Let this be clearly understood, that Christ as the God-Man bought back for us, by His positive perfections and His personal excellence, all that the first Adam had lost in the Fall—and more. Throughout all the days of His flesh He met day by day the crosscurrents of a sinful world, suffered from them, and by His active obedience triumphed over them. He never swerved from the will of God, but became obedient unto death, even the death of the Cross. The struggle was most severe as He met death, but through death He overcame him that had the power of death, and "offered himself without spot to God" (9: 14). This obedience to the will of God, and perfect submission to the penalty of death by One who "knew no sin," made His offering at once vicarious and propitiatory—the ground of expiation for all sin. This perfect offering being voluntary, He was given as a reward of merit the *authority* to administer the salvation which He had procured by His own shed blood; and by His obedience through suffering, He had acquired that *sympathy* necessary to enter fully into the needs of those whom He would save through faith in His vicarious sacrifice. These three things—the *perfected human nature* as a vicarious sacrifice; the *authority* conferred upon Him to administer this salvation as a reward for His voluntary and perfect offering; and the *sympathy*, or capacity to understand by actual human experience those whom He would save—all these had to be acquired by the God-Man, for they did not belong to Him as the eternal Son of God. Herein lies the intense significance of the perfected human nature of Christ as the ground of His mediatorial and priestly work.

2. From the supernatural or divine aspect, the words "having been made perfect" indicate a state or condition transcending that which existed "in the days of his flesh." During His earthly life, Christ was a Partaker of human nature under the effects of sin; and although himself without sin, still it is said that He was made "in the likeness of sinful flesh." The human nature which He had assumed had not as yet been brought to

the perfection for which it was divinely created. Likewise He himself had not reached the destined end for which He had come into the world. Both of these came to their ultimate perfection only when Christ was raised from the dead, assumed a glorified body, ascended into the heavenly sanctuary, and was seated at the right hand of God. He was the First Fruits of our humanity, perfected, exalted, and glorified. In Him our human nature passed from under the curse; in Him it was exalted to the throne of God. Human nature having been perfected in the God-Man, He became the Author of eternal salvation; and from His exalted position on the throne He communicates this heavenly life, and secures obedience for His people in a priestly form, that is, the obedience of faith.

This new humanity in Christ, the God-Man, is called by St. Paul the "new man," and is the nexus of the new and redeemed race, as the "old man" is the nexus of the sinful and depraved race. From the God-Man there flow two streams in His great redemptive work: the new and redeemed humanity, and the Spirit which dwelt in Him "without measure." These are combined in the new life which Christ imparts to them that obey Him, but this life can come to its fullness only when the old self-life is crucified, that Christ may be All in All. Hence we are exhorted to "put off the old man" and to "put on the new man, which after God is created in righteousness and true holiness" (Eph. 4: 24).

Eternal Salvation

The words "eternal salvation" are used by the writer to denote the fourth phase of full salvation as set forth under the provisions of the new covenant. This salvation in Christ is called "eternal" in contrast with the priestly work of Aaron, who was required to make an atonement for sin every year. The ancient Jewish sacrifices could not remove moral defilement or "take away" sin, and therefore could not secure eternal salvation. But Christ's offering was of eternal validity, securing

an eternal deliverance from all sin for those who walk
in obedience to divine light and truth.

He became the author of eternal salvation (5:9b).
The perfected High Priest became the Author of salvation, thus accomplishing through having been perfected
that which without that perfection He could never
otherwise have accomplished. Here again the several
words of this text take on great significance. He "became" *egeneto* (ἐγένετο), not "becomes," for from the
divine side the propitiatory work of Christ had been fully
completed, and for this reason we speak of it as a "finished atonement." The word *aitios* (αἴτιος) does not
occur elsewhere in the New Testament. The word translated "author" (12:2) is identical with the word translated "captain" in 2:10 and is not the same word used
here. As the Author of our salvation, Christ is in the
fullest sense our Saviour in that He has provided it by
His propitiatory offering and administers it through the
Holy Spirit. The word *aioniou* (αἰωνίου) is made emphatic in this sentence; and the word *pasin* (πᾶσιν),
"all," includes all of those, whether Jew or gentile, who,
having been saved by faith, enter into a life of obedience
to Christ.

Them that obey him (5:9c). By our insistence upon
salvation by faith alone we must not be betrayed into
the error of thinking that faith supplants obedience.
Rather it is its source and spring; for that which does not
lead to obedience is not faith but presumption. The
word *hupakouousin* (ὑπακούουσιν) is here used in the
sense of the "obedience of faith." "This is the work of
God, that ye believe on him whom he hath sent" (John
6:29). Salvation is all of grace. There are preliminary
stages wrought by the Spirit in awakening, conviction,
and repentance (John 16:8-11), but these must be
regarded as the conditions of faith. Grace operates only
on the plane of human helplessness. Man must be
stripped of his self-righteousness before he can receive
the righteousness which is of faith; he must let go of all
self-trust before he can trust solely in Christ. While

these preliminary stages of surrender may in some sense
be termed obedience, they are not the obedience of a
Christian. Conversion or the "new birth" alone marks
the beginning of the Christian life, and therefore the
beginning of true obedience.

We must bear in mind, also, that the writer is addressing Christian Jews; they have been converted but
have not yet entered into the full provisions of the new
covenant. In speaking of Christ being perfected, it
appears to be his purpose to prepare their minds for
the later injunction that they too must "go on unto
perfection." The sin problem is not entirely settled at
conversion, for inbred sin is not removed, though it
does not reign. This is the Christian's sin problem, and
multitudes of believers still struggle with it. The full
Christian life does not begin until the entire sin question
is settled; for those who are Christ's under the provisions
of the new covenant have not only put off the works of
the flesh in conversion, but have likewise crucified the
flesh itself as the source of all inordinate affections and
desires. In conversion the power of sin is broken; in the
full sanctification of the believer "the sin" itself with
its inner contradictions is removed by the cleansing
blood of Jesus (Gal. 5: 24; I John 1: 7, 9).

As the obedience of Christ led to death, the death
on the Cross, so also our obedience to Him must lead
to death, the death of the carnal self-life. We are to be
crucified with Christ. Our hands are to be so nailed to
the cross that they do only the will of Christ, our Lord;
our feet so nailed that they no longer walk in our own
ways; our brow so thorn-crowned that it will bow in
humiliation before the boasts of reason; and our hearts
so pierced by the Spirit that nothing will flow out from
them but life and love to Christ and a dying world.

St. Paul uses another illustration closely related to
the idea of crucifixion mentioned here. He says, "For if
we have been planted together in the likeness of his
death, we shall be also in the likeness of his resurrection" (Rom. 6: 5). Now it is evident that the word
resurrection as used here no more refers to the future

resurrection of the body than the being planted in death refers to the death of the physical body. It means death to the carnal mind or the self-life and a resurrection into holiness of heart and life. As the Father gave the Son to the world for its redemption by the blood of the Cross, so also Christ gave himself to the Church for its sanctification and cleansing (Eph. 5: 26-27). And as faith in Christ secures for us the redemption wrought out on earth, so faith in the promised gift of the Holy Spirit secures for us this salvation as perfected in heaven. As the one is received by faith, so also is the other.

THE FOURTH WARNING: AGAINST INDIFFERENCE

The fourth warning is a humiliating rebuke for the dullness of hearing found among the Hebrew Christians. The word translated "dull" is *nothroi* (νωθροί) and is the same word translated "slothful" in 6: 12. The general meaning of the word is "sluggish" and occurs only in these two places in the New Testament. It may be said that the word *nothroi* as used here applies only to a failure to grasp the deeper and more significant truths of Christianity, while in 6: 12 it is a warning against the failure to act upon known truths. The former is concerned with the understanding only; the latter, with the activities of life. This distinction is important.

The Warning Is Addressed to Christians. That those addressed were Christians is evidenced by the fact that they had the faculty of hearing, though dulled by lack of attention; they were infants and therefore capable of growth; they could walk but had made no perceptible progress. In the following chapter they are called the "beloved," and are praised for enduring a great fight of affliction and taking joyfully the spoiling of their goods. They were under the temptation of returning to the externalities of Judaism and needed steadfastness in maintaining the faith. That they were the possessors of spiritual life there can be no doubt, for the writer would not exhort sinners to steadfastness. Rightly interpreted, these words are a rebuke to the sluggishness of the Hebrew Christians.

Why Was This Warning Necessary? The writer had just spoken of Christ as a High Priest, and in doing so had strengthened his expression by the use of the aorist participle, "greeted or designated," of God, as "an high priest after the order of Melchisedec." This new order, far more than that of Aaron, reflects both the greatness and the endlessness of Christ's high priesthood. The significance of this great truth the Jews had overlooked, its depth and mysteriousness lying, not in Melchisedec, but in Christ, whom he foreshadowed. As a type this order was established in Abraham's day, and it was its perfect fulfillment in Christ that constituted Him the Author of eternal salvation. Concerning this the writer says, There is much that "ought to be said," or more literally, "concerning which we should have much discussion," but "hard to be uttered, seeing ye are dull of hearing" (5: 11).

Babes or Teachers? "For when for the time ye ought to be teachers, ye have need that one teach you again which be the first principles of the oracles of God; and are become such as have need of milk, and not of strong meat" (5: 12). The writer upbraids his readers with sluggishness of mind of which they should be ashamed. He is saying, "Look at yourselves; although you have been Christians for a long time, you are yet but babes, who still need milk and cannot be fed with solid food; and even this light diet must be given you by others!"

Several Greek words are of interest here. The word *chronon* (χρόνον) is a word for time in its extension or length. Whether Palestinian Jews or those of the Dispersion, they must have known the Old Testament Scriptures, which furnish the background for Christian interpretation. The word *gegonate* (γεγόνατε), "have become," used in verses 5: 11 and 5: 12, indicates that they had been alert to the truth at one time but had fallen into sluggishness of mind; and that their present infantile condition was due to degeneracy, from a failure to press on into the fullness of the blessing of Christ (6: 1).

The word *logion* (λογίων) meant at first merely "sayings," then "oracular sayings," and finally "divine
revelation." The word *stoicheia* (στοιχεῖα) means "elements," or "rudiments," here translated "principles."
As used here, the word refers to the simplest elements of
which a thing consists, and is frequently compared to
the alphabet as the first principles of language.

There is another word of importance here, in that it
relates the Christian teaching to the Old Testament.
The word is *arches* (ἀρχῆς) or "the beginning," here
translated "first." The beginnings of the rudiments of
Christianity are found in the Scriptures of the Old Testament. It is not that the Hebrews were unfamiliar with
the symbolism of the Old Testament, but they had not
been able to interpret these symbols as the "principles
of the doctrine of Christ" (6:1). They had not seen that
the insistence of the Jewish Scriptures on repentance
and faith were the beginnings of the Christian doctrine
of the actual forgiveness of sins, or of justification by
faith. They knew of the washings and laying on of hands,
but they had not seen that these washings were to be
fulfilled in actual Christian purity, without and within;
and that the "laying on of hands" indicated the divine
element, the impartation of life and purity through the
Spirit. Then too, it is clear that the Judaism of Christ's
time held to a resurrection of the dead as shown by their
own teachings and the miracles of Christ, and nothing
is clearer than that they believed in the judgment of the
last day.

Inexperienced in the Word of Righteousness. "For
every one that useth milk is unskilful in the word of
righteousness: for he is a babe" (5:13). The writer
uses the inverse form in order to emphasize the fact
that one who has advanced no further than a milk
diet is yet a babe. As such he is "unskilful," *apeiros*
(ἄπειρος), or "inexperienced," and at best can speak
only of childish things (I Cor. 13:11). To this state the
Hebrew Christians had brought themselves. Using their
spiritual senses less and less, their development had
become so arrested as to make them unable to discrimi-

nate between the good and the evil. They were therefore unprepared for the great truths which the writer was about to present to them.

The expression *logou dikaiosunes* (λόγου δικαιοσύνης) or the "word of righteousness" has been the source of various interpretations. Lenski holds that the word "righteousness" as used here is adjectival, and therefore means only that, as babes, the Hebrew Christians were insufficiently advanced to enter into any "right" or proper discussion. The majority of commentators, however, appear to hold that the word is a genitive and refers to the righteousness which Christ imparts through faith. Westcott seems to take somewhat of a middle position in that he regards the word righteousness here as not containing the full Christian doctrine (II Cor. 3: 9), but does indicate that Christ is the Source of righteousness and the Means by which men partake of it. Ebrard puts the matter strongly and applies it to the Hebrew Christians. He says that the train of thought is this: "You still need milk; strong meat does not agree with you. For whosoever (like you) has not yet apprehended even the fundamental doctrine of righteousness in Christ (whosoever still makes his salvation to rest on the services and sacrifices of the temple), needs as yet milk, being yet a *babe*, and standing still at the first elements of Christian knowledge."

The distinguishing between the καλόν and κακόν does not, as some strangely suppose, belong to the *strong meat;* but the habit already acquired of distinguishing the true from the false, is rather the immediate fruit of the right understanding "word of righteousness," and forms, together with the latter, the indispensable *condition* which must be fulfilled ere *strong meat* can be once thought of. He who has taken the milk of the Gospel, i.e., the fundamental doctrine of justification . . . so that he can spontaneously, and by immediate feeling, consequently without requiring any previous long reflection or reasoning, distinguish the right from the wrong, the way in which the Christian has to walk from the Jewish by-paths, the evangelic truth from the Pharisaic righteousness of the law, so that he could, as it were, find out the right path though asleep—he who has so thoroughly seized and digested these elements, that he no longer needs to be instructed in them (the milk), consequently is no longer νήπιος, but τέλειος—may now have the strong meat offered to him—the difficult doctrines of the higher typology of the old covenant, and of the eternal Melchisedec-nature of the New Testament high priest.—EBRARD, *Biblical Commentary on the Epistle to the Hebrews.* p. 194.

Strong Meat for the Perfect. "But strong meat belongeth to them that are of full age, even those who by reason of use have their senses exercised to discern both good and evil" (5:14). The word translated "full age" is *teleion* (τελείων) or "perfect," and is so translated in Phil. 3:15. It appears that the writer introduces this term in order to prepare the minds of his readers for the further discussion of the term "perfection" in the next chapter, where the same root word occurs in the opening sentence, "Let us go on unto perfection." We may say, then, that the writer does not intend to use the milk of the Word in dealing with the Hebrew Christians; but neither does he intend to furnish them with "solid food." His intention is to lead them from a state of infancy to that of the *teleion* or "perfect," here translated "full age [growth]." In spiritual things time is not essential, as it is in nature, for this transition to maturity; for as we shall later show, this relative maturity consists in the wholehearted devotion of a believer brought by divine grace into the full provisions of the new covenant in Christ.

The participial clause is evidently intended to explain the condition of the *teleion* or the "perfect." The word for "use" is *hexin* (ἕξιν), sometimes translated "habit" but not necessarily in the narrow use of the term. The word is from Aristotelian phraseology and signifies a given natural condition or *habitus*. Lenski therefore translates this clause, "those who by reason of their condition have their senses trained (or exercised) for discrimination of both what is excellent and what is bad." Mr. Wesley says that "habit here signifies strength of spiritual understanding, arising from maturity or spiritual age. By, or in consequence of, this habit they exercise themselves in these things with ease, readiness, cheerfulness and profit." The real meaning of the text, therefore, appears to be almost the opposite of the impression made in reading the Authorized Version. The level of the *teleion* (τελείων) or "perfect" is not reached by human effort but by faith in Jesus Christ; and from this spiritual condition the senses, *aistheteria* (αἰσθητήρια), or "organs of sense" are exercised freely and easily in discriminating between good and evil. This position is confirmed by St. John, who says that "the anointing which ye have received of him abideth in you, and ye need not that any man teach you" (I John 2: 27); that is, the indwelling Spirit first furnishes a touchstone for the discernment of truth and then serves as a Guide into all truth. The *teleion* therefore are those filled with the Spirit, and from this inner spiritual condition there flow both discernment and progress.

CHAPTER VI

CHRISTIAN PERFECTION

We come now to the fourth term which our author uses to characterize the spiritual experience attainable under the new covenant. This is commonly known as Christian perfection, and accompanying it is a warning against slothfulness. The writer has just reproved the Hebrew Christians for their lack of progress in spiritual things. That they had been "illuminated," had "endured a great fight of affliction," and had been made a "gazingstock" (10:32-33) is sufficient evidence of their conversion, but they had not gone on to perfection. They were still babes, feeding on the milk of the Word, and had not come to the full stature of Christian maturity. They had in some sense even lost their enthusiasm for the first principles of the oracles of God. This may be interpreted as a failure to properly interpret the symbolical meaning of Judaism. These Christians therefore were in danger of returning to its externalism instead of advancing to the spiritual standards of the new covenant in Christ.

THE PRINCIPLES OF THE DOCTRINE OF CHRIST

The writer, having exhorted his readers to leave the first principles of the doctrine (λόγον), or "word," of Christ and go on unto perfection, first pauses to enumerate those principles upon which this perfection rests. He states them as follows: "Not laying again the foundation of repentance from dead works, and of faith toward God, of the doctrine of baptisms, and of laying on of hands, and of resurrection of the dead, and of eternal judgment" (6:1b-2). These principles are summed up under three main heads, represented by three important Greek terms: (1) metanoias (μετανοίας), "repentance"; (2) pisteos (πίστεως), "faith"; and (3) didaches

($\delta\iota\delta\alpha\chi\hat{\eta}s$), "doctrine" or "teachings." These words are
all in the genitive case, and <u>under the latter, four other</u>
<u>genitives are classified</u>: "of the doctrine of baptisms,"
"of laying on of hands," "of resurrection of the dead,"
and "of eternal judgment." It will be noted that it is
the teachings that attach to such symbols as baptism
and the laying on of hands that give them their value;
while the resurrection and the judgment, being future,
are those things in which the Church finds its consummation, and therefore furnish the object of the Christian's hope. The writer, in enumerating these principles,
places them in three related pairs:

1. "Repentance from dead works, and of faith toward God";
2. "The doctrine of baptisms, and of laying on of
   hands"; and
3. The teachings concerning the "resurrection of
   the dead, and of eternal judgment."

The first pair, repentance and faith, may be regarded
as purely personal. Neither of these is mentioned under
the head of doctrine or instruction. <u>Repentance is the</u>
<u>personal act of turning away from sin, while faith</u>
<u>toward God brings forgiveness or justification.</u> <u>Repent-</u>
<u>ance must be regarded as a condition of faith</u>, for justifi-
cation is solely by faith. The expression "dead works"
occurs again in 9:14, and signifies works apart from
the living God and therefore in the sphere of death.
It is evident, however, that in this instance the reference
is to the Jews and their lifeless ceremonies. From these
the Hebrew Christians must turn away by repentance
in order to have salvation by faith in Christ.

The second pair, baptism (plural, baptisms) and the
laying on of hands, <u>have reference to the public con-</u>
<u>fession of faith</u> and are therefore ecclesiastical in nature.
The historical sequence is followed, <u>for salvation through</u>
<u>repentance and faith must be publicly confessed in the</u>
<u>Church</u>. The <u>laying on of hands in the apostolic age</u>
<u>was a symbol of the bestowal of the Holy Spirit</u>, and

later came to be used in the ordination of elders. It
was however but a symbol, for the Spirit was never
communicated from one individual to another. The
laying on of hands simply marked the candidate as the
object for whom earnest prayer was made.

The third pair, resurrection from the dead and
eternal judgment, are eschatological in nature and have
to do with the believer's outlook on life. The resurrection marks the continuance of the Christian's individual
life in a new and eternal order; while the judgment,
which is eternal, marks the permanence of that order.

Without the knowledge of these foundation truths,
one could scarcely be called a Christian. They are essential at once to a knowledge of God and to the spiritual
experience of the individual. It will be noted also that
these truths span the whole of the Christian life, from
the first scene of repentance and faith to the final scene
of the resurrection and the judgment. Further still,
these foundation principles mark the two stages in the
redemptive work of Christ. Repentance, baptism, and
resurrection belong to Christ under the symbol of Aaron,
the priest of death and atonement; while faith which
brings salvation, the laying on of hands, symbol of the
reception of the Holy Spirit with His gifts and powers,
and the judgment, which is eternal and unchangeable,
belong to Christ under the symbol of Melchisedec, the
priest of life. The former were accomplished through
the earthly ministry of Christ, the incarnate Son being
the Gift of the Father to the world; the latter were accomplished by Christ through the Holy Spirit, and administered from the throne in the heavens. It is to this
profound truth of the Melchisedec priesthood of Christ
and the life of the Spirit that the writer is now about
to direct the attention of his readers.

THE NATURE OF THE PERFECTION TO BE ATTAINED

*Christian Perfection as the Standard of New Testa-
ment Experience.* "Therefore leaving the principles of
the doctrine of Christ, let us go on unto perfection"

(6: 1a). "And this will we do, if God permit" (6: 3). The subject of Christian perfection has been the source of much controversy in the Church. A critical study of this text, therefore, becomes necessary; and on the ground of this exposition, the theological concept of the doctrine and the experience will later be presented. The word *Dio* (Διὸ) may be translated either as "therefore" or "wherefore," and links this verse with the exhortation of the previous chapter which sets forth the shamefulness of the lack of spiritual progress among the Hebrew Christians. The word "leaving," *aphentes* (ἀφέντες), is sometimes translated "having left." The word means a "letting go," not in the sense of discarding, but of taking for granted—a presupposition from which to rise to higher attainments.

The words, "Let us go on," are better translated, "Let us be borne or carried on," for the word *pherometha* (φερώμεθα) is in the passive as denoting the effect. To "be borne or carried on" does not exclude the active use of means. The origin of the term is that of a ship under full sail before the wind. Westcott speaks of it as "a personal surrender to an active power, the power is working, we have only to surrender ourselves to it." The words are very emphatic. All negligence and slothfulness is to be put aside, and the Christians are to be borne on with the full bent of their minds to the goal. The word *epi* (ἐπι) is interesting in that it means to "go on unto" or until arriving at the goal. Put in terse words, the writer is saying, "Now on to perfection!"

Dr. Whedon says, "When Hebrews 6:1 is adduced as an exhortation to advancing to a perfected Christian character, it is no misquotation. It is in the noun form of the Greek adjective rendered full age in chapter 5:14, and signifies adulthood." "The original," says Dr. Adam Clarke, "is very emphatic. Let us be carried on to this perfection. God is ever ready by the power of His Spirit, to carry us forward to every degree of life, light, and love necessary to prepare us for an eternal weight of glory. There can be little difficulty in attaining the end of our faith, the salvation of our souls from all sin, if God carry us forward to it, and this He will do in His own way and on His own terms. Many make a violent outcry against the doctrine of perfection, i.e., against the heart being cleansed from all sin in this life, and filled with love to God and man, because they judge it to be impossible. Is it too much to say of these, that they know neither the Scripture nor the power of God?"

The words "if God permit", cannot be made to suggest that God would forbid a duty that He has enjoined. Rather the words mean, "With God's help," that is, by His Spirit and His guiding providences.

Scriptural Terms Used for Perfection. The word for perfection as here used is *teleioteta* (τελειότητα) and occurs only here and in Col. 3:14, where it is translated "perfectness." The verb *teleioo* (τελειόω) means to perfect in the sense of finishing or completing, and applies solely to the subject under discussion. Thus if a person sets out on a journey to a particular city and reaches his destination, he is said to have completed or perfected his journey. St. Paul uses the term in this sense, but with two widely different objectives in view. He speaks of a resurrection perfection and says, "Not as though I had already attained, either were already perfect" (Phil. 3:12). Here the word is *teteleiomai* (τετελείωμαι). Since resurrection perfection cannot be attained until the time of the resurrection, it is evident that he was not perfected in this sense. However, in verse 15 of the same chapter he speaks of another perfection, using the word *teleioi* (τέλειοι), saying, "Let us therefore, as many as be perfect, be thus minded" (Phil. 3:15). Here he is speaking of Christian adulthood and that stability of character and purpose which holds him steady in his desire to attain the more remote perfection found only in the resurrection of the redeemed. The word *teleiois* (τελείοις) or "perfect" is used by St. Paul in a similar sense of adulthood when he says, "We speak wisdom among them that are perfect" (I Cor. 2:6). Christian perfection therefore means the attainment of the goal of adulthood as it is recognized in the present gospel dispensation. In a spiritual sense this does not so much involve the element of time as the entering into the fullness of the new covenant provided through the blood of Jesus and administered by the baptism with the Holy Spirit. Adulthood thus has not only a chronological but also a legal aspect; it is accomplished, not by growth alone, but by a divine pronouncement.

There is another word translated "perfect" which
must be given brief attention before going on to a consideration of the legal aspect of the term. This New
Testament word is *katarisai* (καταρίσαι), from the verb
kat-artizo (κατ-αρτίζω), which means to perfect in the
sense of "to equip" or "to prepare." The same word is
found in Heb. 13:21, "make you perfect in every good
work"; I Thess. 3:10, "perfect that which is lacking in
your faith"; and I Pet. 5:10, "make you perfect, stablish,
strengthen, settle you." In the sense of "prepare" the
same root word is found in Heb. 10:5, "a body hast
thou prepared me"; and again in II Tim. 3:17, "that
the man of God may be perfect, throughly furnished
unto all good works." The corporate aspect of the term
is emphasized in I Cor. 1:10, "be perfectly joined together in the same mind." It will be seen then that,
while *teleioteta* emphasizes the character aspect or perfection of heart, the word *katarisai* must be viewed from
the functional and corporate aspect. However there is a
close relation between the two terms, for it is "befitting"
that those who have been made perfect in heart by the
Holy Spirit should likewise by that same Spirit be perfectly joined together in the Church, and made "perfect
in every good work to do his will," the Holy Spirit
"working in you that which is well pleasing in his sight,
through Jesus Christ."

The Legal Aspect of Christian Perfection. By Christian perfection we mean spiritual adulthood, or that
maturity of experience which the writer sets over against
infancy or babes in Christ (5:12-14). In the natural
realm, growth and development are so closely associated with maturity that the legal aspect of it is often
overlooked. As the Roman Catholics have confused the
doctrines of justification and sanctification, so also the
reformers have in general confused the doctrines of regeneration and sanctification. Regeneration or the new
birth is the impartation of life to a soul dead in trespasses
and sins; sanctification is a cleansing from that which
would hinder the development of the new life in the

soul. Growth is a factor of spiritual as well as natural life. But when may a growing person be said to be mature? To determine when one has arrived or is supposed to have arrived at this state of adulthood, the laws of our states in general set the age at twenty-one years. Previous to this time one is a minor, for whom others must be responsible; having reached this age, he is said to have attained his majority, and in the eyes of the law has become an adult, with full rights of a citizen, responsible for himself and his own actions. Adulthood in this particular sense is not a matter of growth but of legal enactment.

Christian perfection also has its legal aspect; it is the entering into a covenant with God. This aspect is set forth by St. Paul in the Epistle to the Galatians. Here he speaks of a son as being an heir and yet not having entered in upon his inheritance. Although a son, he is still under tutors and governors until the time appointed of the father (Gal. 4: 1-3). In a spiritual sense, the time appointed of the Father for those who have been born again is the moment of the baptism with the Holy Spirit, by which they are inducted into the fullness of the new covenant. Then it is that they attain their majority or spiritual adulthood. Their hearts being purified from sin, they now act solely from the initiative of divine love; and the law of God being written in their hearts, they serve Him with supreme devotion.

Andrew Murray in his *Holiest of All* says that "manhood, or the full-grown, mature, perfect man, does not as in nature come with years, but consists in the wholeheartedness with which the believer yields himself to be all for God. It is the perfect heart that makes the perfect man. The twenty years needed for a child to become a full grown man are no rule in the kingdom of heaven. There is indeed a riper maturity and mellowness which comes with the experience of years. But even a young Christian can be of the perfect, of whom our Epistle speaks, with a heart all athirst for the deeper and more spiritual truth it is to teach, and a will that has indeed finally broken with sin, and counted all things but loss for the perfect knowledge of Christ Jesus" (p. 199).

The Characteristics of Christian Perfection. The term "perfection" received new emphasis in the teaching of Mr. Wesley, who adopted it because he found it to be a scriptural term, and deemed St. Paul and St. John sufficient authorities for its use. The word and its relatives occur 138 times in the Scriptures, and in at least 50 instances refer to Christian character under the operation of divine grace. The term must be regarded as more specific than the word holiness, which is more general and comprehensive, and refers to salvation from sin and the possession of the moral image of God. Since this "perfection" has been a controversial subject, we give in the following paragraphs what we believe to be the teachings of the Epistle on this important subject.

1. Christian Perfection Is Subsequent to Regeneration. "Therefore leaving the principles of the doctrine of Christ, let us go on unto perfection" (6:1a). We have seen that the redemptive process is twofold because sin is twofold. (1) It is an act which requires forgiveness, and (2) it is a state or condition of the heart known

The attempt has been made to prove that the words "go on unto perfection" do not mean the entering into a deeper spiritual experience in the things of God, but merely the advancing from elementary truths of Christ to those which are deeper and more profound. Ebrard gives one of the most convincing arguments against the latter position. He says: "There are many who do not regard *pherometha* (φερώμεθα) as the *insinuative* first person plural, and the whole passage hortatory, but understand the first person plural as *communicative*, and the whole as an *intimation* on the part of the author that he now intends to pass to a consideration of strong meat." To this latter position he offers the following objections: "(1) The word *Dio* (Διὸ) connects this passage with 5:12-14. How from the fact that the readers, could as yet bear no strong meat, but needed the milk of the elements, could the author with any appearance of reason draw the inference; 'Therefore let us lay aside these elements and proceed to the more difficult doctrines'? (2) That interpretation itself leads *ad absurdum*, for according to it *teleiotes* (τελειότης) must be taken in a completely different sense from *teleios* (τέλειος). In 5:14 τέλειος denoted the subjective state of those who are exercised in the word of righteousness, and in the discerning between good and evil, in order to be able to understand which is more difficult. In 6:1 *teleiotes* (τελειότης) is suddenly made to denote the *objective* difficult doctrinal statements respecting the similarity between the priesthood of Melchisedec and Christ."—EBRARD, *Commentary on the Epistle to the Hebrews*, pp. 194-95.

as inbred sin or inherited depravity, which can be removed only by cleansing. As God gave His only Son to the world for its redemption (John 3: 16), so Christ gave himself to the Church, that through the Holy Spirit "he might sanctify and cleanse it with the washing of water by the word" (Eph. 5: 25-27). And as Christ, the Gift of God, is received by faith, so the Holy Spirit, the Gift of the risen and glorified Christ, is likewise received by faith. It is for this reason that we speak of Christian perfection as "a second blessing, properly so-called."

2. Christian Perfection Does Not Preclude Further Growth. It is ushered in by Christ's baptism with the Holy Spirit, which purifies the heart (Acts 15: 9) and fills it with divine love (Rom. 5: 5). Mr. Wesley states the scriptural position admirably when he says: "Both my brother and I maintain, that Christian Perfection is that love of God and our neighbor which implies deliverance from all sin. . . . It is the loving God with all our

It is not only those of the Wesleyan tradition who hold to a work of grace subsequent to regeneration. Dr. A. J. Gordon, a Baptist preacher and writer of outstanding ability, in his work entitled *The Twofold Life,* says: "The Scriptures seem to teach that there is a second stage in spiritual development, distinct and separate from conversion, sometimes widely separated from it, and sometimes almost contemporaneous with it,—a stage to which we rise by a special renewal of the Holy Ghost, and not by the process of gradual growth. . . . There is a transaction described in the New Testament by the terms, the gift of the Holy Ghost, the sealing of the Spirit, the anointing of the Holy Spirit, and the like. The allusions to it in the Acts and Epistles mark it unmistakably as something different from conversion." Dr. Gordon further says that he came to this conclusion after a "fresh study of the Acts of the Apostles, and from the conviction begotten by such study, that there is more light to break out of that book than we have yet imprisoned in our creeds."— A. J. Gordon, *The Twofold Life,* p. 12.

Andrew Murray, who differs in many points from Wesleyan theology, has through his deep devotional spirit come to a recognition of the need of an experience beyond that of regeneration. He says: "I cannot with too much earnestness urge every Christian reader to learn well the two stages of the Christian. There are the carnal and there are the spiritual; there are those who remain babes, and those who are full-grown men. There are those who come up out of Egypt, but then remain in the wilderness of a worldly life; there are those who follow the Lord fully, and enter the life of rest and victory."

Rev. John McNeil says: "This being filled with the Spirit is a definite blessing, quite distinct from being born of the Spirit. . . . to have the Spirit, and to be filled with the Spirit are two different things."

heart, mind, soul and strength. This implies that no wrong temper, none contrary to love, remains in the soul; and that all the words, thoughts and actions are governed by pure love" (*Works*, VI, 500). This love not only becomes the compelling motive of life, and the fulfillment of the law (II Cor. 5:14), but is susceptible to eternal increase and all the fruits of the Spirit. This state in which perfect love rules the heart, the Scriptures call spiritual adulthood or Christian perfection. As previously indicated, the word *teleioteta* (τελειότητα) is also found in Col. 3:14. Here love is called the "bond of perfectness." This means that love not only brings all the individual graces or virtues to their perfection, but that it then binds all these separate factors into a united whole, so that love in its very nature has assigned to it all the collective virtues, which it wears as an upper garment. "He is then fit to mingle in the society of archangels," says Dr. Daniel Steele, "and in this court dress to be presented to King Jesus Himself."

3. **Christian Perfection and Degrees of Maturity.** We have seen that love is capable of infinite increase. Here we return to the aspect of growth and development. The life imparted in regeneration is a holy life and embraces all the graces of the Spirit. When through the purifying act of the Holy Spirit the inner contradictions and obstacles to growth, or whatever hinders the increase of love, are cleansed away, the spiritual life expands more rapidly. This is the meaning of Jesus when He said, "Every branch that beareth fruit, he purgeth it, that it may bring forth more fruit" (John 15:2b). Hence St. John tells us that in this experience of Christian perfection there are little children, young men, and fathers. Little children are those who have recently entered the experience but have not yet become estab-

---

John Fletcher defines Christian perfection as follows: "The pure love of God shed abroad in the heart by the Holy Ghost given unto us, to cleanse us and keep us clean from all filthiness of flesh and spirit, and to enable us to fulfil the law of Christ, according to the talents we are entrusted with, and the circumstances in which we are placed in the world."

lished in grace; young men are those who have so pro-
gressed in the knowledge of God as to overcome the evil
one in the battles of life; while only those who have
gone through the mellowing, enriching experience of
the years are entitled to be called fathers in spiritual
things. Christian perfection is an experience which
may be immediately entered by faith, but maturity
comes only with the enrichment of the years.

4. Christian Perfection Does Not Remove Natural
Infirmities. A sharp distinction must be made between
sin and infirmity. Christ never took upon Him our sins
in the sense of himself becoming a sinner, for He was
"separate from sinners"; but He did assume our weaknesses and infirmities and was himself crucified through
weakness. This distinction is based upon a difference
between sin and its consequences. Sin, whether in act
or in state, is removed in this present life by the all-
atoning blood of Jesus; but the consequences of sin
manifest in weakness and infirmity will be removed only
at the time of the resurrection. Here we may find Christian perfection, which is love out of a pure heart; but
in the resurrection perfection the redeemed enter into
glory and are made like the glorified Christ. To call
innocent mistakes in judgment, lapses of memory, and
a lack of understanding due to weakened human powers
sin is to open the floodgates to all kinds of actual sin.

5. Christian Perfection Does Not Supersede the
Need for Atonement. After one is brought under the
atoning blood of Christ by a crisis experience which
cleanses from all sin, that same atoning Blood sustains
a state of cleanness in the soul of him who walks in the
light. We see therefore at once a crisis of cleansing and
a continued state of purity. Thus in I John 1: 7 we have
the word *katharizei* (καθαρίζει), which, being in the
present tense, means to cleanse and keep cleansed, as a
present experience, all who "walk in the light," while in
the same chapter (I John 1: 9) we have the words *aphei*
(ἀφῇ), "forgive," and *katharisei* (καθαρίσῃ), "cleanse,"
both of which are aorists and denote definite acts in the

past. Mr. Fletcher says: "To say that the doctrine of
Christian Perfection supersedes the need of Christ's
blood, is not less absurd than to assert that the perfection
of navigation renders the great deep a useless reservoir
of water" (*Last Check*, p. 574).

THE FIFTH WARNING
AGAINST SLOTHFULNESS AND THE DANGER OF APOSTASY

The second division of this chapter (6:4-12) opens
with one of the most debatable passages in the entire
Epistle. It reads, "For it is impossible for those who
were once enlightened, and have tasted of the heavenly
gift, and were made partakers of the Holy Ghost, and
have tasted the good word of God, and the powers of the
world to come, if they shall fall away, to renew them
again unto repentance; seeing they crucify to themselves the Son of God afresh, and put him to an open
shame" (6:4-6). This passage is related and in some
sense a continuation of that found in 5:11-14, and cul-
minates in the warning against slothfulness and lack of
progress in spiritual things (6:10-11). In order to point
out the dangers of slothfulness, the author reviews the
whole scope of Christian experience, from the first dawning of spiritual light to the experiencing of the powers of
the world to come. Thus he not only rebukes slothfulness in going on to Christian perfection, but also, with
the preparation which this experience brings, in failing
to press on to the glory of the resurrection perfection,
wherein we shall see and be like the glorified Christ.

In a series of chapel talks extending over a period of
weeks, Dr. Phineas F. Bresee used these verses as a
basis for his expository and doctrinal studies. He made
it clear that they not only reveal Christian perfection
as the normal standard of spiritual experience, but also
the high level of living which should characterize holy
men and women. The following is a brief summary of
his positions concerning this controversial passage, positions which our later studies fully sustain.

(1) *Enlightenment and Awakening.* This he regarded as the prevenient work of the Spirit, given unconditionally to all men as a result of the universal atonement.

(2) *"Tasted of the Heavenly Gift."* This is the gift of eternal life. The Scriptures are plain here. This is regeneration, or what we commonly call conversion.

(3) *"Made Partakers of the Holy Ghost."* This is the coming of the Spirit as a Comforter in His sanctifying power.

(4) *"Tasted the Good Word of God."* "The good word of God" has reference to the fullness of life resulting from the cleansing of the heart from all sin. It is the life of holiness resulting from the act of sanctification.

(5) *"The Powers of the World to Come."* These powers refer to the manifestations of the Spirit in answer to obedient faith. The preceding has reference to the nature or character of the life; this, to the activities of that life.

(6) *The Danger of Apostasy.* When those who have made such advances in grace as are mentioned in the five preceding propositions turn away from God, it becomes impossible to renew them to repentance—and for this reason: "they crucify . . . the Son of God afresh, and put him to an open shame." They therefore reject the atoning mercies of the Cross, through which alone salvation is possible.

1. *"Those Who Were Once Enlightened."* These words have reference to that operation of the Spirit by which men are awakened to a sense of sin and the need of salvation. They are based upon the words of Jesus, who said of the Comforter, "When he is come, he will reprove the world of sin, and of righteousness, and of judgment" (John 16: 8). Without this Spirit of grace, given preveniently to all men, salvation would be impossible. The word for "enlightened" as here used is *photisthentas* ($\phi\omega\tau\iota\sigma\theta\acute{\epsilon}\nu\tau\alpha\varsigma$) and means literally to "emit light," or to so shine upon something as to bring it to the knowledge of men. In common Greek the word was

applied only to objects, but in Hellenistic Greek it is also applied to persons in the sense of instruction. This is its meaning here.

The word for "once" is *hapax* (ἅπαξ), and is used more frequently in this Epistle than in the remainder of the entire New Testament. As used here it does not mean "once" in the sense of a preparation for something to follow, but in the sense of "once for all." It should be noted also that the word "once" does not modify merely the first participle, "enlightened," but applies to all the following participles. There is therefore the idea of gradation or amplification which enters into the whole passage, and this makes necessary the experience of all the factors before apostasy can occur. It is not the smallness but the greatness of the attainments and privileges that marks the doom of the apostate.

2. *"Have Tasted of the Heavenly Gift."* "The gift of God is eternal life through Jesus Christ our Lord" (Rom. 6: 23*b*; cf. John 3: 15; 10: 28; 17: 2). Our Lord spoke of this life as "living bread" and "living water"— the one a symbol of His flesh (John 6: 51), the other a symbol of the Spirit (John 7: 38-39). There is first the bread from heaven, and then the water of life; first Calvary and then Pentecost. This new life is imparted by the Spirit in regeneration and is therefore scripturally known as the "new birth" or the "birth from above."

The word *geusamenous* (γευσαμένους), translated "tasted," has been a very controversial term, and the ideas attached to it are of great importance to the right understanding of this passage. The word has been interpreted to mean tasting lightly as with the mere tips of the lips. Calvin thus interpreted it and held that the individuals here mentioned had tasted but a little of the grace of God and received some sparks of light; and the Reformed church, always concerned about the final perseverance of the saints, has strenuously adhered to this idea. Lindsay says that it rather means tasting "in the sense of partaking, receiving fully and copiously." He then calls attention to the use of the word in 2: 9, where it is said that our Lord tasted of death, which "certainly does not mean that He had only the slightest touch of suffering, but rather that He felt the full bitterness of dying."

Other of the great commentators take the same position. Alford interprets "tasted" as "personally and consciously partaken of"; Grimm says that it means "to feel, to make trial of, experience"; Westcott regards it as expressing "a real and conscious enjoyment of the blessing apprehended in its true character"; Adam Clarke says that "to taste, signifies to experience, or to have full proof of a thing"; while Cremer says that it means "practically and in fact to experience anything." These words, therefore, cannot be weakened down to mean a mere mental or aesthetic appreciation of Christ by an unregenerate observer. No! it means the gift of spiritual life to a soul dead in trespasses and sins—a life such as only the truly regenerate know.

3. *"Were Made Partakers of the Holy Ghost."* Our Lord's last discourses were concerned with the coming of the Comforter or the gift of the Holy Ghost. "I will pray the Father," He said, "and he shall give you another Comforter, that he may abide with you for ever" (John 14: 16). Following these words are three references to the Comforter of great significance. (1) The Comforter is said to be the Gift of the Father (John 14: 26); (2) He is said to be the Gift of the Son (John 15: 26; 16: 7); and (3) He is said to come in His own right (John 16: 13). As Christ was God's redemptive Gift to the world, so the Holy Spirit is Christ's sanctifying Gift to the Church (Eph. 5: 25-27). As the One is received by faith, so also is the Other. To be made partakers of the Holy Spirit, then, is to receive Him as a personal, indwelling Spirit, the Promise of the Father and the Gift of the risen and glorified Christ. When received, the Spirit manifests himself *in* us as a *sanctifying* Spirit, *through* us as a *charismatic* or gift-bestowing Spirit, and *upon* us as an *anointing* or *empowering*

Spirit. The Holy Spirit is often spoken of as a Seal, His gifts and powers being an evidence of the exaltation and glory of Christ, a testimony to the believer's acceptance, and the pledge of a future inheritance.

Westcott regards "the heavenly gift" and "partakers of the Holy Ghost" as a twofold blessing, the former describing the conscious possession of the principle of life, the latter a sense of fellowship in a vaster life. The first element is that which a believer has personally in himself; the second, that which he has by partaking in something which has a far wider action (*Epistle to the Hebrews*, p. 150). The word *metochous* (μετόχους) is sometimes translated "companion," especially when used as a substantive in the genitive denoting a person. It is rightly translated "partakers" in this place because there is a mystical communion between Christ and believers, and the Holy Spirit and believers. When therefore the word is combined with these names in the genitive, the word "partaker" is proper in that something is received from them.

4. *"Have Tasted the Good Word of God."* The writer again uses the word "tasted" but not because of poverty of language. It is rather his purpose to re-emphasize the experience of testing and enjoying the fullness of a new and abounding life. This comes from the Holy Spirit, who by His act of sanctification purifies the heart from sin (Acts 15:9) and makes possible a life of holiness. The term *hrema* (ῥῆμα) is sometimes used to denote the whole Word of God, but here it is used more especially to denote the promises, which to those who embrace them become the source of continued life and power. The use of the word *kalon* (καλόν) or "good" would seem to favor this position. When the Word of God is expressed by the term *logos* (λόγος), it has reference more particularly to the message or content of the Word; but when expressed by *hrema* (ῥῆμα), it refers primarily to the Word as uttered or spoken. The former emphasizes the message, the latter the speaker. Through the Holy Spirit as the Spirit of truth, God speaks to us

afresh through His Word, making the promises vital, rich, and real, and thus we taste "the good word of God."

5. *"And the Powers of the World to Come."* If tasting of "the good word of God" has reference to the life of holiness which flows from being "partakers of the Holy Ghost" in His sanctifying power, then "the powers of the world to come" have reference to the activities of that life. To the Jews "the world to come" meant the coming of the Messianic age with its miraculous gifts and manifestations; to us however it can mean nothing short of the millennial age and the eternal order. Even here the glories of that upper Kingdom break through into the realm of consciousness; and while we now behold them as in a glass darkly, "then shall the righteous shine forth as the sun in the kingdom of their Father" (Matt. 13:43). Christianity is a religion of a future world, and has power to elevate the present. We are therefore, with open face, to behold as in a glass the glory of the Lord, and be "changed into the same image from glory to glory, even as by the Spirit of the Lord" (II Cor. 3:18).

The Danger of Apostasy

Having pointed out the nature of Christian experience under the new covenant, the Apostle further states that if such fall away it is impossible "to renew them again unto repentance; seeing they crucify to themselves the Son of God afresh, and put him to an open shame" (6:4-6). Since this great truth, or the perversion of it, has disquieted many a timid and overscrupulous believer, we shall give careful attention to the grammatical structure of the text, and follow this with a discussion of some of the errors which have attached to it.

The Grammatical Construction of the Text. Dr. Adam Clarke quotes Macknight, a Calvinist scholar, as giving one of the most scriptural interpretations of these verses. He says: "The participles *photisthentas* (φωτισθέντας), 'who were once enlightened'; *geusamenous* (γευσαμένους), 'have tasted'; and *genethentas* (γενηθέντας), 'were made partakers,' being aorists, are properly rendered by our translators, in the *past* time; wherefore *parapesontas* (παραπεσόντας) ought likewise to have been translated in the past time, 'have fallen away.' Nevertheless our translators, following Beza, who without any authority from ancient manuscripts, has inserted in his version the word *si* ('if'), have rendered this clause 'If they shall fall away,' that this text might not appear to contradict the doctrine of the *perseverance of the saints*. But as no translator should take upon him to add to, or alter, the Scriptures, for the sake of any favorite doctrine: I have translated *parapesontas* (παραπεσόντας) in the past time, 'having fallen away,' according to the true import of the word, as standing in connection with the other aorists in the preceding verses."

It is clearly evident therefore, from the grammatical structure of this text, that the author intends to say that it is possible for Christians, even after high spiritual attainments, to fall from the grace of God into total apostasy. Concerning such, he says that it is impossible "to renew them again unto repentance." The key to this impossibility lies in the two following participles—not now aorists but present and durative. The first is *anastaurountes* (ἀνασταυροῦντας) and the second is *paradeigmatichontas* (παραδειγματίζοντας), the former translated as "crucifying," and the latter as "exposing to public ignominy," as did the Jews with Christ on Cal-

Dr. Adam Clarke in commenting upon this exposition says: Dr. Macknight was a Calvinist; and he was a thorough scholar and an honest man; but, professing to give a translation of the Epistle, he consulted not his creed, but his candor. Had our translators who were excellent and learned men, leaned less to their own peculiar creed in the present Authorized Version, the Church of Christ in this country would not have been so agitated and torn as it has been with polemical divinity." Continuing the thought he says: "It appears from this, whatever sentiment may gain or lose by it, that there is a fearful possibility of falling away from the grace of God; and if this Scripture did not say so, there are many that do say so. And were there no Scripture expressed on this subject, the nature of the personal state of man, which is a state of *probation* or *trial* must necessarily imply it. Let him who most assuredly standeth, take heed lest he fall."—ADAM CLARKE, *Commentary*, on Heb. 6:6.

vary. What the writer says therefore is that it is impossible to renew again to repentance those who have fallen away, "while they are still crucifying the Son of God afresh for themselves" (ἑαυτοῖς); and "while they are still exposing Him to ignominy and shame."

In simple words, if a man should be stranded on an island and there was furnished but one means of transportation to the mainland, this being rejected, there would be no other possibility of escape left to him. Now, since "there is none other name under heaven given among men, whereby we must be saved," (Acts 4: 12) it is evident that repentance is impossible while one crucifies for himself the Saviour, and while he still villifies the name by which alone he may be saved. Doubtless in all sin there is a continuous hardening process which may finally bring one to the place where penitence is impossible, but in this text there is implied a judicial act of God, a condemnation of the apostate that permits no return. There is a sin against the Holy Spirit which our Saviour said "hath never forgiveness," and which finds its culmination in total apostasy.

The Warning Against Apostasy Drawn from Old Testament History. As in a previous chapter the writer of this Epistle used Canaan as a type of spiritual rest, so now he finds in the rebellion at Kadesh-barnea the ground of one of his severest warnings. On the very

Since this portion of scripture has been used by the enemy of souls to discourage many, especially young Christians, a clear distinction should be drawn between backsliding and total apostasy. Here the words of Dr. Adam Clarke are much to the point. He says: "Before I proceed to explain the different terms in these verses, it is necessary to give my opinion of their design and meaning. (1) I do not consider them as having any reference to any person *professing Christianity*. (2) They do not belong, nor are they applicable to *backsliders* of any kind. (3) They belong to *apostates* from Christianity; to such as reject the whole *Christian system*, and its *Author*, the Lord Jesus. (4) And to those of them only who join with the blaspheming Jews, call Christ an impostor, and vindicate His murderers, in having crucified Him as a malefactor; and thus they render their salvation impossible by *wilfully* and *maliciously* rejecting the Lord that bought them. No man, *believing in the Lord Jesus* as the great sacrifice for sin, and acknowledging *Christianity* as a *Divine Revelation*, is here intended; though he may unfortunately have *backslidden* from any degree of the salvation of God."—Dr. Adam Clarke, *Commentary*, Heb. 6:4.

eve of entering in upon their promised inheritance, the Israelites refused to go forward and turned back into the wilderness. This refusal was no ordinary failure; it was rebellion of the most extreme kind. Isaiah says of it, "They rebelled, and vexed his holy spirit: therefore he was turned to be their enemy" (Isa. 63:10). Turned back into the wilderness, a whole generation, save Caleb and Joshua, perished, their carcasses falling in the wilderness (Heb. 3:17).

It will be readily admitted that the Hebrew Christians were peculiarly liable to apostasy, having lived from infancy under a law which had the outward sanction of God's name and which was held to have been given by the dispensation of angels. The Jews generally regarded themselves as God's only true people, and therefore there must have been a constant temptation to those of the Christian Church. Hence the severity of the warning. If such fearful consequences followed the rejection of the symbols and shadows under Moses' dispensation, "Of how much sorer punishment," the Apostle says, "suppose ye, shall he be thought worthy, who hath trodden under foot the Son of God, and hath counted the blood of the covenant, wherewith he was sanctified, an unholy thing, and hath done despite unto the Spirit of grace?" These are solemn words indeed and are intended to warn the Hebrew Christians against the fearful state of perdition that could result from being led away from Christ, either by the persuasions of their countrymen or by the fear of persecution. It is further evident that the irrecoverable depths into which an apostate may sink can be measured only by the Christian heights from which he has fallen.

Errors Connected with This Text. We have seen from the grammatical construction of this text that the participle "having fallen away" admits of no denial of the grave possibility of apostasy. This being true, in order to support the doctrine of "final perseverance," countrymen or by the fear of persecution. It is further now generally known as "eternal security," false interpretations are advanced concerning the words "enlight-

The import of this interpretation is an attempt to prove
that these verses do not refer to one who is *altogether*
a Christian, but only to one who is an *almost* Christian.
Ebrard points out the absurdity of this position. He
says: "But whoever is not blinded by dogmatical prejudices must perceive, that the aim of our author is evidently and assuredly not to say: the *less* one has tasted
of the gifts of grace the more easily can he be irrecoverably lost, but precisely the reverse, the *more* one has
already penetrated into the sanctuary of the state of
grace, by so much more irrecoverably is he lost in case
he should fall away." (Cf. *Hebrews,* p. 200.) Then,
how can one be renewed again to repentance who has
never truly repented? This is idle talk. And what a
fearful doctrine it would prove to be, that if one were
almost persuaded to be a Christian and relapsed from
that point, he could never be brought again to repentance! Such are some of the futile attempts to harmonize
clear scriptures with others misinterpreted, and all in
the interest of a dogmatic position flatly contradicted
by the whole tenor of the Scriptures.

An Illustration from Nature. "For the earth which
drinketh in the rain that cometh oft upon it, and bringeth forth herbs meet for them by whom it is dressed,
receiveth blessing from God: but that which beareth
thorns and briers is rejected, and is nigh unto cursing;
whose end is to be burned" (6: 7-8). The writer now
turns to a common illustration from the material realm
—doubtless suggested by our Lord's parable of the soils
—and advances to the divine judgment necessarily involved. The husbandman sows the seed in a field, one
portion of which proves fruitful and the other barren.
Both portions were equally tilled, and likewise received
the same blessings from heaven. They both drank in
the rain (aorist: fact) which came often upon it, that
is, "keeps coming down" (present participle: iterative);
and the one that "keeps bearing herbs" (present participle) for them by whom it is dressed receives blessing
from God; while the other, although every means was

used to make it fruitful, "thrust forth abundantly, thorns and briers." Spiritual barrenness is never alone, but always accompanied with the thorns and briers of sin. The author says of the latter portion that it "is nigh unto cursing." He cannot be understood to say that the curse results in the burning of the land and its noxious products. This is a judicial visitation of God. The illustration makes clear that those who have been once enlightened and passed through the rich experiences of the Spirit, and "have tasted the good word of God" with its many infallible proofs, and then fall aside into apostasy, must bear the threefold punishment of rejection, the curse, and the burning. The writer offers no further comment.

Words of Confidence and Comfort. "But, beloved, we are persuaded better things of you, and things that accompany salvation, though we thus speak. For God is not unrighteous to forget your work and labour of love, which ye have shewed toward his name, in that ye have ministered to the saints, and do minister" (6: 9-10). Having spoken of the dangers of apostasy in words of earnest warning, the writer now turns to words of encouragement and comfort. These he introduces with the word "beloved" the only place where this word occurs in the entire Epistle. He would not have the readers think him harsh in using the strong words of warning, for he is persuaded (perfect tense, "we still have the persuasion"—himself and others) that they are faithful in that they manifest the evidences which accompany or pertain to salvation. Probably this is a reference to the rich herbage of the fruitful field which he sees in them, instead of the thorns and briers that tend toward the curse. The writer recalls that in the past they have received Christ's ministers with

Lenski holds that the writer is speaking of the same field, at first productive and then so degenerated as to bring forth only thorns and briers. This argument he bases on the use of the present participles found in the text. That this is possible those know full well who live in arid countries brought into productiveness by irrigation. The water which at first brings an enormous yield, unless proper subteranean drainage is provided, soon "goes wet" and becomes worthless.

joy, and have shared their reproach even to the spoiling
of their goods. Because for the love of the Name they
have ministered to the saints and still continue to minister, he assures them that God is not unrighteous to
forget their work and love. While showing anxiety for
them, the writer makes it clear that he in no wise classes
these Hebrews with the apostates, for he sees in them
an active love—an evidence that God is still with them.

*The Culmination of the Warning Against Slothful-
ness.* "And we desire that every one of you do shew
the same diligence to the full assurance of hope unto
the end: that ye be not slothful, but followers of them
who through faith and patience inherit the promises"
(6: 11-12). The word translated "slothful" is the same
as that previously used concerning dullness of hearing
(5: 11). The writer fears that the same dullness which
has found lodgment in their hearing might also affect
their lives and prevent further progress. Instead, he
earnestly desires that the same zeal which they have
previously manifested in their charities shall also characterize their spiritual advancement. They are called
to be followers or "imitators" of those who through
faith and patience inherit the promises. Slothfulness
has done them much harm; and after having warned
them concerning the fathers who refused to go forward
into the land of promise, but turned back into the wilderness, he now encourages them to follow those who,
having inherited the promises, entered in to possess the
land. The writer now turns attention to Abraham, to
whom the promises were made.

THE ABRAHAMIC COVENANT

The writer, having warned his readers against the
danger of apostasy, and exhorted them to "be not slothful, but followers of them who through faith and patience
inherit the promises," now turns their attention to the
faith of Abraham, who after patient endurance "obtained the promise." He selects for consideration the
last of a series of four events, in which the unwavering

faith of Abraham met every crisis of his soul, and was rewarded with a promise confirmed by the solemn oath of God. These events are as follows:

(1) There was the call of Abraham, "Get thee out of thy country, and from thy kindred, and from thy father's house, unto a land that I will shew thee." This was a call out of idolatry; for Terah, Abraham's father, was an idolater. Here the promise was given that in him shall all the families of the earth be blessed, but no oath was attached to the promise (Gen. 12: 1-4, 7).

(2) Next follows Abram's offering of consecration. A deep sleep falling upon him, he beheld a smoking furnace and a burning lamp passing between the pieces, hallowing the whole burnt offering to God. Added assurance was thus given to the fulfillment of the promise, but still no oath was attached (Gen. 15: 8-18).

(3) Following this, and doubtless closely related to it, was Abram's call to perfection. "The Lord appeared to Abram, and said unto him, I am the Almighty God [El Shaddai, 'the Nourisher or Sustainer']; walk before me, and be thou perfect" (Gen. 17: 1-8). Here the promises are called a covenant, and the name "Abram" is changed to "Abraham," "the father of a multitude." The close connection between the terms "perfect" and "covenant" anticipate the perfection of the new covenant, to which our author directs our attention in the subsequent chapters of the Epistle. Still no oath attaches to the promises, even when considered as a covenant.

Dr. Adam Clarke gives an interesting account of the theories attaching to the change of names from Abram to Abraham. The word Abram means "high or exalted father"; and Abraham as used here means a "father of many nations have I made thee." This has led some to maintain that the word is from Ab-hamon-goyim, "a father of a multitude of nations," while others think that it is a contraction of the word Ab-rab-haman, which means "the father of a great multitude." The same writer commenting on the words "be thou perfect" says that the Hebrew words veheyeh tamin mean. "And thou shalt be perfections, i.e., altogether perfect; be just such as the holy God would have thee to be, as the Almighty God can make thee, and live as the All-Sufficient God shall support thee; for He alone who can make the soul holy can preserve it in holiness." Our blessed Lord appears to have had these words pointedly in view when He said, "Ye shall be perfect, as your Father who is in heaven is perfect" (Matt. 5:48). (ADAM CLARKE, Commentary, I, 79.)

(4) The last event selected by the author is Abraham's offering up of Isaac, his only son. The angel of the Lord, having called out of heaven and stayed the hand of Abram, called a second time and said, "By myself have I sworn, saith the Lord, for because thou hast done this thing, . . . that in blessing I will bless thee, and in multiplying I will multiply thy seed as the stars of the heaven, and as the sand which is upon the sea shore; . . . and in thy seed shall all the nations of the earth be blessed" (Gen. 22: 16-18). Thus says Bishop Chadwick, "After the sacrifice of Isaac, when the triumphant faith of the patriarch had overcome all that makes such promises to be conditional, he was given the further assurance, the first recorded oath of God."

The Oath of Confirmation. The word "oath" is from the Greek *horkomosias* (ὁρκωμοσίας) and may mean either the oath itself or the taking of an oath in a sworn statement. Here it refers primarily to the latter. "For when God made promise to Abraham, because he could swear by no greater, he sware by himself, saying, Surely blessing I will bless thee, and multiplying I will multiply thee. And so, after he had patiently endured, he obtained the promise. For men verily swear by the greater: and an oath for confirmation is to them the end of all strife" (6: 13-16). By common usage, men take a solemn oath as in the presence of God, and this oath is their last resort against gainsaying, controversy, and strife. God therefore in like manner, because He

Men swear by a being who is greater than they, who possesses omniscience enabling him to know the perjured person, and power and justice to punish him. The oath consists in this, that the person who swears calls the higher being to witness at once the promise and its fulfilment or non-fulfilment, and to be the eventual avenger of the latter. (Hence with the purified Christian every word is a tacit oath, inasmuch as it is spoken in the consciousness of the testimony of the all-present and all-knowing God. And hence Christ forbids swearing by inanimate things (Matt. 5:34), and puts that state of mind in which every yea is yea—i.e., in which every word, whether God be called to expressly witness it or not, is spoken in the consciousness that God is witness—in the place of that swearing which was alike superstitious and false. Christ does not therefore forbid the oath, but He wills that the Christian should speak *only oaths,* and that in this way the difference between swearing and not swearing should find an end).—EBRARD, *Biblical Commentary on the Epistle to the Hebrews,* pp. 206-7.

could swear by no greater, sware by himself, and thereby confirms His promises with the most solemn and sacred of all oaths. Since God, who cannot lie, affirms His own promises with a solemn oath, this affirmation should awaken in us the deepest appreciation of His condescending love.

The Purpose of the Oath. "Wherein God, willing more abundantly to shew unto the heirs of promise the immutability of his counsel, confirmed it by an oath" (6: 17). Wherein, that is, "this being so," or "in connection with the oath," God was willing more abundantly to show to the heirs of promise by an overwhelming evidence the immutability of His counsel. The word "counsel" is used in that it is the word of infinite wisdom. This was therefore a determinate act of God, which He determined in himself, not to make His counsel unchangeable, but to declare that it is so, that His promise should be without reservation and His purpose unalterable. There appears to be even a deeper meaning of the oath here than that expressed in verses 13-16. God is said to have "intervened" or "interposed" himself, the verb being *emesiteusen* (ἐμεσίτευσεν). Thus God is not only the Maker of the oath but its Witness as well, pledging himself as Security for the fulfillment of the promise. The Jewish oath if carried out in full would read, "If I fulfill not the promise, then I am not God"; or, "The promise shall stand as long as the eternal God liveth," and therefore is both perfect and permanent. God wishes in an abundant manner to fully satisfy every fear and doubt on the part of each and all of the heirs of promise.

The Two Immutable Things. "That by two immutable things, in which it was impossible for God to lie, we might have a strong consolation" (6: 18a). The two immutable things are the promise and the oath. Of God, who made *promise* to Abraham, it is said that it was impossible for Him to lie; and concerning the *oath*, God sware by himself and therefore interposed himself and all the perfections of the Godhead as a pledge for

the fulfillment of the promises. This oath points to another which our author is about to introduce, the oath
which attached to the covenant with Christ, namely,
that He should be "a priest for ever after the order of
Melchisedec" (7: 21). The one oath parallels the other.
That made to Abraham and his seed confirmed the
redemptive promise; that made to Christ, the Seed of
Abraham (Gal. 3: 18), confirmed the priestly agency
by which the promises were brought to their fulfillment.
The one attaches to the nature of the covenant, the
other to its administration; and as two immutable things
attached to the first, so the writer is about to show that
two attach to the second. For the one incarnate Son
is from the divine aspect the "minister of the sanctuary,"
and from the human aspect the "surety" of the covenant. The promise therefore rests securely on the covenant with Christ, who as our propitiatory Offering made
it possible for God to still be just and the Justifier of
him who believes in Jesus. Thus God has given to the
heirs of the promise the double assurance of the validity
of the covenant and the infallibility of its administration.
And the heirs are not merely the natural descendants of
Abraham but his spiritual progeny; for in Christ, his
Seed, who is the Heir of all things, shall all the nations
of the earth be blessed.

The two immutable things furnish the ground for
strong consolation to the heirs of promise. It will be
noted that the writer says, "We might have a strong
consolation," using the first person instead of a general
statement, and thus includes himself within the promise.
The word for "consolation" is *paraklesis* (παράκλησις),
another reference to our word Paraclete or Comforter,
the term which our Lord used of the Holy Spirit, who
was to come on the Day of Pentecost. The American
Revised Version has the word "encouragement" instead
of "consolation." This seems more in keeping with the
thought of the writer, whose purpose it is to encourage
his readers to hold on by faith and hope in the oath-
bound promise of God until the thing promised is re-

ceived. For our assurance, three illustrations are given: (1) The Refuge of Hope, (2) The Anchor of the Soul, and (3) The Divine Forerunner.

The Refuge of Hope. This is evidently an allusion to the cities of refuge in Israel, to which one who was instrumental in the death of another might flee from the avenger of blood. Reaching the city, he was safe within its walls, and upon the death of the high priest was again at liberty. While the Authorized Version reads, "who have fled for refuge to lay hold upon the hope set before us," making the infinitive *kratesai* (κρατῆσαι) one of purpose, the grammatical construction makes it possible to be translated as an infinitive of result. It would then read, "we who found refuge so as to hold fast to the proffered hope." Christ is our Refuge, and the use of the words "have fled" indicates the urgency of fleeing to Christ for salvation. It is in Christ that the hope is set before us upon which we are to lay hold. Hope may be either objective as a goal set before us or it may be subjective in the sense of an inward grace or disposition which animates our souls. Here it appears to be used in both senses: (1) as an object in the words "set before us," a thing for which we hope; and (2) as subjective in the words "to lay hold upon," which necessitate an inner experience or faith and patience. Hope is therefore at once both the gift of God and the inner experience of man.

The Anchor of the Soul. "Which hope we have as an anchor of the soul, both sure and stedfast, and which entereth into that within the veil" (6:19). This is a nautical reference and is the scripture which furnished us with the anchor as the symbol of hope. The word "anchor" does not occur in the Old Testament, and in the New Testament only here and in the description of Paul's shipwreck on the island of Melita (Acts 27:29, 40). The anchor as the familiar symbol of hope, says Bishop Chadwick, has "passed into the very fibre of our thought, so exactly does it express our conception of the promise, firm itself, strong, but requiring . . . that we . . .

should firmly lay hold upon that which lays hold upon eternal things." As the heavy iron anchor sinks into the great deep and fastens itself to the immovable rocks, holding the vessel "sure and stedfast," so hope, the Christian's anchor, reaches upward and "entereth into that within the veil." But what is it that lies within the veil? It is the substance of that of which the earthly holy of holies was but the shadow. There is the throne of authority and power, whereupon Jesus is seated at the right hand of the Father, having himself become our propitiatory Offering and thus able to purge the people from their sins with His own sacrificial blood. Here the promise has come to fulfillment, and the types and shadows are lost in eternal verities.

The figure of the anchor is sometimes used in another sense. We are told that in many of the inland seas in ancient times there were great stones imbedded in the ground along the shore, where smaller craft were usually moored. But often because of adverse winds the larger vessels were not able to reach the harbor by means of their own sails. Then it was the practice to lower a small boat and send a forerunner ashore with a strong cable, which he fastened to one of these stones known as *anchoria,* and holding fast to that line the ship could be brought safely to its moorings. The uniqueness of the Christian's hope then lies in this, that it finds no anchorage in the shallow waters of this world, but reaches within the veil, and by the strong cords of grace

It is from this passage that our symbolic use of the anchor is derived; for an anchor is never mentioned in the Old Testament; nor elsewhere in the New except in its literal sense in connection with the shipwreck of Paul. And yet it has passed into the very fibre of our thought, so exactly does it express our conception of the promise, firm in itself, strong, but requiring (as the beginning of this chapter affirmed so solemnly) that we for our part should firmly lay hold upon that which lays hold upon eternal things. Little avails the anchor when the chain has parted. It is not the anchor, but the sure and stedfast hope, which is said to enter within the veil (so that the charge of mixed metaphor is baseless), yet the expression is somewhat influenced by the thought of the reliance of the mariner on that which has passed beyond his vision, but which grasps realities underlying the shifting tides, realities he knows and trusts even if he cannot define them. So has our hope passed within the veil. And more is there to be relied upon than any hope.— CHADWICK, *The Epistle to the Hebrews,* p. 82.

and truth is bound to the heavenly *anchoria,* the eternal throne of God. The Holy Spirit is the Spirit of grace and truth, and holding fast in obedience to Him, we shall in our own time be brought safely to the golden strand and the shores of eternal light and love. This is the Christian's hope, made "sure and stedfast" through the promise and the oath.

The Divine Forerunner. "Whither the forerunner is for us entered, even Jesus, made an high priest for ever after the order of Melchisedec" (6:20). From the previous thought of hope as the anchor of the soul, the writer now turns his attention to Him who carries that hope within the veil. Bruce points out that most commentators fail to perceive, or at least fail to adequately express, the significance of the term *prodromos* (πρόδρομος) or "forerunner," which in this verse takes on new spiritual significance and becomes the crowning thought of the chapter. Christ has been shown to be the Captain of our salvation, leading us into the rest of faith as our earthly inheritance, and on toward the eternal rest of our heavenly inheritance. Here however a new idea is expressed in that Christ as our Forerunner has entered and opened the holy of holies for us. The Levitical high priest entered the most holy place but once each year, and that merely as a representative of the people. He entered in their stead, and not as a forerunner. The glory of the new covenant and its privileges lie in this, that Christ has not only entered the holy of holies as our great High Priest, but He has rent the veil that we too may enter. Thus Christ is not only our Moses to lead us out of bondage, and our Aaron to atone for us, but in Him are blended both of these offices in a new and eternal order, that of Melchisedec, who was at once a king and a priest. It is specifically stated that this twofold office He exercises for us. During His humiliation on earth He was our propitiatory Offering and shed His blood for us that we might be cleansed from all sin and unrighteousness. Now that He has entered within the veil, His offering is still all for us.

From His mediatorial throne He ministers the Spirit, which He has promised His disciples, a promise which was fulfilled on the Day of Pentecost. This marked the inauguration of a new spiritual dispensation, one in which we live and serve through the power of the indwelling Spirit. Calvary without Pentecost is incomplete.

The entrance of our "forerunner" within the veil carries with it this deep and far-reaching significance: (1) that it establishes the perfect worship, of which Judaism was but the shadow; and (2) it provides for the universal and unrestricted fellowship with the Father and with the Son through the Spirit. Thus it does away with the localization of places technically termed holy. Jesus said to the Samaritan woman, "The hour cometh, when ye shall neither in this mountain, nor yet at Jerusalem, worship the Father. But the hour cometh, and now is, when the true worshippers shall worship the Father in spirit and in truth: for the Father seeketh such to worship him. God is a Spirit: and they that worship him must worship him in spirit and in truth" (John 4: 21, 23-24). Then too, it is not until this fellowship of perfect love out of a pure heart is established that Christianity comes to its full expression. This the writer tells us is accomplished by, and in, our divine-human *prodromos* or "forerunner." It is significant that the writer when speaking of His triumphant entrance into the heavens uses the word Jesus, His human name, and not the divine title "Lord." He who was the God-Man on earth is in some true sense the Man-God in the heavens, and thus it is that we have One of our own on the mediatorial throne. Since Deity and humanity are so closely related in the one Person of our divine-human Forerunner, we too may have in Him the closest and most unrestricted fellowship with the Father and the Son through the indwelling presence of the Holy Spirit.

Furthermore, the term "forerunner" is expressive of the relation which Christ bears to His people. The term means (1) a "forthrunner," one who runs to convey tidings. Thus Cushi outran the official messenger and came to David crying, "Tidings, my lord." Christ came out from the heavens singly and alone to be the Propitiation for our sins; He returns in triumph crying, "Behold I and the children which God hath given me." (2) The word also means a "quartermaster," one who goes before to prepare for an army. Our great Quartermaster has gone before to prepare for the sacramental hosts, which the Old Testament describes as "fair as the moon, clear as the sun, and terrible as an army with banners." In God's great army, every soldier has won his badge of bravery in service, which as a banner he carries in testimony of his faithfulness. (3) Again, the word means a "harbinger," or one who goes ahead to prepare for royalty. The Church of Christ is not only described as "brethren" from the viewpoint of the *family,* or as an army marching in triumph against the *enemy,* but also as a nation of *"kings and priests unto God."* "But ye are a chosen generation, a royal priesthood, an holy nation, a peculiar people; that ye should shew forth the praises of him who hath called you out of darkness into his marvellous light" (I Pet. 2: 9).

CHAPTER VII
THE SURETY OF A BETTER TESTAMENT

In this middle chapter of the Epistle the writer begins a thorough study of the new order of priesthood and its relation to the Aaronic covenant and the Mosaic law. He has already awakened interest in the subject by his threefold reference to the priesthood "after the order of Melchisedec" (5: 6, 10; 6: 20), and now takes up the subject in earnest. This study continues through the greater part of three chapters, and deals with the various aspects of the priesthood. This new order of priesthood, therefore, becomes the central and pivotal point on which the writer builds his great, thematic argument for the priesthood of Christ. He draws his material from an obscure event in early Hebrew history—three verses in Genesis (14: 18-20) and a single verse in the Psalms (110: 4). Of the references to Melchisedec we may say that the Genesis account is historical; the reference in the Psalms, prophetical; and that in Hebrews, doctrinal (7: 1-10).

THE ORDER OF MELCHISEDEC: AN ETERNAL PRIESTHOOD

The argument which the writer advances for the superiority of the Melchisedec order can be appreciated only by those who understand how tenaciously the Hebrews of that day held to their ideas of the Levitical priesthood and its importance. To have failed here would have destroyed the very foundation of the author's teaching concerning the superiority of Christ over Aaron.

The Historical Event. The writer sums up the entire historical passage in Genesis (14: 18-20) in one long sentence (7: 1-3). These verses in Genesis are the sole historical source of our author's argument; and strange as it may seem, much of the argument is drawn from what is not said, rather than from that which is recorded. Several things stand out clearly here. (1) The name Melchisedec is from *Malchi tsedek* and signifies a righteous king, probably from the righteous character of his government. His title, "King of Salem," signifies a peace king. Westcott points out that the genitive in each case indicates the characteristics of the sovereign; he is a "righteousness-king," and a "peace-king," one in whom and through whom righteousness and peace are realized. "The personal character of the priest-king leads to the notice of the kingdom which he administered; being righteous in himself, he kept peace under his sway." (2) He was without recorded genealogy. "Without father, without mother, without descent, having neither beginning of days, nor end of life." Thus the whole history of Melchisedec except this one recorded event is closed against us, and doubtless by divine intention. The ground of the argument, therefore, is that Melchisedec stands out as a priest-king, not by inheritance or descent, but in his own right. Furthermore, there being no record of the beginning or ending of his kingdom, it becomes a worthy symbol of the eternal priesthood of Christ. (3) The author says further that Melchisedec was "made like unto the Son of God." Thus his life and the life of Abraham in relation to him show the providential ordering which lays the foundation for an eternal priesthood outside the Levitical order, and one in which the kingship and priesthood are con-

Suppose those three verses in Genesis to have been non-existent, the narrative in other respects remaining unchanged. Suppose that we now learned for the first time, by the deciphering of some old inscription, that the father of the faithful, to whom all Judaism looks back as its founder, the recipient of the promises which are its title deeds, that he, to whom as we assert God came by direct revelation, and who alone is called the friend of God, was actually in communication with an older priest of his own religion, paid him tribute and bent his head under his benediction, what use would the assailants of the faith make of a disclosure such as this? What agonies of alarm would torture those good people who were weak enough to grow pale when we learned that just about this time Hammurabi promulgated a code of law which may have influenced the laws of Israel? And yet we know that such an alarm would be ridiculous and baseless. All good is of God, and His saints in the Old Testament and in the New welcome it and profit by it all.— CHADWICK, *Epistle to the Hebrews*, p. 97.

joined in one Person. These are the arguments which the writer will later develop. It is a significant fact that the seeds of Israel's decay and the inauguration of a new order lie hidden in the literature held sacred and divinely inspired by the Jewish people.

The Prophetical Psalm. "The Lord hath sworn, and will not repent, Thou art a priest for ever after the order of Melchizedek" (Ps. 110:4). This prophetical psalm is the sole link between the historical event of Genesis and its application in the Epistle to the Hebrews. This the writer uses to the fullest extent. To him, every word is important: the word "for ever" with its finality; "made like unto the Son of God," as revealing the providential guidance that brought Melchisedec into conformity with the coming Redeemer; the "oath" which confirmed the priesthood of the Son of God; and the silence concerning the genealogy of Melchisedec, which not only speaks of the eternal priesthood of Christ but creates an atmosphere of mystery which lifts the whole event from the natural to the spiritual realm. Outstanding of course is the conjunction of kingship and priesthood, a thing not known in Israel, where the priesthood depended wholly upon descent. The dispensation or economy being a covenant, the high priest

The person of Melchisedec has been the source of much speculation. As early as 135 B.C., Rabbi Ismael advanced the theory that Melchisedec was Shem, the son of Noah, who had preserved the true religion in his own person and kingdom. Philo held that Melchisedec was merely the divine reason functioning in a priestly manner, exercising control over the passions, and inspiring exalted thoughts of God. Origen, of the early Christian period, thought Melchisedec to be an angelic being—some said the angel Michael. Perhaps the first to suggest a theory which has received some acceptance in modern times was Hierakas, about the third century A.D., who held that Melchisedec was a temporary incarnation of the Holy Spirit—a theophany with special reference to the Third Person of the Trinity. Among the earlier heresies in the Church was that of the Melchizedekites (c. A.D. 200), who made him the original of which Christ was the Copy. The text does not mean that Melchisedec had no father or mother, but that he was without (recorded) father, or (recorded) mother, and there was no record of his birth or death. This marks a decided contrast to the custom of the Semites, who kept careful records, as is shown by the genealogical chapters in the Bible. Probably the truth lies in this, that the true religion of Noah was carried down through the line of Shem to Melchisedec and his kingdom, who embraced in himself the patriarchal priesthood.

is of necessity the central figure, for the dispensation is in some sense a priesthood. The order of the priest is therefore all-important.

For this reason, when the old and new covenants are brought into sharp contrast, the contrast focuses in the differing orders of priesthood. The new covenant is to the old as the priesthood after the order of Melchisedec is to the Levitical priesthood. However the phrase "a priest for ever" is probably of greatest importance in the mind of the writer, for it becomes the seal of finality as to Christ's priestly acts in sanctifying the people (10:10), and of the eternity of the covenant (7:22), both of which belong to Him by virtue of His indissoluble life (7:3, 8, 16). This He has because He is the Son of God (7:3). The priesthood therefore resolves itself into the nature of the person. As Melchisedec is presented without any genealogical connections, and yet was a priest, so also Christ is a Priest in His own right, by virtue of His qualifications, and not by virtue of human relationships, as was the Levitical priesthood.

The Greatness of Melchisedec. "Now consider how great this man was" (7:4a). The word "consider" carries with it the thought of diligent contemplation, or looking intently into the things that are about to be spoken. The writer would have us consider Melchisedec in his dignity and pre-eminence. He leads his readers on step by step. He knows that a right understanding of him who was "made like unto the Son of God" will bring about a deeper appreciation of the new order of priesthood, which through a new covenant brings to perfection all that was anticipated but not realized under the old covenant. We are thus brought to the very heart of the Epistle, the priesthood of the Son of God,

---

When David in the spirit of prophecy sees of the seed promised him, that like Melchisedec, he will unite kingly with priestly dignity, he surely does not predict in these words a merely outward and mechanical conjunction of the two dignities, but he has before him the figure of a man, in whom, as in Melchisedec, the kingly power would be consecrated and penetrated with the sanctifying virtue of the priestly dignity and work, the form therefore, of a king who would truly govern in peace.—OLSHAUSEN, *Biblical Commentary on the Epistle to the Hebrews*, p. 218.

which abideth forever. The writer will show that Melchisedec is greater than Abraham (7:4-10); greater than Aaron and the Levitical priesthood (7:11-14); and greater than Moses and the law which was given by the dispensation of angels (7:15-19).

In the Jewish mind a halo of glory seemed to surround Abraham, the ancient patriarch. He was the father of the Hebrew nation; to him were given the promises that made them God's chosen people; through him was to come the Seed in whom all the nations of the earth should be blessed; and the abode of the blessed dead was known as Abraham's bosom. This greatness the writer freely acknowledges, but Melchisedec is greater. This superiority he argues from the two priestly acts performed by Melchisedec in relation to Abraham. Thus was Melchisedec oriented into Hebrew history in a manner which in no wise could be set aside. These two priestly acts were: (1) Abraham paid tithes to Melchisedec; and (2) Melchisedec blessed Abraham.

1. *Abraham paid tithes to Melchisedec.* It was an ancient custom among many of the earlier peoples to consecrate a tenth of the spoils taken in war to the objects of their worship. This tithe was not according to any provision of law, but a eucharistic offering to those whom they thought had given them the victory. The author's argument may be summed up in the following manner: (1) Melchisedec, who belonged to no priestly class entitled by law to receive tithes, acted, not by law, but in virtue of the greatness of his person. (2) The Levites receive tithes of their brethren, and yet they are men who die; but Abraham paid tithes to one "of whom it is witnessed that he liveth." (3) Combining the above, the writer clinches his argument by the statement that Levi himself must have acknowledged this superiority; and while unborn, in some sense he may be said to have paid tithes in Abraham.

2. *Melchisedec blessed Abraham.* The writer assumes that his readers will accept without contradiction that the less is blessed of the greater. The blessing pro-

nounced upon Abraham by Melchisedec and the fact that Abraham accepted this blessing put their relative positions beyond question. The nature of this blessing is not here considered. The writer aims only to show the superiority of Melchisedec over Abraham. However, St. Paul in his rugged Epistle to the Galatians evidently refers to this when he says, "That the blessing of Abraham might come on the Gentiles through Jesus Christ; that we might receive the promise of the Spirit through faith" (Gal. 3:14). The writer buttresses his argument by saying that the promises were made to Abraham and his seed, and interprets this seed as Christ. "He saith not, And to seeds, as of many; but as of one, And to thy seed, which is Christ" (Gal. 3:16). He concludes by saying that "if ye be Christ's, then are ye Abraham's seed, and heirs according to the promise" (Gal. 3:29). As Abraham bowed in submission to receive the blessing of Melchisedec, so we are to bow in humble submission to Jesus, our "priest for ever," and receive by faith His blessing, which is the gift of the Comforter, the indwelling presence of the Holy Spirit.

It is interesting to note that the writer to the Hebrews makes no mention of the bread and wine which are so closely connected with the priesthood in the verse, "And Melchizedek king of Salem brought forth bread and wine: and he was priest of the most high God" (Gen. 14:18). He may have understood the historian to regard this bread and wine as merely a refreshment for Abraham and his men, or it may have been aside from the purpose of his argument; but even so, the bread and the wine so closely connected with the priesthood may well have been a prophecy of the sacramental elements which our Lord was to use as emblems of the new covenant. The similarity lies in this, that it was after the refreshments of the Passover supper—though Jesus did not partake of it—that He "took bread, and gave thanks, and brake it, and gave unto them, saying, This is my body which is given for you: this do in remembrance of me. Likewise also the cup after supper, saying, This cup is the new testament of my blood, which is shed for you" (Luke 22: 19-20). The sacramental churches, of course, make much of this; but even in those churches where the sacraments are not so strongly emphasized, they become memorials of the whole work of Christ. Thus are opened to us wide vistas of accomplishment under the new order of priesthood, which shall find their perfect fulfillment in His glorious second coming.

THE SUPERIORITY OF THE NEW ORDER: A SPIRITUAL PRIESTHOOD

Having proved the superiority of Melchisedec to Abraham, the next task is to prove him superior to Aaron and the law which was received under the Levitical priesthood. The argument is divided into two sections: (1) the failure of the Levitical order (7: 11-13) and (2) the rise of a new priesthood after the order of Melchisedec (7: 14-19).

The Failure of the Levitical Order. "If therefore perfection were by the Levitical priesthood, (for under it the people received the law,) what further need was there that another priest should rise after the order of Melchisedec, and not be called after the order of Aaron?" (7: 11)

1. *Perfection was not attained by the Levitical priesthood.* The writer's purpose is not now to discuss the nature of perfection; this he has done in earlier chapters. He aims simply to show that it could not come by the Levitical priesthood. Davidson points out that "perfection is always a relative word. An institution brings perfection when it effects the purpose for which it was instituted, and produces a result that corresponds to the idea of it" (*Hebrews,* p. 136). What the writers thought of perfection as used here is clearly stated in verse 19, that of drawing near to God. This the Levitical priesthood could not accomplish because it could not take away sin, for sin cannot approach the flaming holiness of God. There must be a better priesthood in order to a better hope.

2. *The parenthetical clause.* The parenthetical expression, "for under it the people received the law," is introduced by the writer to point up and emphasize the original question. The Aaronic priesthood was indeed divinely given to the Jews, but it was constituted on the basis of law. While the words "under it" as found in the Authorized Version best express in English the formal or shaping power of this law concerning the priesthood, the words in Greek are *epi autes* (ἐπ᾿ αὐτῆς), which mean literally "above" or "on top of it." Hence we are to understand, not that the people received the law from the priests, but that the priesthood itself was constituted and held intact by the laws which God imposed upon the people in order to maintain its authority. The people therefore were said to be "lawed" or "subjected to law"; and the word *nenomothetetai* (νενομοθέτηται), "had received," being in the perfect tense, indicates that this condition continued to the present time. It is thus easy to understand why the writer declares that a priesthood which must be maintained by law is far inferior to that which flows from the power of an endless life.

3. *The author's query.* "What further need was there that another priest should rise after the order of Melchisedec, and not be called after the order of Aaron?" It is because God himself has provided a different order or kind of priesthood, having announced it through the prophet David and confirmed it by an oath. This fact indicates at once the failure of the Levitical priesthood to attain its goal and the introduction of a new and transcendent order which brings in a better hope. Aaron was a type of Christ as well as Melchisedec, for Christ was called of God as was Aaron (5:4). But Aaron's work was only typical, not spiritual. Hence a new order or kind of priesthood was necessary: (1) to make real in spiritual experience that which was typified by Aaron and the Levitical priesthood; and (2) to carry the priesthood beyond the limits of the earthly life of Christ. (a) Aaron typified Christ in His humiliation; Melchisedec, His glorified life in heaven. (b) Aaron was a priest

of death; Melchisedec, a priest of life. (c) Aaron represented the Cross; Melchisedec, the throne. (d) Aaron represented the finished atonement of Christ on earth; Melchisedec, His continuous intercession on the throne in heaven. (e) Aaron could not carry through to completion or perfection by reason of death; but Christ has an unchangeable priesthood—He is "a priest for ever after the order of Melchisedec."

It now becomes clear that there is a vast distinction between the two orders of priesthood fulfilled by Christ: one which He accomplished in humiliation on earth as an Atonement for sin, the other administered in power from His throne in the heavens. But the work of our great High Priest is one; and the lesser, that which is symbolized by Aaron, is comprehended in the greater, that which is symbolized by Melchisedec. The converse is equally true; for that which is accomplished by Christ on the throne is by virtue of that which in His humiliation He accomplished on the Cross. The work wrought by Christ under the symbol of Aaron has reference to the removal of sin; that under the symbol of Melchisedec, to an eternal increase of life and love.

The truth expressed in this symbolism is frequently stated in more abstract terms, as the negative and positive aspects of the one experience of entire sanctification. By the former is meant the cleansing from inbred sin; by the latter, the fullness of divine love. Both are accomplished by the Holy Spirit, who purifies the heart that He may take up His abiding presence there. Nor

Sanctification is more than a negation of sin, it has an unlimited positive side, in which moral health promotes growth, strength and enlargement. . . . There is a difference in entire sanctification in its beginnings, in its infancy, and in its maturity as an advanced, established and confirmed state of purity. . . . Sanctification does not put a finality to anything within the heart except the existence and practice of sin. Perfection in quality, as is the case in perfect love, does not exclude increase in quantity.—J. A. WOOD.

It will be remembered that we have found sanctification to imply both *the death to sin,* and *the life of righteousness.* And when we speak of entire sanctification as to the former part of it, we say that it may be attained at once—*it is an instantaneous work.* . . . But in relation to the latter part of this great work, viz., the life of righteousness, embracing all holy affections, and pious efforts, it is regarded as entirely progressive.—PECK, *Christian Perfection,* p. 212.

should we forget that it is not by the holy heart that
the work of God goes forward, but by Him who dwells
within the holy heart. In Him, and not in what He has
wrought within us, lies the secret of progress in the
divine life. Failure to recognize this great truth prevents
many from entering into this full privilege in Christ,
while at the same time it gives rise to grave errors in
doctrine.

There are those who, having entered into this gracious experience of entire sanctification, have had their
minds so occupied at first with the marvelous cleansing
wrought within that for a time they have failed to grasp
the full extent of their privileges in Christ. Thus far
Christ was only their Aaron, not the fullness of the
Melchisedec priesthood. What a glorious revelation it
was to my own soul, while studying this precious Epistle,
when this great truth broke in upon me like a sunburst
from heaven! Christ is a Priest forever! His priestly
work did not cease when we were cleansed from sin;
His purpose is to make our hearts His divine presence
chambers, where His glory shall be revealed more and
more. As when a commercial house fails, it is said to
go into the hands of a receiver, who takes complete
charge of its affairs, so I saw that our lives from henceforth are to be lived through a Divine Receiver, our
great High Priest, who as a Son has been perfected
forevermore. What a change that worked in my thinking; what a burden it lifted from my heart; what comfort
and assurance it brought to my life! Nor has He ever

Sheridan Baker says that soon after he entered the sanctified life he
began to turn his attention away from what had been "done for him"
to what "he saw before him." He saw, as have many others, that a
state of purity and general fullness of the Spirit were small matters
compared with "all the fulness of God," and "living in the realm of the
'exceeding abundantly above all that we ask or think.' " Since that
time, he says, "I have been a seeker, continuously, not for pardon or
purity, or the grace already received, but for more and more of the
Christ nature."—SHERIDAN BAKER, *Hidden Manna.*

It was this grasp of the fullness of grace in the Melchisedec priesthood of Jesus that led the saintly John Fletcher to say, "With me it is a
small thing to be cleansed from all sin. I want to be filled with all the
fulness of God." William Bramwell, one of the early Methodist preachers,
exclaimed, "To be justified is great; to be sanctified is great; but, oh, to
be filled with all the fulness of God!"

failed to guide me by His Spirit in times of perplexity, or to strengthen me by His power in all of life's conflicts and sorrows. What a joy to know that He cares for us better than we can care for ourselves! This was no new work of grace; it was a fresh grasp of truth through the Spirit, one of the glorious surprises from the consecration of the "unknown bundle."

There are grave errors in doctrine also that flow from a failure to grasp the scope of this great truth. There are those who seek the baptism with the Holy Spirit as a gift of power for service under the symbol of Melchisedec, and overlook Christ's preliminary work of cleansing under the symbol of Aaron. But the work of Christ on the throne is by virtue of His work on the Cross, and the Blood shed there was for the cleansing from sin. Nor can Christ fully reign in the heart without this cleansing, for the carnal mind is not subject to the law of God. Another error is the limiting of sanctification to the work of cleansing, and viewing the baptism with the Holy Spirit as an additional work of grace, or at least a gift of power. But sanctification is more than cleansing; it is cleansing in order to indwelling. There can be no sanctification without the sanctifying presence of the Holy Spirit.

4. *A changed priesthood necessitates a changed law.* "For the priesthood being changed, there is made of necessity a change also of the law. For he of whom these things are spoken pertaineth to another tribe, of which no man gave attendance at the altar" (7: 12-13). Since the Levitical priesthood was constituted, regulated, and maintained by law, a change in the kind or order of priesthood would necessarily make a change in the law which supported that priesthood. This is self-evident. The writer approaches this subject cautiously, using such mild and general terms as *metatithemenes* (μετατιθεμένης), "being changed," and *metathesis* (μετάθεσις), "a change"; but having taken this initial step, he will show later (7:18) that this change means a complete disannulment of the law affecting the constitution and service of the Levitical priesthood. Concerning

the word *meteskeken* (μετέσχηκεν) in verse 13, which in the Authorized Version is translated "pertaineth to," and sometimes is equally well rendered "has part in," Bishop Westcott says: "The choice of this word points to the voluntary assumption of humanity by the Lord. It is not said simply that He was born of another tribe; He was of His own will so born" (*Commentary*, p. 184).

The Rise of the New Order of Priesthood (7:14-19). The argument for the new order or kind of priesthood is presented in two sections, the first marked by the words "It is evident," the second by the words "And it is yet far more evident." To set off these arguments more distinctly, the writer uses two different Greek words. For the first he uses the word *prodelon* (πρόδηλον), which means evidenced by facts; and for the second, the word *katadelon* (κατάδηλον), which expresses a conclusion drawn from proper inferences.

1. "For it is evident that our Lord sprang out of Juda; of which tribe Moses spake nothing concerning the priesthood" (7:14). Here the evidence is one of fact, plainly supported by the genealogical records so meticulously kept by the Jews. Again, nothing is more plainly set forth in the Scriptures than that the Messiah was to be of the lineage of David and of the tribe of Judah; and yet of this tribe Moses said nothing concerning the priesthood. There can be but one conclusion: the introduction of a new order or kind of priesthood drawn from the kingly line meant the exclusion of Aaron and his house from the priestly office.

2. "And it is yet far more evident: for that after the similitude of Melchisedec there ariseth another priest, who is made, not after the law of a carnal commandment, but after the power of an endless life. For he testifieth, Thou art a priest for ever after the order of Melchisedec" (7:15-17). This further evidence is to be found in the declaration of the Scriptures that God himself testifies of One who is a Priest forever after a new order or kind, that of Melchisedec. This word of scripture no Jew would question. The new order is spiritual rather than legal, royal rather than sacerdotal, and

eternal rather than transitory. The writer introduces the thought also that, while perfection was not only unattained by the Levitical priesthood, it was never intended that it should be attained by this order. He will show later that this priesthood supported by law was but the shadow of things to come (10:1) and looked forward to the priesthood of Christ, whose atoning sacrifice alone could cleanse men from all sin and bring them into the presence of God. He does not say that this law had no value; he merely says that it was weak and therefore could only pave the way for something better. St. Paul seizes upon this thought and calls the law "our schoolmaster to bring us unto Christ" (Gal. 3:24).

This advanced argument makes the transitoriness of the Levitical priesthood to rest upon two striking contrasts: (1) that between law and power, and (2) that between a carnal or fleshly commandment and that of an endless life. In the first contrast it is shown that the Levitical priesthood rests solely upon positive law. By positive law is meant a secondary enactment intended to protect or perpetuate something more fundamental. It is therefore transitory and may be revoked when its purpose is fulfilled. Thus the Levitical priests were merely "law-made," while the true Messianic priesthood of Christ rested upon the fundamental law of spiritual qualification and inherent fitness for the office.

The second contrast carries the thought still further. Here the word "commandment" is used, for the writer evidently is not referring to the whole Mosaic law but only to that portion which concerns the priesthood. The word "carnal" or fleshly calls attention to the fact that all the requirements for the Levitical priesthood were of a physical or fleshly nature. No mention is made of moral or spiritual fitness. It was marked by outward descent, bodily perfection, and ceremonial purity. A commandment, therefore, based solely upon fleshly requirements of a body subject to death must of necessity be transitory in its very nature. Over against this is set, in contrast, an endless or indissoluble life. Christ indeed laid down His life as a Sacrifice for sin, but he had power also to take it again (John 10:18). "Thou art a priest for ever" not only means that in looking forward the priesthood will never cease, but also in looking backwards that it had never had a beginning. The priesthood of the Son rests in the eternity of God. A Priest forever, He lives and works in the power of divine life.

The Disannulling of the Commandment. "For there is verily a disannulling of the commandment going before for the weakness and unprofitableness thereof" (7:18). This marks the writer's conclusion concerning the Levitical priesthood. We note briefly the stages in the argument. (1) It began with the simple question, What need was there of another kind of priesthood? (2) Then follows a self-evident truth, that if the priesthood be changed, there must also be a change in the law that constitutes and regulates it. (3) The evidence for a new order of priesthood is then presented, (a) from the fact that the new priesthood was to spring from Judah, which is not of the Levitical order; (b) from the scripture statement that God testified to His Son, "Thou art a priest for ever." (4) The argument is then reduced to the fundamental character of the two orders of priesthood: the Levitical priesthood being made after the law of a carnal commandment; the Messianic, after the power of an endless life. To this may be added (5) a general summary, "For the law made nothing perfect," which serves as a transition to the next subject, "the bringing in of a better hope." As in verse 16 there is

Every reader of verses 18, 19 is reminded of Gal. 4:9; Rom. 8:3. "No one can doubt that it is one of those coincidences which could hardly take place where there was not community of thought and diction." (Alford) We think, however, that we trace still more; even nothing less than a common author. The likeness of our context extends to a likeness between verses 16 and Romans 8:2, where: "the law of the Spirit of life in Christ Jesus hath made me free from the law of sin and death," seems to be the very truth expressed by calling Christ: "A priest raised up not according to a law of carnal commandment, but according to power of life indissoluble." It is the same truth doing service in Romans 8, among Gentile Christians, as here it does service among Jewish Christians. It is but the same Author speaking in two situations, as it is the same truth for two different relations.—LOWRIE, *An Explanation of the Hebrews*, pp. 247-58.

likewise in these two verses a double contrast, in which the commandment is superseded by a better hope; and its weakness and unprofitableness, by the power through which we draw nigh to God.

A clear distinction must be made between the moral law which flows from the nature of God, and was in force from the time of man's creation, and what is here called the commandment, by which the Aaronic priesthood was instituted and regulated. St. Paul is referring to the moral law when he says that "the law is holy, and the commandment holy, and just, and good" (Rom. 7:12); and the author of this Epistle is referring to the ceremonial law as it concerned the priesthood of Aaron, when he says it was disannulled because of its "weakness and unprofitableness." The law can make nothing perfect—either the moral or the ceremonial law, but for very different reasons. The moral law is perfect in that it is God's will for man, but it was weak through the flesh (Rom. 8:3). Such were its standards that sinful men could not render perfect obedience. It could therefore only condemn the disobedient, not help him. On the other hand, the ceremonial law was weak in itself, and being imperfect itself, it could not make "the comers thereunto perfect."

To understand the differences, then, between the Aaronic and the Melchisedec orders of priesthood and their consequent covenants, it is necessary to set life over against law. God's creatures act according to the nature of the life given them. A good tree brings forth good fruit, and an evil tree evil fruit. So also man in his original state acted according to the holiness of his life. But man was created a moral and spiritual being and capable of a probationary choice between right and wrong. When man fell into sin, his life became perverted, and therefore we are told that the law "was added because of transgressions"; that is, a law called the "commandment" was added to enforce another law. Law is, then, an evidence of a life that is wrong, but it is powerless to correct it. A holy life will manifest itself in holy thoughts and deeds. Holiness always manifests

THE EPISTLE TO THE HEBREWS

itself in love; love, when genuine, always leads to holiness. Aaron was a priest after a "carnal commandment"; Christ is a Priest after the "power of an endless life."

Now we are told that the law and the commandment were "holy, and just, and good." The work of Christ, therefore, is not to add more law, but to so change the life as to bring it into harmony with the law of God. Only as we see that this new order of priesthood acts as a life within us, our very own life, do we begin to appreciate the depths of the Melchisedec order of Christ's priesthood. Our lives are so strengthened by the inbreathing of Him who is "the life" that His life within becomes our life; and in its outflow, our life is His life manifested through us. When the carnal self-life is crucified, then and then only can we say with the Apostle Paul, "Nevertheless I live; yet not I, but Christ liveth in me: and the life which I now live in the flesh I live by the faith of the Son of God, who loved me, and gave himself for me" (Gal. 2: 20). We may say, then, that Aaron ministered from without; Christ ministers within. Aaron ministered through typical sacrifices; Christ ministers the Spirit. The ministry of Christ is the outflow of holiness and righteousness from His inmost being; and since His is an "endless life," there need never be an interruption or a breakdown on the part of those in whom He dwells.

The Better Hope. "For the law made nothing perfect, but the bringing in of a better hope did; by the which we draw nigh to God" (7: 19). While the law made nothing perfect, it did serve to introduce a better hope. Since hope is at once objective and subjective, this "better hope" must be so considered.

1. *The objective hope.* This better hope brings in that perfection which God provided for man through the Lamb slain from the foundation of the world (Rev. 13: 8); and includes a cleansing from all sin and a restoration to perfect fellowship with God. This was accomplished by our great High Priest through His death on the Cross, His resurrection, His ascension, and His

session at the right hand of the Father. The blood of beasts offered by the Levitical priesthood could not take away sin, but the expiating blood of Jesus Christ, God's Son, cleanses from all sin (I John 1: 7). The ceremonial sacrifices were weak in that they were wholly dependent for their efficacy on the blood of Christ, which was yet to be shed. Those saved under the Old Testament were not saved by those priestly sacrifices, but by faith in the all-atoning blood of Christ, which those sacrifices typified. When therefore the blood of Christ was shed on the Cross, the whole ceremonial system of sacrifices, together with the priesthood by which they were offered, having served their "going before" or typical purpose, were disannulled. They were lost in the better hope, the expiating blood of Jesus Christ, the Son of God, our great High Priest.

2. *The subjective hope.* The writer, having presented the objective hope as the expiatory sacrifice of Christ, gives attention also to the subjective hope in the words "by which we draw nigh to God." Under the Levitical priesthood, God appeared outwardly in the form of a fixed commandment; under the new order of priesthood, God unites himself with man in the person of His Son, who assumes our nature and dwells within it (2: 16b). Thus the better hope brings men into the presence of God through Jesus Christ (I Pet. 3: 18). The words "draw nigh to God" also point the way to the writer's deeper truths which are to come, concerning the rent veil and the entrance into the holy of holies, where dwell the harmony and fellowship accomplished through the Holy Spirit.

THE SURETY OF A BETTER TESTAMENT: A PERPETUAL PRIESTHOOD

The next parallel which the writer draws between the Levitical and Melchisedec orders of the priesthood is concerned with the oath by which the latter order is confirmed. "And inasmuch as not without an oath he was made priest: (for these priests were made without an oath; but this with an oath by him that said unto him, The Lord sware and will not repent, Thou art a priest for ever after the order of Melchisedec:) by so much was Jesus made a surety of a better testament" (7:20-22).

We have traced the steps by which the writer proved the "weakness and unprofitableness" of the Levitical priesthood; and starting from this, it may be well to note briefly the steps by which he reaches the conclusion that Christ is the Surety of a better covenant, which makes possible the uttermost salvation. (1) The Levitical priesthood failed to attain perfection, and therefore any change in the priesthood demands a change in the law. (2) The new priesthood, being one of life rather than law, necessarily finds expression in a new covenant. (3) The perpetuity of the priesthood is confirmed by an oath; therefore this priesthood makes possible a better covenant. (4) This better covenant rests upon the continuity of intercession; therefore this better covenant makes possible an uttermost salvation.

Three things demand consideration here: (1) the nature of the oath; (2) the meaning of the term "surety"; and in the remaining verses of this section (7:23-24), (3) perpetuity of the covenant. These together form the basis for the next main topic, "The Uttermost Salvation."

The Nature of the Oath. "And inasmuch as not without an oath he was made priest" (7:20). In verses 1-10 it was shown that the priesthood after the order of Melchisedec is by the Psalmist represented as a type of the Messianic priesthood, and therefore superior to the Aaronic order. In verses 11-19 the writer proves that the Levitical priesthood and the Mosaic law by which it was constituted and regulated, being typical and preparatory, were but an imperfect stage, destined to be abolished. In verses 20-24 and 28 the writer will show that Jesus is the Messiah; and therefore in opposition to both the Levitical priesthood and the Mosaic law, He is the perfect Priest, who introduces a "better testament" or a perfect covenant.

The word "oath" is from the Greek *horkomosias* (ὁρκωμοσίας) and may mean either an oath or the taking of an oath, in the sense of a sworn statement. The words *pros auton* (πρὸς αὐτόν) are in the Authorized Version translated "unto him," and in the American Revised Version "of him." Westcott points out, however, that these words have a double meaning in relation to the two parts of the verse quoted. The first part has Christ as its Object, i.e., "in regard to him," while the second is addressed directly to Him and is therefore correctly rendered "unto him."

But what need is there for an oath? Is not God's word of itself as infallible and immutable as an oath can make it? Several reasons may be given. (1) This new priesthood, instituted with the solemnity of an oath, which did not obtain in reference to the Aaronic priesthood, indicates that it was a more important appointment, and therefore introduced a better testament. Since it is a time-honored custom to verify our more important transactions with a sworn statement, it is evident that God intended to indicate by these solemn words the importance of the Messianic over the Levitical priesthood. (2) Its importance lies also in the statement to which the oath attached, viz., that Christ was a Priest forever—the unchangeable priesthood of an indissoluble life. Of the Levitical priesthood, God made no mention of perpetuity. (3) To those with deep spiritual insight, the oath marks the difference between the covenant of works and that of faith, between the obedience of the law and the glorious promises of the gospel. Referring again to the oath which God sware to Abraham saying, "By myself have I sworn, saith the Lord . . . that in blessing I will bless thee, and in multiplying I will multiply thy seed as the stars of the heaven, and as the sand which is upon the sea shore" (Gen. 22:16-17), God says, "I will do it." Thus the condition of works which marked the failure of the first covenant is replaced by the law of faith. No merit accrues to man, for all boasting is excluded by this law of faith (cf. Rom. 3: 26-28). Righteousness is the gift of God through Jesus Christ our Lord (Rom. 5: 17).

The Surety of a Better Testament. "By so much was Jesus made a surety of a better testament" (7: 22). The Greek word *egguos* (ἔγγυος), translated "surety," is found only here in the New Testament, and is likewise rare even in classical Greek. The origin of the word is obscure, but the use of its kindred terms clearly fixes its meaning as "a surety." But what is the importance of this word "surety" and what is its meaning? As to its importance, this is indicated by the relation of the word "inasmuch" (v. 20) to the words "by so much" in the present verse. "Inasmuch as not without an oath he was made priest . . . by so much was Jesus made a surety of a better testament." Thus the oath marks both the priesthood and the surety as being eternal and unchangeable, and the superiority of this testament over the old is what Dr. Whedon calls "the measure of the unmeasurable veracity of God." This "better testament" of which Jesus is a Surety was confirmed and established with His own blood (Heb. 9: 15-17).

The word "surety" has been the source of much

Concerning these verses, Dr. Sampson says: "The fact that the Apostle, an infallible expositor, draws this argument from this circumstance, favors the highest theory of the inspiration of the Scriptures. It seems to indicate that we are to consider every trait of the sacred language, every phrase, every word, as placed on record by a divine intention, and as having its meaning."—SAMPSON, *Commentary on the Hebrews*, p. 275.

As the word surety (ἔγγυος) has been often abused or used in an unscriptural and dangerous sense, it may not be amiss to inquire a little further into its meaning. The Greek word means a pledge, and is supposed to be so-called from being lodged with or in the hands of a creditor. It is nearly of the same meaning as bail . . . In this sense therefore, the word which we translate surety, cannot be applied in the above case, for Christ never became surety that if men did not fulfil the conditions of this better covenant, i.e., repent of sin, turn from it, believe on the Son of God, and having received grace, walk as children of light, and be faithful unto death; that He would do all these things for them Himself! This would be both absurd and impossible; and hence the gloss of some here is both absurd and dangerous, viz., "That Christ was the surety of the first covenant, to pay off the debt; and of the second, to perform the duty."—ADAM CLARKE, *Commentary*, Chapter 7.

error in theological thought and needs therefore to be given careful consideration. It should be noted (1) that Jesus is not a Surety to God for man's good conduct, but a Surety of a covenant which God has made with man. Hence, as Dr. Adam Clarke points out, the teaching "that Christ was the surety of the first covenant, to pay off the debt; and of the second, to perform the duty," is both absurd and dangerous. The "better testament" or new covenant is not one of works which demands two sides—that was the weakness of the first covenant; this is a covenant in the sense of a testament, in which God through the death of His Son has made provision for His people to be received solely by faith. Thus the weakness of the flesh is overcome by the power of God, which Jesus communicates through the Holy

What was this oath of God? and when was it given? An old commentator answers, this is none other than the purpose, by no means to be subverted, of the divine decree. He is right. But perhaps we may recognize in it also the immutable assurance given by the Eternal Father to the consciousness of the Eternal Son, whom He addresses. It has no date in time, and is not so much an event as an abiding certainty made manifest. And this gives a sublime force to the present tense "Thou art." "By so much the surety of a better covenant is Jesus," says the Epistle, holding back the proper name to the end for emphasis, employing for the same object the word "surety" (which is not elsewhere in the New Testament in Greek or English) instead of "mediator"; which is frequent, and introducing the thought, new in this connection, of a Covenant to attest, instead of a cause to plead. This also is among the thoughts to be presently renewed and amplified.—CHADWICK, Epistle to the Hebrews, pp. 101-2.

Macknight says that the word is not applicable in this sense (i.e., surety for the good behavior of another) to the Jewish high priests; for to be a proper surety, one must have either power to compel the party to perform that for which he has become his surety; or in the case of his not performing it, he must be able to perform it himself. This being the case, will any one say that the Jewish high priests were sureties to God for the Israelites performing their part of the covenant of the Law? Or to the people for God's performing His part of the covenant? As little is the appellation, surety of the new covenant, applicable to Jesus. For since the new covenant does not require perfect obedience, but only the obedience of faith; if the obedience of faith be not given by men themselves, it cannot be given by another in their room; unless we suppose that men can be saved without personal faith. I must therefore infer, that those who speak of Jesus as the surety of the new covenant, must hold that it requires perfect obedience; which not being in the power of believers to give, Jesus has performed it for them. But is not this to make the covenant of grace a covenant of works, contrary to the whole tenor of Scripture? For these reasons I think the Greek commentators have given the true meaning to ἔγγυος in this passage when they explain it be mediator (μεσίτης). (Quoted by Dr. Adam Clarke in his Commentary on this verse.)

Spirit in answer to simple faith in the atoning blood of Christ.

(2) The text does not say that Christ *will be* a Surety of the covenant; He *is* our Surety. This was accomplished by His incarnation—His life, death, resurrection, and ascension. But since it is the priesthood that is under consideration, only His intercession is mentioned as the consummation of the Incarnation. He is the Surety of a better testament, for in His glorified humanity He has entered into the presence of God for us. "A surety for the most part," says Bishop Westcott, "pledges himself that something will be; but here, the ascended Christ witnesses that something is; the assurance is not of the future, but of that which is present though unseen. It must be noticed that Christ is not said here to be a surety for man to God, but a surety of a covenant of God with man" (*Commentary*, p. 191).

The Perpetuity of the Covenant. "And they truly were many priests, because they were not suffered to continue by reason of death: but this man, because he continueth ever, hath an unchangeable priesthood" (7:23-24). The writer has shown that the new priesthood is superior to the old in that it was confirmed by an oath; and being a better priesthood, it ushered in a better testament or covenant—one of faith instead of works. Now he adds to these by the conjunction *kai* (*καὶ*) another aspect of the new covenant, i.e., its perpetuity. The words "and they truly," referring to the many priests of the old order, are intended as an emphatic declaration of that which could not be disputed, in that "they were not suffered to continue by reason of death." The argument is presented, however, not only to account for the many priests, but also in proof of the temporary nature of the order, due to weakness and infirmity. The whole system of the Levitical priesthood and the covenant which it represented was marked by change, weakness, and death. In contrast with this, Jesus has an unchangeable priesthood by virtue of His indissoluble life. His office is perpetual. It can never

THE SURETY OF A BETTER TESTAMENT

pass to another. Thus in these three sections is shown the supreme dignity of Christ's priesthood in that it was confirmed by an oath; it is shown that He is the Author of a better testament in virtue of the power of an indissoluble life; and He is supreme in ability, in that His is a perpetual priesthood, uninterrupted in administration and without a successor.

THE UTTERMOST SALVATION: AN EFFECTUAL PRIESTHOOD

In our interpretation of the spiritual experiences which attach to the different aspects of the person and work of Christ, we have discussed the following: (1) In connection with the *Deity of Christ,* we have the *Great Salvation,* and the consequent warning against *Neglect.* (2) In connection with the *Humanity and Humiliation,* we have *Sanctification,* with a warning against *Hardening the Heart.* (3) Concerning Christ as an *Apostle,* we have the *Rest of Faith,* and a warning against *Unbelief.* (4) Concerning His *Priesthood,* we have *Eternal Salvation,* and a warning against *Indifference* or dullness of mind. (5) As it concerns the *Better Promises,* we have *Christian Perfection* and a warning against *Slothfulness* or lack of progress.

(6) We now approach that aspect of spiritual experience known as the *Uttermost Salvation,* but here we have no warning. Instead, the verses which follow enumerate the perfections of Christ, who, as an effectual Priest, is able to save to the uttermost. There are two additional aspects and warnings to follow: (7) the *Holiest of All* in connection with the work of the High Priest in the sanctuary. Here it is that the Blood of the atonement is mentioned, and the warning that follows is against *Sinning Willfully.* (8) Finally, we have the simple word *Holiness* and the injunction to "follow peace with all men, and holiness [or 'the sanctification'], without which no man shall see the Lord" (12:14). This is further summed up in the supreme purpose of the Epistle: "Wherefore Jesus also, that he might sanc-

tify the people with his own blood, suffered without the gate. Let us go forth therefore unto him without the camp, bearing his reproach" (13: 12-13). Here we have the warning, *See that ye refuse not him that speaketh* (12: 25-29). Since this is spoken in connection with our eternal inheritance and the final judgment, it may well be considered a warning against *Final Apostasy.*

Saved to the Uttermost. "Wherefore he is able also to save them to the uttermost that come unto God by him, seeing he ever liveth to make intercession for them" (7: 25). This verse is introduced naturally by the preceding one, which sets forth the unchangeable priesthood of Christ; and it is because he "ever liveth to make intercession" for us that He is able to save us "completely," "perfectly," or "to the uttermost." The writer has shown that perfection does not come by the Levitical priesthood, but he does say in effect, if not in words, that perfection does come through Christ. He does not use the term perfection, *teleiosis* (τελέιωσις), but the more general term *sozein* (σώζειν), "to save;" to which is added the phrase *eis to panteles* (εἰς τὸ παντελές), which means "completely," "perfectly," and "to the uttermost," as indicated above. This is a strong expression ascribing to Christ a salvation which includes all possible perfections, all beneficent ends, pardon of sins, sanctification, our "fruit unto holiness, and the end everlasting life" (Rom. 6: 22). This verse justifies the reference to Jesus as the Sanctifier as given in 2: 11, and this sanctification in its wider meaning includes the cleansing from all sin and the indwelling of the Holy Spirit.

Another Use of the Word Uttermost. The Greek words *eis to panteles,* here translated as "to the uttermost," are found in one other place in the New Testament (Luke 13: 11). It was said of the woman who was bowed together by the spirit of infirmity for eighteen years and could in no wise lift up herself, the Greek words being identical with those above. She could not lift up herself "wholly" or "to the uttermost." As through the miraculous healing she was enabled to lift up herself to her full height physically, so the writer of this Epistle tells us that Jesus also enables men to lift themselves up to their full height spiritually. God never destroys in man any faculty which He has created, nor does He add any; but He does so cleanse from all sin and unrighteousness that a man may stretch himself up to his full height. To what heights the Spirit of holiness may raise and sustain the soul that is fully committed to Him we cannot know; but we do know that whatever heights are attained are due to the new humanity, perfected in Christ by obedience and suffering, and now imparted to His people by the power of the Holy Spirit.

The Power of Intercession. The word "intercession," which reveals the means by which Christ saves to the uttermost, is fraught with deep spiritual meaning and comfort. The Greek word *entugchanein* (ἐντυγχάνειν), found also in classic usage, means primarily "to meet with" or "to deal with" another in matters of common concern. It is found in connection with the word *hyper* in Rom. 8:26, where the Holy Spirit is said to make intercession for us with groanings which cannot be uttered. Unlike the Levitical priests, who needed to offer sacrifices daily for themselves, Christ made one supreme sacrifice forever; and this He did when through the eternal Spirit He offered himself without spot to God (9:11). Hence because of His perfection in character and sacrifice, He needs now only to speak the word and the work is done. As He spoke the worlds into existence and now upholds all things by the power of His word, so also by that word He is able to save from the uttermost to the uttermost. If with such ease our Lord in the heavens ministers to the needs of His people, should we not more frequently and in all confidence boldly approach the throne of grace, that we may obtain mercy and find grace to help in time of need? (4:16)

THE CHARACTERISTICS OF THE NEW ORDER: A QUALIFIED PRIESTHOOD

The writer now passes to his climax and describes for himself and for us the Ideal Priest, which is Christ (7:26-28). The High Priest which becomes us, or is suitable to our needs, must have a threefold perfection: (1) the perfection of character, (2) the perfection of His offering, and (3) the perfection of intercession. Before considering these qualifications, however, it will be well to note that this is the first time our author uses the term high priest in connection with the Melchisedec order. Previous to this, it is used solely in connection with the Aaronic priesthood. Christ is not only the Antitype of the Aaronic high priesthood; He is also a Priest of an entirely different order. When therefore these two aspects of Christ are combined as they are here, their distinctness must not be confused. The writer is about to speak of the great atonement of Christ, His supreme sacrifice, and His entrance through the veil into the presence of God for us. He will thus show that Christ fulfilled the symbolism that attached solely to the Aaronic high priesthood. But Christ was also a Priest of a new order, the distinctness of which lies in this: (1) Aaron was a priest which had infirmity; Christ is the eternal Son of God. (2) Aaron had a "worldly" or earthly sanctuary; Christ ministers from His throne in the heavens. (3) The blood of animal sacrifices, which could never take away sin, was done away in the sacrifice of the body of Christ once for all. Hence Christ becomes the Minister of a heavenly sanctuary, and the Surety of a better covenant. Let us now notice the threefold perfections of this Ideal High Priest.

Christ Was Perfect as to His Character and Calling. "For such an high priest became us, who is holy, harmless, undefiled, separate from sinners, and made higher than the heavens" (7:26). There are five statements here concerning the perfection of Jesus, our great High Priest, and each of them is in apposition with the word *toioutos* (τοιοῦτος), "such an one." (1) He was "holy" within and without. The word for holy is not *hagios* (ἅγιος), which means separated unto God, but *hosios* (ὅσιος), which is a separation from pollution. (2) He was "harmless." The Greek word is *akakos* (ἄκακος), the negative of badness, and therefore asserts that nothing base or even inferior attached to Him. He was without "guile" in every manifestation of His life. (3) He was "undefiled," from *amiantos* (ἀμίαντος), "without a stain," not bearing any of the blemishes due to sin. Perhaps this has reference to the necessity of bodily perfection in the Old Testament sacrifices. (4) He was "separate from sinners"; and while truly human, as a Man among men, He kept himself free from their sins. It will be noted that all the foregoing are but varying emphases of the one supreme quality of holiness as freedom from sin. To these has been added that (5) He was "made higher than the heavens"—doubtless a reference to the high priest's entrance into the holy of holies on the great Day of Atonement. It will be shown later that it is one of the chief characteristics of our High Priest that He ministers from the throne in the heavenly sanctuary.

Christ Was Perfect as a Sacrificial Offering. "Who needeth not daily, as those high priests, to offer up sacrifice, first for his own sins, and then for the people's: for this he did once, when he offered up himself" (7:27). This is the second evidence of His perfection. Unlike the Levitical high priests, He had no sin for which to atone, and therefore became solely a Propitiation for others. The contrasts are sharply drawn. The Levitical priests offered sacrifices daily; He, only once forever. Their sacrifices could not make the comers thereto perfect; His shed blood cleanses from all sin and unrighteousness. As in the previous verses we have the first mention of a High Priest in connection with the order of Melchisedec, so here we have the first mention of Christ as a Sacrifice. The words "offer up" must be completed by the words "to God," thus indicating that Christ offered himself on the altar of God. He was both Offerer and Offering. In 2:9 it is said that Christ "was made a little lower than the angels for the suffering of death," and thereby "crowned with glory and honour." Here we see that glory and honor manifested in tasting death for every man.

Christ and His Perfect Intercessory Work. "For the law maketh men high priests which have infirmity; but the word of the oath, which was since the law, maketh the Son, who is consecrated for evermore" (7:28). This verse is a recapitulation of truths previously presented, but here summarized and stated in their final form. (1) The law makes men high priests who have infirmity or weakness. The weakness here mentioned includes both the natural limitations of finite men and the personal imperfections of the high priest. (2) The word of the oath, by which is meant the "taking of an oath," was subsequent to the law, and therefore must take cognizance of that law. This it does by abrogating it (verse 18); for a change in the priesthood necessitates a change in the law (verse 12). (3) This greater High Priest is a "Son, who is consecrated for evermore." The word "Son" is used here without the article and refers to the incarnate sonship of Christ. This usage the writer has made clear in the earlier chapters of his Epistle. The Word or "eternal Son," having become incarnate as the God-Man, lived the life of a Man among men during the days of His flesh, and through His human experience became "a merciful and faithful high priest in things pertaining to God, to make reconciliation for the sins of the people" (2:17).

The word "consecrated" as used here is very unfortunate, and greatly confuses the thought. The Greek word *teleleiomenon* (τετελειομένον) is the perfect passive participle of *teleioo* (τελειόω), and means "has been perfected" and still continues to be perfect. Perfection, *teleiosis* (τελείωσις), was not attained by the Levitical priesthood, but was attained by the Son, who has been perfected forevermore. Thus the perfection of the Son becomes the direct antithesis of the lack of perfection in the Aaronic priests. But how did Christ attain this perfection? He "learned obedience by the things which he suffered; and being made perfect, be became the author of eternal salvation unto all them that obey him" (5:8-9). But now, having met and overcome death as the last enemy, and thus become the First-born from the dead, He has ascended on high, carrying His humanity—and ours—in its glorified state to the very throne of God. On the ground of His finished atonement on earth, and His intercessory presence at the right hand of the Father, he received the Holy Spirit as a Gift to His Church, by which means He dwells within His people in sanctifying power. When He shall come the second time, we too shall rise in resurrection power and glory, and "be like him; for we shall see him as he is" (I John 3:2). What a marvelous triumph of the Christ! What a glorious hope for His people!

CHAPTER VIII

THE BETTER MINISTRY AND THE NEW COVENANT

In the previous chapters the writer has proved the necessity of a new order of priesthood, based scripturally upon the Old Testament references to Melchisedec. He is now about to show the necessity of a new order of service, based upon a comparison between Aaron and Christ. This new section is usually considered as extending from 8:1 to 10:18, and includes a discussion of the two ministries (8:3-6); the two covenants or dispensations (8:7-13); the two tabernacles (9:1-12); the two offerings (9:13-28); and the two sacrifices (10:1-18). The two veils (10:19-22) must also be considered, but these verses are usually classified in the hortatory section. The present chapter will be considered under the four following divisions: (1) The Transition; (2) A Minister of the Sanctuary; (3) The Mediator of the Better Covenant; and (4) The Provisions of the New Covenant.

THE TRANSITION

The writer, having gathered up the thought of the previous chapters concerning the perfection of Christ's priesthood, turns immediately to a discussion of the perfection of His ministry. "Now of the things which we have spoken this is the sum: We have such an high priest, who is set on the right hand of the throne of the Majesty in the heavens" (8:1). These transitional verses concerning the kingship and priesthood of Christ are based on Psalms 110, the first on the words, "Sit thou on my right hand, until I make thine enemies thy footstool"; and the second on the statement, "Thou art a priest for ever after the order of Melchizedek."

The Sum or Chief Point of the Argument. "Now of the things which we have spoken this is the sum" (8:1). The word *kephalaion* (κεφάλαιον) has been used by both ancient and modern commentators in two different ways: (1) as "sum" in the sense of a summary; and (2) as "sum" in the sense of the chief or main point of the argument. Vaughan elaborates the latter point as a capital, chief, or crowning particular, a main point, and thus interprets this portion of the verse, "As a capital upon the things which are being said—a thought, forming the headstone of the argument"; and again, "As a main point crowning our statement." This crowning point is expressed in the words, "We have such an high priest." The word "such" signifies the dignity and glory of Christ's person, previously described as "holy, harmless, undefiled, separate from sinners, and made higher than the heavens" (7:26). It is such a Priest as this that becomes us, or is suited to us.

Glorious as is this truth, it is too often regarded merely as a doctrinal statement and not as a practical way of life. But the writer is not dealing with abstractions. He is rather disclosing to the hearts of his Hebrew brethren and to all mankind the fullness of God's great salvaion, and seeking to rightly direct their faith. He would have them understand that if by their confession of the crucified but risen and ascended Lord they had become outcasts from the commonwealth of Israel, and no longer worshipers in their earthly courts, they were not therefore without the great High Priest of their confession, who ministers in the heavenly sanctuary. Ministering in the heavens, all that Jesus is and does is heavenly; and this heavenly life Jesus reveals in the hearts of His people by His indwelling through the Holy Spirit. "The throne of the Majesty in the heavens" is therefore no longer to be contemplated at a distance and with dread; rather the people are brought nigh to God in filial affection. Our High Priest is such that we can make a full committal of our lives to Him, and day by day live our lives through His priestly intercession. We have "such an high priest" not only in theory, but in personal experience, and by Him live in the presence of God within the veil.

"The Right Hand of the Throne." The statements made concerning the High Priest and His ministry appear to have been grouped together, in order to be immediately grasped and properly related to each other. Hence we have the throne, the Majesty, and the heavens representing His kingly authority; and closely related, His priestly functions in the true tabernacle, likewise in the heavens. The words "is set on the right hand of the throne" suggest a voluntary act, of One who takes His seat by virtue of a task accomplished or a purpose fully achieved; while the "right hand" suggests the place of honor and power, as well as of satisfaction and delight. Christ's right to the throne is the reward of His personal achievement. We have seen that the Son was made man "for the suffering of death, crowned with glory and honour; that he by the grace of God should taste death for every man" (2:9). He has therefore received a twofold glory: one by right, that of becoming man; and one by the grace of God, that of personal achievement (cf. John 12:28). Concerning the first, Jesus said of His human life, "I have power to lay it down, and I have power to take it again" (John 10:18). While it is also said that He was raised "by the glory of the Father," and again, "by the exceeding greatness of his power," it is clear that Jesus participated in His own resurrection as He did in His incarnation, and that neither of these was by a power wholly external to himself. The Father gave Him to have life in himself (John 5:26). When He arose from the dead, He had by personal achievement triumphed over death as the last enemy, and therefore had both the right and the power to take His seat at the right hand of the throne, where He was crowned with glory and honor.

"The Majesty in the Heavens." At this point everything turns towards the heavens. The attention is directed upwards. Here the writer brings before us a

series of contrasts, based on two levels, the heavenly substance and the earthly shadow. The expression "in the heavens" can but refer to the abode and manifestation of the glorious presence of God, the place where the will of God is done in that perfection that excludes all sin. Jesus is said to have passed through the heavens (4:14); to have been made higher than the heavens (7:26); and to be seated on the throne in the heavens (8:1). The suffering and tears in the days of His flesh, His death on the Cross, by which atonement was made for sin, are over; and from His throne in the heavens He now reigns with authority to put into effect the salvation wrought out on earth. As High Priest, He represents atonement for sin; as King, the power of redemption. As a Priest, He reigns with the dignity and authority of a King; as a King, He administers the covenant wrought out for us in the days of His humiliation. As High Priest in His glorified humanity, He represents man to God; and in His divine nature, He represents God to man. All that He does, whether as Priest or King, is heavenly; and this heavenly life He communicates to us through the Spirit. Thus it is that He sets up within the hearts of His people the kingdom of Heaven, which in its initial stage is described as "righteousness, and peace, and joy in the Holy Ghost" (Rom. 14:17).

A Minister of the Sanctuary

The kingly aspect of Christ having been presented, attention is now turned to His ideal priesthood. He is "a minister of the sanctuary, and of the true tabernacle, which the Lord pitched, and not man" (8:2). Though seated at the right hand of the throne of God, Christ is still a Priest—a Priest clothed with royal authority, a King with the gentle forbearance of a Priest. A priest must not only bring an offering; he must also have a sanctuary in which he ministers, a place of approach to God. Christ's sanctuary is in the heavens, in the true tabernacle which the Lord pitched. He ministers the spiritual realities of heaven. It is there that He meets

His people and brings them into the presence of God through the Spirit. The word used here for "sanctuary" is not the ordinary term *ho naos* (ὁ ναός), but *ton hagion* (τῶν ἁγίων), "of the holies"; and since Christ's priestly functions attach to the whole of the divine indwelling, the more general term *skenes* (σκηνῆς) or "tabernacle" is added. "The general thought," says Westcott, "is that of the immediate Presence of God (τὰ ἅγια), and the scene of His manifestation to His worshippers (ἡ σκηνή)." Christ having entered the holy of holies by His own blood, the writer will later show that thereby He has prepared a new and living way into the holiest, and lives within the veil. We too may enter by the Blood within the veil, where dwells the sanctifying presence of the Holy Spirit. It is to such a life of holiness that the writer bids us enter.

The High Priest and His Offering. "For every high priest is ordained to offer gifts and sacrifices: wherefore it is of necessity that this man have somewhat also to offer" (8:3). It follows therefore that Christ, being a High Priest, must have "somewhat" to offer, and the writer has told us in a preliminary way that this "somewhat" is himself (7:27). But only as he takes up the matter of the greater and more perfect tabernacle can the writer bring his thought to completion, and set forth in any adequate manner the supreme offering of Christ. This he does under the symbolism of the great Day of Atonement. Leviticus 16 must ever be associated with Hebrews 9 and 10— the former the great atonement chapter of the Old Testament, the latter the great atonement chapters of the New Testament. It is interesting to note that in the Greek the above text (8:3) sets forth a great truth not always fully recognized in the English translations. The word *prospherein* (προσφέρειν), meaning "to offer," as applied to the Jewish priests, is an iterative, present infinitive, signifying that they brought their offerings over and over again, never ceasing to bring them from year to year. The word, however, as applied to Christ's offering, is *prosenegkei* ($\pi\rho o\sigma\epsilon\nu\acute{\epsilon}\gamma\kappa\eta$), the same root word but here used in the aorist subjunctive, and therefore punctiliar, signifying but one offering on the part of Jesus, and not a repetition of offerings. This fact the writer treats more fully in chapters 9 and 10.

The Heavenly Sanctuary. The next verse marks a further step in the progress of the argument. "For if he were on earth, he should not be a priest, seeing that there are priests that offer gifts according to the law" (8:4). The Levitical priests were divinely appointed to serve in the earthly Tabernacle; hence it would be unlawful for another, even though superior, to serve in their place. The argument is as follows: (1) Christ could not be a priest on earth, for He was not of the Levitical line. The writer is emphatic. He would not even be a priest (literally, "having been being a priest") of any kind, much less a high priest, to whom alone belonged the *prosphora* ($\pi\rho o\sigma\phi o\rho\acute{a}$) or "offering" of blood in the holy of holies on the great Day of Atonement. (2) The gifts and sacrifices of the Levitical priests were also prescribed by law, this law being understood as divine authority for the institution as a whole, including the ritual as well as the duty. Since Christ could not be a priest on earth, nor could the "somewhat" which He had to offer be acceptable in the earthly Tabernacle, it is clearly evident that His superior priesthood demanded a heavenly sanctuary, and His offering a "greater and more perfect tabernacle." Thus the necessity of a heavenly sanctuary is set forth by the inefficiency of the earthly priesthood and the inadequacy of the earthly Tabernacle.

The Substance and the Shadow. The progress of thought continues with reference to the Levitical priests, "who serve unto the example and shadow of heavenly things, as Moses was admonished of God when he was about to make the tabernacle: for, See, saith he, that thou make all things according to the pattern shewed to thee in the mount" (8:5). This verse is a reference to Exod. 25:9, 40, where it is clearly stated that the

Tabernacle and its furniture made by Moses was but a copy of that shown him in the mount. It is the heavenly sanctuary that is the substance; the earthly Tabernacle was but a copy or a shadow. For this reason the writer describes the Levitical priests as doing service in a realm of shadows and in a shrine made by human hands. But while the earthly Tabernacle service was but a shadow of the heavenly reality, it was at least that. Its priests typified the one great Priest; and its sacrifices, the one great Sacrifice on the Cross. The writer further assumes that as there was a priesthood with a system of sacrifices set up by Moses, so there must be a Priest in the royal sanctuary (verse 1), and the One who fills it must have "somewhat" to offer (verse 3). The true realities therefore are a High Priest after the eternal order, a heavenly sanctuary, and an offering acceptable to God. This latter we have seen was *himself*, which, through the eternal Spirit, He offered without spot to God.

A Christian Apologetic. The preceding verses furnish a strong apologetic for the Christian position as over against that of Judaism. The Jews might argue (1) that the Aaronic service with its splendid ritual had been their inspiration since childhood, and (2) that the Christian Priest was so far away and invisible that there was nothing to inspire worship. The strength of "the wizardry of a spectacular service, an elaborate apparatus of robes and incense and a visible sacrifice," says Bishop Chadwick, "the church has always felt, and too often has tried to incorporate these methods with her own." The writer of this Epistle points out a better way. This better way places the "spiritual over against the magnificent, and meets all such influences by quickening faith in the invisible," until Christ's offering becomes the more impressive because it is offered behind the veil, too great indeed to have its sphere on earth. Christ is where the Psalmist foretold that He would be, "seated on the right hand of God," and is invisible to us because He has taken that awful seat in light unapproachable; and will remain there expectant until His enemies are made His footstool.

THE MEDIATOR OF A BETTER COVENANT

The writer brings his discussion of Christ's ministry to a climax in the words, "But now hath he obtained a more excellent ministry, by how much also he is the mediator of a better covenant, which was established upon better promises" (8:6). This verse marks the transition, not to a discussion of the offering or the sanctuary, as one would suppose, but to Christ as the Mediator of a better covenant. The writer has already spoken of Christ as the "surety" of the covenant, by which he means a guarantee of its validity; he has also spoken of Christ as the "minister of the sanctuary" in which we are to draw nigh to God. Now he speaks of Christ as the Mediator of a better covenant, without which Mediator sinful man could not stand in the presence of God.

Christ as the Mediator of the Better Covenant. "No idea is more fundamental in Christian theology," says Dr. Pope, "than that of Mediation; and none so obviously depends for a right conception upon its relation to the one and indivisible Person of Christ. With reference to our present purpose the term may be viewed under three aspects. In the union of His Divine and human natures, our Lord is in the highest sense of the word, and in virtue of His twofold nature, a Mediator; but this only on the ground of a mediatorial reconciliation of two parties through His sacrifice as a Third between the Two; and, combining these, His incarnate Person is the Mediator of the Christian covenant in all His acts. Hence our doctrine may be referred to the Incarnation, the Atonement, and the Redeeming ministry of Christ" (POPE, *The Person of Christ*, pp. 43 ff.). Following the outline of the above writer, and lifting into prominence some of his further rich thought concerning the importance of the Mediator, we offer the following.

1. In the Incarnation, mediation has its highest and fullest meaning. Human nature is actually brought into fellowship with the Divine Being in the person of Christ. In the conjoining of God and man, peace becomes "an

accomplished and blessed reality." "Too much stress
cannot be laid upon this, provided only we remember
that the eternal pledge of reconciliation was given to man
only on the presupposal of an atonement which in human
nature Christ should offer for our race."

2. Christ, being both God and man in one Person,
became the Reconciler; for the human nature that He
assumed He offered as a sacrifice on the cross of Calvary to make atonement for the sins of the people. His
human nature, therefore, became the instrument as well
as the pledge of our redemption. "But this is the mystery
of the mediating Person, that each nature gives its own
virtue to His propitiatory work, while that virtue is
the result of His intervention as a Third Person. It is
Divine in its worth, human in its appropriateness,
Divine-human as reconciling God and man." The divinity of Christ's divine-human person gives the offering which He presented on the Cross unlimited value
and acceptance; the offering itself was the ransom price
paid "in that fine gold of the sanctuary, His human life."

3. Christ thus becomes our living Redeemer. His
offering in the highest sense was a living sacrifice, for
the law of His being was such that even in dying He
should live. This is the broader aspect of mediation
"which represents Christ's Person as achieving on earth
and in heaven, the union between God and man." "We
rise, if such word may be used, from the Incarnation as
a pledge of peace, and the Atonement as the redemption
of that pledge, to the Mediatorial ministry of our Lord
Himself in which both are united."

The "Better Promises." The first covenant was established on human promises of obedience to law, but as
St. Paul points out, this failed through the weakness
of the flesh (Rom. 8:3). The new covenant is established upon "better promises," that is, the promises of
God alone, and these confirmed by an oath. It is therefore a covenant of grace instead of works, in which
God's faithfulness is substituted for human weakness.
However, in speaking of the "first covenant," as the

term is used here, it should be borne in mind that previous to the Mosaic covenant there were a number of other covenants. (1) There was first the implied covenant between the Creator and the creature, God assuming certain responsibilities for man, and laying upon him the response of obedience and trust. (2) The first expressed covenant was with Noah (Gen. 9: 8-17), of which the rainbow was given as a sign. So long as there are rainbows, this covenant will stand. (3) The next covenant was with Abraham and his seed, and was of a personal nature, given in the nature of a promise and conditioned on faith. This covenant, St. Paul tells us, "the law, which was four hundred and thirty years after, cannot disannul, that it should make the promise of none effect" (Gal. 3: 17). (4) The next covenant was the Mosaic, which was the first national covenant. For this reason it is known as the "first" or "old" covenant, though the meaning would be more exact perhaps if the word *prote* (πρώτη) had been translated "former." However, it was common in Greek usage for the term "first" to be used in contrast with *deutera* (δευτέρα), and this may account for its usage here.

   The Failure of the First Covenant. The writer here indicates that the first covenant was a failure, and that this failure furnishes the ground for the seeking out of a place for a new covenant. In the words "for finding fault with them," there are two readings. The first is *autous* (αὐτούς), which in the Authorized Version is translated "them"; the second is the neuter form *autois* (αὐτοῖς), found in the Vatican text, and translated "it." If the former reading be preferred, it means that the failure of the old covenant was due to the Israelites alone; if the latter, the reference is to the particulars of the law, which was not able to bring to a consummation the purposes of God for mankind. That one of its weaknesses lay in disobedience is clearly stated in the divine pronouncement, "They continued not in my covenant, and I regarded them not" (8: 9b). But since a new covenant was to be sought, it is evident that some degree of faultiness attached to the covenant itself. This is seen under two aspects: (1) it had no power to enable men to perform the obedience which they had promised; and (2) it could not do away with the sins which followed the disobedience of their covenant vows. It was inadequate, and while divinely given, it was not God's ultimate purpose for men. Hence the making of a new covenant must be interpreted to mean one with finality, one in the giving of which must be included the final consummation. This consummation Christ accomplished when, by His own blood shed on the cross of Calvary, He entered into the heavenly holy of holies and became our High Priest forever.

The Old Testament Oracle and the New Covenant. To indicate that the covenant of God with Moses must be lowered in value by another and later covenant would appear to most Jews as nothing short of sacrilege. They would inquire, "How could it be said that the first covenant was not without fault when it was known to have been divinely given?" The author must sustain his position by a reference to their own sacred Scriptures, and therefore brings forward Jeremiah's oracle which declares, "Behold, the days come, saith the Lord, when I will make a new covenant with the house of Israel, and with the house of Judah" (8: 8; Jer. 31: 31). It should be observed that these words are not merely an inference from the oracle, but God's own assertion. God himself says, "I will make [or consummate] a new covenant"; and the writer argues that if the first covenant had been faultless, or adequate, there would have been no desire for a second. The new covenant is therefore superior in that it works an actual inward experience of holiness through the gift of the Holy Spirit; and it is not limited to a nation, but susceptible of universal diffusion. St. Paul expressly mentions both of these points when he says that "the law . . . was weak through the flesh" (Rom. 8: 3); and, "They which are of faith, the same are the children of Abraham," and therefore heirs of the promise (cf. Gal. 3: 7). He further states that this blessing of Abraham which comes upon the gentiles through Jesus Christ is "that we might receive the promise of the Spirit through faith" (Gal. 3:14). The new covenant therefore occupies a place not filled by the first, and comprehends the whole will of God for men.

A Comparison of the Old and New Covenants. "Not according to the covenant that I made with their fathers in the day when I took them by the hand to lead them out of the land of Egypt; because they continued not in my covenant, and I regarded them not, saith the Lord" (8:9). The words "not according to" are to be understood in the sense of "not after the likeness or pattern" or "not on the scale" of the former covenant. The new covenant was not even to resemble the old, being of an entirely different nature. The words "with their fathers" convey the idea of a benefit for the fathers. "In the day when I took them by the hand to lead them out of the land of Egypt" is a figure derived from a helping hand given to a child or aged person. It suggests the thought that the covenant made with Moses was for an immature people, and not intended to be the ultimate plan of God for His people. The last clause, "because they continued not in my covenant, and I regarded them not, saith the Lord," is a quotation from Jer. 31:32 as it appears in the Septuagint, and is expressed in different words from our Authorized Version. Bishop Chadwick points out that the Hebrew reads, "Though I was a husband to them. Alas, I was!" Estrangement and divorce are in the words, which he says more than justify the expression, "I regarded them not." The tense of *emelesa* (ἠμήλησα) expresses a single act of abandonment, "I gave up caring for them."

Since the new covenant was in no wise to resemble the old, we may note briefly and with profit the following contrasts before taking up more thoroughly the provisions of the new covenant.

1. The first covenant was not faultless; the new covenant is perfect. The first was temporary and made with reference to Another which was to come; the second is the final and enduring expression of the grace of God.

2. The old covenant was national and dealt with men in the aggregate; the new covenant deals with the individual, and rests ultimately upon the promise made to Abraham personally, and to his seed as individuals.

3. The former covenant had reference to material things and was based upon secular promises. There was to be a material inheritance, the land of Canaan. The Lord would deliver His people's enemies into their hands and enlarge their borders. The new covenant is spiritual, for material things cannot satisfy the souls of men.

4. The Mosaic covenant set up a standard or rule of life, but could give neither the power nor the disposition to obey the commands which it imposed upon the people. In the new covenant the law of God is written within, and therefore not only illumines the mind with the possibility of knowing God but gives the disposition to obedience within the heart.

5. The former covenant could not with its continual offerings take away sin. The priests offered that which cost them nothing. The new covenant was established by Christ, who "once in the end of the world hath appeared to put away sin by the sacrifice of himself" (9: 26).

6. The old covenant was limited to the sons of Abraham after the flesh; the new covenant is universal in its scope, for they that are Christ's are "Abraham's seed, and heirs according to the promise" (Gal. 3: 29). Since true faith was the sole condition of Abraham's acceptance, it is therefore the only condition required of the spiritual sons of Abraham, and the Mosaic covenant of works is forever set aside as the basic condition of acceptance with God. "It is of faith, that it might be by grace" (Rom. 4: 16).

THE PROVISIONS OF THE NEW COVENANT

The several lines of thought traced by the writer of this Epistle find their focal point in the glorious truth of the new covenant. The provisions of this covenant are first set forth as an accomplishment of the Mediator

(8: 10-12); and again as they concern the benefits accruing to the people (10: 15-18). In the present account (8: 10-12) the accomplishment of the Mediator is presented preparatory to a consideration of the perfect oblation of Jesus Christ, presented under the symbolism of the great Day of Atonement. This latter was the highest priestly exercise under the Levitical dispensation and a symbol of what was actually accomplished in bringing us to God.

The best outline of these verses, perhaps, is that of Andrew Murray, who arranges them in a threefold division: (1) The Central Blessing of the Covenant; (2) The Crowning Blessing of the Covenant, and (3) The Initial Blessing of the Covenant. This outline follows the scriptural pattern, and illustrates also the general method of presenting the truth. Thus our Lord in His conversations with Nicodemus presented the necessity of the new birth, and later His own death as the means of making it available. St. Peter sets forth the blessings of Pentecost, and then the manner in which this grace is obtained, and St. Paul follows the same order in his speech at Antioch in Pisidia. This order has the endorsement of both scripture and reason, for men must ever be convinced of the blessings of the goal before serious effort will be put forth for its attainment. We must now give attention to the threefold division of the new covenant in a more particular manner.

The Central Idea of the Covenant. "For this is the covenant that I will make with the house of Israel after those days, saith the Lord; I will put my laws into their mind, and write them in their hearts" (8: 10a). The law of God written in the hearts and minds of His people forms the central idea of the covenant. In the first covenant the law was imposed from without and failed because there was no disposition of heart to obedience. The law was good but the heart was not right. In the new covenant, God transforms the external law into an inner life, and through the gift of the Holy Spirit so purifies and renews the heart that from its inmost being it does by nature the will of God. Furthermore, the law being put into the mind suggests such a communication of divine truth as enables its possessor, not only to love the Lord with all the heart's affection, but to intelligently interpret and express that love in holy living. Since the vital feature of the new covenant is spiritual life in the innermost being, the heart is thus opened to God, and given an inner sense of what is pleasing to Him. This leads immediately to a personal knowledge of God, and to know God is to love Him who is himself Love. This love which the Holy Spirit sheds abroad in the heart purified by the blood of Jesus becomes the energy which is the spring of joyful obedience to God's law. Love is thus the fulfilling of the law, and in no sense does it lower the divine standard or weaken the moral law.

The Crowning Idea of the Covenant. "And I will be to them a God, and they shall be to me a people" (8: 10b). The crowning blessing of the new covenant is personal fellowship with God. God becomes the supreme Object of His people's affection; His people are given the inward assurance of belonging wholly to God. This glorious fellowship is accomplished by means of the law written in the minds and hearts of His people. Since, however, the carnal mind is not subject to the law of God (Rom. 8: 7), the heart must be purified before it can be perfectly attuned to the will of God. It is only the "pure in heart" who see God, and without holiness no man shall see the Lord (12: 14). This purifying of the heart from sin and the writing of the law of God within it is a conscious, personal experience, wrought in the soul by the Holy Spirit. But we do not rest in the experience; we rest in God, whom the experience of heart purity has enabled us to see, and with whom the indwelling Spirit of holiness brings us into conscious fellowship. Thus the heart so purified and renewed becomes the presence chamber of God, whom alone we worship and serve.

The Initial Idea of the Covenant. "For I will be merciful to their unrighteousness, and their sins and their iniquities will I remember no more" (8:12). Since mercy is the ground, not only of the remission of sins, but of the law of God written upon the heart, and consequent fellowship with God, it is in reality, logically, the first blessing of the covenant, followed by the central and crowning blessings. If the remission of sins appears to be a mere appendage in both of these accounts of the new covenant, it must be borne in mind that Israel had been redeemed from the guilt of sin by the blood of the Passover lamb sprinkled on the doorposts, and led out of bondage by a strong hand and a stretched-out arm. The Epistle to the Hebrews does not date from the Passover as previously explained, but from the sprinkling of the blood upon the book and the people at Sinai (Exodus 24); and it is the purpose of this Epistle to reveal the possibilities shut up in the true Passover Lamb, which culminate in the great Day of Atonement. The term "remission of sins" as used here may refer primarily to actual transgressions, for Israel grievously sinned in the wilderness, but the term is broad enough to extend to the cleansing from all sin, original as well as actual. It has been suggested that the reference, "I will be merciful to their unrighteousness," is a revelation of divine grace; and "their sins . . . will I remember no more," to the divine oblivion into which these sins are cast.

The term *hileos* (ἴλεως) or "merciful" must be given further consideration. It has a deeper meaning here than is commonly attributed to it, and means in fact to be propitious. When the publican (Luke 18:9-14) beat upon his breast and said, "God be merciful to me a sinner," the word used is *hilastheti* (ἱλάσθητι), which means to propitiate, that is, to show mercy on the ground of penalty for which a substitute has been offered. In effect he said, "I am the sinner, not the lamb offered on the brazen altar; therefore for the sake of the substitute which has died for me, be propitious or merciful to me, the sinner." There are instances in the Old Testament where mercy was shown without exacting the legal penalty for sin, as for instance, Abner and

Absalom, and in either case the results were disastrous. But under the new covenant, Christ himself has become our Propitiation (ἱλαστήριον), so that God can still be just and the Justifier of those who believe in Jesus (Rom. 3:24-26).

The Conclusion of the Chapter. "In that he saith, A new covenant, he hath made the first old. Now that which decayeth and waxeth old is ready to vanish away" (8:13). The Greek has two sets of terms to express the old and the new. The words *kainos* (καινός), "new," and *palaios* (παλαιός), "old," are relative terms—a thing being new when it is added to something already existing. Thus the new covenant is *kainos* or new in that it was made at a later date than the former covenant, which now becomes *palais*, or old. The words *neos* (νέος) and *geraios* (γεραιός) mean that a thing is new in the sense of being young or fresh in itself, or old and aged in itself. Both words for "old" are used in this text. When God spoke of a new covenant (*kainos*) about 600 B.C., He thereby declared the first covenant old (*palais*). It was not Jesus who made the first covenant old, for it had been old for centuries. The writer then uses the word *geraios* when he speaks of this covenant as being aged, and ready to vanish away. The author is saying to his readers indirectly, "Do you wish to go back to the old covenant, which is becoming aged and is about to vanish away? Jesus is the Mediator of a better covenant; and from the heavenly sanctuary ministers not only the words but the Spirit."

The words, "I will put my laws into their mind," are further amplified in the statement, "And they shall not teach every man his neighbour, and every man his brother, saying, Know the Lord: for all shall know me, from the least to the greatest" (8:11). In the more immediate sense, it is through the remission of sins and the writing of the law of God within the heart that the believer comes to know God in personal experience. This is not merely knowledge about God, such as might be obtained by the hearing of the external law, but an acquaintance with God himself in Christ. There is also a more objective sense in which this verse may be interpreted. In the Old Testament the revelation was not complete, but was made at sundry times and in divers manners; thus the words of the prophets from Moses onward must be passed along to ever larger companies. Then too, the law of Moses, being given in precepts and commands, required interpretation and led to the formation of the scribes, who devoted themselves to this end. In Jesus Christ however the revelation became complete, and through the Holy Spirit given at Pentecost the word was rapidly heralded abroad. But the word, thus transmitted orally for a time, was soon fixed into a canon of Scriptures, inspired by the Holy Spirit. Our Bible is therefore at once the Word of God and a Record of that Word, and this alone becomes the basis of our faith and practice. By this Word alone, which is of no private interpretation, we may even judge those who stand up to preach. In this sense then we may say that from the small to the great, from the children to the theologians and interpreters of the Scriptures, God's Word in its saving capacity is accessible to all.

CHAPTER IX

THE GREAT ATONEMENT CHAPTER

We come now to the most solemn chapter in the Epistle to the Hebrews, the great atonement chapter of the New Testament. We have considered Christ as the Surety of a better covenant, and as a Minister of the sanctuary, these together making possible the better covenant established upon better promises. Of this better covenant, Christ is the Mediator, as He said at the Last Supper, "This cup is the new testament in my blood, which is shed for you" (Luke 22: 20); and here it is said that "by his own blood he entered in once into the holy place, having obtained eternal redemption for us" (9: 12). We are now brought face to face with a consideration of Christ's great atoning sacrifice, the shedding of His own precious blood on the cross of Calvary for our redemption.

Previous to this we have been told that, as our great High Priest, Christ had "somewhat" to offer, and that this "somewhat" was himself. But while reference has often been made to it, there has been no mention of Blood until the present chapter, where it is mentioned twelve times: (1) as opening the holy of holies for a propitiatory offering (9: 11-14); (2) as the inauguration of the new covenant (9: 15-22); and (3) as the purifying of the heavens, where Christ now appears for us in the presence of God (9: 23-28).

As we have seen, the real distinction between the old and new covenants lies in this: that the former was external and material, the latter internal and spiritual. The Minister of the sanctuary, therefore, requires a "greater and more perfect tabernacle," in which His service is to be rendered and His offering presented. Hence the writer turns to a consideration of the highest service rendered in the ancient Tabernacle, that of the great Day of Atonement, and from this presents Christ as serving in the heavenly sanctuary, there to appear in the presence of God for us (9:24). This great atonement chapter should be studied with the deepest reverence.

The First Covenant: Its Ordinances and Sanctuary

The writer now passes from a comparison of the two covenants to a consideration of the two sanctuaries. He introduces the subject with the words, "Then verily the first covenant had also ordinances of divine service, and a worldly sanctuary" (9:1). It must be borne in mind, however, that in referring to the Tabernacle and its service he does so to bring out more clearly their bearing upon Christ's great sacrifice, and to more powerfully portray His supremacy as our great High Priest. The writer refers only to the original Tabernacle, the pattern of which was given to Moses in the mount, and which gave form to the later temples. He in no wise

It is characteristic of the Epistle that all the arguments from the divine worship of Judaism which it contains are drawn from the institutions of the Tabernacle. These, which are treated as the direct embodiment of the heavenly archetype, are supposed to be still preserved in the later forms and to give force to them. They were never superseded even when they were practically modified. The Temple indeed no less than the Kingdom, with which it corresponded, was the sign of a spiritual declension. Both were endeavors to give a fixed and permanent shape, according to the conditions of earthly life, to ideas which in their essential nature led the thoughts of men forward to the future and the unseen. God was pleased to use, in this as in other cases, the changes which were brought about by the exigencies of national life for the fulfilment of His own counsel, but the divine interpreter of the Old Testament necessarily looked beyond the splendors of the sacred buildings (Matt. 24:1ff.), and the triumphs of the monarchy of David, to the sacred tent of the pilgrim people and the heavenly sovereignty.— Westcott, *The Epistle to the Hebrews*, p. 235.

The Tabernacle was a peculiar combination of beauty and barrenness, of preciousness and worthlessness, of glory and vanity. It was pitched upon the shifting sand of the barren and sterile desert. No marble pavement separated the furniture overlaid with gold from the naked ground; and yet these strange contradictions convey to us in symbol the nature of our Lord Jesus Christ, who was at once the Son of God and the Son of Man. In Him all the contradictions of life meet and find their perfect solution. He was the Ancient of Days and the Babe of Bethlehem; the Scepter Bearer of heaven and the Burden Bearer of the world; the Lion of the tribe of Judah and the Lamb of God that taketh away the sin of the world. In Him every tangled skein of life will someday be unraveled, every mystery be made plain, every thwarted ambition realized, every blighted hope fulfilled, and every unrealized purpose of His holy people be brought to a glorious fruition. Here then is the mystery that hath been hid from the ages, but is now made manifest—"Christ in you, the hope of glory."

seeks to detract from its glory; contrariwise, he concedes its greatness in order to set out in bolder relief the exceeding greatness of the heavenly sanctuary into which Jesus has entered to appear for us.

The Sanctuary or Holy Place. "For there was a tabernacle made; the first, wherein was the candlestick, and the table, and the shewbread; which is called the sanctuary" (9:2). In 8:2, *ta hagia* (τὰ ἅγια) or "the holy" refers to the heavenly sanctuary, the neuter plural being idiomatic; in 9:1, *to hagion* (τὸ ἅγιον) or "the holy" refers to the whole earthly sanctuary, with its divisions separated by the inner veil. The front part or place of entrance was called the *hagia* (ἅγια) or the "holy place"; and beyond this the *hagia hagion* (ἅγια ἁγίων), known as the "holy of holies." In Hebrew this most holy place is the "Holiness of Holinesses." Here

In Exodus 38:21 ff. there is given an official summary of the materials used in the construction of the Tabernacle. These have been estimated by some modern writers as follows: gold, 2,400 pounds; silver, 8,400 pounds; brass, about the same as silver. In addition to this there was about 2,400 square yards of linen, goat's hair, ram skins, and badger (perhaps porpoise) skins for the Tabernacle and other hangings. The total cost is generally estimated at about $2,000,000. It was therefore no crude structure of cheap materials and poor workmanship, but one of exquisite beauty and richness, such as would be worthy of its Divine Artificer.

The Tabernacle was constructed on the general plan of an Egyptian home. This consisted (1) of an open court in front of the house, (2) a semiprivate place where friends could be entertained, and (3) the innermost center reserved for the family alone. The Israelites, being familiar with this type of architecture, would readily understand its significance. The Tabernacle was surrounded by a court 75 feet wide by 150 feet long. The walls of the court were linen, 7½ feet high, and held in place by pillars of brass with silver fillets (perhaps silver rods). These pillars were set in sockets of brass and staked within and without by means of cords and brass stakes. Brass symbolizes the judgment of God, and anything which touched the earth was of brass, even the pillars which formed the door of the Tabernacle. Silver symbolizes redemption, as for instance in the matter of the half-shekel tax, paid by both rich and poor alike. The linen curtains as well as other hangings were suspended from silver rods. To touch the linen of the courtyard was to incur the penalty of death. Everything outside the Tabernacle, even including the pillars at the door, was all of brass—the brazen altar and the laver. The Tabernacle was made of acacia boards covered with gold and set in sockets of silver. They were held together by five rods, four visible and one invisible, running through the center of the boards. The four rods symbolized the four relationships of life; the inner, the spiritual unity. Everything inside the Tabernacle was of gold, or acacia wood covered with gold. The wood symbolized the humanity of Christ, the gold His deity.

however each compartment is called a tabernacle (9:2-3), but the first (ἡ πρώτη) describes merely its situation as being the first to be entered, "and after the second veil, the tabernacle which is called the Holiest of all." The verb *kateskeuasthe* (κατεσκευάσθη), "was made," is a comprehensive term and includes the preparation of the Tabernacle, its workmanship, its furniture, and all that "fitted it" for the divine service.

The holy place, here called the "first tabernacle" or "sanctuary," was fifteen feet wide, fifteen feet high, and thirty feet long. It was entered from the east, the coverings being supported by five pillars made of acacia wood, covered with gold, crowned with golden chapiters, and set in sockets of brass. Between the golden chapiter and the socket of brass hung the veil of blue and purple and scarlet, known as the door of the Tabernacle. In this holy place where the priests ministered daily was

Each of the boards of the Tabernacle had two tenons which fitted into two sockets of silver. There were two sockets for every board, and each socket of silver weighed ninety-four pounds. It is said that when these sockets were placed together they appeared to furnish a solid foundation of silver.

There were also four coverings to the Tabernacle. (1) The outward was of badger skins (probably porpoise skins, a form of porpoise which abounded in the Red Sea). This rough protective covering was symbolical of Christ, of whom the prophet wrote, "He hath no form nor comeliness; and when we shall see him, there is no beauty that we should desire him." (2) The next veil was of ram skins dyed red (literally the skins of red rams), and speaks of the obedience of Christ which led Him to the Cross. (3) The next was a covering of goatskins, which likewise speaks of the atonement but in a different manner. The offering for the people on the great Day of Atonement was two goats—one which was slain to pay the penalty of our sins; the other the scapegoat, who bore them away. It was the latter of which John spoke when he said, "Behold the Lamb of God, which taketh [or beareth] away the sin of the world." Here it is evident that not only were sins forgiven, but sin itself was taken away. (4) The inner covering was of fine-twined linen, embroidered with beautiful angelic figures. Perhaps it was from this that we have the words "the angels desire to look into."

The five pillars at the door of the Tabernacle were of acacia wood, covered with gold, set in sockets of brass and crowned with a gold capital. Thus St. Peter speaks of "the sufferings of Christ, and the glory that should follow." The inner pillars which supported the veil proper were the same, but set in silver, and, it is said, had no crowns of gold, symbolizing that Christ was cut off from among the people.

It is interesting to note also that the length of the curtains surrounding the court (280 cubits) was the exact length of the ten curtains which formed the tent proper. These ten curtains were each 28 cubits in length (or about 420 feet in all).

the golden candlestick, or more properly candelabra, adorned with flowers, pomegranates, and almond-shaped vessels for the oil. This was located on the south side and symbolized Christ as the Light of the World (John 8:12). On the north was the table of shewbread with its double crown and its twelve loaves, symbolizing Christ as the Bread of Life (John 6). Next to the inner veil stood the altar of incense, a square altar made of acacia wood and covered with gold, hence known as the "golden altar." On this altar incense was offered daily, symbolizing prayer, intercession, and worship (John 4:24).

The Holiest of All or the Holy of Holies. "And after the second veil, the tabernacle which is called the Holiest of all; which had the golden censer, and the ark of the covenant overlaid round about with gold, wherein was the golden pot that had manna, and Aaron's rod that budded, and the tables of the covenant; and over it the cherubims of glory shadowing the mercyseat; of which we cannot now speak particularly" (9:3-5). The holy of holies was a perfect cube fifteen feet square. It was marked off from the holy place by the inner veil, which was suspended from four gold-covered pillars set in redemptive silver. We are told that these pillars had no chapiters, indicative of the fact that Christ was "cut off out of the land of the living," that by His own blood He might open to us the holy of holies, where dwelt the Shekinah of God's presence.

The writer's mention of the golden censer being in the inner sanctuary has been the source of much discussion. He does not mention the golden altar of incense. The problem has involved much discussion, for it is not merely a verbal but a theological question. The Greek word used here is *thumiaterion* ($\theta\upsilon\mu\iota\alpha\tau\acute{\eta}\rho\iota\omicron\nu$), from *thumiama* ($\theta\upsilon\mu\acute{\iota}\alpha\mu\alpha$), "incense," and means that upon

That there was a direct ritualistic connection between the altar of incense and the holy of holies is found in the statement of Moses' instructions, where God said, "Put it before the veil that is by the ark of the testimony, before the mercy seat" (Exod. 30:6); and again, "Set the altar of gold for the incense before the ark of the testimony" (Exod. 40:5). In I Kings 6:22 it is said of Solomon that "the whole altar that was by the oracle he overlaid with gold."

which the incense is laid, which may be either an altar or a censer. The Septuagint translates this the "altar of incense" instead of "golden censer," as found in the Authorized Version. The solution of the problem appears to lie in the fact that the author is viewing the furniture and utensils, not from their actual location in the Tabernacle, but from their place in the ritualistic service. For this reason he uses different words to express his position. In verse 2 we have the words *en hei* (ἐν ᾗ), "wherein," while in verse 4 we have the word *echousa* (ἔχουσα), "which had," in the sense of belonging to. Thus the golden altar was located in the holy place, but in its ritual associations it "belonged to" the holy of holies. It may be readily understood how the latter term can include both the altar of incense in front of the veil and the ark of the covenant behind the veil. When therefore the priest offered the incense of prayer on the altar, he faced the mercy seat, and though it was hidden by the veil, God had said, It is there "I will meet with thee." When the veil was lifted for the high priest to enter the holy of holies, the altar (of incense) with its cloud of incense was seen to be a part of the ritual of the inner sanctuary. Perhaps the translation "golden censer" comes from a tradition that a special golden censer was used only on the great Day of Atonement, and that the high priest took coals off the altar for the censer and, reaching under the veil, swung it before the mercy seat until, veiled by the cloud, he himself was permitted to enter.

The Ark of the Covenant. The ark of the covenant, so called because in it were the tables of the law, was the central object of the Tabernacle, and therefore the most perfect symbol of Christ's person and work. Here was the place of propitiation and communion, and here burned the Shekinah as the center of God's glory. Hence St. Paul says, "It pleased the Father that in him should all fulness dwell" (Col. 1:19); and our author himself speaks of Christ as the effulgence of "his glory, and the express image of his person" (Heb. 1:3). The ark itself was made of acacia wood and covered with gold within and without (Exod. 25:11). It also had a crown of gold round about, evidently intended to hold in place the mercy seat. The cover of the ark was called the propitiatory or mercy seat. It was made of solid gold, and at either end there was attached a cherub—all of which, being made of beaten gold, symbolized the sufferings of Christ. The cherubim were angelic figures whose feet pressed the propitiatory and whose wings overshadowed it. Their faces were turned toward each other, and their gaze was fixed upon the mercy seat. They are called "cherubims of glory"—not "glorious cherubims," for the genitive is not attributive but possessive, and hence must be translated "cherubim belonging to God's glory." It is interesting to note that Ezekiel mentions "the anointed cherub that covereth" in connection with his prophecy concerning Tyre; but this cherub fell, through his wisdom and beauty, and rebelled against God (Ezek. 28:14 ff.). Here we have two cherubim so guarding the blood-sprinkled propitiatory that they become a prophecy of the eternal ages, the redemptive recovery of that which man lost through the Fall. The mercy seat was in reality a propitiatory, where such a full atonement was made that mercy could be extended and God still be just and the Justifier of those who believe in Jesus. The Shekinah of God's presence shone above the mercy seat between the cherubim (Exod. 25:22), where God met and communed with the high priest on the great Day of Atonement. The Shekinah is generally supposed to symbolize the Holy Spirit; in reality it is the glorious inner relations of the Trinity, manifested by the Holy Spirit.

The Contents of the Ark of the Covenant. "Wherein was the golden pot that had manna, and Aaron's rod that budded, and the tables of the covenant" (9:4b). The pot of manna symbolized Christ in His life-sustaining power. He is the Bread of Life to His earthly people, and through the eternal ages will be the Heavenly Food of a redeemed and triumphant people (Rev. 2:17). Aaron's rod that budded sets forth the resurrection of Christ, and conveys the thought of vitality and fruitfulness. The tables of the covenant are the symbols of Christ, who said, "I delight to do thy will, O my God: yea, thy law is within my heart" (Ps. 40:8); and again, "Then said I, Lo, I come (in the volume of the book it is written of me,) to do thy will, O God" (Heb. 10:7). These sacred objects also represent three things that every true Christian desires; they are all provided in Christ, hidden beneath the propitiatory Blood, and made effective by the presence of the Holy Spirit. (1) A Christian desires an abundant spiritual life, and for this he has the hidden manna. (2) He desires to be useful; and for this he has the power of the Spirit that caused Aaron's rod to blossom and bear fruit in a single night. (3) He desires to live a life of inward holiness and outward righteousness, and for this God has written the law in his heart and mind, so that, by a new and redeemed nature, he delights to do the will of God.

"Of Which We Cannot Now Speak Particularly," or "Concerning which it is not now in order to speak" (9:5b). The writer calls attention to these sacred objects in order to furnish a background for comparing the service of the priests with the superior ministry of Christ. He realizes that many things could be said about the furniture of the Tabernacle, but such were not now in order. There were teachers in that day who instructed the people in these vital matters; but in order to make these teachings forceful and effective in this day, there is need for thorough instruction in the things which in that day were well understood.

It is clearly evident, however, that the purpose of the writer in this brief description of the Tabernacle is to emphasize the fact that there are two stages in our access to God and two degrees of the divine nearness. The outer tabernacle was known as the holy place, and was entered through a veil known as the door of the Tabernacle. Beyond this was a second veil, through which the high priest, once a year only, passed into the holy of holies. Dr. Bresee was accustomed to call the first veil "the veil of actual sins," and the second "the veil of sin conditions." When a sinner is converted and new life imparted by the Spirit, his pardon admits him through the outer "veil of actual sins" into the holy place, where he finds light, life, and communion with God, symbolized by the golden candlestick, the table of shewbread, and the altar of incense. But as he prays and worships God at the golden altar, which is before the second veil, he realizes that there is something "deeper down and further back," to use Fletcher's strong expression, that prevents him from entering the holy of holies, where dwells the Shekinah of God's presence. This something is "the second veil of sin conditions," the inbred sin that remains even in the regenerate, and must be cleansed by the blood of Jesus before one can enter through the veil into the presence of God. Only the pure in heart see God. Nothing can be stated more clearly than that the two compartments of the Tabernacle represent two realms of service, one wrought at a distance with a veil between, the other in the full light of His countenance; and that there are two degrees of fellowship with God, one as a sinner who has been pardoned and received into sonship, the other as a son who has fully consecrated all his redeemed powers to God.

THE LEVITICAL SERVICE AND ITS FUTILITY

After this inventory of the Tabernacle furniture, the writer lifts into prominence but one detail, the meaning of the veiled holy of holies, and then passes on to a description of the priestly service. This, he says, "stood only in meats and drinks, and divers washings, and carnal ordinances." What a contrast! We read of golden candlesticks, of tables and altars overlaid with gold, of the ark of the covenant, the cherubim of glory over the mercy seat, and the rich hangings of the sanctuary; then of gifts and sacrifices which could never take away sin, nor make the worshipers perfect as pertaining to the conscience!

The writer describes this service as follows: "Now when these things were thus ordained, the priests went always into the first tabernacle, accomplishing the service of God. But into the second went the high priest alone once every year, not without blood, which he offered for himself, and for the errors of the people" (9: 6-7). This entire section is a reference to the service on the great Day of Atonement, when the high priest laid aside his garments of "glory" and "beauty," and in the plain linen garments of the ordinary priest, slew the sacrifice with his own hands—not now a menial but a priestly act. Amidst a cloud of incense, he then entered through the veil with the blood which he sprinkled before and upon the mercy seat; and this he did first for himself and then for the people. At the close of the service, the high priest again put on his garments of "glory" and "beauty" and appeared at the gate to bless the congregation which had waited there in fasting and prayer. But this service, though awe-inspiring, was yet inadequate and futile. It could not make the worshipers perfect as pertaining to the conscience, and it could not bring them into the presence of God. The result was spiritual bankruptcy.

The Way into the Holiest Veiled Under the First Covenant. The entrance of the high priest into the holy of holies but once a year is explained to be purely symbolical—"The Holy Ghost this signifying, that the way into the holiest of all was not yet made manifest, while as the first tabernacle was yet standing" (9: 8). The Spirit here shows us the restrictions which bound the worshipers under the first covenant. The people worshiped only at the gate, or at utmost within the courtyard. They had no access to the Tabernacle itself. The priests worshiped in the holy place, which was but the vestibule to the holy of holies. There they trimmed the lamps, changed the shewbread, and offered incense upon the golden altar; but always with the sense that between them and the Shekinah of God's presence there was a heavy, though beautifully adorned, veil. Beyond that veil they could not go, on pain of death. Once each year, and once only, the high priest was permitted to enter, though "not without blood, which he offered [first] for himself, and [then] for the errors of the people."

While the veils remained, the people were separated both from the Object of their devotion and from the fellowship of His presence. But fleshly ordinances and outward washings can never reach the depths of the conscience or satisfy the hearts of men. The cry of the soul is far deeper and more intense; it is the cry for a clean heart and a right spirit. But this cry can be answered only when the veil of "sin conditions" is removed, and men enter into the divine presence chamber, there to find within the veil the fullness of the divine fellowship and the joy of a devoted service.

The Parable and the Reformation. "Which was a figure for the time then present, in which were offered both gifts and sacrifices, that could not make him that did the service perfect, as pertaining to the conscience; which stood only in meats and drinks, and divers washings, and carnal ordinances, imposed on them until the time of reformation" (9: 9-10). While the Levitical services were futile as to the removal of sin, the writer states that nevertheless they were of divine origin and were intended to serve the purpose of instruction for the time then present. Here the word *parabole* (παραβολὴ) or "parable," which means "to place alongside," is used instead of *tupos* (τύπος), which means a "type" or a "shadow," thus indicating that the emphasis was to be placed upon instruction rather than religious effectiveness. However, the Greek term seems to carry a double significance, in that it was not only a parable for the "time then present," but looked forward to the future, when the dawning of the Christian dispensation should make the parable significant in the actual rending of the veil through the death and resurrection of Christ. These ineffective gifts and sacrifices of the Levitical order were imposed upon the Hebrew people only "until the time of reformation." The Greek word *diorthoseos* (διορθώσεως) means a "reconstruction" and probably refers to the new *diatheke* or covenant, which Christ administers through the Spirit, and thus brings to perfection them that are sanctified. The parable of the Levitical service, then, finds its fulfillment and abrogation in Christ, who administers grace from the heavenly sanctuary.

THE MORE EXCELLENT MINISTRY

"But Christ being come an high priest of good things to come, by a greater and more perfect tabernacle, not made with hands, that is to say, not of this building" (9:11). We come now to a consideration of the high priesthood of Christ, the "greater and more perfect tabernacle," and the "good things to come"; all of which are but introductory to the discussion concerning the Blood of the atonement. Perhaps no section in this Epistle (9:11-14) contains more profound or deeper truths than this, or has given rise to more speculative questions. Among these are: What is the essence of Christ's priesthood? What is the sanctuary in which He serves? and What is meant by the "good things to come"? These demand only a brief discussion.

1. *What is the essence of Christ's priesthood?* The deepest and most fundamental truth in priesthood is the ability to bring men to God. "Christ being come an high priest of good things to come" must first approach God as the divine-human Mediator, and in so doing bring our human nature into that contact with God which He has in himself. This nearness is not merely counted as having taken place, that is, by imputation, but by actual spiritual contact with God provided for all believers through the Spirit. This was the great truth revealed on the Day of Pentecost. But when did Christ become a Priest—while on earth or when He entered heaven?

Gerhardus Vos points out that the priesthood may mean either *appointment* or *function*. If the latter is held, then the appointment must precede it. It is not therefore a question of either-or. While on earth Christ was a Priest under the symbol of Aaron, a priest of death. Had He not acted in the capacity of a Priest, He could not have made an offering, nor could that offering have been the sacrifice of His own body on the Cross.

When the writer states that "if he were on earth, he should not be a priest," the context makes it clear that He could not be a priest of the Levitical order—not that He could not act as a Priest of another order. But there is a deeper meaning in these words. "He could not *be* a priest," that is, His earthly limitations prevented Him from becoming a priest of a universal and eternal order. This could not be accomplished except in a "greater and more perfect tabernacle," that is, in heaven itself. Referring to His death, Christ said, "And how am I straitened until it be accomplished!" and again, "It is expedient for you that I go away: for if I go not away, the Comforter will not come unto you; but if I depart, I will send him unto you" (Luke 12:50; John 16:7). Christ was by both nature and appointment a Priest from the beginning; but only after the great vicarious offering on Calvary, and His exaltation to the right hand of the Father, did He as King-Priest enter into the fullness of His ministry "through the eternal Spirit."

2. *What is the sanctuary in which Christ functions as Priest?* This the Scriptures tell us is the "greater and more perfect tabernacle," that is, in "heaven itself" (9:11, 24). But what, then, is the holy place through

The problem which gave rise to the controversy in the medieval period was this: If sin had not entered the world, would Christ have become incarnate? Some modern scholars take the position—among them Dr. Kuyper, Bishop Westcott, and Bishop Martensen—that Christ would have come even if sin had not entered the world. This is known as the cosmological view. Dr. Kuyper held that even in a sinless universe Christ would have been an unincarnate Priest, being such from all eternity. Since sin entered the world, however, he held that Christ's priesthood cannot be separated from His incarnation. Bishop Westcott, on the other hand, held that since the Incarnation and the priesthood go together, Christ would have come incarnate even in a sinless world. This is essentially the position of Bishop Martensen also. Dr. Olin A. Curtis took the opposite position, maintaining the soteriological view that Christ became incarnate solely because of sin in the world. Here again we do not think that this is an either-or matter; for, granting that Christ became incarnate for our redemption from sin, we still believe that He will come again without sin unto salvation. It may well be that this second coming, this coming without a sin offering, would have been His first, had sin not entered the world. While the author of the Epistle to the Hebrews lays primary stress upon the redemptive work of Christ, he never omits the ultimate purpose of His second coming, that is, to lift man from his probationary state and bring him into a new and eternal order.

which He must have passed, as did Aaron before entering the holy of holies? Some have maintained that, following the pattern of the Tabernacle, the heavens were divided into two parts—one, the lower, where the angels ministered; the other, the upper, in which God dwells in light unapproachable. The view generally held by the ancient fathers, however, was that this holy place was Christ's own body or human nature, the holiness of His life in the flesh being that through which He passed into the celestial sanctuary. This appears to be the more acceptable, for Christ's body was known as a "tabernacle" or "temple." Further still, when we take into consideration that Christ's earthly life began in a mystery, that of the Virgin Birth; and that it likewise closed in a mystery, the Ascension, when He was taken up from them; it appears that the space between the two veils of mystery would answer perfectly to the passage of Aaron through the holy place into the holiest of all on the great Day of Atonement. Objection has been made to this explanation on the ground that Christ's body was as truly a creation as ours. This is true but evidently in a very different sense, for the Scriptures plainly state that "a body hast thou prepared me." Although born of the Virgin Mary, His body was specially prepared, a unique and divine fashioning. Christ was the God-Man—one Person, human and divine, as well in His body as in the union of the two natures.

3. *What is meant by the "good things to come"?* The writer uses the name of Christ in order to emphasize

Concerning "a greater and more perfect tabernacle, not made with hands," Dr. Adam Clarke says: "This appears to mean our Lord's *human nature*. That in which dwelt all the fulness of the Godhead bodily, was fitly typified by the tabernacle and temple; in both of which the majesty of God dwelt. Though our Lord's body was a perfect human body, yet it did not come in the way of natural generation; His miraculous conception will sufficiently justify the expressions used here by the apostle." All depends upon whether the word "through" (*dia*) is considered locally or instrumentally. If the latter, then it was Christ's body which was greater than the earthly Tabernacle or Temple, and that through which He accomplished our redemption. This accomplished, however, He entered into a holy place not made with hands, "but into heaven itself," where He appears for us in the greater and more perfect tabernacle, of which the earthly was but a shadow. (Cf. John 12:19, 21; Heb. 8:1-2; 9:24.)

His office. Since the main verb is found in the following verse, the two verses in this connection must be considered together. Here there are three aorists: a participle, a verb, and a participle. (1) The word *paragenomenos* (παραγενόμενος), "having come," is translated by Moffatt, "Christ came on the scene and all was changed"; and by Vaughan, "having arrived" or "appeared on the scene of fact and history." Stated thus, it refers to the greatest event in all history, "God . . . manifest in the flesh." The expression "to come," found in connection with "good things," is found in two different readings. Westcott uses the word *genomenon* (γενομένων), "are come," as found in the Vatican manuscript; while Vaughan, Moffatt, and others use the word *mellonton* (μελλόντων) as found in the Alexandrine and Sinaitic manuscripts, and translated "about to come." The former interprets the words "to come" as future in respect to the law, but belonging immediately to the Christian dispensation; the latter as future, following the coming of Christ. The first is soteriological; the second, eschatological. Robertson puts the matter tersely when he says that Christ is High Priest both of the good things that have already been received and of those that await us in the glorious future. (2) The second aorist is *eiselthen* (εἰσῆλθεν), "he entered," which is the main verb; and (3) the third is *heuramenos* (εὑράμενος), "having obtained" or better, "obtained."

The three aorists together are "arrived," "entered," and "obtained." As aorists, however, they represent a sequence of relations only, not intervals of time. The writer therefore considers redemption as a total act composed of related sequences. The "good things" are comprehended in the eternal redemption obtained for us, and which makes possible a continuous covenant fellowship with God. It is by and through Christ, our Mediator, that all our prayers, praises, and services are offered to God; and it is by and through Him that all of God's blessings are bestowed upon us. He has entered into "heaven itself, now to appear in the presence of God for us."

The Sacrificial Offering of Christ. From Christ as
our High Priest, ministering good things from His throne
in the heavens, the writer passes immediately to the
sacrifice of Christ by which our redemption has been
accomplished. This sacrifice is presented under three
principal aspects: (1) The Blood of the Atonement
(9: 12-14); (2) The Blood of the Covenant (9: 15-21);
and (3) The Blood of Purification (9: 23-28). Later we
shall see that he speaks further concerning (1) The
Blood of Access (10: 19-22), and (2) The Blood of
Communion (13: 10-13).

THE BLOOD OF THE ATONEMENT

"Neither by the blood of goats and calves, but by
his own blood he entered in once into the holy place,
having obtained eternal redemption for us" (9: 12). The
writer continues his parallel between the two covenants, these verses of this section having but one main
purpose, that of setting in contrast the Christian High
Priest entering the real most holy place in heaven above
and that of the Levitical priests ministering in the earthly Tabernacle below. These contrasts may be thus briefly summarized. (1) The Aaronic priests served in an
earthly Tabernacle which was only a "figure" or parable
of the true tabernacle. Christ served in the greater and
more perfect tabernacle, that is, in heaven itself. (2)
The earthly priests served only in the shadows; Christ
ministered the very substance which cast those shadows,
eternal life and light. (3) The priests of the earthly
Tabernacle offered the blood of unwilling beasts; Christ
offered His own blood. (4) The earthly priests entered
often because they brought the blood of others; Christ
entered once forever because He offered His own blood.
(5) The ministry of the earthly priests was continuously
insufficient; Christ entered once into the holy of holies
and thereby obtained eternal redemption for us. (6)
The earthly sacrifices were free from physical blemish
only; Christ offered himself without spot to God, free
from all moral or spiritual blemish. He knew no sin.

(7) The blessings mediated through the earthly Tabernacle were temporal; those mediated by Christ were spiritual and eternal. Thus the one offering of Christ, "through eternal spirit," was infinitely above the myriads of Levitical sacrifices and their endless succession of priests.

The Priesthood and the Blood. The shedding of the Blood on earth, where Christ is portrayed under the symbol of Aaron, is here connected with His spiritual and heavenly priesthood. How this is accomplished appears to lie in the fact that it is the basic condition for His administration of the good things to come. The attention is directed primarily to the future. It was "through the blood of the everlasting covenant" that God brought again from the dead our Lord Jesus (13:20). Here the Blood is the ground of the Resurrection and the means through which it was accomplished. It was through His own blood that He entered in once into the holy place, having obtained eternal redemption for us (9:12). This is the Blood of access. It is through "the blood of sprinkling, that speaketh better things than that of Abel," that we are cleansed from sin. This is the Blood of the covenant, in which our consciences are purged "from dead works to serve the living God" (9:14). The inner veil having been rent, we too are exhorted to have "boldness to enter into the holiest by the blood of Jesus," where we may constantly abide under His atoning efficacy and in the fellowship of His presence.

"His Own Blood." What wonderful words are these! With what tenderness do they come to every redeemed soul! They are of infinite depth and power! Heaven itself cannot exhaust their praises, for the apostle tells us that there the redeemed sing a new song, saying: "Thou art worthy to take the book, and to open the seals thereof: for thou wast slain, and hast redeemed us to God by thy blood out of every kindred, and tongue, and people, and nation; . . the number of them was ten thousand times ten thousand, and thousands of

THE GREAT ATONEMENT CHAPTER

thousands; saying with a loud voice, Worthy is the Lamb that was slain to receive power, and riches, and wisdom, and strength, and honour, and glory, and blessing" (Rev. 5: 9-12). What wonderful power in the blood of Christ! How great must be the sin of its rejection! Without the blood of Christ there is no remission of sins, no cleansing of the heart; and only the cry, "The Blood! The Blood!" will open the gates of pearl to the city of God.

The emphasis in this text, however, is not so much upon death itself as upon a death through the shedding of blood, and therefore a sacrificial death. God said to Moses, "The life . . . is in the blood: and I have given it to you upon the altar to make an atonement for your souls: for it is the blood that maketh an atonement for the soul" (Lev. 17: 11). We must understand from this that, while there can be no pouring out of the blood apart from death—in fact, the pouring out of the blood is the assured evidence of death—the essential idea of the blood itself is not that of death but of life. This profound truth is fundamental to a correct understanding of this Epistle and of the atonement in general. "Without shedding of blood is no remission" (9: 22). It was for this reason that blood was prohibited as a food in the Old Testament, and so enjoined also in the New Testament (Acts 15: 29). Its mysterious and vital principle was reserved solely for the rites of expiation and purification, and that because of the life that was in it. Thus the pouring out of the blood as an offering to God represents the giving of a life for a life, and is therefore expiation by substitution. The blood of Christ, who was made after the power of an endless life, when poured out in sacrificial death, was that therefore which "obtained eternal redemption for us." Here also expiation is by substitution. "For he hath made him to be sin for us, who knew no sin; that we might be made the righteousness of God in him" (II Cor. 5: 21).

The Efficacy of Christ's Blood as an Atonement. "For if the blood of bulls and of goats, and the ashes of an heifer sprinkling the unclean, sanctifieth to the purifying of the flesh: how much more shall the blood of Christ, who through the eternal Spirit offered himself without spot to God, purge your conscience from dead works to serve the living God?" (9: 13-14) The word "for" introduces a restatement of the comparative value and effect of the animal sacrifices with that of Christ, but it does so in a broader and more personal manner. The blood of the bullock was that offered by the high priest for himself; the blood of the goat was offered for the sins of the people—these together constituting the atonement for sin. Here however another sacrifice is added—the ashes of the red heifer—which was for the individual purification of those brought into contact with death. These sacrifices not only served for outward ritualistic cleansing, but they kept alive in the people the consciousness of sin and uncleanness. Here it is evident that the writer is preparing the minds of his readers for his discussion of the purification of the heavens (9: 23). As we shall see later, the value of all of these sacrifices lay wholly in their connection with the efficacy of the Blood of the new testament, that of "the Lamb slain from the foundation of the world" (Rev. 13: 8).

"How Much More Shall the Blood of Christ?" By putting his explanation in the form of a question, the writer makes it a personal matter with his readers, and calls upon them to answer out of their experience. He is making an appeal to them to see in the blood of Christ a far greater efficacy than that of the Levitical sacrifices, upon which they had been relying. If the latter could so cleanse and sanctify the flesh as to enable the worshipers to appear before God on earth, why could they not see the infinitely greater efficacy in the blood of Christ, which could so purge the conscience that, having no longer a consciousness of sin, they would never again feel the necessity of returning to these fleshly ordinances? It was what Christ was by nature that made His sacrifice of such infinite value. It embodies

all His divine-human nature in its meaning for sinful man. He operated in the realm of absolute reality, and His self-sacrifice, as one has said, "was something beyond which nothing could be, or could be conceived to be, as a response to God's mind and requirement in relation to sin."

The blood of Christ is efficacious for every need of the human soul. This is ably set forth by Dr. A. B. Simpson; the following is a brief summary. The blood on the doorposts was *Redeeming Blood;* the blood on the altar was *Atoning Blood;* the blood on the leper was *Cleansing Blood;* the blood on the book was *Covenant Blood;* the blood on the priests was *Consecrating Blood;* the blood on the mercy seat was *Pleading Blood;* and finally, the blood of Christ is *Living Blood.* "He that eateth my flesh, and drinketh my blood, dwelleth in me, and I in him" (John 6: 56). His disciples said this was a hard saying; but He replied, "It is the spirit that quickeneth; the flesh profiteth nothing; the words that I speak unto you, they are spirit, and they are life" (John 6: 63).

"Through . . . Eternal Spirit." "Who through the eternal Spirit offered himself without spot to God" (9: 14b). The w o r d s *dia pneumatos aioniou* (διὰ πνεύματος αἰωνίου), "through eternal spirit," have been the source of much controversy and many speculative theories. The more important of these, however, may be reduced to two: (1) that the "eternal spirit" is Christ's own spirit; and (2) that the "eternal spirit" has reference to the Holy Spirit. In the first view it is held that the shedding of Christ's blood was accompanied by His eternally divine nature, in the same sense as "the power of an endless [or indissoluble] life." The second view regards the "eternal spirit" as the Holy Spirit or Third Person of the Trinity. While the Greek does not have the definite article which is generally used in referring to the Holy Spirit, it must be granted that even without the article it frequently refers to Him, and hence in the American Revised Version the

word "Spirit" is capitalized. When this position is taken, it can but mean that Christ's offering of himself was in accordance with the will of the Father and accomplished through the Holy Spirit. As Christ is the revelation of God, whether on earth or in heaven, so the Holy Spirit is the power of the inward life which is imparted to believers.

"To Serve the Living God." The cleansing of the conscience from "dead works" is in order "to serve the living God" (9:14d). The term "dead works" is peculiarly applicable here, in that it is set in contrast to the living God, who does not and cannot have any part with death. His works are always those of life, health, purity, and power—the outflow of eternal spirit. The opposite is equally true. "Dead works" flow from a creature devoid of divine life, and the result is disease, deformity, and death. The cleansing of the conscience is not only necessary to fellowship *with* God but also to service *for* Him. The consciousness of sin prevents access to God, and therefore acceptable service for Him. When the term sanctification is used in its primary sense as being fully separated to God, purity is an essential concomitant. The Holy Spirit must first purify the heart before He can take up His abiding presence there, but the act of cleansing and the incoming of the Spirit are never separated in actual experience. To be sanctified wholly is to be "God-possessed," thus making possible the full devotion of the heart.

This full devotion of a cleansed heart must find its expression in service. This is its purpose and its glory. Two conditions characterize this service: (1) It is service *to* the living God. Anything touched with death,

---

The truth will become clearer if we go yet a step further. In men the "spirit" is, as has been said, that by which they are capable of connection with God. But in Christ, who did not cease to be the Son of God by becoming man, the "spirit" is to be regarded as the seat of His Divine personality in His human nature. So far the *pneuma aionion* (or the "eternal spirit") included the limited *pneuma* (or "spirit") of the Lord's humanity. This *pneuma*, having its own proper existence, was in perfect harmony with the "eternal spirit."—WESTCOTT, *Epistle to the Hebrews,* p. 264.

whether it be unctionless preaching, thoughtless prayers, lifeless singing, and indefinite testimonies or other merely formal service, is not acceptable to God. (2) It is service performed in the holy of holies which Christ has opened to us through the veil. Having entered through the Blood of access, we dwell in the presence of the Shekinah, the glory of God manifested through the Holy Spirit. All our service, therefore, is not only to be filled with life but touched with the glory of the Divine Presence. This is the meaning of the words, "Thou art my servant in whom I will cause my glory to burst forth." This is the promise of our Lord when He said, "But ye shall receive power, after that the Holy Ghost is come upon you: and ye shall be witnesses unto me" (Acts 1:8). The Holy Spirit dwelling in a pure heart is a Guide into all truth, the Enduement of power, the Sustainer of spiritual life by fresh infillings of the Spirit, and the Bestower of fresh anointings for every divinely appointed service. There is therefore rich meaning in the words, "Let us keep the glory down."

While much may be said in favor of either theory, it is better to consider the two as together being but different aspects of the one great redemptive truth. The former, however, is the generally accepted position, in that it appears to be more directly in line with the specific purpose of the writer. The words "through the eternal Spirit" lift the whole process out of the fleshly and material realm, and above the limiting conditions of time and space, into the realm of the spirit—into a new and eternal order. The expression therefore signifies the realm of the inner spirit as that in which Christ ministers, whether as Priest or as Offering. Christ was the God-Man, and as such was infinitely higher than the priests of the Levitical order. As the Son of God, He was the Priest of an eternal order; as Son of Man, His offering was different in that it was the body and blood of the God-Man. It was this that gave absolute efficacy to His priesthood, eternal validity and perfection to His offering. The sacrificial blood of

Christ, shed on Calvary's cross, was not only an event in time but also a spiritual accomplishment in the absolute and eternal order. And because it is the work of a sinless Person in the realm of the Spirit, it is efficacious for the cleansing of the human spirit from all defilement. Christ offered himself once only, and that without spot to God, but in that one act He accomplished what myriads of fleshly sacrifices could never obtain— the forgiveness of sins.

The Cleansing of the Conscience. "Purge your conscience from dead works" (9:14c). The word translated "cleanse" or "purge" is *kathariei* (καθαριεῖ) and is an ancient Hellenic verb which was generally used in a ceremonial sense. It is the same word that is found in Matt. 3:12, where it is said that "he will throughly purge his floor"; and in Jas. 4:8, which reads, "Cleanse your hands, ye sinners." This word, aside from the text, occurs in only these two places in the New Testament, and makes it clear that the Blood not only cleanses from actual sins but purges the very sin nature itself. The contrast here is between the ashes of a heifer, which only cleansed outwardly those who had touched a dead body, and the blood of Jesus, which, reaching inwardly to the conscience, purges it from all "dead works." The term "dead" would of course include all crimes and flagrant violations of the law, but this is not what the writer has in mind. He is referring rather to the false observances of religious rites, formal, empty, and performed in the energy of the flesh. They are "dead works" because they can neither impart nor sustain life, and hence are useless in the service of a living God. The writer therefore pronounces the sentence of death upon them, that he may later introduce the new covenant of life and power.

THE BLOOD OF THE NEW COVENANT

"And for this cause he is the mediator of the new testament, that by means of death, for the redemption of the transgressions that were under the first testament, they which are called might receive the promise of eternal inheritance" (9: 15). We have seen that the sacrificial blood of Christ had its result in an eternal redemption, which purged or cleansed the *suneidesis,* that is, the "conscience," or the consciousness of sin; and this was accomplished because it was wrought by a sinless Person, who by nature belonged to the eternal order of spirit. The transition is natural and easy: (1) because His blood is the seal of a new covenant which makes sure the realization of the promised inheritance; and (2) because the cleansed soul, entering in upon a new and spiritual service, necessitates a new contract or covenant. The writer now turns from his discussion of Christ's atoning blood to the benefits of that atonement accruing to His people in a new testament; that is, from the Blood of the atonement to the Blood of the new covenant.

The Mediator of the New Testament. The writer has previously discussed the subject of Christ's mediatorship in connection with the better covenant established upon better promises (8: 6); here he is presenting the mediatorship in connection with the inheritance which God had promised to His people. This is an advance in thought. Christ is the Heir of all things (1: 2), and the inheritance therefore must be mediated through Him. He is represented as having made a testament or will; and then having died to make that will operative, He arose again to become the Executive of His own will. Being still alive, His people now become "heirs of God, and joint-heirs with Christ" (Rom. 8: 17). What greater security could be granted to the heirs of the promise than that the Testator himself should rise from the dead to put into effect His own will! The scope of the mediatorial work, as set forth in this verse, is comprehensive and can be only briefly summarized here.

1. The new testament mentioned in this verse is the putting into effect of the original inheritance promised "to Abraham and his seed"; and St. Paul makes it clear that this Seed is Christ (Gal. 3: 14-16ff.). The word

for "new" as used here is not *neos* (νέος), which means new in point of time, but *kainos* (καινός), which means new in quality or character. The covenant is new because of the freshness and effectiveness given to it by Christ. What is here called the "first covenant" is a reference to the Mosaic covenant, which was given four hundred and thirty years after the time of Abraham (Gal. 3:17-19). St. Paul tells us that it was added because of the transgressions, and that it was intended to serve as a schoolmaster to bring us to Christ, that we might be justified by faith.

2. The new testament was said to be given "by reason of death," or more literally, "a death having taken place." This death was at once vicarious and substitutionary, and put the new testament in force because it was a complete and perfect ransom.

3. The scope of this ransom extended to the sins of the first testament. Here we have the expression *eis apolutrosin* (εἰς ἀπολύτρωσιν), "for the ransoming" or redemption of the sins under the first testament, making it clear that the whole of the past, the present, and the future rests upon the redemptive work of Christ on Calvary. Without His mediatorship there would have been no eternal inheritance, and no people called to receive it. The redemptive work of every age has been made possible through the shed blood of Christ as an expiatory Sacrifice, the Lamb slain from the foundation of the world.

Covenant or Testament. "For where a testament is, there must also of necessity be the death of the testator. For a testament is of force after men are dead: otherwise it is of no strength at all while the testator liveth" (9:16-17). This is a general statement, which will be followed by a specific illustration, drawn by the writer from the inaugurating sacrifice of the old covenant. The word *pheresthai* (φέρεσθαι) is a legal expression, and being a technical term, it carries with it the thought of an "announcement" or even the "proof" of the death of the testator before his will can become effective.

The words *me pote* (μή ποτε) simply mean "never." They are used by St. John in an interrogative form, and following this lead, some of the ancient commentators so interpreted this verse. Thus it would read, "For is it ever valid so long as the testator is alive?" The sense is the same in either case.

The word *diatheke* (διαθήκη) is another difficult term of this Epistle. It is translated both as "covenant" and as "testament," the latter being the meaning in classical Greek, but never in the Greek Old Testament or in the New unless it be here. In either case, however, the word implies a death, but in a very different manner. Based upon the twofold terminology, two explanations have been offered, neither of which alone appears sufficient.

1. The first, which is the Hebrew idea, maintains that the meaning throughout is "covenant," and that the sacrifices which accompanied it were merely representative of the contracting parties. Dr. Adam Clarke says that "where there is a covenant, it is necessary that the appointed victim be exhibited, since a covenant is confirmed over dead victims." Summarizing this position, Bishop Chadwick says that, when the covenant was ratified and the victim slain, each of the parties virtually said, "In respect of this transaction my living volition and free choice are gone: I am in this matter as powerless to retract as are the dead."

2. The second explanation is that of Bishop Lightfoot, who holds that at the end of verse 15, when the inheritance is mentioned, the thought turns toward the idea of a bequest or will, and this is its meaning throughout the remainder of the argument. He says: "Even in the exceptional case (9: 15-17), the sacred writer starts from the sense of a covenant and glides into that of a testament to which he is led by two points of analogy, (1) the inheritance conferred by the covenant, and (2) the death of the person making it."

Moffatt maintains that the answer is given in verses 16ff., where the writer plays on the double meaning of *diatheke,* using it in both the Greek and Hebrew meanings, as does St. Paul (Gal. 3:15 ff.). The point of the writer's illustration lies in the legal use of *bebaia* (βεβαία), "affirmed," and *ischuei* (ἰσχύει), "of force," which makes them applicable to wills as well as to laws. He also uses the words *ho diathemenos* (ὁ διαθέμενος), which is a technical term for "the testator." Since the death of Christ was the chief difficulty of the Hebrews in His acceptance as the Messiah, the writer presents the *diatheke* under both aspects, as covenant and testament, in order to demonstrate its full significance. While Moffatt admits that this position has its defects, nevertheless it appears to be the only true solution. Vaughan admits as much when he says that *diatheke* has the comprehensive sense of *arrangement,* whether of relations (covenant) or of possessions (testament). Although Jesus was then alive, yet a death had taken place and hence a *diatheke* had been made possible, both in the Hebrew sense of a covenant sealed by blood and in the Greek sense of a will or testament, due to the death of the testator. Animal sacrifices could only mark the covenant of two living persons and therefore of necessity a covenant of works; the death of One of the covenant parties, who was the Heir of all things, alone could make possible an inheritance of grace in which we become "heirs of God, and joint-heirs with Christ."

The First Covenant Ratified by Blood. No covenant which God has made with sinful man has ever been inaugurated without blood. We have previously called attention to the scripture which declares that "the life . . . is in the blood," so that the pouring out of the blood was evidence that the death of the victim had actually taken place. The blood on the altar evidenced the further fact that God had accepted the substitute, so that it could be truthfully said that the sins were covered by the blood on the mercy seat. The writer cites the first covenant as an illustration.

1. "Whereupon neither the first testament was dedicated without blood" (9:18). Here the attention of the

Hebrews is called to the fact that the covenant under which they were living was inaugurated by blood; and since the use of blood pertained to practically everything connected with it, they should not stumble at the death of Christ. They should rather recognize that all previous sacrifices were made valid by His all-atoning blood, which alone cleanses from all sin.

2. "For when Moses had spoken every precept to all the people according to the law, he took the blood of calves and of goats, with water, and scarlet wool, and hyssop, and sprinkled both the book, and all the people, saying, This is the blood of the testament which God hath enjoined unto you" (9: 18-19). These verses refer to the "dedication"—better translated "inauguration"—of the Mosaic covenant as found in Exod. 24: 1-8, which took place previous to the construction of the Tabernacle. Several details are added which pertained to the service.

3. "Moreover he sprinkled with blood both the tabernacle, and all the vessels of the ministry. And almost all things are by the law purged with blood; and without shedding of blood is no remission" (9: 21-22). The first covenant was not only inaugurated with blood, but from the beginning to its close, its services were based

The writer here mentions the water, the scarlet wool, and the hyssop as used in the inauguration of the first covenant. (1) Water is a symbol of the Spirit, especially in its purifying and invigorating activities. Jesus said, "If any man thirst, let him come unto me, and drink"; and also that out of His inmost being should flow rivers of living water. This He spoke "of the Spirit, which they that believe on him should receive: for the Holy Ghost was not yet given; because that Jesus was not yet glorified" (John 7:37-39). St. John also testified that when Jesus was crucified, "Forthwith came there out blood and water" when His side was pierced. This was indicative of His atoning work and the gift of the Spirit by which it was to be administered. In the Tabernacle, the first was symbolized by the altar, the second by the laver. (2) The scarlet wool was evidently that dipped in blood or blood and water, and used for cleansing where sprinkling would not avail (Lev. 14:51-52). (3) The hyssop was a small plant or weed which, when tied in bunches, was used to sprinkle the blood upon the unclean. (The sprinkling of the Tabernacle and its vessels mentioned here [9:21] is not mentioned in Exodus 40; but since the oil was never used except when blood had first been applied [Lev. 8:23-30; 14:14-17], it is evident that the writer had sufficient authority for his statement. This means that the Spirit is given only to those who have previously accepted the blood of Christ.)

on sacrificial blood. For this reason the writer now includes the fully developed Tabernacle service with that
which marked the inauguration of the covenant.

4. "Without shedding of blood is no remission"
(9: 22). Almost all things were by the law purged with
blood, but there were a few exceptions, as for instance,
the "water of separation." Death was the penalty of
sin, and sin must be removed before there can be access
to God or fellowship with Him. God sent His only begotten Son to redeem us, but not without blood; and all
the blessings of the new covenant are offered only because of the shed blood of Christ. We should therefore
magnify the Blood and seek to understand to our utmost
capacity the infinite scope of the blessings provided for
us by the substitutionary sacrifice of Christ.

THE BLOOD OF PURIFICATION

"It was therefore necessary that the patterns of things
in the heavens should be purified with these; but the
heavenly things themselves with better sacrifices than
these. For Christ is not entered into the holy places
made with hands, which are the figures of the true;
but into heaven itself, now to appear in the presence
of God for us" (9: 23-24). There appears to be a return
here from the thought of the Blood of the covenant to
the Blood of the atonement as presented in verses 11-12.
The writer has shown the relation of the two, in that
both were valid because a death had taken place—the
first as a Substitute for the remission of sins, the second
as a Testator for the restoration of the inheritance. St.
Paul makes it clear, however, that through the sealing
of the Spirit we have but the earnest of the inheritance
in this life, the fullness awaiting final redemption in the
world to come (Eph. 1: 14). We are redeemed from
sin in this life as individuals, but the racial consequences
of sin will not be removed from His people until the
time of the resurrection. It is for this reason that we
speak of a perfection of love in this life and a perfection
of glory in the life to come.

The Purification of the Heavens. The writer now argues that if the "copies" or "patterns" of heavenly things as reflected in the Tabernacle and its services must be cleansed by blood, then of necessity the heavenly things themselves must likewise be purified; and if temporary sacrifices were needed for the "patterns," then better sacrifices were needed for the heavenly and eternal things. Since the cleansing power of the sacrifices lay in the blood, the writer now uses only the term "sacrifices" instead of the "blood." The plural here must be taken in a general sense for the one sacrifice of Christ, although some hold that the writer had in mind the earthly sacrifices in a life of humiliation as well as the supreme sacrifice in His death on the Cross.

1. But why must the heavens be purified? Many of the great commentators assume that this is merely a figure of speech, in which the purification of man necessary to enter heaven is thereby transferred to the heaven which he enters. Thus Vaughan says that "heaven needs no purifying in itself; the necessity spoken of is relative; to fit it for man's entrance. The purifying spoken of is therefore the sacrifice of Christ for man's sin, and the self-presentation of Christ in heaven as man's high priest." Westcott takes a very different position. He says "that even heavenly things, so far as they embody the conditions of man's future life, contracted by the Fall something which required cleansing." The "necessity"—a strong and emphatic word— is therefore to be found in the holiness of God, and those persons or places which He honors with His presence must be holy. He will neither condone evil nor compromise with sin and uncleanness.

2. To what extent has the entrance of sin disturbed the moral order of the world? The Scriptures indicate that the redemptive work of Christ extends more widely than the salvation of the individual Christian, as great as this triumph may be. St. Paul tells us "that the whole creation groaneth and travaileth in pain together until now" (Rom. 8:22); and that God through Christ, "hav-

ing made peace through the blood of his cross," has reconciled all things to himself, "whether they be things in earth, or things in heaven" (Col. 1: 20). This is a remarkable text. If there are things to be reconciled in heaven, it should not surprise us if there are things also to be purified. However, the Scriptures do not fully reveal to us all the grandeur of Christ's redemption, for they were not written to satisfy our curiosity, but to make us wise unto salvation.

Christ's Entrance into Heaven for Us. "For Christ is not entered into the holy places made with hands, which are the figures of the true; but into heaven itself, now to appear in the presence of God for us" (9: 24). Previously the writer has said that Christ entered by His own blood (9: 12); here it is said that He entered, not for himself, but for us. He is said not to have entered into the holy places made with hands, that is, the earthly Tabernacle, which with all its gold and grandeur was but a copy or shadow of the true tabernacle, now clearly defined as heaven itself. The word for "appear" is *emphanisthenai* (ἐμφανισθῆναι), a participle, translated elsewhere as "to show forth" or "to make manifest"; and the word "presence" is *prosopoi* (προσώπῳ) or "face." Thus it is that Christ was manifested to God's immediate presence or full view; but as God views immediately the face of His Son, so also the Son views likewise the face of God. The aorist indicates a single act of self-presentation by ascension into heaven; the word "now" implies that the condition of manifestation continues; and the words "for us" represent the simplest form of intercession. Christ has only to appear before the face of God and that appearance is solely for us; and that appearance, because of what He is and has done, is our intercessory Presence. What therefore was prefigured in the earthly copy is fully and finally accomplished in the heavenly sanctuary.

The Offering Once for All. "Nor yet that he should offer himself often, as the high priest entereth into the holy place every year with blood of others" (9: 25).

Here the writer contrasts the offerings of the Levitical high priest and Christ. The former, entering with the blood of others, repeated his sacrifice every year; Christ entered once for all through the sacrifice of himself. The priests could enter often because they entered with the blood of others; Christ entered but once because He offered His own blood in a sacrificial death. Christ offered himself in full obedience to the will of God, and therefore a further offering was unnecessary, both because of the efficacy of His sacrifice and because of the glory of His person.

1. The writer pursues his argument still further by saying, "For then must he often have suffered since the foundation of the world" (9:26a). Evidently the Jews questioned the validity of the one offering. Had the offering not been once for all, he says, it would imply repeated suffering—the Incarnation, a life of suffering, and a cruel death—and all this from the foundation of the world. The writer looks solely to the past. Had Christ's offering not been once for all, it would have been valid only for His generation, as was that of the Levitical high priest. His offering therefore must be independent of time and valid as a single act. And further, since His appearance was at the end of the age (αἰώνων), it is evident that His sacrifice was efficacious for all that preceded Him, and marked the ushering in of a new age or dispensation based upon a better covenant and established upon better promises.

2. The purpose of this one offering was "to put away sin by the sacrifice of himself" (9:26b). This is a climactic statement. By it the writer means that Christ has put away sin and all that is connected with it—its nature and effects, its roots and its fruits. He has removed its guilt, destroyed its power, and cleansed away its very being. Sin was apostasy from God. No man was able to destroy it. But Christ appeared to put away sin by the sacrifice of himself. His atonement has abrogated and disannulled "the law of sin and death" and brought in "the law of the Spirit of life in Christ

Jesus" (Rom. 8:2). Here is an inner transformation by the Holy Spirit that puts the life in harmony with the will of God and makes true obedience possible. The words "put away sin," therefore, declare not only His purpose, but affirm its effects. He was manifested to take away our sins (I John 3:5, 8), and this purpose He has fully and triumphantly accomplished.

Death and the Judgment. "And as it is appointed unto men once to die, but after this the judgment" (9:27). This is a transitional verse, the first half being an affirmation of the efficacy of the one death of Christ, while the second is a glimpse into the future when Christ shall come again without sin unto salvation. Two things are specified as appointed to men, death and the judgment. The word translated "appointed" is *apokeitai* (ἀπόκειται) and means "to lay off," or "to be reserved," and thus made sure. It has therefore the force of unalterable law, which cannot be transgressed, and applies equally to both death and the judgment. Death closes the door upon the history of life in this world and opens up to it the world to come. What is not done before death must be left forever undone in this world. The particle *de* (δέ), "but," has the force of certainty—that if death takes place, judgment must follow, and this too is an irrevocable decision. It would seem that, to be in line with the writer's thought, this judgment should follow immediately after death; but many commentators hold that, instead, it refers to the awe-inspiring scene that marks the close of this world's history. Probably the first judgment refers to an *initial* judgment, which determines the saved or unsaved state of the individual, and must of necessity take place at death; and the other to the *general* judgment, at which men are rewarded or punished in the degree that their works demand.

CHRIST'S SECOND APPEARANCE

"So Christ was once offered to bear the sins of many; and unto them that look for him shall he appear the second time without sin unto salvation" (9:28). The writer now draws his parallel to a close. When the high priest had finished the service on the Day of Atonement, he put on again his garments of "glory" and "beauty" and appeared at the gate to bless the waiting congregation. So also Christ, after He had made the one offering for sin and entered once into the holiest of all, will come again, not now in His humiliation, but in His garments of glory and beauty, transformed into brightness above that of the sun shining in his strength. "For as the lightning cometh out of the east, and shineth even unto the west; so shall also the coming of the Son of man be" (Matt. 24:27), and so shall He gather together His redeemed, who anxiously await Him.

The word "offered" is *prosenechtheis* (προσενεχθείς), a passive participle, "having been offered," and is but another way of saying "having offered himself." Christ was both the Offerer and the Offering; at once the High Priest and the Sacrifice. This whole sentence, "So Christ was once offered to bear the sins of many," is remarkable in that both the words *prosenechtheis* (προσενεχθείς), "having been offered," and *anenegkein* (ανενεγκείν), "to bear" or "to carry up," are both from the same root word, the prepositions *pros* ("forward") and *ana* ("up") being the sole difference, except that the former is in the passive voice. Cowles gives us this paraphrase, "Christ was once *brought forward* (i.e. before the world and the universe), that He might *bear away* before all heaven and earth (so the word signifies), that He might visibly, publicly, *bear away* the sins of many." Vaughan holds more strictly to the technical meaning of the last term, as the "carrying up" or "bringing up" the sacrifice to the altar, which with Christ was the Cross. He then paraphrases the whole expression as "having been brought to the altar of sacrifice that He might bring up to it in His own person the sins of many." Thus was the cross of Calvary the public demonstration of Christ's sacrifice for the sin of the world.

The word *pollon* (πολλῶν), or "the many," has no reference to the "many as chosen from the whole number," but of "the many" in contrast with the *one* Christ and the *once*-for-all offering. These words cannot be perverted to teach a "limited atonement"—a theological doctrine out of harmony with the entire tenor of the Scriptures, and expressly so stated in John 1: 29, "Behold the Lamb of God, which taketh away the sin of the world"; and again in II Cor. 5: 15, where it is clearly stated "that he died for all." Here the word used is "all" ($\pi\acute{a}\nu\tau\omega\nu$) and not "many" ($\pi o\lambda\lambda\hat{\omega}\nu$). Since in the preceding verse (9: 5) the word *anthropois* ($\dot{a}\nu\theta\rho\acute{\omega}\pi o\iota s$) is used, meaning mankind in general, the word "many" could be properly applied to those who believe and thereby avail themselves of the benefits of the atonement. In theological terms, "The atonement is sufficient for all men, but efficient for only those who believe." The atonement extends to all men universally, but those who by their own will reject its provisions thereby limit its significance to those who through faith have availed themselves of its redemptive power.

The words "without sin" must also be given consideration. "Unto them that look for him shall he appear the second time without sin unto salvation" (9: 28b). Christ was himself "without sin" and "separate from sinners"; and yet it is said, "He hath made him to be sin for us, who knew no sin; that we might be made the righteousness of God in him" (II Cor. 5: 21). Whatever interpretation is put upon this verse as to His being made sin, His second coming in the same sense will be "without sin." If this text be interpreted to mean that Christ came as a Sin Offering, then the second time He will come without a Sin Offering. If He came as a Sin Bearer the first time, He will come the second time as having put away sin. And if He came out of compassion for sinners in His humiliation, He will come the second time in glory to judge the earth.

The words "unto salvation" refer to the ultimate consummation of all things. Whatever theories of the millennium attach to His second coming are not here taken into account. "When the Son of man shall come in his glory, and all the holy angels with him, then shall he sit upon the throne of his glory." Then shall

He say unto the righteous, "Come, ye blessed of my Father, inherit the kingdom prepared for you from the foundation of the world"; but unto the wicked He shall say, "Depart from me, ye cursed, into everlasting fire, prepared for the devil and his angels" (Matt. 25: 31, 34, 41). "Then cometh the end, when he shall have delivered up the kingdom to God, even the Father; when he shall have put down all rule and all authority and power" (I Cor. 15: 24)—then it is that all things come to their final estate in a new and eternal order.

CHAPTER X

THE NEW COVENANT AND THE LIVING WAY

This chapter marks the author's final verdict on the whole Levitical order, and introduces the new covenant and the living way. The word "for" does not necessarily imply a continuance of the argument, but only a general connection with the preceding discussion. Bruce in his *Epistle to the Hebrews* views the writer as making a pause in order to deliver his final verdict on Leviticalism. This he does in "a solemn, deliberate, authoritative manner. This verdict we have here rapid in utterance, lofty in tone, rising from the didactic style of the theological doctor to the oracular speech of the Hebrew prophet, as in that peremptory sentence: 'It is not possible that the blood of bulls and of goats should take away sins.' The remarkable thing about this chapter," he continues, is "the series of spiritual intuitions it contains, stated or hinted, in brief, pithy phrases: the law a shadow; Levitical sacrifices constantly repeated, inept; the removal of sin by the blood of bruit beasts, impossible; the only sacrifice that can have any real virtue, that by which God's will is fulfilled." This chapter therefore, rightly considered, is the peroration of a weighty discourse.

The Law as a Shadow. "For the law having a shadow of good things to come, and not the very image of those things, can never with those sacrifices which they offered year by year continually make the comers thereunto perfect" (10:1). The "substance and the shadow" have been previously discussed as pertaining to the two tabernacles (8:5); here however the contrast is between the "law" and the "good things to come." In the expression "good things to come," the word used is *mellonton* (μελλόντον), which means "good things about to come." This may have a more immediate and a more remote meaning. The things immediately subsequent to the law are those which in Christ are made available to us in this life; those more remote are the good things in store for us in the future state. This position appears to be borne out by a further contrast in which it is said that the former services could not make the worshiper "perfect" (9:9), while of Christ it is said that "by one offering he hath perfected for ever them that are sanctified" (10:14).

The Greek words used in this comparison are *skian* (σκιὰν), "shadow," and *eikona* (εἰκόνα), "image." The word "image," however, is not a mere copy or reflection, but is used in the sense of the form in which actual things exist. The writer uses the metaphor of a statue and the shadow which it casts, terms well chosen to show that Judaism was but a mere shadow of the realities in the gospel dispensation. Among the Greeks, however, the *skia* was understood by patristic commentators as the first sketch of a picture, and *eikon* as the finished picture after the colors were put in. Westcott points out that this is one of the few illustrations from art found in the New Testament. As a shadow has some value in that it indicates the existence of a real substance, so Judaism had its value as a shadow of that which became a reality in Christ.

The writer, however, is not averse to repeating his former statements in order to reinforce his argument. Having said that the law was but a shadow of the coming realities in Christ, he sums up his argument thus: (1) Its services and sacrifices could never "make the comers thereunto perfect," that is, bring them to the goal that God intended for His people (10:1b). (2) Had these sacrifices brought the people to perfection, "then would they not have ceased to be offered?" (10:2a) (3) Had the worshipers been actually purged, would they not then have been no longer conscious of sin? (10:2b) (4) Instead, did not the sacrifices made every year bring again a remembrance of sins? (10:3) Lastly, there comes the final pronouncement in brief, but strong and authoritative, terms, "Impossible [it is] for [the] blood of bulls and of goats to take away sins" (see 10:4).

The Two Sacrifices Compared. "Wherefore when he cometh into the world, he saith, Sacrifice and offering thou wouldest not, but a body hast thou prepared me: in burnt offerings and sacrifices for sin thou hast had no pleasure" (10: 5-6). "Wherefore," that is, because there was no inherent possibility that animal sacrifices should take away sin, a new sacrifice is demanded—the self-sacrifice of the body of Christ. "When he cometh into the world" refers primarily to the Incarnation. The word is *eiserchomenos* (εἰσερχόμενος), a participle which means literally "being born." It is the most general term for entering the sphere of human existence, and in rabbinic language was the usual expression for "being born." However the words have a wider meaning as seen in the prologue to St. John's Gospel, where it is said of the preincarnate Logos, that He "lighteth every man that cometh into the world" (John 1: 9). These words are a clear indication that the writer believed in the pre-existence of Christ. When these words are conjoined with "he saith," they indicate a posture of activity—"he cometh" and "saith."

1. The writer finds his authority for the better sacrifice in a quotation from the fortieth psalm (Ps. 40: 6-8); and though spoken first by David, it is here said to be spoken by Christ. Vaughan states it as a principle of interpretation that, where that is written of a *man* which no *man* can satisfy, there lies under it a reference to One who is not man only. Delitzsch states the matter clearly. He says, "It is not as if Christ and *not* David speaks; but Christ, whose spirit already dwells and works in David, and who will hereafter receive from David His human nature, now already speaks in him." It is David, the type, speaking words which make them authoritative in Christ, the great Antitype. The writer has said that it is impossible for the blood of bulls and of goats to take away sin; here he finds his supreme authority in the words of Christ himself.

2. "Above when he said, Sacrifice and offering and burnt offerings and offering for sin thou wouldest not, neither hadst pleasure therein; which are offered by the

law" (10:8). The writer now offers his comments on the preceding quotation, these comments taking the form of an analysis of the text. The word "above" as used here does not merely mean that which precedes, as we commonly use it. The word is *kephalis* (κεφαλίς), which means "little head," and was a technical term for the often highly ornamented knobs on the ends of the rods upon which the scrolls were rolled. Hence they came to stand for the rolls themselves, or as we understand it, the Scriptures. The writer emphasizes his point by calling attention to the fact that the negative statement, both in the psalm and in the quotation, is placed ahead of the positive statement concerning God's will. Here he is specific and mentions all classes of the Levitical offerings: (1) from the material standpoint, animal sacrifices or blood offerings, and meal or vegetable offerings; and (2) from the standpoint of types, the whole burnt offerings (eucharistic or praise offerings) and sin offerings. These, it is said, God did not desire (A.V., "require") and did not approve, in the sense that He had no pleasure in them. They were therefore not according to God's will; and hence the writer looks forward to that which is the will of God, which was to be perfectly accomplished in the body of Christ. He closes this verse with the emphatic statement, "He taketh away the first," which was not according to the will of God, "that he may establish the second," which is the will of God. One concessive statement however is made: the first sacrifices were by the law, though but a shadow of that which was to be perfectly accomplished in Christ.

3. Christ coming into the world and saying, "Lo, I come to do thy will, O God," gave utterance thereby to the great truth that the only true sacrifice which man can offer to God is that of heart obedience to His will. The only way to God is through the will of God; and in His will alone man finds "righteousness, and peace, and

Christ did not come into the world to be a good man; it was not for this that a body was prepared for Him. He came to be a great High Priest, and the body was prepared for Him, that by the offering of it He might put sinful men forever into the perfect religious relation to God.—DENNY, *The Death of Christ*, p. 234.

joy in the Holy Ghost." Sin and the whole tragedy of the human race came through man's disobedience. Man sinned by turning from God's will to his own; Christ redeemed man by turning from His own to God's will. We may say, then, that the will of God as expressed here is that a body should be prepared for Him who was the eternal Logos, and in that body He should voluntarily assume all that was required for the expiation of sin. To do the will of God is for the writer a sacrificial act which should involve Jesus in an atoning death, the tasting of death for every man.

The Perfect Will of God. "Then said I, Lo, I come (in the volume of the book it is written of me,) to do thy will, O God" (10:7). We are given an insight here into the conversation in heaven, in which the Son voluntarily offers to assume a human body, and in this state of humiliation to carry into effect perfectly the will of the Father. His submission is further shown in that He uses the Father's own words written concerning Him "in the volume of the book," and in this filial manner expresses His desire and delight to do the will of God. Having quoted these words, the writer calls attention to certain outstanding facts in the text.

1. "Then said he, Lo, ['Behold'] I come to do thy will, O God." This is not a mere repetition. He says, "Behold," and thereby calls special attention to this redemptive Person. His desire is that every eye should be fastened upon the Son, and every ear be opened to hear His words. This is a matter of utmost importance, for without the substitutionary death of Christ, there could be no atonement for sin; and without the rending of the veil, there could be no fellowship with God in the holy of holies.

2. Concerning the relation of Christ's coming to the Levitical order, the writer gives us this exegesis. If God "wouldest not," or "willed not," the ancient Levitical sacrifices (10:8); and indicated that He willed something else, i.e., that the body of His Son should fill out, complete, and annul all previous sacrifices; then it is

evident that "He taketh away [annuls or abrogates] the first, that he may establish the second" (10:9b). The "first" is the entire Jewish offerings of blood and meal sacrifices; the "second" is the establishing of God's will through that obedience which led to His death on the Cross, a sacrifice in which He tasted death for every man.

3. Christ's death on the Cross marked the completion of His perfect obedience which he offered to God in His divine-human person. The word eireken (εἴρηκεν), "he said"—literally, "then hath he said"—is an abiding declaration that the will of God will be continuously fulfilled; and the words "I am come" mark the immediacy of His response. It was His own obedience, and yet being the obedience of the God-Man gives to it that infinite value which made it vicarious for the whole human race. As an obedience unto death, it became the ground of our justification; and as a voluntary sacrifice of self-surrender, it became also the ground of our sanctification. As an appointment of God, this satisfaction provided by divine love must therefore be viewed on the one hand as an expiation of sin and guilt and on the other as a propitiation of the divine displeasure. This reconciliation was also twofold: (1) it is a work of Christ by which God is reconciled to the whole race of mankind through the Blood of the atonement; and (2) this general reconciliation is the provision by which individual men may become reconciled to God. This individual reconciliation is but the personal assumption through faith of the benefits made provisional in the general reconciliation.

"A Body Hast Thou Prepared Me" (10:5b). The contrast here is between unwilling animal victims and the one sacrifice of Christ, which was freely offered for all. The writer follows the Septuagint in this text, as does our Authorized Version, but the Hebrew text reads, "Mine ears hast thou digged." The explanation however does not lie in a mistranslation in which soma (σῶμα) or "body" is substituted for otia (ὠτία) or "ears." Delitzsch is probably right when he says that the translators of the Septuagint sought to make the expression "digged mine ears" more intelligible to their Greek readers by translating it "shaped a body for me." Since the main purpose of the writer is to emphasize the necessity of doing God's will, this is made equally clear whether rendered "digged mine ears" to hear God's will, or the Septuagint's rendering, "shaped me a body" to respond to that will. The term "body" is more comprehensive than that of "flesh and blood"; and especially since blood is the symbol of earthly life, it appears to have no place in the resurrection (cf. Luke 24:39; I Cor. 15:50). Thus the one life of Christ is equally manifested under the "body of His humiliation" and the body of His glory. Likewise man bears a twofold relation to the body of Christ, for "as we have borne the image of the earthy, we shall also bear the image of the heavenly" (I Cor. 15:49).

Any denial of the virgin birth of Christ is of necessity a denial of His true deity. The very wording of the text, "A body hast thou prepared me," implies that His body was specially prepared (or shaped) by God, who was His true Father, and therefore out of the ordinary line of generation. He was the eternal Son of the Father, the preincarnate *Logos* become flesh; He received His entire humanity from the Virgin Mary, who through the power of the Holy Spirit was given power to conceive —and thus two natures, the divine and the human, were forever conjoined in one Person, the God-Man. This prepared body, representing as it does the whole of humanity, made possible His expiatory sacrifice to the holiness of God. Dr. Pope says that "the soul of the sinner could not be at once offered in death and accepted as living; could not be at once a sin-offering doomed to destruction, and a burnt-offering, well-pleasing to God. But in man's Representative at the holy altar, these most gloriously meet. He presented a sacrifice which was a veritable endurance of the consequence of transgression: *He died unto sin once.* But that death was also a living Sacrifice of our human nature, given back to God again in perfection. . . . These seem to be paradoxes; but they express the very secret and mystery of redemption. "

Sanctification as the Will of God. "By the which will we are sanctified through the offering of the body of Jesus Christ once for all" (10:10). The writer, having shown that the will of God was perfectly manifested in Christ's offering of himself, now turns his attention to the future results of this sacrifice. The word *hegiasmenoi* (ἡγιασμένοι), "sanctified," is the periphrastic perfect passive indicative of *hagiazo* (ἁγιάζω), "we have been sanctified"; that is, we are included in the will which was made operative by the one perfect offering of the body of Christ. Here also is to be seen in a new light the writer's teaching concerning the inheritance administered through Christ as the Heir of all things, in that it has as the first item of the will that we should be sanctified. The offering of Christ is modified by the adverb *ephapax* (ἐφάπαξ), "once for all," which is a stronger term than the common word *apax* (ἅπαξ), found in 7:27 and 9:28. Some have attached this word to the offering of Christ which was "once for all," but it is clearly evident from verse 14 that the "once for all" offering brought a "once for all" result in the sanctification of the people.

Christ in His high priestly prayer says, "For their sakes I sanctify myself, that they might also be sanctified through the truth," that is, in truth or "truly sanctified." Christ was given a prepared body, that in that body He might live a sanctified life, that is, a God-possessed life. Jesus had no sin from which to be cleansed and therefore could of His own will offer himself to be fully possessed and used by the Father. Man however has a sinful nature, which remains even in the regenerate, and this must be cleansed before there can be full divine possession. As we speak of justification and regeneration as being concomitant, or two aspects of the general term "conversion," so purification and divine possession are concomitant in the one experience of entire sanctification. Logically however the act of cleansing by the Spirit must precede the fullness of the indwelling Spirit in the one experience, in the same sense that all Protestantism holds that justification as a change of relations must logically precede the new birth in the one experience of conversion. Only the fullness of the Holy Spirit in His purifying and anointing power enables the Christian to render the highest and most effective service to the living God.

The Exaltation and Finished Atonement of Christ. The writer has not yet reached the climax of his argument. There is one more weakness of the priests to be presented, and in contrast, the crowning statement concerning the exaltation of Christ and His finished atonement.

1. The Levitical priests were "standing priests." "And every priest standeth daily ministering and offering oftentimes the same sacrifices, which can never take away sins" (10: 11). The sacrifice of the high priest on the great Day of Atonement did not provide for a continuous state of sanctification; hence the common priests stood, offering day by day, oftentimes the same sacrifices. This offering was not limited to the daily morning and evening sacrifice, but included also the same sacrifice for each type of sin, and this over and over again without end. It was a tiresome routine. Each new sin required a new offering; hence the conclusion that these sacrifices could never take away sins. We have seen that even the service of the high priest on the Day of Atonement only pointed to Christ and His one all-atoning sacrifice; so also the sacrifices of the common priests had their validity solely in the acceptance by faith in Him who was to come. It will thus be seen that the writer by his reference to the common priests intensifies his teaching that these sacrifices, in and of themselves, can never take away sin.

2. *Christ as the seated Priest.* "But this man, after he had offered one sacrifice for sins for ever, sat down on the right hand of God" (10: 12). The attitude of sitting is indicative of authority. The Levitical priests stood because their work was never done; but Christ was a Priest of another order, the order of Melchisedec, and therefore a King-Priest. He sits as one whose task is finished and whose work is complete. However, the

purpose of the writer is not so much to restate Christ's
work as Priest as to emphasize His exaltation as King.
By His one sacrificial offering, He has carried our humanity from its lost and sinful condition to the very
throne of God! What a glorious triumph! In the presence of the God-Man we have a Representative, "One of
our own folks" on the throne. The God-Man is a Priest-
King. As Priest, He is at the right hand of God as our
intercessory Presence; as King, He has set up His initial
kingdom in the hearts of His people—a kingdom of
"righteousness, and peace, and joy in the Holy Ghost."
But the writer hastens on to show that this initial Kingdom shall yet become a universal Kingdom, all things
shall be subjected to Him.

3. "From henceforth expecting till his enemies be
made his footstool" (10:13). The writer refers again to
the 110th psalm, where it is written, "The Lord said
unto my Lord, Sit thou at my right hand, until I make
thine enemies thy footstool" (Ps. 110:1). He infers that
Christ now has only to await the time when all enemies
shall be put under His feet. The contrast here is between
the attitude of a priest who stands, ever ready to offer
another sacrifice, and Christ, who sits in solemn confidence "awaiting" (for this is the meaning of the word
"expecting") the ingathering of the fruits of His triumph. While this is a militant figure, the writer does
not say who the enemies of Christ are, for this is not in
line with the trend of his argument. Nor should we think
that the attitude of sitting, while one of confidence, is
also one of quiet indifference. Instead it means the full
exercise of power and majesty. Regardless of what may
be the order of events attending the millennium, it seems
evident from 9:28, which marks the close of the service
on the Day of Atonement, and from many other scriptures, that Christ will appear the second time for the
salvation of His people, previous to the day mentioned
here, which is the day of judgment. Then every knee
shall bow, and every tongue confess that Jesus Christ
is Lord, to the glory of God the Father. St. Paul tells us
that the last enemy to be destroyed during Christ's reign

is death (I Cor. 15: 23-26); and that the resurrection will occur in stages: (1) "Christ the firstfruits"; (2) "they that are Christ's at his coming"; and then of course (3) the resurrection of the wicked. Death must be entirely conquered in the resurrection before there can be a general judgment. The word "until" is interesting as used here, in that it shows how far the sacrifice reaches.

Sanctification and Perfection. "For by one offering he hath perfected for ever them that are sanctified" (10: 14). This marks the climax of the work of Christ as High Priest. It is stated in a simple explanatory clause, "For by means of a single offering [or sacrifice], He has perfected [brought to completion] forever [in perpetuity] them that are sanctified." In 10: 10 the words "we have been sanctified" show what Christ has accomplished objectively, and that we with Him have been included in the will. Here the words are *tous hagiazomenous* (τοὺς ἁγιαζόμενους), "them that are sanctified," an articular participle in the accusative case, present passive of *hagiazo* (ἁγιάζω), "to sanctify" or "to make holy." These words affirm not only that the heirs are included in the will, but that they have been brought actually into possession of that which was bequeathed them. They "are sanctified" as a present, inner, spiritual experience wrought by Christ through the one great sacrifice of himself. Furthermore, the writer links the term "sanctified" with the *teleiosis* (τελείωσις) or "perfection" which the Levitical system could never achieve, but which now has been accomplished by Christ. The word used here is *teteleioken* (τετελείωκεν), the perfect active indicative of *teleioo* (τελειόω), "He has perfected and continues to keep perfect."

A further word needs to be said concerning the expression "them that are sanctified." Since the word "sanctified" is in the form of a present participle, it may easily be translated in different ways, and hence we are warned that "grammar speaks to exegesis here with no decisive voice." (1) As a present participle, the word "sanctified" may be regarded as durative; that is, the time element enters into it. It would then be translated "being sanctified," in the sense of being in the process of sanctification. This position is held by those who regard sanctification as a process carried on through life, and not as a single definite act of faith in the blood of Christ. (2) As a present participle, the word may also be regarded as iterative, or a timeless act repeated, and would then mean those who from time to time are sanctified by a definite act of faith. Robertson states that the present participle used in the expression "such as were being saved" (Acts 2:47) should be regarded as iterative and translated "those saved from time to time" . . . "for here repetition is clearly the point of the present tense." So also it seems to me that the true meaning of "being sanctified" is also iterative and can only refer to those who are being sanctified from time to time. Otherwise it appears inconsistent for the writer to say that he has perfected or completed those who are as yet only in the process of being sanctified. The most conclusive evidence of this position, however, is found in the words of our Lord's high priestly prayer,

Dr. Ross E. Price cites the following authorities as to the use of the present participle in the iterative sense. (1) Dr. Moll in Lange's *Commentary* (p. 170) says that *tous hagiazomenous* means "those who are being sanctified, or who are sanctified from time to time." (2) Whedon (on verse 14) says, "He has fully and forever potentially and conditionally perfected all; but the full reality takes effect only in those who are sanctified through Him." Marcus Dods says that this expression "literally means those who are being sanctified, all those who, from age to age, through faith (verse 22) receive as their own that which has been procured for all men." In his *Prolegomena* (p. 126), Moulton says that, "like the rest of the verb, outside the indicative, it has properly no sense of time attaching to it; the linear action in a participle, connected with a finite verb in past or present time, partakes in the time of its principle. But when the participle is isolated by the addition of the article, its proper timelessness is free to come out." Again, "The present participle with the article becomes virtually a noun" (p. 127). E. V. P. Nunn says: "The present participle may also be used simply to define its subject as belonging to a certain class which does or suffers the action denoted by the verb from which it comes. In this case it becomes equivalent to an adjective. It is generally preceded by an article, and it is best translated into English by a relative clause" (pp. 123-24). Burton in his *Moods and Tenses* (p. 56) takes the same position. "The present participle used without reference to time or progress, simply defining its subject as belonging to a certain class, i.e., the class of those who do the action denoted by the verb. The participle in this case becomes a simple adjective or noun and is like any other adjective or noun, timeless and indefinite." Robertson in his *New Testament in the Light of Historical Research* (p. 892) notes that, with the article, "the present participle has often the iterative sense."

"Sanctify them through thy truth: thy word is truth"
(John 17: 17). Here the word for sanctify is *hagiason*
(ἁγίασον), which is a first active imperative, and cannot
possibly mean an incomplete process but a definite act
of sanctification. Certainly the writer of this Epistle
means to say that what our Lord prayed for has actually
been accomplished.

We have presented the teaching of this Epistle under
various aspects, as the great salvation, sanctification, the
rest of faith, the uttermost salvation, and Christian perfection; and perhaps may now be allowed to give a
brief statement of the latter in the words of another.
Perhaps no clearer or more exact and scholarly statement of the doctrine of Christian perfection, as set forth
in this Epistle, has ever been made than that of the
great English theologian William Burt Pope, in his *Compendium of Christian Theology*. We can give here only
a few brief extracts, but the full account is well worth
careful perusal. He says: "The word *Perfectionism* is
sometimes applied satirically to those who hold the
doctrine we here maintain; they who bear it, bear it in
the reproach of Christ. The term *Perfection*, being alone,
should not be adopted without qualification; but with
its guardian adjectives Christian or Evangelical it is
unimpeachable. It is the vanishing point of every doctrine, exhortation, promise and prophecy in the New
Testament. Christian Perfection is relative and probationary, and therefore in perhaps an undefinable sense
limited."

1. *Relative.* "This may be viewed in relation to the
final consummation. In the hope of that last *tetelestai*
(τετέλεσται) 'perfection' all Christians unite: when Holiness unto the Lord shall be the eternal law of the glorified man in his integrity. In this life, *the body is dead
because of sin* (Rom. 8: 10); it not only perisheth itself,
but, in the words of the Apocryphal Wisdom, *the corruptible body presseth down the soul, and the earthly
tabernacle weigheth down the mind that museth upon
many things* (Wisd. 9: 15). Christian perfection is the
estate of a spirit every whit whole, but still in a body

the infirmity of which is the main part of its probation. Each has its own order. With regard to physical resurrection St. Paul says: *That was not first which is spiritual, but that which is natural.* This order is inverted as to the resurrection of the soul: first *that which is* spiritual. But when the perfection of the soul is reached, the body has still to submit to the dust: the spiritual eye sees *the King in his beauty . . . in the land that is very far off;* the natural eye goes down to *see corruption.* And the body on its way to dissolution impairs in ten thousand ways the absoluteness of the deliverance of the spirit. Perfection under this and every aspect is relative."

2. *Probationary.* "Christian perfection at its best is that of a probationary estate. There is no reason therefore why it may not be lost again, and utterly lost, even after the fruition of the result of long years of heavenly blessing on earthly diligence. The principle of sin, extinct in the soul, may be kindled into life as it was kindled in Eve. There is no reason why it should not and ought not. Such a second fall would be a fall indeed. It is not probable that it was ever witnessed. It is only our theory that demands the admission of its possibility."

3. *Individual.* Probation is "that of the individual person whose relation to the race remains. Though personally in Christ, and altogether in Christ, during probation he is still under the generic doom of original sin, with a concupiscence which is not sin but the fuel of it always ready to be rekindled, and generally under the law of probation which is peculiar to our race . . . the inheritor of a sinful nature which, cleansed in himself, he transmits to his own children uncleansed. He does not altogether lose his connection with the line of sinful humanity. We never read of an entire severance

---

Dr. Adam Clarke in his comment on I Thess. 5:23-24 says: "Hence we learn (1) that body, soul and spirit, are debased and polluted by sin; (2) that each is capable of being sanctified, consecrated in all its powers and made holy; (3) that the whole man is to be preserved to the coming of Christ, that body, soul and spirit, may be then glorified forever with Him; and (4) that in *this* state, the whole man may be so sanctified, as to be preserved blameless, till the coming of Christ. And thus we learn, that the sanctification is not to take place *in, at* or *after* death."

from the first Adam as the prerogative of those who are found in the Second."

4. *Ethical.* "Once more, it is a probationary perfection inasmuch as it is always under the ethical law. . . . It is a state to be guarded by watchfulness, which is subjected to an infinite variety of tests, and must be maintained by the habitual and, by Divine grace, perfect exercise of all the virtues active and passive."

5. *Mediatorial.* "Hence this perfection needs constantly the mediatorial work of Christ; it demands His constant influence to preserve as a state what is imparted as a gift. The mediatory intercession is never so urgently needed as for those who have so priceless a treasure in earthen vessels; the height, the grace and the more finished the sanctity, the more alien it is from the surrounding world, the more hateful to the tempter, and the more grace does it require for its guard" (III, 54-60).

THE RESTATEMENT OF THE NEW COVENANT

The writer, having brought the argument concerning the futility of the Levitical covenant to a close, now restates the new covenant in a somewhat freer manner than previously. Here he follows his usual plan of omitting any reference to the human agent in revelation, and assigns the words directly to the Holy Spirit, who inspired them. His simple faith in the inspiration of the Scriptures and his unquestioned confidence in their authority as the Word of God are worthy of emulation. The statement, "Whereof the Holy Ghost also is a witness to us," is sometimes attached to the preceding verse, making it a witness to sanctification; but the Revised Version makes it the transition point for the introduction of the new covenant. Here we read, "And the Holy Spirit also beareth witness [or testifieth] to us; for after he hath said, This is the covenant that I will make with them after those days, saith the Lord." This is the Spirit's objective authority for the establishment of a new covenant as given in the Scriptures.

"The Holy Ghost Saith." In addition to the Spirit's objective authority for the new covenant, ministered through the Word, it has also a subjective aspect in that it is administered immediately by the Spirit himself. As there is an inward witness of the Spirit to the sonship of believers (Rom. 8:16), so also the Spirit witnesses to His own incoming in the hearts of believers (I John 4:13). This new and spiritual covenant was ushered in and became effective on the Day of Pentecost, the great inauguration day of the Holy Spirit. Our King-Priest, seated at the right hand of the Father, began on that prophetic day His spiritual reign within the hearts of His people, purifying them from sin (Acts 15:9) and anointing them with the power of the Holy Spirit (Acts 1:8). This St. Peter acknowledged in his Pentecostal sermon, saying, "Therefore being by the right hand of God exalted, and having received of the Father the promise of the Holy Ghost, he hath shed forth this, which ye now see and hear" (Acts 2:33). From His throne in the heavens Christ ministers not only the words of the covenant, but its inner spirit; and therefore by the Spirit writes the law of God in our minds that we may understand it, and puts the love of it within our hearts that it may be the inner, impulsive power of obedience. Here again St. Peter says, "Elect according to the foreknowledge of God the Father, through sanctification of the Spirit, unto obedience and sprinkling of the blood of Jesus Christ" (I Pet. 1:2). True sanctification results in obedience and the sprinkling of the blood of Christ, and the sprinkling of that Blood so purifies the heart that it can render to God the obedience of perfect love.

The Two Approaches to the New Covenant. The quotation from the prophet Jeremiah found in Heb. 8:10-12 is here repeated in a somewhat abbreviated manner and with certain verbal changes. However the purpose of the two statements is very different, and the verbal changes are intended to accentuate these differences. The first statement was made to show that God intended to abrogate the old Levitical law and replace it with a new and entirely different type of covenant; the second is to show that this new covenant is ratified by the blood of Jesus Christ, and through the Spirit made so effective that it will remove the very remembrance of sins and iniquities. Previous to this the writer has presented the work of Christ under two aspects: (1) His work on earth as the "surety of the covenant"—not that He guarantees our obedience to God, but God's faithfulness to us; and (2) His work in heaven as the "minister of the sanctuary," by which through the Spirit the provisions of the covenant are made effective in the lives of men. From the standpoint of the "surety of the covenant," the progress is from earth heavenward: "I will put my laws into their mind," (the words of the covenant) "and write them in their hearts: " (the spirit of the covenant) "and I will be to them a God, and they shall be to me a people" (the goal of the covenant). From the standpoint of the "minister of the sanctuary," the progress is from heaven earthward: "I will put my laws into their hearts," (their inmost being) "and in their minds will I write them;" (the outward expression of the inner spiritual consciousness) "and their sins and iniquities will I remember no more." Thus the covenant in Christ spans man's upreach to the presence of God, and God's downward reach to man in the removing of even the remembrance of sins and iniquities.

The writer concludes this section, and in a sense the entire argument, with this clear and positive statement: "Now where remission of these is, there is no more offering for sin" (10:18). The word *aphesis* (ἄφεσις), translated "remission," means literally "to send away"; and here it is said that God has sent our sins so far away that even His memory does not recall them. Two things, it is clear, the Holy Spirit witnesses to in the new covenant: a work done for us and a work done in us. The former we call justification, the latter sanctification; and sanctification in its deepest, fullest sense is that of a heart cleansed from sin and "lawlessness," a life so filled with the Spirit that it may truly be said to be "God-possessed." These glorious truths are now considered proved. The argument does not admit of further questions. Not only is no further sacrifice needed, but no further presentation of a sacrifice. This, the writer testifies, is witnessed by the Holy Ghost.

THE HOLIEST OF ALL

"Having therefore, brethren, boldness to enter into the holiest by the blood of Jesus, by a new and living way, which he hath consecrated for us, through the veil, that is to say, his flesh" (10: 19-20). From the beginning of chapter seven the writer has given himself to a continuous argument, based on the exposition of certain Old Testament scriptures; and having completed the argument in triumph, he turns to an extended series of exhortations designed to make a practical application of his doctrinal positions. However, the first two verses of this hortatory section have also an important doctrinal import and must be given due consideration.

"The Holiest of All." The writer now presents a new aspect of the fullness of salvation as purchased by Christ, which he represents as a life within the holy of holies, or literally, the holiness of holinesses. In his inventory of the Tabernacle furniture (9: 1-5), he mentions the two veils of the sanctuary: the outer as the "door of the tabernacle," and the inner as the "veil of separation." These are appropriately called veils in that they shut off from view the glories of the sanctuary to all except those who enter by the sprinkling of atoning blood. By anticipation we have spoken of the outer veil as that of *actual sins* or personal transgressions, and the inner veil as that of *sin conditions* or inherited depravity. Before a sinner can enter the holy place, he must find forgiveness at the Blood-sprinkled altar, and cleansing from guilt and acquired depravity at the laver of cleansing. This experience in the language of the court is *justification;* in the language of the family, the *new birth;* and in the language of the Temple, *initial sanctification.*

Then and then only has one liberty to enter through the outer veil into the first tabernacle, where in Christ he finds life and light and love.

But the newborn Christian soon finds that he still has a sin problem—not now his own sins, but the sin nature inherited from the race. He soon finds that he has life, but not the abundance of life; that he has light which too often is mixed with worldly wisdom; and that he has love, but not the perfect love that casts out fear (I John 4: 17-18). This veil of an inherited sinful nature prevents his entrance into a deeper communion *with* God, and touches with pollution even his best service *to* God. This veil of a sin nature must be rent; the "flesh," as the carnal self, must be crucified (Gal. 2: 20; 5: 24); the "old man" must be "put off" (Eph. 4: 20-24; Col. 3: 9-10); and the "sin" as a condition of the heart must be cleansed and purified (I John 1: 7-9). The way through the veil is the way of death to the carnal self. There is no other way. Then and then only can one enter within the veil and dwell in "the Holiest of all"—in the presence of God through the Spirit.

The Exhortation. "Having therefore, brethren, boldness to enter into the holiest by the blood of Jesus" (10: 19). The writer addresses his readers as *adelphoi* (ἀδελφοί) or "brethren," as previously he has addressed them as "holy brethren" (3: 1). He is not writing to sinners, but to Christians. They had through forgiveness of sins passed through the outer veil into the holy place of life and light and love in Christ. Now they are invited through the inner veil of sin conditions into the holy of holies, the Holy Spirit witnessing that the way is no longer closed, but opened through the sacrificial blood of Jesus. The word *parresian* (παῤῥησίαν), sometimes translated "liberty," is here better expressed by the stronger term "boldness," or "confident trust." The word *eisodon* (εἴσοδον) means an "entrance," or sometimes the "act of entering." It therefore not only signifies the way itself, but carries with it the thought of using the entrance, and that with "boldness" because entering through the sprinkling of the Blood.

"The Holiest of All" in Christian Experience. But what is the meaning of the holiest of all as here set forth? It does not mean heaven in the sense of a place above us, separate and distinct from the earth, as many seem to think. Heaven is any place where God manifests himself, for wherever God is, there is heaven. In this sense heaven is not limited by time and space as are things on earth, but is as omnipresent as is God himself. The "Holiest of all" in Christian experience is that place which is out beyond the sin question, a place where the soul is cleansed from all sin by the blood of Jesus. It is a place of spiritual purity with Christ, our great High Priest, where we live and work in the presence of God, our Father. It is the fullness of the Spirit, the promise of the Father, and the gift of the risen and glorified Christ. It is a life within the veil, where burns the Shekinah of God's presence over the mercy seat, illuminating the mind, satisfying the heart, and shedding its radiance throughout all the wide expanses of man's being.

This glorious experience, purchased by the blood of Jesus and made effective by the gift of the Holy Spirit at Pentecost, is the New Testament standard for the Christian life. Many have testified to its satisfying fullness, but perhaps none more effectively in this particular connection than Andrew Murray in his *Holiest of All* (pp. 355-56) where he says: "Oh, the blessedness of a life in the Holiest! Here the Father's face is seen and His love tasted. Here His holiness is revealed and the soul made a partaker of it. Here the sacrifice of love and worship and adoration, the incense of prayer and supplication, is offered in power. Here the outpouring of the Spirit is known as an ever-streaming, over-flowing river, from under the throne of God and the Lamb. Here the soul, in God's presence, grows into more complete oneness with Christ, and more entire conformity to His likeness. Here, in union with Christ, in His unceasing intercession, we are emboldened to take our place as intercessors, who can have power with God and prevail. Here the soul mounts up as on eagle's wings, the strength is renewed, and the blessing and the power and the love are imparted with which God's priests can go out to bless a dying world. Here each day we may experience the fresh anointing, in virtue of which we can go out to be the bearers, and witnesses, and channels of God's salvation to men, the living instruments through whom our blessed King works out His full and final triumph."

The New and Living Way

We have seen that it was by the blood of Jesus that the new covenant was ratified, and the new and heavenly sanctuary opened; now the writer presents the Blood as opening "a new and living way" into the holiest of all. The word *prosphaton* (πρόσφατον), "new," is found only here in the New Testament, and originally meant "freshly killed or slaughtered"; but having lost its significance as a freshly killed sacrifice, it is now translated as "newly" or "freshly" made, and in this text simply as "new." The expression is intended to set in contrast the Old Testament service on the Day of Atonement, which lasted in its results for only a year, with that of Christ, which is not only fresh and new, but "everlastingly fresh and new." The word *enekainisen* (ἐνεκαίνισεν), "consecrated," used here and also in 9:18, means literally "to bring into use for the first time," and therefore to inaugurate or dedicate. The word *zosan* (ζῶσαν), "living," marks the contrast between the offering of dead victims under the law and the living sacrifice of Christ. The word does not mean either a way into life or a way of life; instead it means living in the sense of a living Person, and is a reference to Christ as "the way."

The Veil of His Flesh. The rending of the veil of His flesh is a reference to Christ's physical death on the Cross, and meant on the one hand the shedding of His blood as a vicarious atonement for sin; and on the other, the opening of a new and living way into the holiest of all. This was symbolized at the time of the Crucifixion by the rending of the Temple veil from top to bottom, thus marking the close of the law dispensation and the opening of a new and spiritual order. The fall of man was marked by a withdrawal of the Holy Spirit, leaving him without spiritual life, and therefore in death with its defilement and decay. It is evident, therefore, that the impartation of spiritual life in the new birth, and the cleansing of the heart from defilement in sanctification, can be brought about only by the restoration of the Holy Spirit to the human race.

But how can the Spirit be brought again into the sinful race of mankind? There appears to be one way, and one only. The Son of God must become incarnate, and in His own person bring the Spirit again into human life. Hence we read that "God giveth not the Spirit by measure unto him" (John 3: 34); and that "in him dwelleth all the fulness of the Godhead bodily" (Col. 2: 9). This Spirit, shut up within the incarnate Christ, could not come as the "promise of the Father," or the gift of the glorified Christ, until the veil of Christ's flesh was rent by His death on the Cross and the Spirit thereby set free. It is for this reason that St. John says, "The Holy Ghost was not yet given; because that Jesus was not yet glorified" (John 7: 39b). As the Eternal Son took upon Him a human nature that He might become our Redeemer, so the Eternal Spirit dwelling in Christ the God-Man took upon Him a human experience that He might become our Comforter or Paraclete. Christ

It was this specific relation of the Son that made it possible, becoming and appropriate, that He should be the Redeemer of the fallen race; a truth that may be pondered profitably, if it is not perverted into the doubtful notion of a necessary incarnation, apart from sin, of the Second Person. But this doctrine is incomplete without the addition of the supernatural gift of the Holy Ghost; if that may be called supernatural which belonged to the union of God with His Elect Creature. . . . He did not add the moral image, but He guided the principles of action of man's soul created in that image. This solves the difficulty sometimes expressed as to the creation of a character which, it is said, must of necessity be formed by him who bears it.—POPE, *Compendium of Christian Theology.* I, 427.

is our Intercessor above; the Holy Spirit is our Intercessor within. The one has His seat at the right hand of the throne of God; the seat of the other is within the Church. Thus the entire Trinity—Father, Son, and Holy Spirit—is engaged in the salvation of mankind.

A Great Priest over the House of God. "And having an high priest over the house of God; let us draw near" (10: 21-22a). The words *hiereus megas* (ἱερεὺς μέγας), "a great priest," frequently occur in the Septuagint as synonymous with *archiereus* (ἀρχιερεύς) and hence appear here as "high priest," and in 4: 14 as a "great high priest." We have now reached the last of the four heavenly things which the writer has had under consideration: the shed Blood, the heavenly sanctuary, the living Way, and now the presence of the great High Priest himself. Great as is the work which Christ has done *for* us, the fellowship *with* His person, and life *in* His presence, are most precious of all; for it was these that formed the goal of His suffering and triumph. The primary emphasis of the exhortation, however, appears to be this: that, having made provision for our complete salvation, He now stands as the "living way" to care for our every need. Salvation does not come through effort and struggle, nor by human strength and worldly wisdom; it is not a matter of creeds and confessions, but simple, heartfelt trust in a living Person—the One who now presents himself as worthy of our confidence, and lovingly awaits our faith in His infinite grace.

But there is a further meaning in these words. He is also a great "high priest over the house of God," of which the writer has previously said, "Whose house are we, if we hold fast the confidence and the rejoicing of the hope firm unto the end" (3: 6b). We having committed ourselves and our all to Him, He becomes to us the Priest of life, and henceforth we are to live our lives through Him. We have seen that the Son became man for our redemption; and that the Holy Spirit, dwelling in the God-Man, took upon Him a human experience to become our Comforter or Paraclete. The Spirit therefore not only searches the deep things of God but knows our human nature to its very depths. The word Paraclete is from *para,* "with," and *kletos,* the "called," and hence means one who goes along with the called to do anything that needs to be done. He who led Jesus as the Captain of our salvation all the way from the cradle to the throne has been given to us as the "Spirit of truth" to lead us through the tangled ways of life to our eternal home. Here, as St. Paul tells us, "we walk by faith, not by sight"; He also says that to be at home in the body is to be absent from the Lord, expressing his desire rather "to be absent from the body, and to be present with the Lord" (II Cor. 5: 7-8). Soon, like Christ, we too shall have the veil of our flesh rent, and then we shall see Him face to face in His glorified state, for we too shall be glorified with him. Then shall we find in supreme measure that "in thy presence is fulness of joy; at thy right hand there are pleasures for evermore" (Ps. 16: 11).

The Exhortation to Draw Near. "Let us draw near with a true heart in full assurance of faith, having our hearts sprinkled from an evil conscience, and our bodies washed with pure water" (10: 22). This exhortation is similar to that in 4: 16, where we are told to come boldly to the throne of grace. We regard the statements in this verse as setting forth the conditions of entrance into the holy of holies, and not the marks of a true worshiper already within the veil. These the writer sets forth in the verses which follow. There is a certain symmetry in this verse which needs to be recognized in order to its better understanding. (1) There are two *subjective conditions,* both expressed by prepositions with their objects and modifiers—a true heart, and full assurance of faith. Then (2) there are two *preliminary objective states,* which not only furnish the ground but, as is implied, also provide a stronger incentive for approach. These are expressed by two perfect passive participles, each with an accusative and a modifier; and being perfect tenses, they indicate that the effects of a past act continue to the present time. These objective states are: a heart sprinkled from an evil conscience and a body washed with pure water.

1. *The Subjective Conditions.* These are (1) "a true heart," by which is meant one of sincerity as opposed to unreality and hypocrisy. God always looks at the heart and sees through any pretentions or superficialities. A true heart is honest before God, and earnestly and unfeignedly desires to be made holy. (2) The "full assurance of faith," that is, a faith which shuts out every doubt and fear, and rests alone by faith on the atoning work of Christ.

2. *The Preliminary Objective States.* The participles used here refer to past events and therefore are not so much a part of the exhortation as the ground upon which it is based. The writer evidently refers to the two functions of the ancient priesthood, the sprinkling of blood and the washing with water; and these he interprets in a Christian sense as "having our hearts sprinkled from an evil conscience, and our bodies washed with pure water." These participles are important, therefore, in that they indicate clearly that only the regenerate are qualified for entrance into the holy of holies; and while the invitation is to all, in the language of the Temple, only those who pass through the holy place may approach the rent veil and enter into the holiest of all.

The participle *errantismenoi* (ἐρραντισμένοι), "having been sprinkled," is by Vaughan more clearly rendered, "our hearts being already sprinkled [with the atoning blood] from [so as to remove] a bad conscience." The word for "evil" is *poneras* (πονηρᾶς), meaning also a "wicked" or "bad" conscience, that is, a conscience burdened and clogged by the sense of unforgiven sin. This "bad" conscience is purged by the sprinkling of the Blood; for that Blood which has put away even the remembrance of sin on the part of God puts away sin in us also, and thereby removes the evil conscience that not only condemns us but hinders our approach to God.

The second factor, "our bodies washed with pure

water," is also typical of regeneration. Here the term used is *lelousmenoi* (λελουσμένοι), "washing," which means a washing, not of parts of the body only, but of the whole body. St. Paul speaks of salvation "by the washing of regeneration, and renewing of the Holy Ghost" (Titus 3:5), and also of a "washing of water by the word" as an element in sanctification (Eph. 5:26). Some have regarded this statement as referring to water baptism, but the grammatical construction will hardly allow this. Without question, however, it means that there must be a conformity of the outward life with the inner spiritual nature, and this whether in regeneration or in sanctification. A spiritual nature must express itself in a spiritual life, and the character and quality of this life is determined by the Word of God. Bonar sums up this text well when he says, "As with the water, so with the blood, for they are for inward as well as outward application."

The exhortation, "Let us draw near," takes on new meaning now that the writer has told us the manner of approach. We have seen that the way into the holiest is that of a true heart and a confident faith, or perhaps in more familiar terms, the way of consecration and faith. As we are justified by faith alone, so also we are sanctified by faith alone; and as the precondition of faith in the former is repentance, so also in the latter it is consecration. Since we are studying in the language of the Temple, the writer tells us that we enter by the blood of Jesus, but before this we must be "justified by his blood" (Rom. 5:9). In Biblical terminology the word heart is used in the broad sense to include the whole of the inner life, especially from the standpoint of activity; and the body as the outward life—the two together constituting the whole man. It is not then that the heart and body may be cleansed separately; the cleansing must affect the entire man. And for this purpose there flowed from the wounded side of Christ on the Cross both water and blood—blood to atone for our sin, water to cleanse from its defilement.

Since God has joined inseparably together a fully cleansed heart and a fully washed body, we enter into the holy of holies, not in spirit only, but with the body as well. The whole life, outward as well as inward, is to be lived in the presence of God. Perhaps this explains why some who have sought so earnestly to enter into the holiest have failed; they have some idol of the heart which has not been cast down, or it may be some bodily practice which has not been brought under the sprinkling of the Blood. Perhaps we have not yet fully realized how our eating and drinking, the manner in which we dress or conduct ourselves in public and social life, our daily duties, and our seasons of recreation affect our spiritual lives. These things wisely used under the illumination of the Spirit are a source of spiritual blessing; used wrongly or to excess, they steal our fire, dampen our enthusiasm, and chill our ardor. As Christ was given a body that He might sanctify it, and so yield it as to be God-possessed, we too are given bodies that they may be sanctified, so that every thought of the mind, every power of the being, all the love of the heart, our gains and our losses, our tears and our triumphs, shall be offered up to His glory.

THE HOLY LIFE

We have now come to a section (10: 23-25) which deals with the life and walk of a Christian who has entered into the holy of holies. When the expression "full assurance of faith," previously treated as one of the conditions of entrance into the holiest, is seen also to belong to the life "within the veil," then this whole section will be found to be built upon the three fundamental virtues—faith, hope, and love. Further still, it must be noted that the four exhortations here cover every phase of the Christian life. (1) "Let us hold fast the profession of our faith" refers to our relation with God; (2) "Let us consider one another" concerns our relation to our brethren; (3) "Not forsaking the assembling of ourselves together" presents the negative aspect of the corporate life of the church; and (4) "Exhorting one another daily" speaks of the positive means for spiritual advancement.

The Exhortation to Steadfastness. "Let us hold fast the profession of our faith without wavering; (for he is faithful that promised;)" (10:23). The use of the word "faith" is an innovation, but was probably used with the thought in mind of a "confession of faith" or "creed," which some, like Seeberg, hold was an early catechism adopted by the churches. The Greek word is *elpidos* (ἐλπίδος), or "hope," and is so translated in the American Revised Version. The word *katechomen* (κατέχωμεν), "we should hold fast," differs from the word *kratomen* (κρατῶμεν), 4:14, which means to use our strength in holding fast to our profession. Faith and confession are always conjoined, and the latter must always be held without wavering. Here the word is *akline* (ἀκλινῆ), which means "steadfast" or "unbending." Wycliffe translated it, "Hold we the confessioun of oure hope bowynge to no side." The figure evidently is that of a banner to be held high and not allowed to droop. In the midst of discouragements, doubts, ridicule, or persecution, we are to hold fast our confident expectation; and this for the best of reasons, "he is faithful that promised."

An Exhortation to Thoughtfulness. "And let us consider one another to provoke unto love and to good works" (10:24). The word *katanoomen* (κατανοῶμεν), when translated "consider," as pointed out in 3:1, is an astronomical term and one of great intensity. It means to "observe carefully" or to "fix the attention" steadily upon an object. Here it means setting one's mind on the brethren and developing a thoughtfulness concerning them. This not only concerns the influence of our attitudes and conduct upon them, but suggests the thought that the care for the needs and claims of our brethren will open up in our own hearts a full stream of love and practical helpfulness. The word for "provoke" is *paroxusmon* (παροξυσμὸν), from which we have the

English word paroxysm. It is therefore an intensely strong word. Used in a bad sense, it means to incite others to anger, bitterness, or revenge; here it is used in the good sense of possessing such an intensity of love as will fire others with enthusiasm and incite them to good works. There is no thought of mere competition in the matter of good works.

An Exhortation to Corporate Worship. "Not forsaking the assembling of ourselves together, as the manner of some is" (10:25a). The writer is no rugged individualist. He sees in Christianity even a broader social life than that of Judaism. He sees also that, in order to incite others to good works through an overflowing enthusiasm and the intensity of divine love, there must be public assemblies. Corporate worship is a necessity in the Christian life, and fellowship one with another has ever been regarded as one of the chief means of grace. The word *episunagogen* (ἐπισυναγωγὴν), "assembling together," may mean either the formation of the assembly or the act of assembling together. So also the word *egkataleipontes* (ἐγκαταλείποντες), "forsaking," has been very differently interpreted. It may mean either the abandoning of the assemblies altogether or it may mean merely a laxity in attendance. A number of commentators take the former position, maintaining that the writer meant a defection from Christianity to Judaism. The great majority, however, take a milder position, that is, simply becoming careless in attendance. "As the manner of some is" may refer to the Gnostics, who held that the "enlightened" were sufficient of themselves and did not need the help of others. As for the careless and indifferent, one writer suggests that, if the real reasons were recorded, they might be easily recognizable in the modern Church.

An Exhortation to Mutual Helpfulness. "But exhorting one another: and so much the more, as ye see the day approaching" (10:25b). It has been suggested that the words "one another," which are supplied here by the translators, should be considered as the object of the word "exhorting" or "encouraging"; the text would then read, "But exhort [or encourage] one another to attend on these assemblies." However it is likely that the exhortations are to be taken in a broader sense as covering the whole field of Christian life—in relation to God, in relation to the world, in relation to the Church, and in relation to individual Christians.

The reason given for this exhortation is found in the words "and so much the more, as ye see the day approaching" (10:25b). The "day" refers to the "day of the Lord," an expression which does not always mean the final day of judgment. Jesus explained to His disciples that there were two different periods—one, the judgment of Israel, which took place at the destruction of Jerusalem, and from which time they should be trodden underfoot until the close of the gentile age (Luke 21:24). But the gentile age shall also end in judgment, when the Lord shall come in glory and all His holy angels with Him. Let us then hold fast to the hope of His glorious appearing; and as the end of the age approaches, let us not forsake the assembling of ourselves together, for at His coming these assemblies shall find their glorious consummation in the fellowship of "the saints in light."

THE SIXTH WARNING: AGAINST SINNING WILLFULLY

It is the mention of "the day of the Lord" with its judgments that forms the transition to the severe warning which follows. "For if we sin wilfully after that we have received the knowledge of the truth, there remaineth no more sacrifice for sins" (10:26). Previously the writer has warned against neglect, hardening of the heart, unbelief, indifference, and slothfulness, but for the first time the word sin is used, and this because it is set over against the atoning blood of Jesus. "To sin against law is great, to sin against light is greater, but to sin against love is the greatest of all sins." To reject the one and only remedy for sin, that provided by the love of God through the shed blood of Christ, is forever to cut one's self off from any hope of salvation, either here or hereafter. One can but note the similarity of this passage to that of 6: 4-6; but as Riggenbach has pointed out, there the passage is *psychological* in that repentance and renewal are declared impossible; here the passage is *soteriological,* there being no more sacrifice for sin. So fearfully important is this verse that the exact meaning of the words needs to be carefully determined.

A Critical Study of the Words of This Text. In the expression "For if we sin wilfully," the word *hekousios* (ἐκουσίως), "wilfully" or "willingly," is in the Greek order placed first for emphasis. The word for sin is *harmartanonton* (ἁμαρτανόντων), "having sinned"—a present participle which means, not a single sin alone, but a continuous practice of sin. These words therefore can only mean deliberate and determined sinning, committed with willful intention, and marking a constant decision against light and truth. The expression "after that we have received the knowledge of the truth" makes clear the twofold aspect of truth, as given by God and as received by man. The word *labein* (λαβεῖν), "after the receiving," is an aorist infinitive and therefore means "actually having received" the truth. The word for "knowledge" found here is not the common word *gnosis* (γνῶσις) but the compound word *epignosin* (ἐπίγνωσιν), which means a full or complete knowledge, and is a characteristic word in St. Paul's later Epistles. It is a knowledge of Christ in personal experience, revealed to them by the Spirit, and made their actual possession. Delitzsch says, "By the very choice of the word, the writer gives us to understand that he means, not merely a superficial historical knowledge about the truth, but a living perception of the same by faith, which had seized upon it and fused it into oneness with itself." Westcott regards the use of the word "we" as softening the severity of the warnings with a touch of deep sympathy, as if, dwelling on the dangers of others, he does not forget his own. By the same reasoning, however, the word must apply to all true Christians; for though the warnings of this and the following verses are in opposition to many false notions of security and cherished dispensational opinions, there is but one honest way to deal with them; that is, to apply them to real children of God.

The Expectation of the Adversaries. "But a certain fearful looking for judgment and fiery indignation, which shall devour the adversaries" (10:27). The word for adversaries is *hupenantious* (ὑπεναντίους), which means "the opposite" or "adverse"; and what is said in this and the following verses is said of those who rejected the atoning Blood and continued in willful sin. After this repudiation the writer tells us that there remains only "a certain fearful looking for of judgment." The word for fearful is *phobera* (φοβερὰ), "frightful," and intensified by the Greek word *tis*, becomes a thing very frightful. This may mean that the judgment itself is frightful, or the thought of it, or both. The word *ekdoche* (ἐκδοχὴ), "looking for," is found only here in the New Testament, and is used in the sense of "expectation"; that is, what awaits the sinner is a frightful expectation of judgment. This judgment is characterized as a "fiery indignation" (cf. Isa. 26:11), from *puros* (πυρὸς), "fire," and *zelos* (ζῆλος), "fervor" or "zeal"—or even "fierceness"—and means that judgment shall be administered with the fierceness of fire. The word *zelos*, from which we have our word zealot, is sometimes used as the "fervor of love" (Isa. 9:7), but as used here suggests a love that has been spurned. Once again, this fire is pictured as a living thing with open mouth, ready to fiercely devour every adversary.

An Illustration from the Mosaic Law. "He that despised Moses' law died without mercy under two or three witnesses: of how much sorer punishment, suppose ye, shall he be thought worthy . . . ? (10:28-29), and following this is a description of the adversary or apostate. The certainty and righteousness of God's judgments are here established by a reference to the law of Moses, a law with which the Hebrews were perfectly familiar (Deut. 17:2-17). The man or woman who turned from the covenant of God to the worship of idols, when testimony was borne to this apostasy by two or three witnesses, was to be stoned to death. Irrespective of compassion, the execution was to be carried out, the witnesses themselves casting the first stones. The argument here is from the less to the greater, and the writer answers with a parenthetical question, How much sorer [worse] punishment, suppose ye, shall be meted out to those who reject the love of God, the blood of Christ, and the tender wooings of the Holy Spirit? The appeal is made to the intelligence of his readers, and he leaves each to judge for himself. The word *axiothesetai* (ἀξιωθήσεται), "counted worthy," is generally applied to a person of honor; but here applied to *timorias* (τιμωρίας), "retributive justice or punishment," it takes on striking significance.

The Threefold Sin of the Adversaries. "Who hath trodden under foot the Son of God, and hath counted the blood of the covenant, wherewith he was sanctified, an unholy thing, and hath done despite unto the Spirit of grace?" (10:29b) It should be noted that the adversary not only turns away from God in His triune being as Father, Son, and Holy Spirit; but he manifests this aversion in a threefold manner: (1) as an act, "trampled upon"; (2) in thought, "counted . . . unholy"; and in direct assault, "done despite." These severe words are even more frightful when their original meanings are clearly understood.

1. "Who hath trodden under foot the Son of God." The word *katapatesas* (καταπατήσας), "trampled upon," when applied to a person, denotes the worst form of contempt possible. Some understand it to mean that form of contempt which ignores another, treating him as of no more account than the dust upon which he walks. The enormity of this appears in that it was not merely the law of Moses that was trampled underfoot but the Person who gave the law—the infinite and exalted Son of God, who is himself God.

2. "Counted the blood of the covenant, wherewith he was sanctified, an unholy thing." The word *koinon* (κοινὸν), "common," means without sacredness, and therefore unholy. This Blood which was accounted unholy was the Blood of the new covenant, which secured for us the gracious privilege of redemption from sin and eternal fellowship with God. Further still, it was this very Blood by which the adversary himself was sanctified—*hegiasthe* (ἡγιάσθη), first aorist passive participle, "was at one time sanctified"; but now he considers it merely as the blood of another person, even the malefactors who were crucified with Christ. This would seem to be the height of sacrilege!

3. "And hath done despite unto the Spirit of grace." The word *charitos* (χάριτος), "grace," used here with the word "Spirit," is a paraphrasis for the "Holy Spirit," who is "the Spirit who is grace." This evidently was intended to emphasize the personal and gracious nature of the Spirit. The word *enubrisas* (ἐνυβρίσας), "despite," is used only here in the New Testament and is a strong word. Even without the preposition, the word *hubris* (ὕβρις) is defined as a combination of "insult and injury, wanton outrage" (Vaughan), which becomes especially obnoxious when set in contrast with the graciousness of the Spirit. It is the Spirit who administers the grace of Christ and performs the work of sanctification in our hearts, and to insult a tender Spirit like this is a heartless outrage. It has been clearly seen that when the blood of Christ is rejected, there remains no further sacrifice for sins; so also after the grace of the Spirit has been spurned, there is no further way of approach. This is the sin against the Holy Ghost which shall never be forgiven (Matt. 12:31-32; Mark 3:28-29; Luke 12:10).

The Certainty of Penalty. The certainty of penalty is emphasized in two passages of scripture from Deuteronomy: (1) "For we know him that hath said, Vengeance belongeth unto me, I will recompense, saith the Lord" (Deut. 32:35, cf. Rom. 12:19). (2) "And again,

The Lord shall judge his people" (Deut. 32: 36, cf. Ps. 135: 14). The first rather emphasizes the fact that the judgment will be an exact requital, for in it absolute justice will be rendered; while the second refers more to the extent of the judgment as including all, even the people of God. The expression "we know him" indicates that both the writer and those whom he addresses know by experience the true character of God. Both the warnings and the exhortations belong to the gospel, and God will make sure His every word. There are those who present only the "mercy aspect" of the gospel and forget that justice belongs also to the Christian concept of God. The word "vengeance" means to exact justice, and "recompense" has the force of paying back what is due. As the righteous shall receive the rewards of grace, so also the wicked shall be paid "what is due" in justice. The Septuagint reads, "In the day of vengeance I will give due return." While the term judgment as applied to the people often means their vindication, here evidently it must mean that so universal is the judgment of God that even His own people are included. These words of doom are closed by what appears to flow from deep and profound reflection on the part of the writer, leading to the exclamation, "It is a fearful thing to fall into the hands of the living God."

Words of Consolation

The writer now turns from words of sternest warning to those of consolation and assurance. This section has frequently been the basis of the argument for the Pauline authorship of the Epistle as addressed to the Hebrew converts at Rome, and it appears to me as having much to substantiate this theory.

The Call to Remembrance. "But call to remembrance the former days, in which, after ye were illuminated, ye endured a great fight of affliction" (see 10: 32-34). Memory is an important factor in religion, and recalling the victories of the past gives strength to the present. The writer asks them to call to remembrance the persecutions which followed soon after their conversion, and the strength of their new-found faith which enabled them to bravely endure these afflictions. These afflictions, he reminds them, were partly due to the insults and injuries to which they were subjected, as well as the unjust accusations of crime and vice. More particularly, these stinging taunts and sneers had to be borne in the open. The Christians had been made a gazing-stock or a "theatrical show," horribly held up by the populace to the extent of reproaches and afflictions and all manner of indignities. The afflictions were partly also because the Hebrew Christians had not shunned the shame of loyalty to their companions in the faith, voluntarily assuming the responsibility of ministering to the persecuted and imprisoned.

Then again, they had taken joyfully the spoiling of their goods—not merely with patience but joyfully, and this whether by authoritative decree or by the plundering of riotous mobs. This, the writer tells us, they did because of their rich heritage in Christ, which made the things of the world seem small by comparison—for their citizenship was in heaven. The word *hyparxin* (ὕπαρξιν), "possession," is used for the heavenly and abiding possessions, and therefore is placed over against the word *hyparchonton* (ὑπαρχόντων), used to designate the earthly possessions which had been taken away from them. The word "knowing" has a judicial aspect, that is, "you as judges pronouncing the sentence that you for yourselves have property more abiding than that which they had lost." The participle is iterative, "making this judicial pronouncement every time one of your homes was looted." Since the sustaining of material loss was by many of the ancients the sign of a higher philosophic mind, this gave the Christians a place of high regard in the minds of thoughtful men.

An Exhortation to Perseverance in the Faith. "Cast not away therefore your confidence, which hath great recompence of reward. For ye have need of patience, that, after ye have done the will of God, ye might receive the promise. For yet a little while, and he that shall come will come, and will not tarry" (10:35-37). Here again we have the word *parresian* (παῤῥησίαν), "confidence," previously translated "boldness." The word for recompense is *misthapodosian* (μισθαποδοσίαν), a "payoff" which is due us and said to be "great"; and the word translated patience is *hypomones* (ὑπομονῆς), "perseverance or endurance," and means literally, "to carry the load bravely" and not shrink away from it or give up under pressure. We are therefore to have boldness to carry our load bravely, that we may receive (or carry off) the great pay-gift promised us. True, this is not due us by virtue of our works, but by the promise of grace; and yet in a sense it is due us, in that it is to be received only by those who fulfill the necessary conditions, those who have done the will of God.

There is another incentive to perseverance presented by the writer, the coming of Christ in a little while. The word for "little" is *mikron* (μικρὸν) and means "a very little while." Since the previous words, "ye see the day approaching," (10:25b) have frequently been regarded as a reference to the fall of Jerusalem, the incentive is thought to be that of a cessation of persecution on the part of the Jews. However it seems more probable that it refers to Christ's second coming, which was the all-absorbing concern of the early Christians. This verse is quoted freely from the Septuagint, which reads, "Because the Coming One will come, and will by no means delay long. If any man draw back, my soul has no pleasure in him; but the just shall live by faith in me." As the ancient prophet (Hab. 2:3-4) tells of a vision that would come and would not tarry, so the writer applies this to the strain upon the faith of the people of God previous to the fall of Jerusalem, and which our Lord tells us will tax our faith even more, previous to His coming at the close of this age.

The Transitional Verses. "Now the just shall live by faith: but if any man draw back, my soul shall have no pleasure in him" (10:38). This and the following verse mark the transition to the great faith chapter. The writer has shown that both faith and patience are necessary to inherit the promises, but he has named only a few of the outstanding representatives of the Old Testament. Now he will turn his attention to a great list of ancient worthies, and show not only the various aspects of faith which characterized them, but also the great patience which they endured. He then closes with a great rallying cry of confidence, "But we are not of them who draw back unto perdition; but of them that believe to the saving of the soul" (10: 39).

CHAPTER XI

THE HEROES OF FAITH

The eleventh chapter of this Epistle is one of the great chapters of the entire Bible. It is best viewed as a gallery of portraits, each drawn with a master hand, and all set in a magnificent grouping. Here are the ancient heroes and martyrs which the Hebrews delighted to honor, the pride and glory of every son and daughter of Abraham. These all believed the promises of God, and trusted the unseen, for which they patiently hoped and waited. Testimony is borne to their faith in promises greatly delayed in outstanding achievements, in painful tortures and even martyrdom—counting not their lives dear to themselves.

The writer appears to have had his Old Testament open before him, and beginning with Genesis, he searched past history for the names of the ancient worthies of faith, and these he inscribed on an immortal scroll. It appears that he had in mind the making of a complete list, but so great became the number that he found it impossible to continue. Then without mentioning the names, he proceeds to arrange them in groups—first, as to their great achievements; and second, as to their patient endurance—closing the list with the mention of a great company who wandered in deserts, and in the mountains, and in the dens and caves of the earth. All these, he says, received a good report through faith. After a preliminary word concerning the nature of faith, the writer then proceeds to name these historical witnesses to the faith, apparently lifting into prominence the chief names selected from the several periods of Israel's history.

THE NATURE OF FAITH

This famous chapter begins with the words, "Now faith is the substance of things hoped for, the evidence of things not seen. For by it the elders obtained a good

report" (11: 1-2). The American Standard Version
reads, "Now faith is assurance of things hoped for, a
conviction of things not seen. For therein the elders
had witness borne to them." The Revised Standard Version has this rendering, "Faith is the assurance of things
hoped for, the conviction of things not seen. For by it
the men of old received divine approval." Then there
are the important marginal readings: "the ground or
confidence of things hoped for" (A.V.); and "the giving
substance to things hoped for, a test [the putting to the
proof] of things not seen" (A.R.V.).

The reason for these variations is the fact that the
chief words are used in such a variety of ways in Greek
literature. The word "substance" is *hupostasis* (ὑπόστασις) and is variously rendered as "substance," "assurance," "confidence," "firm confidence," "ground,"
"solid ground," and "firmly grounded confidence." The
word "evidence" is *elegchos* (ἔλεγχος) and is translated
"evidence," "conviction," "demonstration," "putting to
the proof," "actual proof," and even as "title-deed." It
is easily understood, then, why some regard this verse
as a description of faith, while others see in it a definition of faith itself. But these terms are not mutually ex-
clusive; rather, each is a matter of emphasis. The one
regards faith from the standpoint of what is accomplished; the other, from what faith is in itself; and the
one is not complete without the other. It is therefore
important, not only that the writer should present faith
as the rule by which men live, but that he also should
clearly define what he means by the term.

Faith is necessarily subjective, as are also the terms
used to express it, "confidence" and "conviction"; and
yet all three of these words imply an objective aspect.
Faith in its simplest form is an act of trust in someone
or something. It does not rest in itself; it rests in its
object. Faith is not mental effort or struggle; faith
comes only when these cease. It is Christ, the Object
of our faith, who saves us; and this He does by grace
through faith. Grace operates on the plane of human
helplessness, and it is only as the soul lets go of all

self-trust and casts itself wholly upon the grace of God that faith is born. The difference between true and false faith does not lie in the act of trust itself, but in the worthiness or unworthiness of the person or thing in which that trust is placed. Eve believed the lie of Satan and was deceived; those who trust Christ wholly find Him wholly true. There are three essential elements in faith: the assent of the mind, the consent of the will, and what the older theologians termed recumbency or reclining, but which is more simply expressed by the word trust. Faith is therefore the act of the whole being under the influence of the Holy Spirit. This full trust, this reclining wholly upon Christ, deprives the soul of any claim to merit, whether of works or of the self, and thus makes it necessary to ascribe all the glory to God through Jesus Christ. With these words of explanation and caution, we turn now to a further exegetical study of the text.

The Text as a Description of Faith. Those who regard the first verse of this chapter as a description of faith maintain that the writer is not so much concerned with what faith *is* as with what it *does.* The second verse, therefore, becomes a transition to the illustrations drawn from the ancient worthies of faith, in order to prove that this attitude toward life, this frame of mind which looks upon spiritual things as the actual realities of life, is that which obtained for them a good report. Bishop Chadwick says, "Clearly this is a description of faith, not a definition," but admits that even as such it requires some explanation. He considers the marginal reading of the Revised Version as most nearly expressing the meaning of the original text, and paraphrases it

Faith has both a negative and a positive aspect, that is, it is both receptive and active. As negative, faith makes the whole soul empty and ready for Jesus; as active, it reaches forth with all its powers to embrace Him and His salvation. Faith in its negative aspect may be regarded as the understanding affecting the heart; in its active aspect, it is that of the understanding affecting the will. The former is the operation of the Holy Spirit, convincing the mind of sin and awakening in the heart strong desires after salvation; the latter, the active instrument by which the soul lays hold of Christ, and is enabled to believe unto the salvation of the soul.—WILEY, *Christian Theology*, II, 370.

as follows: "Faith is that which gives substance, body, reality to our hopes, and which puts unseen things to the test."

Faith is used here in the sense of confidence or assurance, and knows that it rests upon a secure foundation. Faith is the capacity for seeing those realities which are invisible to the natural eye; but unless awakened by something from without, it lies dormant, like the eye without light or the ear without sound. Christ has sent the Holy Spirit to convince "the world of sin, and of righteousness, and of judgment" (John 16:8); and He it is who by His prevenient grace takes the initiative and awakens the soul to a knowledge of the truth. If this truth is submitted to and not rejected, faith becomes active, and brings into clear realization the invisible and eternal things; and these having been brought near, the unseen becomes an active power in the Christian life. Faith may be specific in that it leads to justification or sanctification; but it is here used in a more general and comprehensive sense, and thus the faith which saves becomes the faith which is the law of our being, or the permanent attitude of the soul. As God bore testimony to the faith of His ancient people, so the writer implies that those to whom he writes are to do something more than revere the memory of the fathers or gild their sepulchers. They must walk obediently as the fathers walked, and thereby live again the heroic faith and the patient endurance that shall win for them also the divine approval.

The Text as a Definition of Faith. Delitzsch says: "It seems to us that a more complete and accurate definition of faith, and one that is more generally applicable, could not be devised than that which is here given. . . . If this is not a definition, pray, what is it?" He then adds that it seems necessary at the beginning of such a historical summary as is found in this chapter that "a com-

---

Things which in the succession of time are still "hoped for" as future have a true existence in the eternal order; and this existence Faith brings home to the believer as a real fact. So also things unseen are not mere arbitrary fancies: Faith tries them, tests them, brings conviction as to their being.—WESTCOTT, *The Epistle to the Hebrews*, p. 353.

prehensive and general definition of what faith is in itself" should be added, and "that this was the only definition suitable and possible." The word "substance" in the Authorized Version goes back to Thomas Aquinas, who translated the word *hupostasis* (ὑπόστασις) as *substantia* (Vulgate) instead of *fundamentum,* on which the marginal note, "ground" or "confidence," is based. The Latin word *substantia* is not as sharply defined as the Greek term, in that it includes both the idea of *ousia* and *hypostasis.* It was this confusion of terms that gave rise to the long-drawn-out controversy between the Eastern and Western churches on the subject of the Trinity.

1. The first term in this definition is the word "substance." This word, however, cannot be used in the sense of *ousia* or "being"; that is, faith does not impart reality in the sense of giving creative existence to its future objects; they have their reality from God, who created them. The word *substance* therefore can be understood only in the sense of *hypostasis,* the laying of a foundation in the soul, or the "substantiating" to us of those things which already are by the fiat of God. Faith can be called substance, then, only in the sense that it makes eternal things real in the experience of the believer. Plummer calls it "the reflex of eternal realities or rewards promised by God . . . the faith by which a good man lives."

> Faith is an affirmation and an act,
> That bids eternal truth be present fact.

But faith therefore is "not merely a subjective persuasion," says Ebrard, "that those possessions although unseen are yet present; but it is an *act* which in itself gives *knowledge* and *proof* of the existence of those

---

Man lives and moves and has his being, as a spiritual creature, in an element of belief or trust in the unseen; in that sense also, "we walk by faith, not by sight." Belief is a primary condition of all knowledge and of all reasoning on knowledge. It may be said that without it there can be no full assent given to any proposition that deals with other than the matter of sense. Hence the propriety of Anselm's "*crede ut intelligas,*" in opposition to Abelard's "*intellige ut credas,*" the two watchwords of the Christian faith and rationalism respectively.—POPE, *Compend. Chr. Th.* II, 377.

things *not seen.* The *fact of faith* is *itself* the proof of
the *reality of its object.* In faith the actual *power* of the
thing believed is already manifest. Thus the author has
had reason for using in the first member, precisely the
word *hupostasis* (ὑπόστασις) as 'grounding' or the 'state
of being grounded.' He will represent faith not as a
theory but as *life-power,* which, inasmuch as it actually
grasps at the future and unseen possessions, is thereby
actually *assured* of them." He continues by saying that
the nature and characteristic quality of faith lie in this,
"that it begins not with theories and arguments, but
with acts." This life-power, then, is man's ability to
transcend the perception of the bodily senses and perceive that which is invisible. Andrew Murray in his
Holiest of All has this practical and devotional injunction. He says: "Faith is the unceasing reaching out
heavenward of that spiritual sense to which things future
and unseen reveal themselves as near and present, as
living and powerful. Faith must in the spiritual life be
as natural, as unceasing, as our breathing and seeing
when we are doing our ordinary work . . . it is an unceasing intercourse with the unseen world around us"
(p. 423).

2. The second term, found in the latter half of this
verse, is the word *elegchos* (ἔλεγχος), translated "evidence" (A.V.) and "conviction" (R.V.). It is in some
sense parallel with the former term, but is more comprehensive and emphasizes more strongly the evidential
aspect of faith. Mr. Wesley says of this verse that it
means literally "a divine evidence and conviction. . . .
It implies both a supernatural evidence of God, and the

As the new-born child does not first receive instruction on the necessity of breathing, and then resolve to breathe, but first breathes and then
grows to the youth who learns to understand the process of breathing,
so also must that which is born of the Spirit in us inhale in deep in-
spirations the heavenly breath of life, ere it can grow up to the full
knowledge. And as the drawing of the breath itself is the surest proof
of the existence of a life-bringing atmosphere which we breathe, so is
the act of that faith which *lays hold* on the future and unseen possessions,
and draws *strength* from them, the most satisfactory proof of the fact that
these possessions are more than mere fancies and chimeras.—EBRARD, *Biblical Commentary on the Epistle to the Hebrews,* p. 328.

things of God; a kind of spiritual light exhibited to the soul, and a supernatural sight or perception thereof."

The mention of a divine element in faith brings us at once to the question, Is faith the gift of God? Dr. Adam Clarke gives us perhaps the clearest and most reasonable answer. He says: "Is not faith the gift of God? Yes, as to the grace by which it is produced; but the grace or power to believe, and the act of believing are two different things. Without the grace or power to believe no man ever did or can believe; but with that power the act of faith is a man's own. God never believes for any man, no more than He repents for him: the penitent, through this grace enabling him, believes for himself. Nor does he believe necessarily or impulsively when he has that power; the power to believe may be present long before it is exercised, else, why the solemn warnings with which we meet everywhere in the word of God, and threatenings against those who do not believe? Is not this the proof that such persons have the power but do not use it?"

That faith must be regarded as a form of knowledge is explicitly set forth in the writer's previous statements concerning the new covenant. In each of these it is said that the law of God is written in our minds and in our hearts—in our minds that we may know it, and in our hearts that we may love it. It is the conjoining of these two that makes possible a true obedience of faith. Christ's dwelling in the heart through the Spirit is itself a witness to the reality of spiritual things, and this is accomplished through faith. No form of knowledge can be more certain than this.

The Sphere of Faith. "Through faith we understand that the worlds were framed by the word of God, so that things which are seen were not made of things which do appear" (11:3). Before describing the records of the

---

Bishop Weaver simplifies this position by saying that we have the power to walk; that power is the gift of God. We have the power to see; this is also the gift of God. But God does not walk for us, nor see for us. We may refuse to walk, or we may close our eyes. See Weaver, *Christian Theology*, p. 158.

ancient worthies, the writer pauses to point out that the very world in which these witnesses lived and showed their faith is the outcome of that which is invisible, and that this conviction is itself an act of faith. Faith therefore deals not only with the future but also with the past and the present. Creation, being the first revelation of God to man, thus becomes the supreme proof of faith.

1. It is well known that this entire Epistle is written in the finest Greek, but in this text particularly the writer's choice of words is superb. In the first portion of the text the word for faith is used in the dative case, *pistei* (πίστει), which signifies an act of faith, or faith in its direct exercise. As in the first verse, it refers to that power in man by which he is enabled to see the invisible, and therefore differs from mere sense perception. The word *nooumen* (νοοῦμεν), translated "understand" or "apprehend," is from the word *nous* (νοῦς), the "mind," and indicates a mental act. In current Hellenistic Greek it was the word used for the apprehension of God in nature (Rom. 1:20). Over against this is *noesis* (νόησις), which signifies perception by means of the senses, and thus furnishes a marked contrast to *pistis* or faith. The word *katertisthai* (κατηρτίσθαι), "framed," means "to fit perfectly," or "to adjust"; and being in the perfect tense signifies the permanence of creation. This term is particularly well chosen in that it "expresses the manifoldness and the unity of all creation; and by the tense marks that the original lesson of creation remains for abiding use and application" (Westcott).

The word for "worlds" is *aionas* (αἰῶνας), literally "ages" or "aeons"; but since the Greek word is often used in the sense of a metonomy or figure of speech to express, not only vast periods of time, but all that exists in those ages, it is properly translated "worlds." St. John in his prologue uses the simple word *panta* (πάντα), "all things," to express the creation of existent material things; but this writer by the use of *aionas* furnishes us with a grander concept in that he not only includes the material creation but all that enters into these aeons to make up the worlds. The "word" of God as used here is not *logos* but *hremati,* which means a spoken word or "utterance." It is an exact term and retains its full meaning as a single expression of the divine will. Thus we understand through faith that the worlds were framed solely by the "utterance" of God, and that the things seen have not come into being out of the things not apparent.

2. The second part of this verse has been the source of much perplexity to the commentators. We have seen that the words *pistei nooumen* exhibit faith as a spiritual power or organ by which we apprehend truth, but in this case the ground of belief as to the existence of the world rests wholly on the Scriptures as the Word of God. When the translators of the Authorized Version rendered the words *to me ek phainomenon* (τὸ μὴ ἐκ φαι-νομένων) as "things which do not appear," they evidently had in mind that the world was created out of nothing or *ex nihilo.* But "things not apparent" might also mean "things not now apparent though real," and this interpretation gave rise to widely different scientific and philosophic views. The specific words of the writer seem to indicate that he had in mind the refutation of such false views. Some, like the Gnostics, because of their belief in the inherent evil of matter, distinguished between the creator of the world as a demiurge, and the supreme God; some held that the invisible things referred to the chaos of Gen. 1: 2, and others to the Platonic or Philonic system of ideas. The use of the negative μή instead of οὐκ makes it clear that creation was not only out of things that did not appear, but which by their very nature could not appear. The word *blepomenon* (βλεπομένων) means the thing discerned by the eye, and although singular in form is yet a collective term that gathers up all the particulars of visible being into one whole. The statement of the writer is, therefore, that the visible universe was not made of things that either did or could appear. The great Architect had no materials to work upon, and therefore the visible universe

arose into being from the word—the eternal wisdom and energy of God; causalities that lie hidden in the nature of God, made visible only in their creative effects.

It is clear, therefore, that the writer by the use of the negative μή refers solely to a spiritual realm, which is not and cannot be visible to the senses, but apprehended by faith alone. Furthermore, this text is not only an affirmation of creation *ex nihilo;* it is an assertion that the spiritual realm is the only *ultimate real.* The writer has previously indicated this in his view of the Tabernacle as a shadow of the real, and the Levitical priesthood as ministering only in the shadow. True worship must be spiritual; and the worshipers, to be acceptable to God, must worship Him in spirit and in truth. Thus must the worshiper rise from the things seen to the unseen things of the Spirit; and in the "things made" discern His eternal power and Godhead.

The Witness of Faith

It has been thought that this chapter was originally prepared as a separate document to stimulate the faith of those Jewish Christians who under the stress of reproach and persecution were seriously considering a return to Judaism. Whether this theory be true or not, the chapter is without doubt an integral part of this Epistle, and is introduced by the words, "For by it the elders obtained a good report" (11:2). It should be noted also not only that the names of the ancient wor-

---

Here again we must refer to the excellent work of Ebrard in distinguishing between the use of *me* (μή) and *ouk* (ούκ), both of which are negatives and rightly interpreted by the word "not." He says ὄν denies the *existence;* μή, the quality. Ού says that a thing is *not* objectively; μή denies a thing as conceived or conceivable. Ούκ ὄν denotes that which does not exist, which is not; μή ὄν, that whose existence, in respect of its quality, is a nonexistence, a thing unreal. In short, ού before adjectives is generally rendered by "not," μή before adjectives generally by "un-." Thus the ού βλεπόμενα are things which *are* not *at present* seen; μή βλεπόμενα would be things which, under no condition, and at no time, *could* be seen. Ού φαινόμενα would be things which (at the time or in the circumstances spoken of in the context) do not come into appearance; μή φαινόμενα are things which, from their nature, *cannot* come into appearance. See Ebrard, *Biblical Commentary on the Epistle to the Hebrews,* p. 331.

thies are mentioned, but that they are also catalogued according to the chief periods of Israelitish history. Thus we have (1) the *Antediluvian Period*—Abel, Enoch, and Noah; (2) the *Patriarchal Period*—Abraham, Sarah, Isaac, Jacob, and Joseph; (3) the *Period of the Exodus*—Moses; (4) the *Period of the Conquest*—Joshua (not mentioned by name, but known by the fall of Jericho) and Rahab; (5) The *Period of the Judges*—Gedeon, Barak, Samson, Jephthae; and (6) the *Period of the Kingdom*—David, the only king mentioned; Samuel and the prophets. (Samuel marked the transition from the judges to the kings, and his books are sometimes known as the Books of the Kings.) After this the writer deals solely with groups, the achievements of faith and the endurance of faith, and closes with the wanderers and exiles—all these forming the "cloud of witnesses" mentioned in the following chapter.

So rich and varied is the work of faith set forth in this chapter, so worthy of close and intensive study, that whole books have been written on this chapter alone. But both time and space fail us, and we must of necessity confine ourselves to lifting into prominence only the distinctive features of the faith which the Scriptures attribute to those on God's honor roll. Laying aside any further reference to the historical periods, we shall follow the order of the Scriptures in our study of this inspiring chapter.

The Faith of Abel. "By faith Abel offered unto God a more excellent sacrifice than Cain, by which he obtained witness that he was righteous, God testifying of his gifts: and by it he being dead yet speaketh" (11:4). It is a significant fact that in the roll of those to whom God bore testimony, Abel led the way with his "sacrifice of faith." Thus at the very dawn of history, faith is revealed as the power of righteousness. Now faith is taking God at His word, and any worship to be acceptable to Him must be inspired by faith. But in what way was the will of God revealed? Doubtless through the *protevangelium* given to Adam and Eve—The Seed of

the woman shall bruise the serpent's head, and the
serpent shall bruise His heel (Gen. 3:15). Thus the
mystery of sin and the mystery of redemption met at
the very gates of Eden. Abel with his spiritual insight
recognized in this promise the coming of a Redeemer,
who by His suffering and death should make an atonement for sin. He therefore chose as his offering the
firstlings of the flocks "and the fat thereof," while Cain
brought the fruit of the ground. In offering the lamb,
Abel offered himself with it, confessing his own unworthiness and his faith in the acceptance of the offering, and thereby "obtained witness that he was
righteous."

1. Abel shows us that the approach to God is
through faith, through sacrifice, and through death—a
truth that finds its full realization only in Christ. All
access to God is through the propitiatory offering of
Christ, that sure trust in His shed blood which alone
brings the forgiveness of sins and the impartation of
divine life. To this the Holy Spirit bears witness that
we are the children of God. But faith cannot enter into
this new experience of life without entering also into
the deeper significance of sacrifice itself. This new life
in the Spirit reaches out for full conformity to Christ,
and this it sees can be accomplished only by the death
of the carnal self. Only when we are crucified with
Christ does He live fully within us. But the blood of
Christ is not only atoning Blood; it is also cleansing,
sanctifying Blood. "For by one offering he hath perfected for ever them that are sanctified." The veil
having been rent, faith now has the boldness to enter
into the holiest by the blood of Jesus, into the presence
of God and into fellowship with Him through Christ,
our great High Priest.

2. Abel was the first man to suffer physical death,
which sin brought upon the race as a penalty; but the
writer tells us that "he being dead yet speaketh." It is
frequently said that Abel's blood crieth for vengeance;
Christ's blood for forgiveness. While this may be in-

ferred from Heb. 12:24, it is not the emphasis which the writer puts upon the text. Here it is Abel that speaks, not his blood; and he speaks, not to God, but to us. The text appears to mean simply that the faith of Abel as recorded for us in the Scriptures still speaks to us through the Word, and will do so until the end of time.

The Faith of Enoch. "By faith Enoch was translated that he should not see death; and was not found, because God had translated him: for before his translation he had this testimony, that he pleased God" (11:5). The historical account is, "And Enoch walked with God: and he was not; for God took him" (Gen. 5:24). In the Hebrew the words "he walked with God" are in the Septuagint rendered "he was well-pleasing to God." Enoch therefore represented the "walk of faith" (Hebrew), and the "life of faith" (Greek). The primary emphasis in this text is that Enoch by means of faith escaped from death by translation. Abel, a righteous man, suffered a violent death at the hands of his brother; so also Christ suffered a violent death at the hands of His people. Enoch by his translation represented Christ's resurrection and ascent into glory. Thus the first two recorded witnesses of faith set forth in symbol the full sweep of Christ's redemptive work. It is probable, had not sin entered the world, that the probationary state of Adam and Eve would have ended as did that of Enoch in their translation into a new and eternal order. Most certainly, however, it is a prophecy of our final triumph over death as revealed in Christ, the First Fruits of the resurrection glory. We have therefore before us the sacrifice of faith, the walk of faith, the life of faith, and the triumph of faith.

From the faith of Enoch the writer makes certain observations of value to his readers. God says that without faith it is impossible to please Him, and no man should attempt God's impossibilities. Cain made the attempt and failed, and all who have followed him have likewise failed. Our faith must rest in a personal, prayer-answering God. Faith rests in another, and unless that other be an understanding person, our faith is vain and our prayers unheard.

The Faith of Noah. "By faith Noah, being warned of God of things not seen as yet, moved with fear, prepared an ark to the saving of his house; by the which he condemned the world, and became heir of the righteousness which is by faith" (11:7). This verse is a condensation of the entire Flood account as found in Genesis. "Noah was a just man and perfect in his generations"; he "walked with God" and "found grace in the eyes of the Lord." He alone of all his contemporaries was pronounced righteous. The word "warned" carries with it the significance of a divine revelation, and being a participle, may well be translated, "having received a divine communication." The second participle expresses the subjective aspect of Noah's faith, "being moved with godly fear," because of both the severity of the impending judgment and the condescension of God in sparing him and his family. That a flood of waters should cover the earth was by Noah's unbelieving generation unthinkable, and even more so that a small vessel should ride its turbulent waters. But moved by this godly fear, Noah prepared an ark "to the saving of his house." Noah therefore becomes a representative not only of the "work of faith" but also of the "endurance of faith"; for it was much in his favor that he stood the strain of long delay and yet exemplified his faith by his works. Christ is the Ark of our salvation, in whom we rise above the flood tides of worldliness and sin; and even in our greatest disasters, through the "upper window" we may still hold communion with our Lord. The writer makes two observations concerning the faith of Noah.

1. Noah by his faith "condemned the world." The perseverance in the work God had assigned him was doubtless the primary source of condemnation, although St. Peter speaks of Noah as a "preacher of righteousness" (II Pet. 2:5). During this period God was long-suffering, His Spirit striving with men; but men heeded

not and continued in their sin until the day that Noah entered the ark (Matt. 24:38-39). We may say then that Noah's work condemned the world, his life condemned them, and his warnings of impending judgment condemned them.

2. Noah "became heir of the righteousness which is by faith." As Noah was given a revelation of the impending Flood, so we have it revealed to us that "the day of the Lord will come as a thief in the night; in the which the heavens shall pass away with a great noise, and the elements shall melt with fervent heat, the earth also and the works that are therein shall be burned up. . . . Wherefore, beloved, seeing that ye look for such things, be diligent that ye may be found of him in peace, without spot, and blameless" (II Pet. 3:10-14). As Noah believed God's word concerning the impending Flood, so we are to believe God's word concerning the fiery judgment that is to come upon the earth; and we too face the same unbelief that obtained in Noah's day. Let us then by the seriousness of our mission condemn the world's frivolity, by our persistence in our commission condemn its unbelief, and by our ceaseless warnings condemn its insensibility to truth. So shall we too become the heirs "of the righteousness which is by faith."

The Faith of Abraham. It is but natural that the writer should give special attention to Abraham, who was known as the "father of the faithful" and revered alike by Jews, Christians, and Mohammedans. His faith is summarized in four different manifestations: (1) his call to a future inheritance, (2) his sojourn in the land of promise, (3) his promise of an Heir in whom all the nations of the earth should be blessed, and (4) his offering up of Isaac as a sacrifice.

1. The call of Abraham represents the "obedience of faith." Leaving his native land with its high civilization but idolatrous practices, leaving his father's house and much that was precious to him, and all this to dwell in tents and live the life of a wanderer, was a great crisis

in his life. Yet he obeyed and "went out, not knowing
whither," for the goal of his journey was not revealed
to him until he left Haran. The word for "called" is
the present participle *kaloumenos* (καλούμενος) and emphasizes the immediacy of Abraham's act of obedience;
that is, "he obeyed the call while (so to say) it was still
sounding in his ears" (Westcott). But with this call
there was a twofold promise: (1) of temporal blessings
—a numerous offspring, and a land in which they should
dwell; and (2) of a spiritual blessing—that through him
should come the "seed of the woman," in whom all the
nations of the earth should be blessed. This call of God
meant the complete breaking with the former life and
the abandoning of all self-trusts, that he might learn
the lesson of full trust in God, and in God alone.
Promptness of obedience and the simplicity of trust in
the invisible God, these are the lessons we must learn
if we would walk in the steps of the "faith of Abraham;
who is the father of us all" (Rom. 4: 12-16).

2. The sojourn of Abraham in Canaan represents
the "patience of faith." "By faith he sojourned in the
land of promise, as in a strange country, dwelling in
tabernacles with Isaac and Jacob, the heirs with him of
the same promise: for he looked for a city which hath
foundations, whose builder and maker is God" (11: 9-
10). There were many cities in Canaan, ancient and
wealthy, but Abraham's spiritual insight saw that these
were subject to decay, as also any city would be which
he himself might establish. These material things did
not meet the grandeur of his ideal. His faith carried
him beyond the things earth might offer, to that spiritual
and heavenly realm above the fleeting things of time.
For this reason he was content to dwell in tents without
any fixed abode, for faith always takes the long view.
Abraham was old when Isaac was born, and in extreme
age at the birth of Jacob; yet throughout this long
stretch of time his faith never wavered. He was content
to regard his earthly life as a transient state, for he
desired a "better country, that is, an heavenly."

God leads His people in the way of faith by presenting first a nearer goal, which, being realized, is found to be but a revelation of something better farther on. Abraham began by seeking an earthly inheritance, only to find that this was but a stage in the onward movement of faith; for faith rises in its demand as experience grows broader and deeper. Material things can never satisfy the soul. Like Abraham, we must refuse to be crushed by disappointment, that our faith may rise from the earthly and temporal to the heavenly and eternal.

3. Abraham and the promised Heir. Here Abraham's faith is represented as the "faith of influence." Beginning with the call of Abraham, faith is not so much associated with personal righteousness as with its relation to the social structure and the building up of the Messianic kingdom. St. Paul makes much of both of these aspects in his doctrinal treatises. Abraham and Sarah had been promised a son, but they were long past the time of nature, and Sarah, becoming discouraged, was rebuked with the words, "Is any thing too hard for the Lord?" (Gen. 18: 14) While Sarah's faith is not mentioned in the Genesis account, this writer calls special attention to it, saying, "She judged him faithful who had promised." Now it is evident that her faith, in part at least, was inspired by that of her husband, so that from Abraham's standpoint it may rightly be called the "faith of influence." As to Sarah, when her thoughts were lifted from herself to God, faith prevailed and that strength was restored to her which she had lost through age. The birth of Isaac was not merely of the flesh, for both were "as good as dead"; it was a miraculous birth, and Isaac was the child of promise. Through him there were to spring so many "as the stars of the sky in multitude, and as the sand which is by the sea shore innumerable."

4. Abraham and his offering up of Isaac as a sacrifice. Here we have both the "test of faith" and the "sacrifice of faith," the trial proving the reality of his faith, and

the sacrifice pointing to the death and resurrection of Christ. Doubtless this was a severer strain on Abraham's faith than any of the previous tests. He was not unmindful of the destinies which hung on the thread of that single life. The promises were to be fulfilled in Isaac, and now came the strange command to destroy the very means through which the promises were to be fulfilled. However, there seems to have been no hesitancy on the part of Abraham, or no thought of a last-minute intervention. The word *prosepheren* (προσφέρεν), being in the imperfect tense, indicates that the sacrifice was performed "step by step"; while the present participle *peirazomenos* (πειραζόμενος), "being tried," seems to suggest the promptitude of the offering. The reason given for the steadfastness of Abraham's faith is that it accounted "that God was able to raise him up, even from the dead." While God intervened to prevent the death of Isaac, as far as Abraham was concerned he had tasted the full bitterness of the act as already completed. The structure of the Greek makes this clear; for the word *prosenenochen* (προσενήνοχεν), "has offered," is a perfect active indicative, and thus expresses completeness of the act. The text then reads, "By faith Abraham, when he was tried, 'has offered up' Isaac." The act is complete; the offering is perfect. It should be noted that the "oath" which attached to the promise made to Abraham concerning the priesthood of Christ is found only in this text. Thus the death and resurrection of Isaac, in a figure, becomes a prophecy of Christ's death, resurrection, ascension, and eternal priesthood at the right hand of the Father. Is it any wonder then that Abraham cried *Jehovah-jireh,* "The Lord will provide"? Thus he stamped upon every mount of emergency the promise that the angel of the Lord will appear, the sacrifice will be there, and thus there will be a way of escape in every temptation or trial.

The Faith of Isaac, Jacob, and Joseph. Since the blessings of these three were pronounced near the close of their lives, this faith has been called "deathbed

faith." This however is not to be thought of in the
sense of a "deathbed repentance" at the close of a
wasted life, but of that faith which has been the rule
of a long life, the roots of which have struck so deeply
into the past that it triumphs over the weakness of
nature and burns with a clear-cut, steady flame until
crowned by death. Isaac and Jacob, like Abraham,
their father, continued to dwell in tents and refused to
seek a fixed abode on earth, while all three spoke only
of things to come—the farsightedness of their faith. Out
of the checkered lives of these men, only the events
closely associated with their last days are chosen; for
the purpose of the writer is to show that all these died
in the faith.

1. "By faith Isaac blessed Jacob and Esau concerning things to come" (11:20). The birth of Isaac was
miraculous, and to him the promise was again given.
Trusting with fullest certainty that the things not then
present would come to pass, Isaac blessed both Jacob
and Esau. His faith rested solely in God and His word.
That Jacob is mentioned first may have reference to the
wealth of the birthright given him. But there is a touch
of tenderness in these words, and a suggestion of Isaac's
early fondness for his nature-loving son, in that he was
not left without a father's blessing. Isaac's faith saw
beyond the then present enmity of his sons to a time
of their reconciliation. But stretching far into the future,
he saw that the time would come when Esau would
throw off the yoke and rule over Jacob's descendants
(Gen. 27:40), a prophecy which was fulfilled when
Herod the Idumean ruled in Jerusalem.

2. "By faith Jacob, when he was a dying, blessed
both the sons of Joseph; and worshipped, leaning on
his staff" (11:21). The writer has taken two events in
the life of Jacob and condensed them into a single verse.
No mention is made of the sons of Jacob at this time;
but a blessing was pronounced upon Ephraim and Manasseh, the sons of Joseph whom he adopted as his own
(Gen. 48:5), that they might have a portion of their

inheritance in the land of promise. Here we see the blessing passed on to the fourth generation. Jacob, being near death, knew that he could not see the promise fulfilled; but in faith he saw that Ephraim and Manasseh would not remain in Egypt but, departing with the Israelites, would be the founders of two tribes in Canaan. In the account of Jacob's worship, the Septuagint, from which this text is taken, has the word "staff," which appears to be more correct than the Hebrew pointing which makes the text read "bed." In Gen. 32:10 there is mention of the staff that Jacob carried from the time he left Canaan, and which therefore came to be a symbol of his life's experiences, witnessing to the goodness of God and the realities of faith. It is significant, therefore, that in the last hours of his life he worshiped "leaning on his staff"—a stroke of the writer which not only completes the picture of the pilgrimage of Jacob, but marks the beginning of the end of Israel's life as a nomadic people.

3. "By faith Joseph, when he died, made mention of the departing of the children of Israel; and gave commandment concerning his bones" (11:22). Joseph lived all his life as an Egyptian, the second in rule over all the land. Doubtless at his death his body was mummified and laid in an expensive tomb in Egypt. But Joseph believed the Abrahamic promises, and like his father, Jacob, gave instructions that on Israel's departure he should be taken with them and buried in Hebron. Here faith overcame darkness, distance, and death.

The Faith of Moses. Moses owed his life to the strong faith of his parents, who, not fearing the wrath of the king, hid the baby for three months. Here is an outstanding example of one whose glorious career may be traced to the piety of his parents. The very statement appears to draw attention at once to Moses, and without doubt his coming into the home inspired faith in the parents. And so we read, "By faith Moses, when he was born, was hid three months of his parents, because they saw he was a proper child; and they were not afraid of the king's commandment" (11:23). The word "proper" as used here is *asteion* (ἀστεῖον), "beautiful," and is the same word used by Stephen in his address (Acts 7:20), where it is translated "exceeding fair," the words "to God" being also in the Greek text. It was this unusual beauty in the child that led the parents, both of whom were of the tribe of Levi, to believe that God had some promise to be fulfilled in him. The king's edict had gone out that every son born in a Hebrew family should be cast into the river; but the parents, having made an ark of bulrushes, preserved him until he was found by Pharaoh's daughter, who named him Moses because he was drawn out of the water.

1. "By faith Moses, when he was come to years, refused to be called the son of Pharaoh's daughter" (11:24). This is the first recorded act of Moses as a mature man, the faith which he first inspired in his parents being now manifested as an individual "decision of faith." He felt the call of God to devote his life to the redemption of his oppressed people, and disloyalty here would have been for him a sin. He chose rather to "suffer affliction." This Greek term, embodying as it does the root word *kakon* (κακόν), which means "base" or "disgraceful," shows that he identified himself with those who were considered a disgraceful lot. The reason given for this choice is that he esteemed the reproach of Christ "greater riches than the treasures in Egypt: for he had respect unto the recompence of the reward" (11:25-26). The word "recompence" means "to balance in the scales" or "to give back a full equivalent of pay"; and thus placed in the scales, the reproach of Christ infinitely outweighed the treasures of Egypt and the transitory pleasures of its court. Moses knew about Christ, for the idea of the Messiah was implicit in the Abrahamic promise. Our Lord said, Moses "wrote

Josephus in his *Antiquities* (ii, 9:7) tells us that Moses refused Pharaoh's crown when a baby. The daughter of Pharaoh placed her baby in the arms of Pharaoh; and then to please her Pharaoh put the crown upon the child's head. But Moses threw it to the ground and stamped on it, an act which to Pharaoh seemed prophetic of danger to come.

of me" (John 5: 46); and Peter quotes Moses as saying, "A prophet shall the Lord your God raise up unto you of your brethren, like unto me; him shall ye hear in all things whatsoever he shall say unto you" (Acts 3: 21 ff.). This statement is also repeated by Stephen (Acts 7: 37). Moses then knew of Christ when he made his decision, for he was of the faith of Abraham, Isaac, Jacob, and Joseph.

2. "By faith he forsook Egypt, not fearing the wrath of the king: for he endured, as seeing him who is invisible" (11: 27). Here we have the "courage of faith." Early patristic exegesis generally referred this to the flight into Midian, probably because it appears in this verse, previous to the Exodus. This can hardly be true, however, for that flight was occasioned by fear. It seems better to refer it to the Exodus, and this position is confirmed by the use of the word *katelipen* (κατέλιπεν), which means to leave, never to return. Moses, who at one time fled in fear of the king, now returns as a fearless leader, demanding of Pharaoh that he "let my people go." The reason for his strength and perseverance is to be found in this—he saw Him that is invisible.

3. "Through faith he kept the passover, and the sprinkling of blood, lest he that destroyed the firstborn should touch them" (11: 28). Here we find the verb *pepoieken* (πεποίηκεν), "has kept" or "instituted," the Passover, not merely as a single act of deliverance, but as a perpetual witness of that deliverance. Before that the events are described in the aorist tense as past—he refused, he chose, he accounted, he looked for, he forsook, and he endured; and likewise of the events following the institution of the Passover. Here the faith of Moses took on magnificent proportions. Being driven from the face of Pharaoh, he was commanded by God not to return. Instead the Passover was instituted. A lamb was to be slain and its blood sprinkled on the doorposts—in reality a challenge to the superstition of the Egyptians. Moses knew that the slaying of the firstborn of Pharaoh's house to that of the maid behind

the mill, and the first-born of all animals, would arouse the king's anger and perhaps bring on a massacre of the people. Hence they were commanded to eat "with your loins girded, your shoes on your feet, and your staff in your hand; and ye shall eat it in haste" (Exod. 12:11). Thus the people escaped while the Egyptians were in confusion and sorrow over the death of their first-born. But Moses was careful to protect his people, for they were saved from the "destroyer" only by the blood on the doorposts, and were led out only by "a mighty hand and . . . a stretched out arm."

"By faith they passed through the Red sea as by dry land: which the Egyptians assaying to do were drowned" (11:29). As the Passover and the flight from Egypt marked the beginning of the Exodus, so the passing through the Red Sea marks its close as far as Egypt is concerned. The fate of the Egyptians which followed them is given in a simple relative clause, "which the Egyptians assaying [or 'presuming'] to do were drowned [literally were 'drunk down']." These two words mark the power of *faith* and the fate of *presumption,* and this because the Israelites had the promise of God, while the Egyptians, having no promise, were moved merely by human expediency and a false courage. "Faith saves us; presumption lets us drown."

The Passover is mentioned in this chapter as indicating the manner in which the Hebrew slaves were delivered from their bondage in Egypt under the leadership of Moses. So great was this deliverance that a memorial feast was instituted, to be observed annually in celebration of the event. The crossing of the Red Sea marked the full deliverance from Egypt, and with this no further mention is made of Moses and his work. Yet great things were accomplished at Sinai under the administration of Moses. Here the law was given and the people organized into a nation; here was the formation of the "church in the wilderness" with its priestly services; and here also there was the uniting of the tribes into a peculiar or unique people by the "blood of the covenant." By this Jehovah alone became their God, and they His people. Other than the historical event of the Passover, which marked the deliverance from Egypt, as indicated in the Introduction, there is no further reference to the Passover nor to the institution of the Lord's Supper. This Epistle deals with a people already delivered from Egypt and on their way to the promised land of Canaan. Two more events are necessary, however, to complete the full history of faith from the promise made to Abraham to the actual entrance into the promised land: the faith of the conquest by Joshua, and the faith of Rahab which preserved her and her house from destruction in Jericho.

The Faith of Conquest. "By faith the walls of Jericho fell down, after they were compassed about seven days" (11:30). With Moses began the faith of leadership, as over against the faith of patient waiting for the promise. The forty years in the wilderness had marked the founding of the nation and the institution of religious services, and had also served to discipline the people by the hardships of their desert wanderings. These years are passed over in silence by the writer. Joshua had now become the leader of Israel in the conquest of a land which had been divinely promised them. Their first point of attack was Jericho, a walled city and adequately manned. The Israelites had nothing with which to attack, but in obedience to the command of God they marched around the walls and shouted, and the "wall fell down flat," so that every man went up into the city straight before him (Josh. 6:20). It was by faith in the promise of God that they conquered, and it is by faith that Christians down across the centuries have likewise won their victories. The weapons of our warfare are not carnal, yet they are "mighty through God to the pulling down of strong holds" (II Cor. 10:4).

The Faith of Rahab. "By faith the harlot Rahab perished not with them that believed not, when she had received the spies with peace" (11:31). Rahab was a gentile woman who kept an inn on the walls of

Jericho, as is evidenced by the fact that the spies found lodging there. At the risk of being considered a traitor, she gave them shelter; and while all the inhabitants of Jericho were doomed to destruction, she alone was saved because she believed the word of God's messengers and acted upon her belief. Thus by faith she was the only inhabitant of the city to save herself and her house. There is no clearer evidence of salvation by faith than this event, and that this salvation is for the gentiles also. Rahab was later married to Salmon and became the mother of Booz, who married Ruth; their son, Obed, was the father of Jesse; and Jesse was the father of David, the king (Matt. 1:5).

The Power of Faith

From the call of Abraham to the occupation of Canaan, faith takes on the nature of a discipline; and for this reason the writer is careful to mention the names of the ancient worthies and to indicate the nature of their faith. This is primarily the period of religious faith; but with the signal victory at Jericho, and the sparing of Rahab, the writer appears to regard this period of disciplinary faith closed. It is interesting to note that the last-named person of this period is a gentile woman and an outcast, typical of the redemptive faith in Christ and the universality of His coming kingdom. The writer now turns to the national period in Israel's history, and confines himself to the summarizing of the power of faith under two main heads, (1) the faith of achievement and (2) the faith of endurance.

The Faith of Achievement. "And what shall I more say? for the time would fail me to tell of Gedeon, and of Barak, and of Samson, and of Jephthae; of David also, and Samuel, and of the prophets: who through faith subdued kingdoms, wrought righteousness, obtained promises, stopped the mouths of lions, quenched the violence of fire, escaped the edge of the sword, out of weakness were made strong, waxed valiant in fight, turned to flight the armies of the aliens" (11:32-34),

There were three classes of leaders in the Canaan period: (1) the judges who ruled under the theocracy, (2) the kings of the kingdom period, and (3) the prophets in both the period of the judges and the kings. The judges are not mentioned in the historical order, and the names of Gideon, Barak, Samson, and Jephthah are perhaps chosen because in the period of conquest they overcame different enemies, viz., Midianites, Canaanites, Philistines, and Ammonites.

The power of faith in its various manifestations is ably set forth by Westcott in three sets of triplets, each marking a progress within itself, and a progress in the succession of groups toward that which is more personal. The *first triplet* describes the broad results which believers obtained: (1) material victory ("subdued kingdoms"); (2) moral success in government ("wrought righteousness"); (3) spiritual reward ("obtained promises"). The *second triplet* notices forms of personal deliverance from (1) wild beasts ("stopped the mouths of lions"); (2) physical forces ("quenched the violence of fire"); (3) human tyranny ("escaped the edge of the sword"). The *third triplet* marks the attainment of personal gifts: (1) strength ("out of weakness were made strong"); (2) the exercise of strength ("waxed valiant in fight"); and (3) the triumph of strength ("turned to flight the armies of the aliens"). The writer, assuming that his hearers have a knowledge of early Biblical history, makes no attempt to name the personal heroes who achieved these victories.

The Faith of Endurance. "Women received their dead raised to life again: and others were tortured, not accepting deliverance; that they might obtain a better resurrection: and others had trial of cruel mockings and scourgings, yea, moreover of bonds and imprisonment: they were stoned, they were sawn asunder, were tempted, were slain with the sword: they wandered about in sheepskins and goatskins; being destitute, afflicted, tormented; (of whom the world was not worthy:) they wandered in deserts, and in mountains, and in dens and caves of the earth" (11: 35-38).

1. Not only were the triumphs of faith won by strong men, but renowned women are also included in the annals of faith. A destitute widow of Zarephath, a heathen town, trusted God to support her if she cared for His servant, and as a special reward her son was restored to life. Likewise the son of the pious Shunammite was brought again from the dead through the prayer of Elisha. Others were tortured, and when offered release, refused in order to obtain a better resurrection. The former were restored merely to their natural lives, while the latter looked for a final resurrection into the heavenly life. Since the word for "others" used here is *alloi* (ἄλλοι), that is, others in the sense of merely a numerical distinction, the reference is probably to the Maccabean mother and her seven sons, each of whom was tortured in a different manner by mutilation, flaying, or burnings before her, and at last she herself burned (II Macc. 6: 21; 7: 27). Others, that is, another group from *heteroi* (ἕτεροι), distinct in the sense of being generically different, were not like the *alloi* put to death, but stood trial by cruel mockings and scourgings; and in addition to these, bonds (or confinements) and imprisonments.

2. The word for "torture" in the first verse of this section is from *tumpanizein* (τυμπανίζειν), "to beat as on a drum," and carrying with it the idea of severe blows, was used in describing the various forms of torture—the breaking on a wheel with its beatings; the stretching on a frame with its excruciating pain, the arms and legs then being broken with heavy clubs; or the beating with leaded scourges. This term is especially applicable to verse 37, which is cast in the form of an *asyndeton* or figure of speech in which the connectives are omitted, and therefore has been compared to sledge hammer blows with their cumulative effect. Thus if these scenes are thrown on the screen with a pause between each, we must read: "they were stoned" . . . "they were sawn asunder" . . . "were tempted" . . . "were slain with the sword" . . . "wandered about" . . . "desti-

tute" . . . "afflicted" . . . "tormented." With all the
horror of torture and suffering, there is something magnificent in the steadfastness of these ancient worthies
and their unwavering faith in Him whom they trusted.
And the writer has so pointed up these pictures, and
has so directed these sledge hammer blows, as to put
to shame the wavering Christians of his time and of all
time.

3. The description of the wanderers who escaped
death forms a fitting climax to the list of those triumphant in their faith. They wandered about in sheepskins
and goatskins, having nothing better with which to
clothe themselves; they wandered in the deserts with
their burning suns, and in the mountains with their
chilling blasts, and had only dens and caves—mere
holes in the ground—for their dwelling places. Three
participles are used to describe them, participles which
express duration or the continuousness of their state.
They were (1) destitute, constantly devoid of food and
drink; (2) they were afflicted, always oppressed; and
(3) they were tormented, being always regarded as evil,
and basely treated. Such heroism can hardly be understood in days of ease and comfort. And all this happened to them because of their faith in Christ. The
world thought them not worthy to live, but the writer
exclaims, "Of whom the world was not worthy." Thus
by the hardships of life were they made conscious of
their need for something that abides. "Wherefore God
is not ashamed to be called their God: for he hath
prepared for them a city" (11:16).

THE REWARD OF FAITH

We have followed the author of this Epistle as he
has eloquently delineated the triumphs of faith, slowly
and deliberately at first as he pointed out the scenes of
faith in the lives of the earlier fathers; and then as the
number of witnesses increased, rushing along with the
speed of a torrential stream until it reaches the climax
—and what an unexpected climax it is! Instead of say-

ing that their faith had realized the promises, that they had been crowned, and had entered into their eternal reward, we read: "And these all, having obtained a good report through faith, received not the promise: God having provided some better thing for us, that they without us should not be made perfect" (11: 39-40).

The reason for the failure of the fathers to receive the promise lies in the purpose of God—"that in the dispensation of the fulness of times he might gather together in one all things in Christ, both which are in heaven, and which are on earth" (Eph. 1: 10). The purpose of God, then, is to bring all things together under one Head, and at the same time. This time is not yet; for beyond His purpose concerning the saints of the Old Testament lie the Incarnation, the coming of Christ as a Sin Offering, and His further purpose to gather out a people of all races and tongues, a new company, the Church of the First-born. A distinction must be made between the promises that have been granted to the people of every age and *the promise* of God, which is far more exalted, and which gathers up into itself the final and supreme fulfillment of all that has been hoped for through all the ages. This can take place only when Christ comes the second time without sin unto salvation. Two reasons are given for this extended delay: (1) "some *better* thing for us," and (2) "that they without us should not be made *perfect.*"

1. The "some better thing" promised to us is closely related to the "perfection" withheld from those of the Old Testament period. We have seen from the previous arguments of the writer that through Christ's death, resurrection, ascension, and intercession we have a "better covenant," established on "better promises," administered by a "better priesthood," and from a "better sanctuary." Two kinds of perfection are attributed to Christ, a perfection through suffering and a perfection in glory. (1) He is said to have been *made perfect* through suffering as a preparation for His redemptive work. His human nature having been perfected by

obedience, and being perfected forevermore, He became our great High Priest, who through the Spirit communicates this new nature to us—His own nature. "For by one offering he hath perfected for ever them that are sanctified" (10:14). This perfection of the individual brings us into the presence of God and so perfects our faith that we "press toward the mark for the prize of the high calling of God in Christ Jesus" (Phil. 3:14). (2) The second perfection is that which Christ mentions concerning himself when He says, "The third day I shall be perfected" (Luke 13:32). This can mean only His resurrection in glory by which He became the First Fruits of them that sleep. When the veil of our flesh shall have been rent by death or rapture, we too shall be made like "unto his glorious body," free from the curse of the race with its attendant infirmities, removed from our probationary state in the first Adam, and enter with Him into the new and eternal order.

2. "That they without us should not be made perfect" in no wise means that their eternal hopes depended upon us, but only that we must be included with them in the final summation of all things. While the perfection promised by our Lord to individuals can by faith be appropriated by every member of the body of Christ, the resurrection perfection cannot take place until the whole body of Christ's people share in this glory. As the ancient worthies looked forward in faith to the coming of Christ as Redeemer, by which the validity of their salvation was sealed, so we are to look forward with the same faith to His coming again in glory. As they endured as seeing Him that is invisible, so only those who by faith endure to the end shall be saved (Matt. 24:13). We have the word as they had it; and our promise is that "as the lightning cometh out of the east, and shineth unto the west; so shall also the coming of the Son of man be" (Matt. 24:27). "When the Son of man shall come in his glory, and all the holy angels with him, then shall he sit upon the throne of his glory" (Matt. 25:31). And while St. Paul tells us that "the

dead in Christ shall rise first" it is only to join with the raptured saints, "to meet the Lord in the air: and so shall we ever be with the Lord" (I Thess. 4: 16-17).

CHAPTER XII

THE CLOUD OF WITNESSES

The writer, having unfolded before the eyes of his readers the splendid achievements of faith accomplished by the ancient worthies, now returns to the exhortation begun in chapter ten, with all the accumulated force gathered in the previous chapter. The word "wherefore" marks the connection with the entire preceding chapter, but especially with the significant transitional verses: "And these all, having obtained a good report through faith, received not the promise: God having provided some better thing for us, that they without us should not be made perfect" (11:39-40). This means, in its simplest form, that the entire roll of the worthies of faith would be incomplete without the addition of the New Testament saints. It means in a deeper sense, however, that perfection came only by the sacrifice of Christ, and this applies equally to those who lived before and those who came after. In this sense they could not be made perfect without us, for the one great sacrifice applies to all people of all time.

The Cloud of Witnesses. The writer, in order to intensify his exhortation to perseverance, pictures himself and his readers as in a great arena, where the rising rows of witnesses appear as a great cloud encircling the amphitheater. The word for witnesses is *marturon* (μαρτύρων), from which we have our word martyrs, although there is no indication that it is used here in this narrower sense. The word means "certified ones" and doubtless refers to the "so-numerous" ones whose victories have been recorded in the preceding chapter. The word for cloud is not *nephele* (νεφέλη), "a single cloud," but *nephos* (νέφος), a mass of cloud that covers the heaven, and was used by both the Greeks and Latins as the symbol of a dense mass of people. The word for "encompassed about" or "encircled" means "lying close-

ly around us" or spread out before us. The Greek word
martus (μάρτυς) had with the ancient Greeks, as it does
with us, a twofold meaning: (1) it may mean persons
who testify to a truth or fact previously known to them,
and (2) it may mean persons who were present at
the scene, whether they testify or not. According to the
former view the term would refer to the ancient believers, who had borne testimony to God's faithfulness
both by their lives and by their too often violent deaths.
However the word used here is "witnesses" and not
theatai (θεαται), "spectators," or even epoptes (ἐπόπτης),
"eyewitnesses." According to the latter view the meaning of this text is that those who have won their own
conflicts are now present to behold those who are still
in the race. Lindsay says that the words "encompassing
us" furnish decisive evidence of "the crowd of witnesses as placed around the Hebrews during their struggle, and the idea of their presence is employed to
stimulate the followers of Christ to unfaltering zeal and
effort." Whichever view may be taken, the real meaning
is that the saints gone on before still testify that faith
was the strength of their lives, in the sense that the
memory of a departed loved one may be even a greater
stimulus to holy living than one still present in the
flesh.

The Christian Race. "Let us lay aside every weight,
and the sin which doth so easily beset us, and let us
run with patience the race that is set before us" (12: 1b).
The writer, having described the arena and the race
course, and taken a glimpse at the cloud of witnesses,
now turns to a consideration of the race itself—its
preparation, its goal, and its obstacles. The word apothe-
menoi (αποθέμενοι), "having laid aside," is a second aorist
middle participle, and has the force and urgency of
prompt action—"Do it and have done with it." This
promptitude has reference to two things: (1) the act
of putting off at once every encumbering weight, and
(2) the act of putting off "the sin" which so easily be-
sets us.

1. The word for "weight" is *ogkon* (ὄγκον) and is here used in the sense of an added encumbrance. The primary meaning of the word is bulk, whether in size or in weight, and therefore has been used metaphorically for undue confidence, such as bombast or pretension. It is doubtful, however, that the word as used here has the sense of putting off excess weight by a course of athletic training; rather it is used in the sense of putting off additional things, such as the flowing garments, or anything which would impede the progress of the runner. In a Christian sense it means anything, whether right or wrong, that is a handicap or hindrance to spiritual progress. Plummer, speaking unmetaphorically, says that such a high end of faith is hardly possible apart from a steady and unflinching resolve to do without certain things. Davidson points out the distinction between "weights" and "sin," and calls attention to the fact that what may be innocent or even commendable in others may to us be a hindrance. He suggests such things as an appetite, though lawful, that tends to gain on one; devotion to some pursuit in danger of absorbing the mind; or an affection that threatens to turn away the heart—these may be weights without being sins. The writer of this Epistle does not, however, make any suggestion as to what these encumbrances may be, but implies that those who set themselves to this solemn race will early discover that which proves to be a hindrance to them.

2. The "sin which doth so easily beset us" is an expression which has been variously interpreted. The word for "sin" as used here is *hamartian* (ἁμαρτίαν), "sin" in the singular, not "sins" in the plural. The word has reference to "sin" itself, the heart condition from which all sins flow. Vaughan says that "the reference is not to one particular sin, as being especially dangerous, but to sin itself. The article is generic." He further states that the rendering of the Authorized Version catches the point admirably until it is perverted into the "besetting sin" as something different from the whole

body of sin. Davidson confirms this position by saying
that what we call a "besetting sin" does not lie in the
passage; the thing spoken of is sin, and it is spoken of
as a thing apt to fold itself about us as a garment, and
impede our running. The word *euperistaton* (εὐπερίστα-
τον), "besetting," is from *statos* (στατὸς) and *peri* (περί).
It is sometimes used in a strict passive, "surrounded";
and sometimes in the middle voice, "standing round."
In its compound form as *eu-peristaton* (εὐ-περίστατον)
it becomes "easily standing round" or "surrounding."

Dr. Adam Clarke says of this passage: "Some understand it to be original sin, as that by which we are en-
veloped in body, soul and spirit. Whether it may be,
the word gives us to understand that it is what meets
us at every turn; that it is always presenting itself to
us; that as a pair of compasses describe a circle by the
revolution of one leg, while the other is at rest at the
center, so this surrounds us in every place; we are
bounded by it, and often hemmed in on every side; it
is a circular, well fortified wall, over which we must
leap, or through which we must break." This sin manifests itself according to temperament, condition, or circumstance; but it is *the sin* itself that we are commanded
to put away promptly—"do it and have done with it."
This, as we have said again and again, is accomplished
by the Holy Spirit through faith in Christ.

3. "Let us run with patience the race that is set
before us." Here we have the word *trechomen* (τρέχω-
μεν), "run," a present imperative, which means "keep
on running." The race is spoken of as a contest because
of the severity of effort and peril involved, although
the milder figure of an athletic event is chosen to represent it. The contest however does not necessarily imply
other contestants, unless, as had been suggested, the
antagonist is "the sin" against which we must strive
(12:4). This race is to be run with, or by means of,
patience, the word *hupomones* (ὑπομονῆς), "patience,"
being used in the sense of perseverance or endurance.
The obstacles in this case are the external hardships of

life and the reproaches of the world. We are not to
allow fatigue to slow us down, nor the disappointments
of life to dishearten us; neither are we to look with
envy upon those whose way seems less difficult, whose
progress appears greater, or whose victories appear to
be more easily won. We are not to compare ourselves
with one another, for in this race all must run, and St.
Paul exhorts us to so run that we may obtain. The
words "set before us" refer to the race track which
stretches out before us, and are placed over against
"the joy that was set before" Christ (cf. I Cor. 9:24).

"Looking unto Jesus." "Looking unto Jesus the
author and finisher of our faith; who for the joy that was
set before him endured the cross, despising the shame,
and is set down at the right hand of the throne of God"
(12:2). The writer, having recorded the faith of the
ancient worthies, and then taken a glimpse at the cloud
of witnesses, now bids his readers to look away unto
Jesus, exalted high above all, and seated at the right
hand of the throne of God. The word for "looking" is
aphorontes (ἀφορῶντες) and means "looking away" from
the things near at hand that would divert our attention,
and consciously fixing our eyes upon Jesus as the great
Goal of attainment. It further means "an all-absorbing
interest," ably expressed in the words "with no eyes for
anything except Jesus." The words "author and finisher
of our faith" have been interpreted in many ways. The
word for "author" is *archegon* (ἀρχηγὸν), "leader" or
"pioneer," and is the same word translated in 2:10 as
"captain" of our salvation. The word "finisher" is *teleio-
ten* (τελειωτὴν), "perfecter" or "completer" (cf. 10:14).
The word "our" before faith is in italics, and as found
in the Greek text is "the faith." However this does not
mean "the faith" in the objective sense, as describing
the Christian system, but faith in the subjective sense,
as the ruling principle of heart and life.

The choice of the word *archegon*, "leader" or "pioneer," instead of *aitios* (αἴτιος), "author," in the sense
of an originator, is very significant. As Davidson points

out, these words as here used "cannot mean that Christ as Author originates faith in us, and as Perfecter sustains it and brings it to a perfect issue"—that is, unconditionally as to both its bestowal and its perfection. Rather the emphasis is upon Christ as the great Pioneer of faith, who in His earthly life, having perfectly realized the ideal and finished the course, is now seated at the right hand of the throne of God. In 2:10 the word *archegon,* as "captain," has special reference to His preparation for leadership; here He has become the Goal of attainment, the Center of all Christian vision. Yet He is still the "Leader," who from His throne in the heavens ministers through the Spirit the strength, the patient endurance, the perseverance, and every needed grace for the conflict; and for those who follow Him with confidence He will become their Perfector, "when he shall come to be glorified in his saints, and to be admired in all them that believe" (II Thess. 1:10).

The writer next turns to a consideration of the humiliating experience of Jesus, vividly portrayed for the readers' encouragement—words which are but the amplification of His work as the "author and finisher of our faith." The author finds here three similarities. For their faith they had endured a great fight of afflictions, partly because they had been made a gazingstock by both reproaches and afflictions, and partly because they had become companions of those that were so used. So also Jesus "for the joy that was set before him endured the cross, despising the shame." This sentence is introduced by the word *anti* (ἀντὶ), which means "to give in exchange," or more especially here, "in consideration of." The word for "joy" is *charas* (χαρᾶς)—not that which He gave up in becoming incarnate, but the joy "lying out before Him." This was the joy of His self-sacrifice for the salvation of men, a self-sacrifice which in itself was a self-satisfying reward. But it meant also the joy of being exalted to the throne of God, and carrying with Him our human nature and His, in His exaltation, thus crowning His redemptive work throughout all

eternity. It was the joy of administering from the throne
His heavenly life through the Holy Spirit, and thus perfecting forever them that are sanctified (10:14). This
was the joy set before Him—a joy that fills all heaven,
and will at His coming again fill the whole earth with
His glory.

What did He give in exchange for this? He endured
the Cross. Here we have again the word *hupemeinen*
(ὑπέμεινεν), previously translated "patience," but here
more aptly rendered "perseveringly endured." The
word for "cross" is *stauron* (σταυρόν), a "stake" or
"post" driven into the ground for the execution of crimi-
nals, but it later came to mean the cross. The words
"despising disgrace" have been called the great paradox.
The word *kataphronesas* (καταφρονήσας), "having despised," is an aorist used to express a single and decisive
act. "Despising the shame" does not mean that He regarded it lightly, but as small compared to the joy set
before Him. Both the words "cross" and "shame" are
used without the article to emphasize the quality—such
a thing as the Cross and the shame; and thus serve to
set in bolder relief the depths of His self-abnegation.
Jesus, being holy in himself, was acutely sensitive to
the shame of the Cross, dying in the eyes of the law as
a criminal, but He did not allow it to daunt His loyalty
to the will of God.

"Consider Him." The writer follows his words of
instruction with another exhortation. "For consider him
that endured such contradiction of sinners against himself, lest ye be wearied and faint in your minds. Ye
have not yet resisted unto blood, striving against sin"
(12:3-4). Many have supposed that the figure changes
here from a racecourse to a pugilistic contest in the
arena, and says that, even though their struggle against
sin is more severe, they have not yet "resisted unto
blood." The writer first used the word "consider" in
relation to the apostleship and high priesthood of Christ
(3:1); here he uses the same strong term in relation to
the sufferings of Jesus at the hands of sinners. It is

evident therefore that, since Jesus was "without sin," the expression "contradiction of sinners" can mean nothing other than that the sin was in those who condemned and crucified Him. Any just comparison must admit that the struggle of his hearers was also objective; it was not sin within themselves, however great the struggle, but sin within those who persecuted them. But severe as their afflictions and persecutions had been, they were not to be compared with those that Jesus suffered. These Christians had not yet "resisted unto blood"; none had as yet suffered martyrdom.

HOLINESS IN RELATION TO PERSONAL EXPERIENCE

From the arena with its racecourse and gladiatorial conflicts, the writer turns quickly to the quiet serenity of the home. The son is now in his father's house, where he is to profit by the wise admonitions and kindly correction of a loving father. The purpose of the illustration however is the same; for though less rigorously and more naturally, it still deals with the problem of holy living. In this section (12: 4-13), the problem is presented under the nature, necessity, and temper of Christian discipline.

The Nature of Christian Discipline. The writer begins this section with a question and a quotation. "And ye have forgotten"—a better rendering, "Have ye forgotten the exhortation which speaketh unto you as children?

My son, despise not thou the chastening of the Lord,
    Nor faint when thou art rebuked of him;
For whom the Lord loveth he chasteneth"
                    (Heb. 12: 5-6).

Here, as is his custom, the writer does not mention the human authorship of this quotation (Prov. 3: 11-12) —which appears to be the words of Solomon to his son, or of some fatherly man to a person in affliction—but sees it as it really is in its ultimate meaning, the very words of God to His children in times of distress and persecution. The word translated "exhortation" is *parakleseos,* "paraclete," the name applied in the New Testament to the Holy Spirit as the "Comforter." Here the Paraclete is personified and discourses with the son in a hortatory or persuasive tone. He says that all afflictions, distresses, and even persecutions are to be regarded as chastenings from the hand of God, and are designed solely for the practical training of His people in the life of holiness. He warns against two dangers, indifference and discouragement.

1. "Despise not thou the chastening of the Lord." These words are a warning against taking too lightly the chastening of the Lord. The Roman writers contemporary with earlier Christianity took a bitter attitude of skepticism concerning any discipline of providence. Strong natures fall easily into this temptation. It is to such as seek to overcome every temptation and endure every affliction by sheer human strength of will that these words are addressed. Such persons fail to see the hand of God in their chastening, and therefore lose sight of the moral and religious value of it; they fail to humble themselves, and thereby lose all the help and blessing it was meant to bring.

2. "Nor faint when thou art rebuked of him." This represents another extreme attitude toward chastening, and therefore another class to be warned. These consider the hand of God as too heavy. They become discouraged in the trials of life, impatient under its vexations, and fainthearted in times of persecutions. They forget that Jesus was perfected through sufferings, and that God sends these trying things to them that they too may receive the highest gain. They have not fully learned to trust the Father's care; they have not learned with St. Paul to say, "When I am weak, then am I strong" (II Cor. 12: 10).

The Necessity for Chastening. "For whom the Lord loveth he chasteneth, and scourgeth every son whom he receiveth. If ye endure chastening, God dealeth with you as with sons; for what son is he whom the father chasteneth not?" (12: 6-7) We readily understand the close connection between disciple and discipline, but it is unfortunate that there is no word in English to show the close connection between child and chastening. The word for children is *paidion* (παιδίον), "little children," while the word for chastening is *paideian* (παιδείαν), from the same root word, and means the training or education of children—hence "instruction, correction, chastening." The writer therefore says children and chastening belong together, and cannot be separated by a wise and loving father. There is a difference however between the word *didaskein* (διδάσκειν), "instruction," and *paideia*, "chastening," the former having reference to mental instruction or the teaching of lessons, the latter to moral training or the disciplining of a child. Westcott points out that "the training by a great master, is something more than his teaching." The word *mastigoi* (μαστιγοῖ), "scourgeth," is a very strong term. Christ warned His disciples that they would be scourged in the synagogues (Matt. 10:17), and He himself was scourged before Pilate. The argument then is this, that as no true father would neglect either the mental instruction or moral training of his children, so neither does God as a loving Father neglect the chastening of His children.

This argument is confirmed by a negative statement in the following verse. "But if ye be without chastisement, whereof all are partakers, then are ye bastards, and not sons" (12:8). Those born out of wedlock, *nothoi* (νόθοι), "illegitimate"—a word found only here in the New Testament—are without recognized position as to their father, and therefore as such are deprived of that moral training which is the right of every true son. Those who love pleasure more than discipline of mind and heart are not, therefore, the sons of God.

The Temper of Christian Discipline. "Furthermore we have had fathers of our flesh which corrected us, and we gave them reverence: shall we not much rather be in subjection unto the Father of spirits, and live? For they verily for a few days chastened us after their own pleasure; but he for our profit, that we might be made partakers of his holiness" (12: 9-10). The writer has shown the necessity for chastening; now he indicates the temper in which such chastening should be received. If we had reverence for our earthly fathers, whose chastening was but for a few days, and dictated by a fallible judgment, how much more should we reverence the Father of spirits and live? Here God as the Father of all spirits is set in contrast to our earthly fathers; and since it is by the spirit that we have access to God and the higher spiritual order, we owe Him much more—the full submission of our entire beings. God has a high ideal for us; He chastens us that we might be partakers of His holiness. Those who have been made holy in heart by the blood of Jesus must now learn to manifest that holiness in every vicissitude of life. St. Paul speaks of this latter as "perfecting holiness in the fear of God" (II Cor. 7: 1). We cannot say too often that it is not by means of holy hearts alone that we are enabled to live holy lives, but by virtue of Him who dwells within those holy hearts.

1. The severity of their chastening is alluded to in the words, "Now no chastening for the present seemeth to be joyous, but grievous: nevertheless afterward it yieldeth the peaceable fruit of righteousness to them which are exercised thereby" (12: 11). Afflictions may be more or less severe, but they are never joyous. Jesus was not joyous when in the garden He sweat as it were great drops of blood. Many a one in deep affliction has wondered if not said, "Why has this happened to me? What have I done to deserve this suffering?" It is only afterward, the writer tells us, that chastening yields the peaceable fruit of righteousness. How light do our deepest afflictions appear in the light of an eternal reward! But God does not reserve all the reward for the future life; we have even here a taste of the peaceable fruit of righteousness, the consciousness of our right relations with God and man. The word "exercise" is a return to the figure of the gymnasium, and marks the transition to the exhortation which follows.

2. The writer reaches his exhortation in the words, "Wherefore lift up the hands which hang down, and the feeble knees; and make straight paths for your feet, lest that which is lame be turned out of the way; but let it rather be healed" (12: 12-13). Here the arena is again brought into view. The hands hang down from weariness in the combat, and the knees are palsied from the tenseness of the race. These are common metaphorical expressions for despair or collapse, and are evidently drawn from Isa. 35: 3, where it is said, "Strengthen ye the weak hands [for service], and confirm the feeble knees [for progress]." The writer of this Epistle issues the same peremptory command. He uses the word *anorthosate* (ἀνορθώσατε), a first aorist, active imperative, variously translated as "lift up," "set right," and "straighten up." Lenski uses the cryptic terms, "Brace up," and, "Go straight."

The words "make straight paths for your feet" (cf. Prov. 4: 26) are a clear indication that there were faltering ones in the congregation, probably due to the vacillating attitude of some who wavered between Christianity and Judaism. The appeal therefore was for each to have care for the other, and all to have special care for those who were weak and discouraged. These latter were called the "lame" from the neuter *to cholon* (το χωλὸν), "the lame thing," which may refer either to some weakness remaining in the individual or, what is more probable, to the lame portion of the congregation. This much-needed help was to be accomplished by making straight paths for the feet—some say "making straight paths by the feet"—thus emphasizing the need for uprightness in the Christian walk rather than the preparation of a straight path. The word *ektrapei* (ἐκτραπῇ) is variously rendered "to turn out," "to twist," and "to put out of joint." Twisted and confused teaching, imprudent conduct, and the habit of indecision, the writer says, "get the lame turned out of the way" (aorist tense). Straightforwardness and spiritual fervor furnish the greatest aid to stragglers. But the word *ektrapei* is also a technical medical term for a dislocated joint; hence the marginal reading, "be not put out of joint." The words "but rather let it be healed" then follow naturally.

HOLINESS IN RELATION TO THE CHURCH

The writer, having given special instructions concerning the mutual care of individuals within the Church, now turns to consider the Church as a corporate body and its wider influence upon the world. This he does by means of two imperatives which serve as a sort of preamble to the instructions and warnings which are to follow.

Sanctification as the Conservative Principle of the Church. "Follow peace with all men, and holiness, without which no man shall see the Lord" (12: 14). This verse expresses both the aim of the Church and its limitations in relation to the world. The word *diokete* (διώκετε), "follow," carries with it not only a desire for peace but the willingness to go far to obtain it; and the word *hagiasmon* (ἁγιασμόν), "sanctification," is an implied warning that we are not to seek peace to the extent of compromising the "sanctification" without which no man shall see the Lord. Thus Westcott says, "The Christian seeks peace with all alike, but he seeks holiness also, and this cannot be sacrificed for that."

The word "follow" is sometimes interpreted to mean the pursuit of a flying goal, hence the seeking of peace which can never be found and the pursuit of holiness which can never be realized. Nothing is further from the truth. The word has reference to a course of action to be followed or a pattern of life to be realized, and this with all diligence. While the word "all" is inclusive of men everywhere, the word *hagiasmon* seems to narrow down the meaning to the "sanctified," especially since the writer avoids the use of the preposition *sun* (σύν), "with," and uses the word *meta* (μετὰ), "along with." The words would then mean that, along with all other Christians, they were to seek that peace and security which come from being fully devoted to God.

The word for "holiness" is *hagiasmon* (ἁγιασμόν) and expresses an action, which together with the article *ton* (τὸν) means "the sanctification," and is so translated in the American Standard Version. As justification is an act which results in peace, so sanctification is an act which introduces a state of holiness. The word *hagiasmos* (ἁγιασμὸς), indicating as it does an act rather than a state or quality, differs in this from the two other forms: *hagiotes* (ἁγιότης), "an agent or source of holiness" (verse 12); and *hagiosune* (ἁγιωσύνη), the quality, state, or condition of holiness resulting from the act of sanctification. The meaning of the writer is therefore that, as much as in us lies, we are to live in peace with all men; and in relation to God, our lives must conform to, and participate in, that holiness wrought within us by the act of sanctification.

The Necessity of Purity in the Church. "Looking diligently lest any man fail of the grace of God; lest any root of bitterness springing up trouble you, and thereby many be defiled" (12: 15). The word for "looking diligently" is *episkopountes* (ἐπισκοποῦντες), from which we have the word "bishop" or "overseer," and is here used in the general sense of a brotherly and continuous care for one another. Two dangers to be guarded against are mentioned: (1) The danger to the individual Christian, "lest any man fail of the grace of God." The word *husteron* (ὑστερῶν) with *apo* (ἀπὸ), "from," cannot mean "falling short of" in the sense of "failing to attain," but "falling short from a thing once attained" (Vaughan). Westcott takes the same position in regard to the use of the preposition *apo* with the participle, the latter "describing a continuous state and not a single defection." Diligent care is therefore urged upon the Church to watch carefully lest a single individual who had received the grace of God should fall away from it. Dr. Adam Clarke thinks that this means an apostasy from Christianity to Judaism. (2) The danger of others' being defiled, "lest any root of bitterness springing up trouble you, and thereby many be defiled." Here the sin of the heart, not having been cleansed, is seen manifesting itself in the lives of those who would bring in alienation, strife, and confusion. The writer probably has in mind an allusion to Deut. 29:18, where it is said, "Lest there should be among you man, or woman, or family, or tribe, whose heart turneth away this day from the Lord our God, to go and serve the gods of these nations; lest there should be among you a root that beareth gall and wormwood." Against such roots of bitterness the Church is to guard itself with all diligence. The warning is, "Resist sin in its very beginnings."

The Danger of the Commonplace. "Lest there be any fornicator, or profane person, as Esau, who for one morsel of meat sold his birthright. For ye know how that afterward, when he would have inherited the blessing, he was rejected: for he found no place of repentance, though he sought it carefully with tears" (12:16-17). The word *bebelos* (βέβηλος), "profane," means literally a path "open to tread," as over against a way "sacred to God." The word "profane" as used here means the counting of holy things as common or irreligious. The word *pornos* (πόρνος), "fornicator," by this same definition, means one who violates the sacredness of the marriage relation, and so becomes a symbol of spiritual unfaithfulness to God. Since the writer has just spoken of a "root of bitterness," it is quite probable that he had in mind the case of Reuben (Gen. 35:22), who was later deprived of his birthright in favor of Levi and Judah, his younger brothers.

The use of the word "or" makes it clear that Esau was not a fornicator in the physical sense, but only in the spiritual sense of adultery toward the nation's covenant-keeping God. He was profane in the sense of failing to justly appreciate sacred things. He sought nothing but savory food to satisfy a physical appetite; and his sin lay in this, that he set sensual gratification over against the spiritual blessings of the covenant, and

chose the former rather than the latter. Later he realized
his loss—and how great a loss it was! His birthright,
—better, "rights of his birth"—was: (1) he was to be
the ruler of the household; (2) he was to be the family
priest; and (3) he was to receive a double portion of
his father's estate. But greater than all these was the
Abrahamic blessing, the blood stream through which
the Messiah should come. All these blessings Esau sold
for one morsel of bread. Later he bitterly repented and
sought to have the inheritance restored, but too late;
it had already been bestowed upon another. There are
some decisions in life the consequences of which are
irrevocable. The word for "sold" is apedoto (ἀπέδοτο
or ἀπέδετο), and being used in the second aorist middle,
indicates that what was sold was actually his. He was
neither a pretender nor deceived. The blame rested
solely upon him. The attitude of irresponsibility which
Esau assumed made it clear that he was both unworthy
and incapable of fulfilling the trust reposed in him, and
therefore God rejected him. This text, like that of
Rom. 9: 10-13, has no reference whatever to future salvation. Whether Esau was saved or lost is not the matter
under discussion, but only whether or not he was fitted
for the position he had inherited.

FINAL CONTRAST OF THE TWO DISPENSATIONS

This section (12: 18-24) is the grand finale to the
series of exhortations intended to hold Christians fast to
their confession. It is presented in the form of a contrast between the two dispensations, set in sharp relief
to better stress the advantages of the gospel era. The
passage is written in masterly Greek, and is rich in spiritual meaning. The nouns are used without the article
"the" and thereby express the quality of being, although
used in a descriptive manner. It is not our purpose to
deal at length with this section, but to endeavor by
means of the bold and vigorous contrasts to set forth
the glories of the New Testament dispensation. Both
Delitzsch and Bengel note that there are seven items

mentioned in each of these descriptions. These may be
set over against each other as follows:

Mount Sinai

1. A material mountain
2. "Burned with fire" (threatenings)
3. "Blackness" (confusion)
4. "Darkness" (hopelessness)
5. "Tempest" (unrest)
6. "Sound of a trumpet" (call to assembly)
7. "Voice of words" (giving of the law)

Mount Sion

1. "The heavenly Jerusalem"
2. "Innumerable company of angels"
3. "General assembly and church of the first-born"
4. God the Father: "Judge of all"
5. "Spirits of just men made perfect"
6. "Jesus the mediator of the new covenant"
7. "The blood of sprinkling"

The Old Testament Dispensation. Here the inaccessible nature of God is presented and His flaming
holiness described in terms of earthly phenomena. As indicated, the complete absence of the article before any
of these terms is clear evidence that they are intended
to be general, and are enumerated, not because of the
particular meaning of each, but because they all agree
in setting forth the awe-fulness of the presence of God.
This section (12:18-21) indicates also by these symbols
the subjective experience of those under the law.

1. "For ye are not come unto the mount that might
be touched." Here the present participle is used, indicating the possibility of the mountain's being touched,
although at this time there were severe restrictions
against approach. It is evident that the writer refers
to Mount Sinai, although this is not mentioned; and the
scene to which he refers is fully described in Exodus 12
and Deuteronomy 4. "It came to pass on the third day
in the morning, that there were thunders and lightnings,

and a thick cloud upon the mount, and the voice of the trumpet exceeding loud . . . And mount Sinai was altogether on a smoke, because the Lord descended upon it in fire: and the smoke thereof ascended as the smoke of a furnace, and the whole mount quaked greatly" (Exod. 19: 16, 18).

2. "And that burned with fire"—literally, "a fire having been enkindled"—is expressed by the perfect passive participle, indicating that the fire in the past burned only for a certain length of time; and while the mount was but an earthly mass of rock, the fire was unearthly, and marked the descent of God. It is evident also that the "thunders and lightnings" are to be included here as the threatenings which formed the sanctions of a broken law. "In that momentous day," says Cowles, "when all Israel . . . stood there in front of its vast wall of rugged rock and frowning precipice, it burned with fire enwrapped in blackness and darkness and tempest—as if a thousand thunder-clouds were condensed into one, and that one begirt this awful mountain in its folds—terrible blackness broken only by the flashes of lightning; and the perpetual roar of the tempest only by the more terrific trumpet-blast and the more awful voice of the Almighty, pronouncing the words of His fiery law. The men who stood there, appalled by that voice never so heard by mortal ears before, besought that they might not hear it more" (COWLES, *Epistle to the Hebrews*, p. 134).

3. "Nor unto blackness." The word for blackness is *gnophoi* (γνόφῳ), from *nephos* (νέφος), a "cloud"; the blackness of a storm cloud, illuminated only by the zigzag flashes of lightning, and symbolical of the confusion of a sinner under the demands of the law.

4. "And darkness"—*skotoi* (σκότῳ or ζοφῳ), a stronger term. It is an impenetrable pall of darkness, the hopelessness of salvation by the law.

5. "And tempest"—*thuellei* (θυέλλη), "to rush," hence a tempest of hurricane, which marks the unrest of the sinner in his striving against the swirling currents

of sin. The mount is material, but the rigor of the elements about it takes on the appearance of unearthliness.

6. "And the sound of a trumpet." These words are quoted from Exod. 19: 16, where it is said to be "the voice of the trumpet exceeding loud." This blast of the trumpet was above the roar of the tempest, which caused all the people in the camp to tremble. It was the call to all Israel, assembled on the great plain of *Er Rahab*, stretching out to the north of Sinai, and symbolical of the final assembling of all people before the great judgment throne of God.

7. "And the voice of words." This quotation is from Deut. 4: 12-13. "And the Lord spoke unto you out of the midst of the fire: ye heard the voice of the words, but saw no similitude; only ye heard a voice. And he declared unto you the covenant, which he commanded you to perform, even ten commandments; and he wrote them upon two tables of stone." As the sound of the trumpet was a call to assemble for judgment, so the voice of words will last be heard in the final sentence—either of reward or of punishment.

Thus it is that every feature of this scene was intended to impress the people with a sense of holy awe and profound reverence. Words such as these, piled up dramatically to express one of the holiest and most terrifying scenes recorded in all history, could but implant deep in the hearts of those people a sense of reverence for the holiness of God, and the necessity of obedience to the commandments spoken audibly from heaven.

The writer then hastens to give us an account of the effects of this terrifying scene. In a parenthetical expression he explains, "For they could not endure that which was commanded, And if so much as a beast touch the mountain, it shall be stoned, or thrust through with a dart" (12: 20). It was the majesty and awe of the Divine Presence that led them to entreat "that the word should not be spoken to them any more"; so also it was the holiness of God that prevented the approach of any unclean thing, even a beast. But the climax is found in the words, "And so terrible was the sight, that Moses said, I exceedingly fear and quake" (12:21). The word for "sight" is "appearance" ("apparition," Matt. 14:25), and means that to Moses all was made apparent to the senses. That Moses himself, the chosen servant of God, could not approach without fear and trembling gives us the highest and most vivid impression of the terror connected with the giving of the law.

The New Testament Dispensation. The transition from an atmosphere of chaos and terror to that of confidence and peace marks clearly the change of dispensations—and what an impressive change it is! "But ye are come unto mount Sion, and unto the city of the living God, the heavenly Jerusalem," and also to all the glorious things which the writer now sets before us in wondrous array. The word *proseleluthate* (προσεληλύθατε), "ye are come," is the writer's favorite term for the approach to God in worship, and being in the perfect tense, has the force of "ye are come and still remain." The recognition of this fact gives color to the entire section; for the words are sometimes used as future, and therefore as applying solely to the heavenly state. The true meaning is that of Christian worshipers on this earth, who, having been redeemed by Christ, now approach God in spiritual worship. But the connection between the present world and the world above us is very close; for Christ on the throne of God ministers the life of heaven to His people on earth through the gift of the Holy Spirit. The earnest of our inheritance which we possess here is the same as that which we shall enjoy in heaven, only more abundantly. Heaven and earth are always close together in true spiritual worship.

1. "But ye are come unto mount Sion, and unto the city of the living God, the heavenly Jerusalem." It is a mistake to separate these two statements, for the writer says that they are come to Sion, on which is the holy city. Here Mount Sinai and Mount Sion are set in sharp contrast. (1) Sinai was in the wilderness with its barrenness and desert storms; Sion was in the promised

land of Canaan, fertile, fruitful, and watered from heaven. (2) God visited Sinai for only a brief season; He is said to dwell in Sion forever. (3) Sinai was a mount of terror and fear; Sion, a habitation of peace. (4) Sinai, of massive rock and steep precipices, stood storm-crowned, alone; Sion was crowned with the city of the living God, the heavenly Jerusalem, where God manifested himself to His people. (5) God gave the law from Sinai; He proclaimed the gospel from Sion. (6) Israel came trembling with fear to a physical mountain; Christians come with confidence to a spiritual mountain, for Sion is the foundation of a spiritual economy, a new and eternal order.

2. "And to an innumerable company of angels." Here the forked streaks of lightning which played with threatening about Mount Sinai are contrasted with the myriad of angels on Mount Sion, each angel a ministering spirit. The word for "general assembly" is *panegurei* (πανηγύρει), the Greek word for a festal occasion. The Authorized Version has attached this word to the clause following, making it read, "the general assembly and church of the firstborn"; but the ancients attached it to the present clause, as do both the Syriac and Latin versions, and some of the Greek manuscripts. The clause then reads, "festal assembly of angels." Some take the word "myriad" as applying to both clauses, an innumerable host of angels and the Church of the First-born, mingling in festal occasion. To the writer, this glorious assembly was a sublime scene, which he would impress vividly upon his Hebrew brethren. What could be more encouraging to a discouraged and persecuted people than the realities of the heavenly world which the gospel offered them—not indeed an empty solitude, but the city of the living God, peopled with myriads of ministering spirits and inhabited by the host of the redeemed who had finished their course and entered through the gates into the eternal city! But the angels of God are concerned not only with those "who have crossed the flood" but with the Church on earth as well. They rejoice over every repenting sinner, minister to the heirs

of salvation, and have already tuned their harps for
the universal song of redemption—"Unto him that hath
loved us, and washed us from our sins in his own blood
. . . to him be glory and dominion for ever and ever.
Amen" (Rev. 1: 5-6).

3. "To the general assembly and church of the
firstborn, which are written in heaven." Christ is the
"firstborn" from the dead (Col. 1: 18; Rev. 1: 5), and
those who bear His image are likewise termed "first-
born" and heirs of the promise. This is the only place
where this term is used with reference to believers, and
as such is to be understood in the sense of rank, rather
than precedence in time. This is the Church on earth,
but its members are enrolled in heaven, and this enroll-
ment does away with all the confusion and uncertainty
engendered at Sinai. The term registered carries with
it the privileges of citizenship, and none may enter the
heavenly Jerusalem whose names are not written in
the Lamb's book of life (Rev. 21: 27).

4. "And to God the Judge of all." The Greek order
is "to the Judge, the God of all." Instead of the deep
darkness and hopelessness occasioned by the giving of
the law at Sinai, those of "the church of the firstborn"
have been "begotten . . . again unto a lively hope by the
resurrection of Jesus Christ from the dead" (I Pet. 1: 3).
No longer do His people stand trembling before the
Judge of the whole earth; but through the redemptive
work of Christ they have become the sons of God, and
dwell securely in the home of the Judge, their Father.

5. "And to the spirits of just men made perfect."
The word for "spirits" is pneumasin (πνεύμασιν) and
may mean either embodied or disembodied spirits; and
the word for "just" is the familiar dikaion (δικαίων),
"righteous." This clause therefore may apply to either
the present or the future state of man, and in a true
sense does apply to both. Dr. Adam Clarke applies it
to the present and says that it means "those who are
justified by the blood and sanctified by the Spirit of
Christ." Plummer points out that the word teteleio-
menon (τετελειωμένων) is added, "not in the sense of

the departed saints but to suggest the work of Christ which included the righteous." It is a reference to the one offering of Christ by which "he hath perfected for ever them that are sanctified" (10:14). But there is a perfection of the saints in heaven—not now from sin, but from all the consequences of sin. They are no longer tempest-tossed; they rest from their labors, perfected in bliss before the throne of God. They have joined the holy fellowship of patriarchs and prophets, and the redeemed of all the ages—all "the pure in heart," whose blessedness it is to "see God."

The Seventh and Final Warning

We come now to the final and most fearful of all the warnings found in this Epistle, the warning against apostasy. From the first warning onward we have noted the rapid and steep decline, and with each step downward the penalty has been intensified. The writer begins this warning with an admonitory section, and follows with a description of the severe judgments to be pronounced against unbelievers in the last time.

The Admonitory Section. "See that ye refuse not him that speaketh. For if they escaped not who refused him that spake on earth, much more shall not we escape, if we turn away from him that speaketh from heaven" (12:25). The reference to the severity of the law of Moses forms the ground for the admonition (10:26-31). The word for "speaketh" is *chrematizonta* (χρηματί-ζοντα) and is the word commonly used for a divine communication of any kind. The writer has just said that the blood of Christ speaks better things than that of Abel, and follows with the same words, thus indicating that the blood of Christ is a message from heaven. The writer therefore admonishes his readers not to think that, because God speaks through the grace of Christ, He will hold them less responsible than those who violate the law. "For if they escaped not"—a conditional clause of fact; they did not escape—"much more shall not we escape," (emphatic, ἡμεῖς) "if we turn away from him that speaketh from heaven." For those who reject the offer of divine love are deserving of a greater penalty than those who transgress the commandments of the law.

The Warning Against Apostasy. The words "if we turn away from him that speaketh from heaven" imply a final rejection of Christ, the sin of apostasy. This is shown by the writer's use of the participle. Thus in 6: 6 we have the word *parapesontas* (παραπεσόντας), "having fallen away"—a "second aorist active participle, in which the catalogue of privileges was closed" (Westcott). The word concerning the Israelites in this passage is *paraitesamenoi* (παραιτησάμενοι), another aorist participle, meaning "refused and continuing to refuse." In order to closely connect this refusal of the Israelites to obey God, the writer uses the same root word in his admonition—*paraitesesthe* (παραιτήσησθε), aorist conjunctive passive, "see that ye refuse not him that speaketh." The final participle in this connection is *apostrephomenoi* (ἀποστρεφόμενοι), present participle middle, "if we turn ourselves away from, and continue in this state of rejection." This "turning away from" is not that of inadvertently falling into sin, but one of deliberate and continuous rejection of God. The necessity of this warning is further accentuated by the writer's use of the word "we" in a specific and emphatic form— "we," that is, "those of us who are turning away," an indication that some were turning back to Judaism with its forms and shadows. But not only did this temptation come to the Hebrews; it still exists in the attractions and allurements of the world.

The Day of Judgment. "Whose voice then shook the earth: but now he hath promised, saying, Yet once more I shake not the earth only, but also heaven. And this word, Yet once more, signifieth the removing of those things that are shaken, as of things that are made, that those things which cannot be shaken may remain" (12: 26-27). The writer refers to the awe-inspiring scene at Sinai, when the mountain trembled as in an earthquake, and its summit burned with the fire of the Divine Presence. But the promise is that the voice of God will cause not only the earth to be shaken again, but heaven also; and the writer hastens to explain that this means the removing of those things which can be shaken, that only the abiding and eternal things may remain.

The foregoing texts are closely related, if not indeed based upon St. Paul's revelation of the Lord Jesus (II Thess. 1: 7-10) and St. Peter's "day of the Lord" (II Pet. 3: 10-13). The latter text reads, "But the day of the Lord will come as a thief in the night; in the which the heavens shall pass away with a great noise, and the elements shall melt with fervent heat, the earth also and the works that are therein shall be burned up." And again, "Looking for and hasting unto the coming of the day of God, wherein the heavens being on fire shall be dissolved, and the elements shall melt with fervent heat." These verses are generally held by most forms of millennialism to mark the great conflagration which occurs at the end of the world. It is the voice of God that removes everything that can be shaken; this is the day which marks the consummation of all things temporal and ushers in the new and eternal order.

The key to these verses is found in the word translated "dissolve." The words *luomenon* (λυομένων), verse 11, and *luthesontai* (λυθήσονται), verse 12, are both from the root word *luo* (λύω), "to loose." It is the same word which Jesus used when He sent the disciples for the colt and said, "Loose him," and bring him to Me. The word "dissolve," therefore, does not mean the annihilation of the earth and of heaven; it means to loose them, to remove them from the bondage under which the whole creation groans and travails, and then through a great cataclysmic process to allow them to emerge from their present and changing state into a new and eternal order. Thus Isaiah says, "Behold, I create new heavens and a new earth: and the former shall not be remembered, nor come into mind" (Isa. 65: 17). From the context, many have thought that this refers to the removal of the curse and the introduction of the mil-lennial period, that transitional period in which the curse is removed as the final stage in the temporal order. For as Christ removes the curse of sin from man in this present world before his transition into the world to come, so also Christ, before His work is completed, must remove the curse from the earth before its transition from the temporal to the eternal order. But concerning the consummation of the temporal order of which the text under consideration speaks, both St. Peter, who looks for it, and St. John, who says, "I saw a new heaven and a new earth," regard it as an emergence, for each uses the word *kainos* (καινός), which means new in the sense of quality, and not *neos* (νέος), which means new in the sense of time, as never having existed before.

A sound eschatology must be based upon a sound Christology. Christ not only died *for* sin, but died also *unto* sin. He saves His people from sin in this world; but only through death and the resurrection does He lift them to a higher than the probationary state of Adam; for He lifts them to a plane beyond the possibility of sin, the plane of *everlasting* life. Now our natural bodies are material substances, earthy and corruptible, as much so as the ground upon which they tread. Is it not possible—rather should we say, is it not God's plan—to remove, through Christ, the curse from the earth with its groanings and travailings (Rom. 8: 22) before the close of the temporal order, and then at last to take this heaven and earth through a cataclysmic process comparable to the death and resurrection of the body, so that out of that baptism of fire there shall emerge an eternal order, a new heaven and a new earth, wherein dwelleth righteousness? Can any environment be proper for the glorified bodies of the saints other than the heavens and the earth likewise glorified? Has Christ not said of the present heavens and the earth that "they all shall wax old as doth a garment; and as a vesture shalt thou fold them up, and they shall be changed: but thou art the same, and thy years shall not fail" (1: 11-12)? What a glorious habitation that will be, in the new heaven and the new earth, when God shall again tabernacle with His people, and all the redeemed of all the ages shall be gathered together in that "better country," in the City of God!

The Immovable Kingdom and the Consuming Fire.

"Wherefore we receiving a kingdom which cannot be moved, let us have grace, whereby we may serve God acceptably with reverence and godly fear: for our God is a consuming fire" (12:28-29). The initial kingdom of God which we receive is that which is within us, a Kingdom of "righteousness, and peace, and joy in the Holy Ghost." It cannot be shaken because God has established it, and of the increase of His kingdom there shall be no end. "Who among us shall dwell with the devouring fire?" inquires Isaiah the prophet; "who among us shall dwell with everlasting burnings?" The devouring flame consumes all the dross of sin and leaves the pure gold of righteousness; and the "everlasting burnings" marks the flaming power of the indwelling Spirit of holiness that protects us from the very approach of sin. It is to such that the prophet says, "Thine eyes shall see the king in his beauty: they shall behold the land that is very far off"—and the ever-widening horizons of the soul shall to all eternity reveal the glory of the Lord and the excellency of His power.

The question is frequently asked, When we reach heaven, shall we still retain our freedom of will? And if so, is there not still the possibility of sin? The Bible tells us that "many shall be purified, made white, and tried"; and the trial is an integral part of our preparation for heaven. Thus as Jesus was perfected through suffering—not in character, but in His function as a Redeemer—so also we, having been delivered from sin, must yet through trial and suffering be prepared for our heavenly abode. It must be kept in mind that, while the purified heart is freed from the tendencies to sin, it is never while on probation delivered from the susceptibilities to sin—else temptation were impossible. When therefore in any trial or temptation a victory is won, we thereby strengthen a motive or group of motives to remain righteous, and exhaust a motive or group of motives which would lead us again into sin. This process continues through life, and by it we are said to be "established" by grace. If then it be possible through grace to remain true to God in an environment of temptation and amidst the allurements of Satan, it is easily understood that when we are removed to the "better country," where temptation and sin cannot come, we shall ever remain there by our own free choice, and that because we have exhausted every motive to leave and strengthened every motive to stay. Whether in Christ or in us, it is the underlying nature that determines the outward act.

CHAPTER XIII

OUTSIDE THE CAMP

The writer has practically completed his argument. He has considered Jesus as our great High Priest, and as the one sacrificial and vicarious Offering for sin; one thing more remains to be considered, the place of His offering—outside the gate. Previous to the inauguration of the old covenant, the "tent of meeting" was likewise outside the camp; but when the blood of the covenant had been sprinkled, the Tabernacle was built, and God dwelt in the holy of holies. So also because of the disobedience of His people under the law, the Blood of the new covenant was shed without the camp. But under the covenant of grace, we look forward to the time when God will again speak to His people with a great voice from heaven saying, "Behold, the tabernacle of God is with men, and he will dwell with them, and they shall be his people, and God himself shall be with them and be their God" (Rev. 21:3).

The scene of this chapter, therefore, is laid without the camp, and its exhortations are to a people who have rejected the world, and in turn been rejected by it. The specific duties mentioned here grow out of this new relation to God; although in the central portion the writer with fresh power again lifts into prominence the supreme purpose of the sacrifice of Jesus; and follows this with a series of obligations pertaining to and flowing from this one great sacrifice outside the gate. The benediction and personal salutations mark the close of this remarkable Epistle.

GENERAL ETHICAL PRINCIPLES

1. *Brotherly Love.* "Let brotherly love continue" (13:1). This virtue lies at the very basis of the Christian social structure. Failure here quickly leads to disintegration. This is especially true under the stress

of persecution and reproach; hence the repeated exhortations to watchfulness and the duty of caring for one
another. Brotherly love will keep the Church both
pure and strong.

2. *Hospitality.* "Be not forgetful to entertain strangers: for thereby some have entertained angels unawares" (13:2). Hospitality was considered a cardinal
virtue in early Oriental life. During the days of persecution, those in the Church who had suffered the loss
of their goods, and those who had been compelled to
flee for protection, were helplessly dependent upon their
Christian brethren. Hospitality thus became a moral
obligation. The writer by his suggestion that some had
entertained angels unawares (Gen. 18:1-8; Judg. 6:
11-24) thereby intimates that these guests may bring
more of spiritual blessing than of material aid received.

3. *Sympathy in Affliction.* "Remember them that
are in bonds, as bound with them; and them which
suffer adversity, as being yourselves also in the body"
(13:3). Here the brethren are exhorted to show the
same sympathy for those in prison as they themselves
would desire in like circumstances; and as to adversity,
they are to remember that they are still in the body and
liable to the same afflictions. Sympathy for the afflicted
is another basic condition of the Christian life.

4. *Chastity.* "Marriage is honourable in all, and
the bed undefiled: but whoremongers and adulterers
God will judge" (13:4). This brief but comprehensive
text makes clear that the race is responsible for the
sacredness of marriage, and for the fulfillment of its
God-given purpose; and furthermore holds that there
are severe judgments in store for its perversion or vio-
lation. The Greek text may be read either "honorable
is marriage," or "honorable let marriage be"; and thus
the text may apply both to those within and those without the marriage relation. The writer evidently intends
to convey a warning against the depreciation of marriage by immorality; and perhaps also a warning against
a certain class of Gnostics who, because of their ascetic

tendencies, held marriage in low esteem or forbade it altogether (I Tim. 4:3). The chief emphasis appears to be upon the necessity for chastity. The writer would have all understand how severe God's judgments are against those who violate His holy ordinance, judgments that frequently occur in this life as well as in the world to come.

5. *Covetousness or Contentment.* "Let your conversation be without covetousness; and be content with such things as ye have: for he hath said, I will never leave thee, nor forsake thee. So that we may boldly say, The Lord is my helper, and I will not fear what man shall do unto me" (13:5-6). As in the Decalogue the sixth commandment against adultery is followed by the seventh against covetousness, so also the writer, having warned against fornication and adultery, follows with a warning against avarice and covetousness. The scriptural use of the word "conversation" is much broader than its present limitations to colloquial discourse. The Greek word is *tropos* (τρόπος) and means "disposition," or as the margin has it, a "turn of mind." This disposition or "turn of mind" the writer tells us must be free from the money-loving spirit, and likewise free from an unwholesome desire for things beyond one's ability to acquire and maintain. Covetousness in its simplest form is an inordinate desire for more, and this lies at the basis of the world's discontent. Covetousness brings its own punishment, for the covetous heart is cursed with discontent, and the discontented mind is cursed with covetousness. Hence the exhortation is, "Be content with such things as ye have." St. Paul calls covetousness idolatry; and we, like him, must learn, in whatever state we are, therewith to be content.

The ground of our contentment is to be found in the promises of God. "For He himself has said"—perfect tense, i.e., what He has said still stands; "in no wise will I leave you"—the word *ano* (ἀνῶ) means to loosen the grasp, and hence "I will never let go of you"; "nor forsake you"—from *egkatalipo* (ἐγκαταλίπω), to leave alone in a contest or a place of suffering; hence, "I will never abandon you." In times of loss, sickness, persecution, or other emergencies of life, God has assured us that He will never loosen His grasp upon us in times of struggle or abandon us in times of poverty or pain. What then is to be our response? We are to "boldly say, The Lord is my helper, and I will not fear what man shall do unto me."

6. *Be Mindful of Your Teachers.* "Remember them which have the rule over you, who have spoken unto you the word of God: whose faith follow, considering the end of their conversation" (13:7). The word for "remember" is *mnemoneuete* (μνημονεύετε) and is translated "be mindful of" in 11:15. These persons, here mentioned three times as rulers (13:7, 17, 24), were their teachers, and by most commentators are regarded as the deceased apostolic missionaries who first spoke the Word of God to them. That they were deceased is argued from the use of the word "spake" in the past tense, and also from the expression "the end of their conversation." Here the word for "end" is *ekbasin* (ἔκβασιν) or "outgoing," and is interpreted to mean the end of their lives or triumphant deaths. But this word does not necessarily mean martyrdom, or even death. It has also the sense of fruit produced out of the soil, and therefore might equally apply to the character and fruitfulness of their present leaders, of whom they were to be "mindful" or thoughtful. However the context seems to indicate that the reference is to their former leaders who had died in the faith. Westcott thinks that it refers to some scene of martyrdom in which the triumphant faith of their leaders was clearly shown. The writer therefore exhorts

This boldness of faith is well illustrated in the experience of John Chrysostom, the preacher with the "golden mouth," who was brought before the emperor, who said, "I will banish thee." He replied, "Thou canst not, for the world is my Father's house." Then said the emperor, "I will kill thee." Again the preacher replied, "That is not in thy power, for my life is hid with Christ in God." The emperor threatened, "I will deprive thee of all that thou possessest." Chrysostom replied, "That too is impossible, for my treasure is in heaven, and my riches are within me." "I will separate thee from all thy companions, and thou shalt not have one friend left." The preacher replied, "Neither canst thou do that, for my Divine Friend will never leave me. I defy thee, proud emperor; thou canst do me no harm at all."

his readers to cherish the memory of those noble and inspiring teachers of the past, whose lives were fully devoted to the proclamation of the gospel, and to consider
attentively their fortitude and courage as they faced
the reproaches of their friends and the persecutions of
their enemies. Such faith, he says, is worthy of imita-
tion—a faith so strong that, like that of their Lord, it
was obedient even unto death.

7. *The Unchangeable Christ.* "Jesus Christ the same
yesterday, and to day, and for ever" (13: 8). This verse
is added without any connectives, and therefore stands
out in a most effective manner. A transliteration in the
Greek order would read, "Jesus Christ, yesterday and
today, the same and to the ages [forever]." The different
versions of our English Bible represent different interpretations of this text. The Authorized Version does
not use the word "is," and separates this verse from
the preceding one by a colon only, making it appear that
the translators regarded the words "Jesus Christ" as in
apposition with the word "end"; that is, Christ is regarded as the "end of their conversation." The Revised
Version reads, "Jesus Christ is the same yesterday and
today and forever." The addition of the word "is" makes
the verse stand out more independently and interprets
the expression "the end of their conversation" to mean
"the close of their godly lives." The word "yesterday"
is here used in a limited historical sense, as referring to
the time when the gospel was first preached to their
former leaders, and not in the equally true but broader
sense of the eternal Logos, or pre-existent and "only
begotten Son."

This is one of the great texts of the Bible, and taken
in its broader sense furnishes a test for a true Christology. As the Logos, the Second Person of the adorable
Trinity, Christ is eternal and existed originally in the
form of God (Phil. 2: 6); and as such in the infinite
depths of sacrificial love was even then "the Lamb slain
from the foundation of the world" (Rev. 13: 8); He took
the form of man (Phil. 2: 7), assuming a human nature
into indissoluble union with His divine nature, and thus

became the God-Man—truly God and truly man in one
Person; He was crucified for our sins and passed into
the realm of the dead, from which He arose on the third
day; He ascended into heaven and today sits at the right
hand of God as our High Priest, as He did yesterday,
and will throughout all eternity. Jesus Christ cannot be
anything but the "same." The question in the mind of
the writer is, Will the faith of his readers likewise remain
the same?

8. *Different and Strange Doctrines.* "Be not carried about with divers and strange doctrines" (13: 9*a*).
The unchangeableness of Christ has been presented as
a test by which to discover and expose error. "What
think ye of Christ? whose son is he?" was the test question proposed by our Lord himself to the Pharisees
(Matt. 22: 42). A changeless Christ necessitates a
changeless doctrine; for as the living Christ He is the
substance of all true teaching. St. Paul was determined
"not to know any thing among you, save Jesus Christ,
and him crucified" (I Cor. 2: 2). The word "divers" is
from *poikilais* (ποικίλαις) and means "many-colored" or
variegated; and "strange" is *xenais* (ξέναις), a stranger
or foreigner. Hence the admonition not to be led aside
from the truth by these "many-colored" doctrines, for
truth is one and unchangeable; and to beware of that
which is alien and odd, which is like strangers and
foreigners who do not present the old, familiar faces but
are suspicious from the very start.

9. *The Established Heart.* "For it is a good thing
that the heart be established with grace; not with meats,
which have not profited them that have been occupied
therein" (13: 9*b*). There were some among the Hebrew
Christians who still clung to the old Temple ritual, some
of whom sought to secure obedience to the Jewish laws
in regard to the eating or abstaining from meats. The
eating of these meats was of course closely connected
with the sacrifices, and therefore a part of the old legal
economy. The body of Christians had not yet been led
aside to these Jewish practices, but many appeared to
be wavering in their position. The writer therefore

seeks to establish their hearts in the Christian position, which will result not only in settled convictions but strength to defend and propagate them. This firmness is to be found in divine grace, not in sacrificial meats. By the term "meats" the writer refers to the whole system of external observances, and warns that no outward ritualistic performances can sustain the inner spiritual life. This comes by grace, and is wrought in us by Christ through the Spirit. It is grace alone that establishes the heart and makes it firm in the Christian way.

10. *"We Have an Altar."* "We have an altar, whereof they have no right to eat which serve the tabernacle. For the bodies of those beasts, whose blood is brought into the sanctuary by the high priest for sin, are burned without the camp" (13: 10-11). Here we have a statement of privilege rather than an exhortation to duty. Furthermore, the text is apologetic in the sense that it is the writer's defense against a supposed deficiency on the part of Christians. Pagans and Jews alike reproached the Christians for their lack of an elaborate cultus, with temple and altars, and an imposing ritual. They were also reproached for not identifying themselves with any earthly polity; and it was this that led Tacitus to say that they were obsessed by "hatred for the human race." Thus the unknown author of the Epistle to Diognetus writes, "The Christians inhabit their own countries, but only as sojourners. . . . Every foreign country is a fatherland to them, and every fatherland is a foreign country."

The writer counters these objections by saying, "We have an altar, whereof they have no right to eat which serve the tabernacle." It is evident however that the writer is more concerned with the sacrifice upon the altar than with the nature and location of the altar itself. This leads him to return again to the ritual of the great Day of Atonement. While the blood of the slain beasts was brought into the sanctuary by the high priest for sin, the bodies of those beasts, being by imputation regarded as sinful, were burned without the camp. Of these the priests could not eat; but Christians may partake of their Sin Offering, which is Christ; and in partaking they have life through His death, and spiritual sustenance through His resurrection and gift of the Holy Spirit. At the Christians' altar there is but one sacrifice for sin, the Blood of the atonement; and one means of sustenance, the indwelling of Christ through the Spirit. Thus there is fully accomplished by the one sacrifice that likeness to Christ and that communion with the Father which could not be attained by those occupied with the meats of the Jewish system. While previously the writer has shown that the Christian does not need the Jewish sacrifices, here it is made clear that he should give them up. This entire section is a protest against mixing spiritual religion with what is material and sensuous.

The Supreme Purpose of Christ's Sacrifice

We have now reached the climax of the entire Epistle, that is, the high and sacred purpose of Jesus to sanctify the people with His own blood; and for this He suffered without the gate. This great theme the writer has developed under various aspects, but with only one thought in mind—the power of Jesus to sanctify, and the actual accomplishment of this purpose through the baptism with the Holy Spirit. In the eloquent words of Dr. Phineas F. Bresee, this baptism "is the crowning glory of the work of the soul's salvation. All that went before it was preparatory to it. Did prophets speak and write; did sacrifices burn; were offerings made; did martyrs die; did Jesus lay aside His glory; did He teach and pray and stretch out His hands on the cross; did He rise from the dead and ascend into heaven; is He at the right hand of God; it was all preparatory to this baptism. Men are convinced of sin, born again and made new creatures that they may be baptized with the Holy Ghost. This work completes the soul's salvation."

The entire Levitical system has been laid under tribute to express the riches of God's grace under the new covenant provisions. Here are the altar and its

sacrifices, the priesthood with its sprinklings and washings, the ceremonies of presentation and dedication, the
hallowing and consecration, the sealing and anointing,
the fasts and the feasts—all these find their culmination
in the one great act of sanctification, by which Christ
purifies the hearts of the people and takes up His abode
within them through the Holy Spirit. The doctrine and
experience of entire sanctification, therefore, occupies
no obscure place among the important truths of the Word
of God. It has a definite and distinct place in the great
organism of Christian truth. Luminous as it is with
divine glory, and conspicuous on every page of divine
inspiration, it is the vital and essential element in man's
salvation; for it is the unchangeable decree of God that
without holiness no man shall see the Lord.

The Supreme Work of Sanctification. "Wherefore
Jesus also, that he might sanctify the people with his
own blood, suffered without the gate" (13: 12). The
word "wherefore" connects this verse with the preceding, making clear the fact that, although the bodies of
the beasts which were slain for the sin offering were
burned without the camp, yet their blood was offered on
the altar as an atonement for sin; even so, that Jesus
suffered without the camp is no argument against the
atoning, sanctifying virtue of His blood. The word for
"sanctify" is the familiar verb *hagiasei* (ἁγιάσῃ), here
found in the first aorist, active, subjunctive, and can
mean only the act of sanctification—that supreme redemptive act by which Christ with His own blood makes
His people holy in heart and life.

The experience of entire sanctification by which the
soul enters in upon a state of personal holiness is a work
of grace so solemn and comprehensive that it must be
approached with the deepest and most profound reverence. To be cleansed from sin and enter into the presence of God within the holy of holies is so awe-inspiring
that, like Moses before the burning bush, we stand with
bowed head and unsandaled feet, "lost in wonder, love,
and praise." "It is evident that the baptism with the
Holy Ghost," says Dr. Phineas F. Bresee, "is the con-

veyance into men and through men, of the 'all-power' of Jesus Christ,—the revelation of Him in the soul"; and again, "The baptism with the Holy Ghost is the baptism with God. It is the burning up of the chaff, but it is also the revelation in us, and the manifestation to us of divine personality, filling our being." Dr. E. F. Walker says, "Perfect purity plus perfect love in the heart by the efficiency of Christ and the power of the indwelling Spirit equals personal sanctification."

The official creedal statement to which we subscribe concerning this important subject is this: "We believe that entire sanctification is that act of God, subsequent to regeneration, by which believers are made free from original sin, or depravity, and brought into a state of entire devotement to God, and the holy obedience of love made perfect. It is wrought by the baptism with the Holy Spirit, and comprehends in one experience the cleansing of the heart from sin and the abiding, indwelling presence of the Holy Spirit, empowering the believer for life and service. Entire sanctification is provided by the blood of Jesus, is wrought instantaneously by faith, preceded by entire consecration; and to this work and state of grace the Holy Spirit bears witness. This experience is also known by various terms representing its different phases, such as 'Christian Perfection,' 'Perfect Love,' 'Heart Purity,' 'The Baptism with the Holy Spirit,' 'The Fullness of the Blessing,' and 'Christian Holiness' " ("Articles of Faith," Art. X).

Over against this scriptural teaching concerning personal holiness as a change wrought in the nature of the soul, thus completing the work of salvation from sin, is a perverted but popular theory of imputation—perverted because untrue both to the Scriptures and to human experience; popular, because it is a plea for sin remaining in the heart. This theory holds that holiness is not imparted to us by the Spirit, but is merely imputed to us, so that by our "standing" we are accounted holy, but as to our "state" or condition we are still in sin. To use Dr. Samuel Chadwick's pertinent phrase, it holds that "God makes man holy by exemption, instead of righteousness." But Christ came, not to exempt us from righteousness, but that "the righteousness of the law might be fulfilled in us, who walk not after the flesh, but after the Spirit" (Rom. 8:4). There is a fine line of distinction between the use of the expression "the righteousness of Christ" imputed to us to cover our sin but not to remove it and "the righteousness of Christ" imparted to us, thus taking away our sin and making us righteous like himself. It is this fine line that marks saving truth from radical error. For this reason Mr. Wesley used these words sparingly. (Cf. note.)

Some sincere but grossly mistaken teachers overlook the simple fact that the Bible says, "The blood of Jesus Christ his Son cleanseth *us* from all sin"; and this word "us" indicates a personal cleansing. They fail to understand the Bible when it says, "Be *ye* holy; for I am holy" (I Pet. 1:16), which can mean only that the quality of being in God which we call holiness must exist in us also. Otherwise the text has no meaning. Holiness as it exists in God, however, is absolute and underived; in us it is derived and relative. "You cannot therefore,

I am myself the more sparing in the use of it ("the righteousness of Christ") because it has been so frequently abused; and because the Antinomians use it at this day to justify the grossest abominations. And it is a great pity that those who love, who preach, and follow after holiness, should, under the notion of honoring Christ, give any countenance to those who continually make Him "the minister of sin," and so build on His righteousness as to live in such ungodliness and unrighteousness as is scarce named even among the heathens.—WESLEY, *Works*, VI, 102.

Scripture holiness is the image of God; the mind which was in Christ; the love of God and man; lowliness, gentleness, temperance, patience, chastity. And do you cooly affirm that this is only imputed to a believer, and that he has none at all of this holiness in him? . . . Nay, but a believer is really chaste and temperate. And if so, he is thus far holy in himself.—WESLEY, *Works*, VII, 22.

But how are we to reconcile this with that passage in the seventh chapter [of Revelation], "They have washed their robes and made them white in the blood of the Lamb"? Will they say, the righteousness of Christ was washed and made white in the blood of Christ? Away with such Antinomian jargon. Is not the plain meaning this: it was from the atoning blood, that the very righteousness of the saints derives its value and acceptableness with God? . . . Without the righteousness of Christ we could have no *claim* to glory; without holiness we could have no fitness for it. By the former we become members of Christ, children of God, and heirs of the kingdom of heaven. By the latter, "we are made meet to be partakers of the inheritance of the saints in light."—WESLEY, *Sermons*, II, 457.

deny," says Mr. Wesley, "that every believer has holiness in, though not from, himself; else you deny that he is holy at all; and if so, he cannot see the Lord."

Outside the Camp. "Let us go forth therefore unto him without the camp, bearing his reproach" (13:13). Capital punishment in the ancient world was always inflicted outside the city; hence Jesus was crucified outside the gate. The word "gate" is used as applying to a walled city, a great historic distance from the ancient camp of Israel; but the writer returns immediately in his thought to the days of the Tabernacle, and therefore in his exhortation uses the word "camp." It is said that Jesus "suffered" outside the gate in order to carry out more fully the analogy with the Day of Atonement. The sacrificial beast was slain at the altar, and only its dead body was burned outside the camp; but Jesus both suffered and died outside the city walls. The writer sees in this event a rich symbolism, which is not merely a denial of Judaism, but a positive call to unworldliness— a rich spiritual fellowship, free from material sacrifices; outside the world with its greed and selfishness, and outside that religion of empty forms which functions within it.

To the writer, the Temple represented the religion of the world; for the atonement was not made at its altar, but outside the gate on the Cross of Calvary. From the day of the Crucifixion, the Temple became a place of obsolete ceremonies; and they who remained there, or who returned from the Cross, must starve their souls on the husks of lifeless Temple ceremonies. The city in which the Temple stood represented the world—that social and political structure concerning which our Lord said of His people that, while living in the world, they were not "of the world." To the Hebrew Christians especially, going outside the camp meant excommunication from their accustomed place of worship, and the loss of citizenship in their city and country. But Abraham was also called out from his country and from his father's house; Moses led the Israelites out of Egypt because he esteemed "the reproach of Christ greater riches than the treasures in Egypt"; and St. Paul found his whole life outside the worldly system. To all who would be loyal to Christ the call still comes to go forth "unto him without the camp, bearing his reproach." But in that reproach they find the radiance of the Cross, which towers above the wrecks of time; and around the sublime head of Him who hung thereon gathers all the sacred story of redemption—redemption from sin in this life, and in the world to come, life everlasting.

The "City Which Hath Foundations." "For here have we no continuing city, but we seek one to come" (13:14). The admonition of the preceding verse is here explained more fully. There is no reason for hesitating to go outside the city gates or to bear the reproach of the Cross, for the present Jerusalem is only a symbol of the temporal nature of earthly things. We can be patient with all the losses and reproaches, for here in this world we have no abiding city, no place of certain rest and satisfaction. We are but wayfarers, here for only a brief time. We are seeking a city to come—one which has foundations, eternal, immutable. The reference is not only to Jerusalem; there is no abiding city here. Christians, having no such city, have therefore nothing to lose. The words "to come" are not to be understood as referring to a city not yet existent, for such is not the meaning of *mellousan* (μέλλουσαν). It means a city that is in existence now, and regarded as future with reference only to believers on earth. It is therefore not to be regarded as a mere hope, but as an eternal reality— "a city which hath foundations, whose builder and maker is God."

RELIGIOUS DUTIES

The writer has previously set forth certain general standards as the basic ethics of the Christian life; and having made his final presentation of the supreme work of Christ, that of sanctifying the people with His own blood, he now lifts into prominence certain specific religious obligations which pertain to, or flow from, this supreme sacrifice. These obligations the writer likewise terms sacrifices.

1. *"The Sacrifice of Praise."* "By him therefore let us offer the sacrifice of praise to God continually, that is, the fruit of our lips giving thanks to his name" (13:15). The word *thusian* ($\theta \upsilon \sigma \iota \alpha \nu$), "sacrifice," may mean either a blood or a fruit sacrifice; here it is used in the latter sense, for the writer quotes from the Septuagint. The Hebrew text, "so will we render the calves of our lips," (Hos. 14:2) was thought to be a peculiar idiom, and the Greeks changed it to "fruit" for better understanding. The words "by him" or "through him" are made emphatic by placing them at the beginning of the sentence. We are not merely to suffer for Christ outside the camp; we owe Him also the sacrifice of praise, expressions of thanksgiving to God and service to man. Such sacrifices are no longer to be administered by the Levitical priests at stated seasons, but continuously, and that through Christ, who alone through the Spirit can make our worship and service acceptable on the altar of God.

Having considered Christ as the Sin Offering, the writer in this text turns his attention to the sweet-savory offerings. The first of these was known as the "peace" offering, which, after the blood had been sprinkled upon the altar, was to be eaten jointly by the priests and the worshipers. It thus became the symbol of restored life and communion with God. The second was the "meal" offering, composed of fine flour and other ingredients, and was the symbol of the nourishment and growth of the new spiritual life. But the highest of these offerings was the "whole burnt offering," one which was entirely consumed upon the altar. In a peculiar manner this offering marked the full devotion to God of the new spiritual life, and is especially associated with praise. Thus during the reformation under Hezekiah it is said that, "when the burnt offering began, the song of the Lord began also with the trumpets, and with the instruments ordained by David king of Israel. And all the congregation worshipped, and the singers sang,

and the trumpeters sounded: and all this continued until
the burnt offering was finished" (II Chron. 29:27-28).
Two things enter into this sacrifice of praise. (1) It
is to be offered continually, and therefore is an inner
attitude of praise to God. Do those who go unto Jesus
without the camp grieve over the loss of the city with
its wealth and pleasures? No, that soul that reaches
Christ in a true and deep experience joins the company
of which the prophet wrote, "Ye shall go out with joy,
and be led forth with peace." In Christ the heart over-
flows with gladness; and so abiding is this inward joy of
the Spirit that in the midst of the deepest trials the soul
can say, "As sorrowful, yet alway rejoicing." (2) This
sacrifice is the "fruit of our lips giving thanks to his
name." The joy of the heart must be given outward expression before the sacrifice of praise is complete. God
has endowed men with speech, and the lips consecrated
to Christ must joyfully speak His praises. The writer
has previously pictured Christ, the Sanctifier, as the
Chief Singer, the Precentor leading the choirs of heaven
and earth, and singing praises in the midst of the Church
(2:11-12). This "joy of the Lord is our strength," and
without it the Church becomes weak and unattractive.
Furthermore, we are told that the highest function of
praise is the confession of the "name," and this because
it is an act of faith. To bear joyful witness to what Christ
has done *for* us, through simple faith, is more effective
in the salvation of souls than that which we are able
to do for Him. Therefore as the high priest brought
the incense within the veil on the Day of Atonement,
let us who have entered the holy of holies through
the blood of Christ by Him also continually bring our
sacrifice of praise to God, having our hearts aflame with
love and our lips attuned to the giving of thanks.

2. *The Sacrifice of Benevolence.* "But to do good
and to communicate forget not: for with such sacrifices
God is well pleased" (13:16). The word *koinonias*
(κοινωνίας), here translated "communicate," means primarily a spiritual communion, a people joined together
in the bonds of faith and love. Those who go unto Christ

without the camp receive this spirit of faith and love
which takes away all undue anxiety for the morrow.
Instead of the desire for merely getting and keeping,
these have found from the Master that "it is more
blessed to give than to receive." They do good and
distribute cheerfully; they are "as poor, yet making
many rich." The pagans were astonished by the care
of the early Christians for their poor, and they marveled
that they were kind even to those who persecuted
them. Lecky in his *History of European Morals* wrote
concerning Christ, "The simple record of three short
years of active life has done more to regenerate and
soften mankind than all the disquisitions of the philoso-
phers, and than all the exhortations of the moralists."
Such sacrifices as these, the Word tells us, are pleasing
to God—sacrifices of praise which cost us something
to confess Christ; sacrifices of giving, when the gift
impoverishes the giver. How different the spirit of those
who go unto Christ without the gate from that of those
who remain in the city of the world! Those bear His
reproach; they rejoice in the Father's love, and have
no fear of the God of judgment, who is a "consuming
fire."

3. *The Sacrifice of Obedience.* "Obey them that have
the rule over you, and submit yourselves: for they
watch for your souls, as they that must give account,
that they may do it with joy, and not with grief: for
that is unprofitable for you" (13:17). The word
"rulers" in verse 7 had reference primarily to their
former leaders; here it is used in verses 17 and 24 with
reference to their present pastors. However, between
these two verses (13:7-17) there is a complete circle
of ideas. The writer begins with the memory of their
former leaders, and brings them forward as examples
of the faith; from this he passes to the faith itself and
its defense against all foreign doctrines; then comes the
establishment of their hearts by grace, and not by
meats; and finally, the presentation of the supreme sacrifice of Christ outside the gate, and the religious obliga-

tions that follow. This brings him again to the need for order in the Church through the gift of pastors ordained of God to watch over the souls of the people.

The word *hupeikete* (ὑπείκετε), "be submissive," is used frequently in classical Greek literature, but occurs only here in the New Testament. "It seems to express that yielding of the self-will to the judgment of another, which recognizes constituted authority even while it maintains personal independence" (Vaughan). The word *peithesthe* (πείθεσθε), "obey," is from the root word meaning to persuade, and is therefore more of a persuasive than a mandatory obedience. The Spirit, who sheds abroad in the heart that faith and love which lead to generosity, creates also in those outside the camp the spirit of humility and submission, obedience and trust. The word *autoi* (αὐτοὶ) is emphatic as it pertains to the leaders. They are not self-appointed, but divinely chosen, as watchmen—the shepherds of the flock who are responsible to the Chief Shepherd; and both the people and their leaders are to look upon themselves as those who must give account to God when their work is done. This the writer hopes may be done with joy and not with grief; for this, he says, would be unprofitable for them.

4. *The Sacrifice of Prayer*. "Pray for us: for we trust we have a good conscience, in all things willing to live honestly. But I beseech you the rather to do this, that I may be restored to you the sooner" (13: 18-19). It is a question whether the word "we" is merely an editorial plural or whether it refers to the writer's associates. The word "I" in verse 19 indicates a purely personal request for prayer. Like praise, thanksgiving, benevolence, submissiveness, and obedience, prayer is also a sacrifice. If Jesus in the garden offered up prayers and supplications, how much more should we live lives of prayer and supplication!

The writer by implication lays down two conditions for successful prayer. (1) The first is sincerity or honesty of purpose. One must be persuaded that he has a good conscience, willing to live honestly before God and man. God will not hear those who regard iniquity in their hearts. A good conscience is one that is enlightened as to its duty and responsibility and fully aware of its just obligations. The word "willing," as used here, is not one of bare consent under persuasion, but an earnest wish or desire in the sense of an intense purpose. The word "honestly" is not as at present limited to integrity in business, or as opposed to that which is deceitful and fraudulent; rather, as Westcott points out, "the adjective *kalos* ($\kappa\alpha\lambda\hat{\omega}\varsigma$) seems to retain its characteristic sense of that which commands the respect and admiration of others." (2) The second condition is that of fervency and persistence, or as St. James puts it, "The effectual fervent prayer of a righteous man availeth much" (Jas. 5:16). The writer had evidently left on some important mission, and for some reason, imprisonment or other, he had been detained from returning to the church. But he knew the power of prayer, and he had confidence in the prayers of his people, and hoped by their intercession to be returned to them soon.

THE BENEDICTION

The writer now approaches the close of this remarkable Epistle. He has had a great purpose in view, and to accomplish this he has poured forth a living stream of argument, warning, and appeal. Having asked for the prayers of the Hebrews that he might soon be returned to them, he now breaks forth into a stately benediction, in which he summarizes the entire Epistle in one sentence—a prayer wish addressed to the Hebrews, but in reality a fervent appeal to God. For the greatest effectiveness this benediction will be presented with but brief comments, that it may stand out in its beauty as a whole; but the careful reader will note that all the high lights of the preceding chapters are here gathered together in one great prayer, a prayer of benediction.

1. *"Now may the God of peace"*—since the article is used, the text reads literally, "God of the peace," or "the God of saving bliss." When the Holy Spirit has accomplished His perfect work, there remains in the heart no friction between the soul and God. This is, therefore, the Christian conception of God as reconciled in Jesus Christ. Peace is here regarded as a state into which we enter, peace *with* God in justification (Rom. 5: 1); the peace *of* God as an enduement of the Spirit in sanctification (John 14: 27). Peace is the normal emotion of the Christian life, peace based on righteousness and rising into a fullness of joy; this constitutes the kingdom of God which is within us (Rom. 14: 17).

2. *"That brought again from the dead our Lord Jesus."* The Resurrection marks Christ's triumph over death and the acceptance of His blood as an atonement for sin. It is the sole but sure ground of our hope for a future life; He alone brought life and immortality to light through the gospel. The resurrected and ascended Christ is seated at the right hand of the throne of God, and as our great High Priest, ministers to us His heavenly life through the Holy Spirit.

3. *"That great shepherd of the sheep."* This familiar Old Testament figure Christ applied to himself, "I am the good shepherd: the good shepherd giveth his life for the sheep" (John 10: 11). The following verse is frequently joined with this, thus indicating that it was through the Blood of the covenant alone that Jesus was raised from the dead. In His death the penalty of sin was paid; and the penalty paid, death could not hold Him. Having given His life for the sheep, He is raised up from death to become the Good Shepherd, the great One who leads His people into the spiritual rest of faith in this life, and eternal rest in the life to come.

4. *"Through the blood of the everlasting covenant."* It was not only by the Blood that our Lord Jesus was brought up from the dead, but having been raised again, He presents His blood as an atonement for all sin—an

atonement sufficient for all men, efficient for all who believe. It is by the Blood that we draw near to God; by the Blood we are cleansed from all sin; by the Blood we enter within the veil into the holy of holies; by the Blood the very heavens are purified for our eternal dwelling place; and like Christ, we too shall be brought again from the dead by the Blood of the covenant, and shall join the glorious company of the redeemed who meet Him in the air, and so shall we be forever with the Lord.

5. *"Make you perfect in every good work to do his will."* Perfection has been one of the great words of this Epistle, and as such, signifies the entrance into the fullness of the new covenant, or what is termed "Christian perfection." However a different word for perfection is used here, the word *katartisai* (καταρτίσαι), which means to fit together in the sense of a well-functioning organism. It is, in fact, a technical medical term implying the replacement of a joint after dislocation. When one is "cleansed from all unrighteousness," God so rectifies the springs of action in the heart that it functions properly in the doing of His will. We must bear in mind that we are not only to do the will of God, but that it is God who fits us to do it. This is accomplished by the Holy Spirit when we rely wholly upon Him, and therefore out of weakness we are made strong.

6. *"Working in you that which is well pleasing in his sight."* The operation of the Holy Spirit in the hearts of men is the gift of the risen, ascended, and glorified Christ. By Him, Christ is enthroned in the heart, the Lord of every motion there. To be well-pleasing to God, it is not enough to emphasize a few particular duties, but to abound to every good work. The test and rule of the duties devolving upon us is the will of God as revealed in the Holy Scriptures, and made effective by the indwelling Christ.

7. *"Through Jesus Christ."* God works in the believer's heart and life through His Son. Christ is the

Surety of the covenant, and the Minister of the sanctuary—the former wrought out on earth, the latter administered from His throne in the heavens. Christ therefore is the sole Mediator between God and man. It is by Him that we have access to God; and it is by Him also that the Spirit ministers to our inner lives, enabling us "both to will and to do of his good pleasure."

8. *"To whom be glory for ever and ever."* The Epistle closes with the doxology, in which the heart of the writer, bursting with adoration, gives utterance to his ecstatic feelings in ascriptions of praise. Without this final note of praise the Epistle would have in no wise been complete; for one who has drunk so deeply of the spirit of truth as has this writer must give expression to the joy of his heart in words of thanksgiving and praise. Having summed up in this benediction the glorious work of Christ, the writer is deeply moved as he presents to his readers the gracious truth that what God has wrought out in Christ, He desires to finish in the Church, which is His body. Let this truth be received humbly and believingly, and from the fullness of the Holy Spirit within, like the incense of old, the flame of God's love will rise heavenward, and the soul itself be "lost in wonder, love, and praise." "To Him be glory for ever and ever"!

9. *"Amen."* This is the Hebrew word for "truth" and is the seal of God's verity, and the confession of our own faith. *Amen*—"so let it be."

THE POSTSCRIPTS

With the benediction this Epistle might have ended, but the writer adds a few personal postscripts, which, it must be granted, appear in the form and spirit of St. Paul. The Epistle being more in the form of a treatise than of a letter, the addition of these postscripts gives it the necessary epistolary character. The writer makes a strong appeal to his readers to give serious heed to his admonitions, indicating that no doctrine is fully understood until it appeals to the conscience, reaches the heart, and thereby affects the manner of living. This hortatory character pervades the entire Epistle. The writer speaks of his exhortation as "in few words," perhaps not with reference to the length of the Epistle, but in proportion to the comprehensive and sublime nature of the subject discussed. For this reason he urges them not to allow its length to prejudice them against it, but to use it to their edification and profit.

Then follows the information concerning the release of Timothy, and if he is not too long detained, together the two plan to visit the Christians soon. The writer sends greetings to those who rule over them and to all the saints, thus furnishing sufficient evidence that this letter was directed to the church as a whole. He includes also greetings from his associates, "They of Italy salute thee." Then in a brief and final word of benediction he prays, "Grace be with you all. Amen." Thus ends this richest of Epistles, written in faultless Greek, and sounding the depth and the height of divine grace as is possible only by one under the illumination and inspiration of the Holy Spirit.

Soli Deo Gloria

INDEX

438